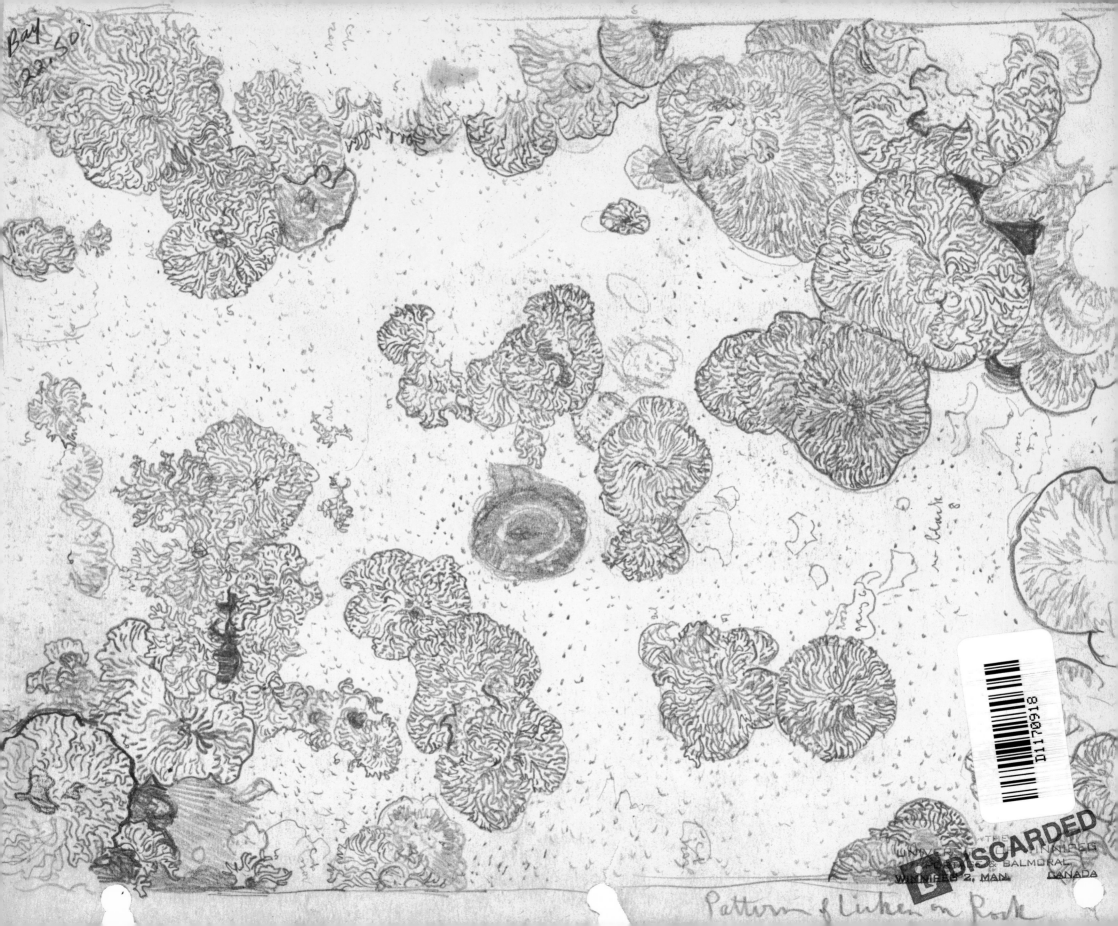

Pattern of Lichen on Rock

A.Y.'S CANADA

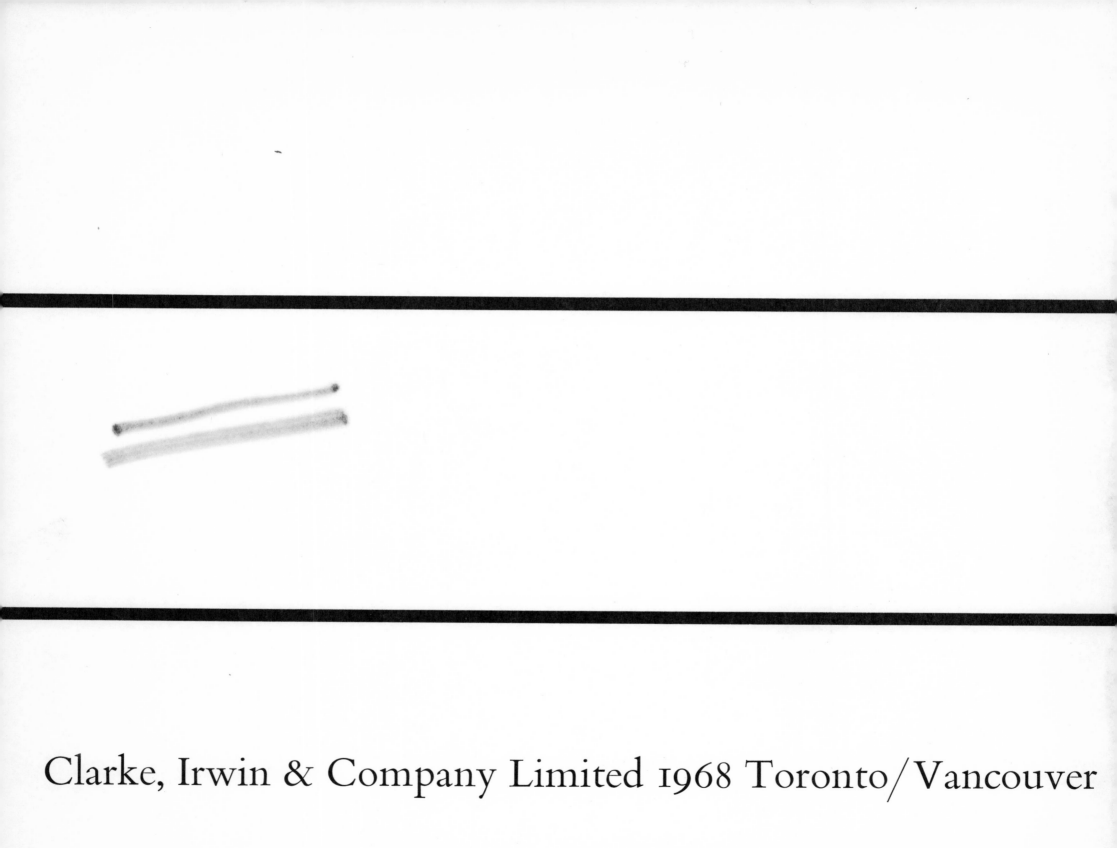

Clarke, Irwin & Company Limited 1968 Toronto/Vancouver

A.Y.'S CANADA

by Naomi Jackson Groves
pencil drawings by A.Y. Jackson

Foreword

AY was to write an introduction to our book which has been such a pleasure to work on together. But he is *hors de combat*, at least for the time being, hence this brief explanatory foreword instead.

Throughout our book, the word *drawing* is used for works in pencil (i.e. black lead graphite) on paper, with the added use on a few occasions of pen-and-ink. The word *sketch* is here reserved, for the sake of precision, for works in oil paint on wood panels, while *canvas* is used for the larger paintings made in the studio with the help of the sketch and the drawing.

Most of the drawings were dated at the time by AY; brackets are used for known dates added here. It is hoped to compile—eventually—a full catalogue of AY's works in all media. Each one already examined has been given its own "njg number," which is included along with the size in the notes at the end of the book. Those notes also provide, for anyone interested, the sources used in the text, and information about vignettes on the text pages.

The fact that AY has always carried a drawing-book with him on his sketching expeditions and used it very often, has only recently become generally known and of particular interest. Perhaps today's sophisticated taste appreciates more intensively the subtleties of the graphic arts and of black-and-white—an antidote to Pop Art and vast vague abstruse abstracts. AY himself often referred to his drawings simply as "notes," and indeed sometimes filled their margins with verbal accompaniments for future reference, such as "pale veiled sunlight . . . source of light from the right."

It may surprise many who read this book to learn that AY usually did the drawing *after* the sketch in oils. To be sure, there were occasions when he began with the drawing, as on Arctic travels when he was always on the move—"we never knew when the ship's whistle would blow for us to leave." In some exciting places he would be given only a twenty-minute stop, no time to paint. Occasionally, when the weather was *too* inclement, he would make copious "notes" to work up later at leisure. But as a rule, in the field he would seize the first effect of his subject in oil colour on the wood panel in his handy little Jackson sketch-box. Then—if it interested him specially—he would proceed to make a drawing as a follow-up, to catch what he has termed "an alternative line for later decision," analyzing and intensifying the composition, rendering certain desired details more sharply or more fully, or jotting down for future use (if for instance the light had changed while he sketched) comments such as "sky lighter . . . whole foreground in bolder relief."

AY's famous "number system" indicates the relative light-dark values of parts of the composition, the range being from 1 to 10, light to dark. He adopted this in France before World War 1, and it stood him in good stead when he was War Records artist at the front, where speed was as essential as accuracy. When not painting on the spot he indicates both colour and tone value, as in "warm grey $7\frac{1}{2}$" or "highlights cool 2." Some drawings show the numbers on the *verso* side, indicating that the paper has been held against the light. A few are "pure drawings" made to capture some fascinating design and not intended for painting; these often show areas of rich black. Rapid studies of people and other animate objects could be used later in a larger context, or are simply for fun, a sign of AY's broad human interests. Spontaneous, unstylized, masterly, an act and not an object, AY's drawings reveal how he takes possession of his subject, gives it his own characteristic imprint, and then puts it aside, to gather a rich patina in the sketch-bag and to lie maybe for years in a casual heap in the studio—rich record of life and land.

The pattern of our present book maintains its unity by swinging through Canada in a great curving circle, rather than by attempting a chronological development of AY's career. Striking changes in the artist's drawing style between early works and late help form a polyphony of time and place.

May I here express on my uncle's behalf and my own our sincere thanks to all who have helped us in the preparation and presentation of *AY's Canada*, both to the private collectors and public galleries that have loaned their treasures for such a long time, and to all who have provided generous information for the text. I am full of gratitude for the patience, encouragement and assistance of our publishers and of my own dear partner through thick and thin here at home.

NAOMI JACKSON GROVES

To the Memory of Henry A. C. Jackson
good brother
good father
good artist–naturalist
good Canadian

Acknowledgements

Grateful acknowledgement is given to the following owners of pencil drawings by
A.Y. Jackson, who have loaned them for reproduction in this book: Mr. and Mrs.
Gerard Brett, Mrs. Robert A. Hamilton, Miss Margaret Perkins Hess, Mr. Walter
Stewart, Mr. Tony Urquhart;   The Art Collection Society of Kingston (Vignette with
Plate 45), Norman Mackenzie Art Gallery, Regina (Plate 2 and Plate 6), J. Gordon and
Wilhelmina Morris McIntosh Collection of the University of Western Ontario (Plate 61).

The author and publisher wish to thank the publishing companies, newspapers and
journals listed here for permission to quote from their works. Complete credit lines are
given in the notes at the back of the book.   *The Calgary Herald* (July 12, 1960 and July 3,
1954);   *CBC Times* (Jan. 29-Feb. 4, 1966);   Clarke, Irwin & Company Ltd., from
*The Fraser, Growing Pains, The Heart of a Peacock, Hundreds and Thousands;   The Globe
and Mail* (Fall 1944);   The Halifax Herald Ltd., from The Halifax *Mail-Star* (Dec. 6,
1965);   Holt, Rinehart and Winston, Inc., from *The Fraser, The St. Lawrence;*   Mr.
Bruce Hutchison, from *The Fraser; Maclean's* (Dec. 19, 1927);   The Macmillan
Company of Canada Ltd., from *Canada, The Downfall of Temlaham, Far Places, Quebec,
Where Ancient France Lingers;*   McClelland and Stewart Ltd., from *Contrasts, A Book of
Verse, Klondike, North of Summer, Remember Yesterday, A Century of Photographs;   The
McGill News* (Sept. 1929); McGill University Press, from *The Living Past of Montreal;
The Montreal Star* (Jan. 30, 1954);   North Carolina Museum of Art, from *Bulletin*
(Spring/Summer 1965);   *The Ottawa Journal* (Nov. 5, 1963);   Queen's Printer, from
The Unbelievable Land;   The Ryerson Press, from *Poems, Son of the North;   Saturday
Night* (Nov. 14, 1953 and June 1967).

Valuable first-hand observations and research materials have been provided by:
Colonel P.D. Baird, Mrs. William Barnes, Mrs. Jack Cloke, Dr. and Mme B.T. Denis,
Miss Mildred Hagar, Dr. and Mrs. Lawren Harris, Miss Marmee Hess, Miss Claire
Jackson, Mr. Kenneth Henry Jackson, Mrs. Duncan de Kergommeaux, the Rt.
Honourable Malcolm MacDonald, Mr. Thoreau MacDonald, Mr. Eric McLean, Mr. and
Mrs. Robert McMichael, Mrs. Geneva Jackson Petrie, Dr. D.B.O. Savile, the Reverend
N.E. Schamerhorn, Dr. and Mrs. R.A. Starrs, Mr. Don Strikefoot, Mrs. Lewis Terrill;
Miss Peggy Blackstock of Shirley Leishman Books, Ottawa, the Reference Librarian and
the Registrar of the National Gallery of Canada, and the Reference Librarian of the
National Library.

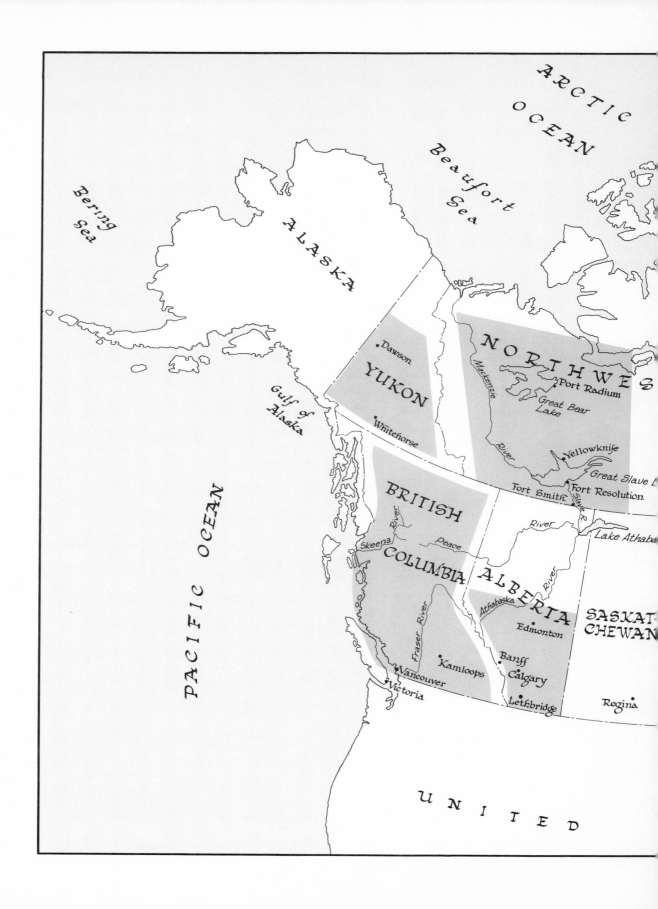

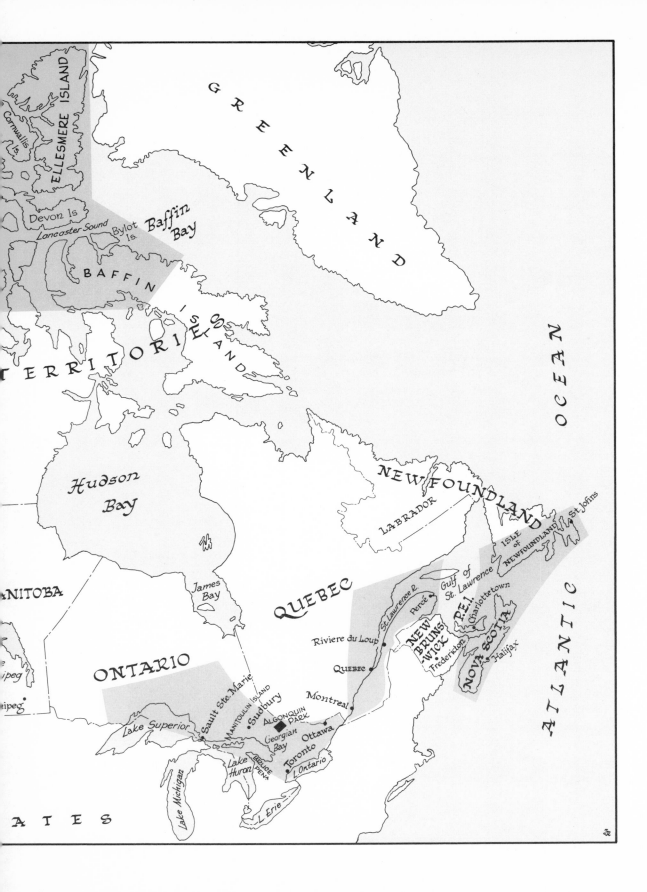

Maynooth
McGregor Bay
Mississagi R.
Mts. of La Cloche
Orrillia
Ottawa
Ottawa R.
Palgrave
Paris
Pembroke
Rossport
Sault Ste. Marie
Serpent R.
Slate Is.
Spragge
Sudbury
Tobermory
Toronto
Western Is.
Willisville

Keithley Creek
Kispiox
Kitwanga
Kitwinkul
Lillooet
Lucerne
Lytton
Maligne L.
Okanagan Valley
Peace R.
Port Essington
Port Simpson
Prince Rupert
Quesnel R.
Rocky Mts.
Skeena R.
The Hundred and Fifty Mile
The-Hundred-and-Twenty-Two
Thompson R.
Tonquin Valley
Yellowhead Pass

PRAIRIE PROVINCES
Athabasca R.
Belly R.
Cadillac
Calgary
Canmore
Carmangay
Carstairs
Castle R.
Cowley
De Winton
Drumheller
Edmonton
Enchant
Fort McMurray
Lake Winnipeg
Lethbridge
Lundbreck
New Drayton
Oldman R.
Peace R.
Pincher Creek
Porcupine Hills
Regina
Rosebud
St. Mary R.
Spring Coulee
Waterton R.
Willow Creek
Winnipeg

YUKON & NORTHWEST TERRITORIES
Bathurst Inlet
Bear R.
Bonanza
Cameron Bay
Chilkoot Pass
Clearwater R.
Contact
Coppermine R.
Dawson
Dease Arm
Dismal Lakes
Dyea
Echo Bay
Fort Chipewyan
Fort Resolution
Fort Smith
Great Bear L.
Great Slave L.
Hay R.
Hornby Bay
Hunter Bay
Kendall R.
Kluane L.
Lac Rouvier
Liard R.
Mackenzie R.
McDonough L.
McVicar Arm
Pine Point
Porcupine R.
Port Radium
Rat R.
September Mts.
Slave R.
Smart R.
Teshierpi Mts.
Walsh Lake
Whitehorse
Yellowknife
Yukon R.

BRITISH COLUMBIA
Ashcroft
Banff
Barkerville
Clinton
Fraser R.
Gitsegyukla
Hagwelget
Haysport
Hazelton
Kamloops

It seems right to launch *AY's Canada* in the farthest corner of the Arctic ever reached (to date, it had better be added) by this sturdy wanderer: the Bache Peninsula on the Kane Basin coast of Ellesmere Island, Canada's most northerly territory, westward from the top of Greenland.

In 1926, a year before AY got there, an RCMP post was established on Bache, about eight hundred miles from the North Pole, to help consolidate Canada's claim to those polar regions. It was maintained by four Mounties and three Eskimos—at that time the sole residents for Ellesmere's 82,119 square miles. Owing to the extreme hazards of approach by ship the post had to be given up within a few years, like so many valiant Arctic projects dependent on sea navigation. Nowadays we simply fly in: "We've grown soft," according to AY.

Jackson was probably the first professional Canadian artist to reach the far North. He travelled twice to the eastern Arctic on the government patrol ship, the rugged little 2,700-ton *Beothic*, with Norwegian-born Captain Falke and a hardy crew from Newfoundland. In the summer of 1927 his companion was Dr. Frederick Banting, the great insulin man, a keen free-time landscape painter who enjoyed getting away on a trip with his artist friend. *A Painter's Country* tells how Banting sat beside AY as he sketched the ice-bound *Beothic* from almost the same angle as in the drawing here. A canvas of this subject was presented by AY to the Department of the Interior which had approved his trip; the picture is now in the National Gallery and seems to have been reproduced more often than any other work by AY.

The present 9 by 12 inch drawing was made in 1930, when the team of Jackson and Harris advanced the Group of Seven's frontiers to the north. "My heart's in the Arctic, my heart is not here," AY wrote in fine fettle on June 25, 1930, as he prepared his gear for the expedition. "Lawren Harris is going with me, so he can take everything on one side of the ship and I everything on the other." Both artists produced a multitude of pencil studies for quick record as the *Beothic* made its rounds; their little cabin served as studio when there was not enough time ashore for painting.

On his 1930 trip AY kept a modest sort of Arctic Diary in a small red notebook, where he recorded that the Kane Basin ice, twenty to thirty feet thick and constantly shifting this way and that, was the worst pack the Canadian government expeditions had ever encountered. The entry for the very day on which he made this drawing reads: "*Wed. Aug. 13th.* Ice all round; made a couple of efforts to get through but the whole bay is full of heavy floe ice. Towards evening it was decided to leave the coal on the shore sixteen miles from the post. L. and I went ashore, carried coal for a while, then went inland over the rocks—not very paintable. Steamer whistled and started back to the protection of Cocked Hat Island. We went back to the shore and followed in the motor boat for five miles. The sea like glass; we circled in and out of ice floes—the most fantastic forms in blue-green and pearl. During the night the *Beothic* moved into Fram Haven. We are getting kind of anxious about the ice."

How often in our North, through the past thousand years or so, have men's eyes rested speculatively on the shape of their ice-bound ship?—the eyes of Frobisher on his twenty-ton cockleshells the *Gabriel* and *Michael;* the eyes of Parry on the stricken *Fury;* the eyes of gallant Franklin, doomed to die as the *Erebus* and *Terror* lay imprisoned in the ice for twenty months; more recently (only fourteen years before AY reached the Arctic) the eyes of Stefansson and Jenness watching the *Karluk* drift away to its fate. . . .

The eyes of the artist, resting on the unromantic, homely *Beothic*, see the situation rather differently, of course, and note how the angular dark ship-form contrasts with the weird fantasies of the ice; how some grey is cold and some has a warm violet tinge; how actually, as the foreground note informs us: "This is the only colorless or opal grey ice."

2

PLATE I

The Beothic *among ice floes off the Bache Peninsula, Ellesmere Island, 1930*

Near Becher Peir
A Y Jackson 1930

This is the only colorless on the greys ice

This dramatic drawing of the coastline looking northward along the east shore of Fram Fiord fits a vast expanse into its modest 7¾ by 10⅞ inches (the size of most of the 1927 drawings). Banting's oil sketch of the same subject, painted from slightly steeper and closer range (perhaps he crouched by those boulders in the middle ground?), is owned by the Art Gallery of Ontario, and is reproduced in AY's little book *Banting as an Artist*.

It is interesting to observe changing reactions in travellers' appreciation of the northern scene. One of the earliest records available is that of John Davis in A.D. 1585, when his little vessel fought its way through the difficult strait that now bears Davis' name, with Greenland towering to the east and Baffin to the west. AY's unpublished Arctic Diary quotes Davis: "A land very high and full of mightie mountains all covered with snowe, no viewe of wood, grasse or earth to be seene, and the shore two leagues off into the sea full of Yce. The lothsome view of the shore and irksome noyse of the yce was such that it bred strange conceits among us."

Later visitors found the view much less "lothsome." In 1899 the intrepid Norwegian Otto Sverdrup manœuvred his *Fram* between drift ice and craggy shore to "a place of anchorage a little west of Cone Island, in a fjord which we called 'Fram Fjord'. The fjord ran due north and south.... A large, fissured glacier covered the bottom of the valley...."

Sverdrup's party found "a wide and smiling valley" on the west side of the fiord. Describing the east shoreline, which we see in AY's drawing, Sverdrup noted the precipitous mountains and the fact that Per Schei, the geologist on his expedition, "as ever, had aspiring tendencies, and was always at the top of some mountain or other, looking down on us and the world."

It was only three decades after Per Schei that AY and Fred Banting stood in about the same spot and also felt "on top of the world" in every sense. AY was not at all averse to heading towards the North Pole to paint, as *A Painter's Country* recounts with great good humour. And Banting matched his friend in rugged energy and northward urge. There are heart-warming records of their sturdy appreciation of each other, as when Banting wrote about their 1927 Arctic adventure in his introduction to *The Far North*, the book of AY's pen-and-ink drawings published in 1928: "Sketching was done under considerable difficulty; cold and wind would have chilled the enthusiasm of a less ardent worker. Jackson cherishes an illusion that the finest colour is generally to be found on the most exposed spots. A restless desire to find what lies beyond the distant hills makes it hard to keep up with him. The barren wastes proved to be rich in form and colour, strange rhythms and unexpected vistas. During our all too brief and exciting scrambles ashore, he would be chuckling and laughing all day—a mood I found contagious."

PLATE 2

The coast of Ellesmere, looking north from Craig Harbour into Fram Fiord, 1927

Clones 10 miles wide

Franz
Fiord

Ellesmere Island
Craig Harbour
1927

looking
north
from Craig
Harbour

On Saturday, August 13, 1927, the Arctic Patrol ship *Beothic* steamed along Eclipse Sound, heading for Pond Inlet on Baffin Island's north-east corner; off to port side lay the south coast of Bylot Island, named after Commander Robert Bylot who sailed those waters with Captain William Baffin in A.D. 1616.

AY saw Bylot Island from all sides in the process of his goings and comings in 1927 and 1930, and considered it "the loveliest island in the Arctic" and "an exciting place to paint."

"No one lives on Bylot," he wrote in the text of *The Far North*. "It is largely snow capped and gleaming with sharp mountain peaks. Glaciers sprawl along its coast, most of them not quite reaching the sea, which seems to be the glaciers' ambition. One corner of it is a rolling pasture land covered with moss and flowers, and here the diminishing caribou still pasture."

AY was never able to climb those 6,600-foot mountains, there being no port of call on Bylot for the *Beothic*, but he made many drawings and notes from on shipboard, those dated on the return journey in 1927 showing a notable increase in freedom and vigour compared to those done on the way north. The present drawing, about $7\frac{1}{2}$ by 11 inches, is a crystal-clear study, with notes for future use about sky, hills, and snow, and especially the tricky combination of ripple and reflection in the water—intended for foreground interest in the painting to come. A lively pen-and-ink version of this drawing, with seals on an icefloe added in the foreground, is reproduced as Plate 14 in *The Far North*. Bylot's clear prismatic forms also delighted Lawren Harris in 1930, and inspired some of his finest sketches and canvases.

A pleasant postscript from the 1960s: With the vast new mining projects of nearby Baffin Island having the unhappy by-product of endangering game and wildlife, it is a comfort to learn that the whole of Bylot Island has been declared a wildlife sanctuary, so that caribou and snow goose can flourish in peace in that "pasture land covered with moss and flowers."

PLATE 3

The south coast of Bylot Island, August 13, 1927

Bylot Island. Aug 13th 27 A Y Jackson

The dramatic area around Pangnirtung Fiord on Baffin Island just below the Arctic Circle has been studied by AY's far-reaching eye on three different northern journeys: in 1927, in 1930, and again recently in 1965. On the first visit, in mid-August 1927, he found the mountain tops obscured by low-lying clouds, so he concentrated upon the Eskimo settlement along the shore. For the second visit, in 1930, the following diary entry tells the tale of how this drawing was made: "*Saturday, September 6th*. A glorious summer day. I went ashore at 8 a.m. It was too serene a day to do anything in the village, so I started for a high hill. After a while I came to a river too deep and swift to cross. Followed it up for a mile, and did some fancy jumping from one boulder to another, and got over. The hills were all moss and boulders. . . .

"From the top of a thousand foot hill there was a great view of pasture land, lakes and snow-capped mountains. I dined sumptuously on a bar of chocolate Housser. The sun blazed down, it was warm. I made some drawings. The *Beothic* looked the size of a toothpick. Went back along a boulder-covered ridge, then had to cross the river again, and had a bad time. Waded across, it was up to my knees and very swift."

In the summer of 1965, thirty-five years after the foregoing was written, having meanwhile attained his energetic eighties, AY returned to the glories of Pangnirtung. Journey III was at today's speedy pace: by D.C.3, only five hours from Montreal-Dorval to Frobisher Bay, then in a five-passenger Otter piloted by Weldy Phipps, a veteran of Arctic air transport, north to Pangnirtung and right up the gap in the fiord ("the wings nearly touching both sides!") to Glacier Lake at the foot of the Penny Highland. There AY, along with a group from the Alpine Club of Canada, plus his niece Geneva and her friend Una as camp cooks *and* a very good medical man as camp doctor, spent a rather cool July—the mean temperature ("really *mean*, away sub-normal") only 40°F. AY had to sleep on the ground in a tent, like everybody else; he never felt really warm. But he still managed to produce a fine crop of oil sketches, though fewer drawings than back in 1927 and 1930.

Baffin is the world's third-largest island. How many of its 184,000-odd square miles are contained in this delicate 9 by 12 inch space! The combination of modest format, vast view, and linear clarity may recall the cosmic landscapes of Pieter Bruegel and other old North European masters of magic realism, discoverers of the delights of alpine vistas. Other Canadians have expressed their enjoyment of the infinite serenity of the northern atmosphere, as for instance W. H. Blake when he wrote "A Christmas Jaunt": ". . . the eye penetrated to the uttermost limits of the horizon through vapourless crystalline air that spared nothing, concealed nothing, drew no veil of distance and mystery over the remotest hills."

Gleaming remotenesses seem to suit today's aerial taste.

8

A Y Jackson
1927.
Pangnirtung

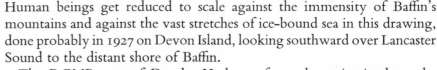

Human beings get reduced to scale against the immensity of Baffin's mountains and against the vast stretches of ice-bound sea in this drawing, done probably in 1927 on Devon Island, looking southward over Lancaster Sound to the distant shore of Baffin.

The RCMP post of Dundas Harbour, formerly maintained on the southeast corner of Devon Island, was the first police post the *Beothic* could reach through the ice on its 1927 trip. Again on the 1930 trip the government ship put three members of the RCMP ashore at Dundas before proceeding west along Lancaster Sound, so AY saw Dundas twice. On the earlier occasion he notes in *The Far North* that "Three police and a family of Eskimos are the sole residents of this extensive island." The three little seated figures in the pen-and-ink drawing *Midnight, Dundas*, Plate 8 in *The Far North*, shown here in vignette in the pencil original from a page of notes, very likely represent that single Eskimo family on Devon Island in 1927. The same can be assumed for the small figures plodding forward in the drawing opposite, against an icy immensity: suggestive, haunting, almost dream-like.

These warm dark specks of humanity silhouetted against the vast frozen ice-field could symbolize all of man's progress through the wildernesses of the world. They could be the first family of all to emerge after the Ice Age; they could be the avant-garde of the Eskimo peoples—*Inuit*, "the people," as they call themselves—gradually working their way eastward in prehistoric times, adjusting to the rigours of climate and terrain, developing their uncanny orientation in travel over the trackless wastes. Or they could be, actually here may well be, the last survivors, on their way out.

In earlier times there were many Eskimo settlements on Devon Island which, though its land-locked icecap is called "the place where the winds are born," has a richly fertile fringe along most of its shore. Great herds of muskox flourished here until the depredations of men with guns. There may well have been Eskimos in this very spot watching brave Parry's little two-hundred-ton *Hecla* and three-hundred-ton *Griper* pass along Lancaster Sound in 1819, and ill-fated Franklin's ships in 1845. In those days ambitious Europeans considered Lancaster Sound a suitable north-west passage to the Orient. But only *Inuit* knew how to cope with the terrible ice and the frozen wilderness. It has taken the rest of us a long time to catch up. . . .

PLATE 5

*Eskimos toting supplies on
Devon Island* [1927]

No location in the entire Canadian Arctic evokes such vivid and poignant memories as does this desolate rim of cliff and gravel where the expedition of Sir John Franklin spent the long winter months of 1845-46 before proceeding westward and southward to its eventual doom. "They fell down and died as they walked..."—but that was not until the summer of 1848, after twenty long months frozen into the ice.

Yet the thoughts of those men of the *Erebus* and *Terror* during the period here at Beechey, when they were ignorant of what lay ahead, may well have been full of satisfaction with what was already accomplished, if we interpret aright the single precious scrap of paper document eventually salvaged in 1858. In the short period since leaving England in early summer 1845 the able commander Franklin had navigated all the way along Lancaster Sound to Beechey (traditionally called Island but actually a promontory or head at the west end of Devon Island, about 160 miles from Dundas Harbour); then on into uncharted seas, up the west coast of Devon to Lat. 77° (150 miles), and back around the far side of Cornwallis Island before returning to winter quarters in the shelter of Beechey's headland.

A small cairn left by Franklin and his men atop this 650-foot cliff before they sailed south-westward in the summer of 1846 was the first trace of them discovered in 1850. By that time a widespread search was under way; there were forty search parties all told. During one period in August 1850 no less than ten search vessels found shelter at Beechey, as Captain, later Admiral, McClintock recalls in his unforgettable work published in 1859, *A Narrative of the Discovery of the Fate of Sir John Franklin and his Companions.*

In hopes that survivors might get back to Beechey, Franklin's winter quarters there were restocked with food and other supplies, and the "decked boat" *Mary* and four smaller craft beached on the shore at the foot of the cliff. On his final visit to Beechey Head, on August 14th, 1858, McClintock reported that the wind had blown open the hut door, but that the *Mary* and the lifeboats were "in excellent order, and their paint appeared fresh, but oars and bare wood were bleached white.... The bears and foxes do not appear to have touched anything." It was on this final visit that McClintock installed the marble plaque prepared by Lady Franklin, with its tribute to the lost gallant souls and its text: "And so HE bringeth them unto the haven where they would be." After that, for many years the dread region lay abandoned.

It was eighty years or so after Franklin's sojourn at Beechey (by now one is tempted to say "only eighty"!) that A. Y. Jackson came that way in the early part of August 1927, as the *Beothic* strove westward in a vain attempt to reach Melville Island and renew a supply cache laid down in 1910. "It is a bleached out landscape," wrote AY in the text to *The Far North*, "bare of vegetation, shale beaches strewn with debris, pieces of boats, canvas, pulleys, and Franklin's water barrels grouped round the roofless house, many of the barrels full of water. Some bore great rips of bears' claws on them." But it was less the passage of time ("nothing ever changes in the Arctic," AY remarked elsewhere) than the depredations of man that had ravaged the shelter and the *Mary*. A grim detail added in *A Painter's Country* recounts how "a trader named James and some Eskimos stripped it of everything useful. Later the Eskimos murdered James."

AY found the barren fog-ridden area poor for landscape painting, but he made several drawings around Beechey. Two of these appeared in pen-and-ink in *The Far North*, including *The Mary, Beechey Island*—"waiting on the desolate shore... a mute reminder of the Arctic's greatest tragedy."

The original pencil version here of the beetling cliff and the pathetically puny hulk at its base shows more vigour than the pen-and-ink version. "Fog, blown against the high cliffs, was pushed upwards out of the funnel-shaped passages, giving the impression that the mass was smoking," AY once said. The vertical format, most unusual in AY's work, unfortunately prevents its being reproduced here in full size with all its grim angularity. An interesting page in AY's voluminous old scrapbook records that soon after his return from the north in September 1927 the Art Gallery of Toronto held a showing of about fifty of his oil sketches and drawings in pencil and pen-and-ink. A generously long article in the *Toronto Daily Star*, with text by C. R. Greenaway, places at the centre of attention this same subject, seen from closer range: the first AY drawing, by many years, to achieve such recognition!

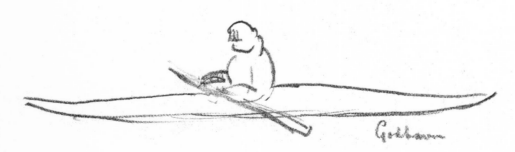

Franklin
wintered here   old floe ice   A.Y. JACKSON BEECHEY ISLAND
AUG 6th/27

PLATE 6

Remains of the Mary *on the
shore at Beechey Head,
August 6, 1927*

Phase I: Away from barren headlands and the dreadful deaths of heroes, over to the Eskimo way of life, here in its early nomadic style, deep in the shelter of Pangnirtung's glorious fiord.

In 1927, when the *Beothic* finally got through the ice to this settlement, AY and Banting felt that they had reached "the metropolis of the North. . . . many Eskimos lived there in skin tents, with hundreds of dogs."

During his second Arctic visit, in early September 1930, AY not only climbed the hills to get the vastest view, but also recorded the shoreline aspects of the not overly crowded metropolis which we see here. On this day he wrote in his journal: "*Friday, September 5th.* Pangnirtung is a neat little burg. From the ship anchored 500 yards out, the white painted Police

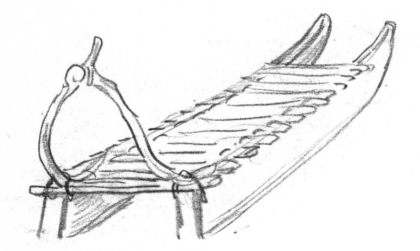

barracks, Hudson's Bay Post and Church Mission and whale oil station make up the entire village. It is only after you land you notice the Eskimo homes—they mix up with the boulders in colour and shape. They look primitive Mongolian, made of skins, canvas, rags, bits of tin, packing cases and other junk. . . .

"The wind has been howling down Pangnirtung Fjord, but it is not cold, and the skies are fine, and we are unloading lumber and other stuff for the Anglican hospital. . . . Dr. Heimbecker is starving four Eskimos for some research he is doing. The massed choirs of Pangnirtung's husky dogs have been giving us a concert. . . . The Hudson's Bay Co. are running a white fox farm across the bay, without much success. The animals, which are blue-grey in summer and white in winter, will not put on their winter costumes; they remain, and probably feel, blue. Neither will they breed— only two that fell into the enclosure and couldn't get out. The vixen had pups but ate them."

One of the drawings from that 1930 trip was entitled *The Stone Age*. It was the ancient and ageless aspects that AY managed to record.

Phase II: But the Stone Age, the age of the nomad hunter with skin tent for summer and snow igloo for winter, is over now for Pangnirtung and for Baffin Land in general. Immense mining operations are projected for the eastern Arctic, with expenditures by oil companies to reach "several hundred millions" and government revenues in the order of "a hundred million dollars annually." No wonder that there "would certainly be more than enough employment to use all the northern natives who could be technically trained for such work. . . ." By 1965, when AY paid Baffin Island a summer visit, the settlement of Pangnirtung had thirty telephones, with some families boasting telephone poles (without phones) as "status symbols." Farther south in the settlement of Frobisher Bay, which did not even exist when AY was north in 1927 and 1930, there are now more than 430 telephones, and a five-mile levelled roadway along which of a fine summer evening the Eskimo teenagers in black leather jackets race one another to the airport on their motorbikes. . . . Not exactly A. Y. Jackson's meat. "I guess I belong to Phase I!" says AY.

PLATE 7

Eskimo tent at Pangnirtung, 1930

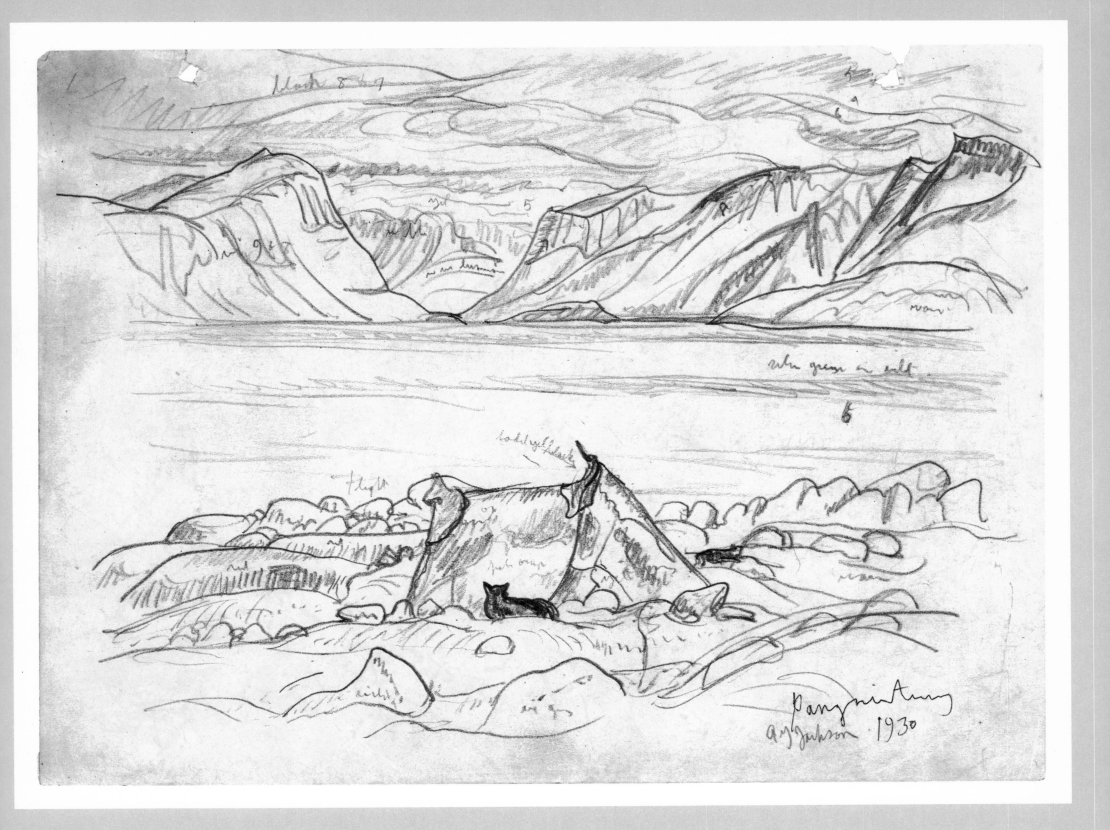

It is lucky for those who like drawings of dogs that AY reached the Canadian Arctic during what might still be called the "dog days," or at least before the transition therefrom diminished the activities of these once vital adjuncts to our northern citizens' way of life. Winter travel and hunting were absolutely essential to survival not so very long ago, and during the present transition phase, as the whites move northward, sledge-dogs are of course still used a fair amount; especially by the RCMP for their winter rounds over many hundreds of miles. But with the advance of all-year-round travel by air (including, for instance, the matter-of-fact delivery of tons of Christmas hampers by parachute and flare), quite apart from snowmobiles, Skidoos and other mechanical monsters, the sledge-dog is bound to become a merely decorative aspect of life in the far North.

On both AY's Eastern Arctic trips (1927, 1930) the *Beothic* was greeted on arrival and departure at every port (and a few times daily in between) with howling choruses from husky throats, as recounted in *A Painter's Country*'s entertaining chapters "An Arctic Holiday with Dr. Banting" and "Second Arctic Voyage." There was also a goodly number of canine passengers on board from port to port, including a "magnificent brute" obtained by trade for a hundred and eighty cartridges at Nerck in Greenland. AY could study his four-legged fellow passengers at close range, and sympathized with the terrified, spray-drenched creatures during the filthy weather on Davis Strait, when they were nearly washed from the deck of the pitching ship.

Enough to fill a whole dog-book has been written about the anything but unsung heroes of the north, whose many bones accompany those of their masters away back in the Old Bering Sea Culture, according to Diamond Jenness in 1926. Parry devotes eleven pages to his dogs; Sverdrup has many wonderful dog-admiring passages and a pathetic photograph of "Adam and Eve moulting." In fact each Arctic explorer seems to enjoy finding appropriate names for his helpers, while the Eskimos sometimes name them after relatives! Memorable in recent times are the little pup who was so ugly that "Cleopatra seemed the obvious name for her," and the black and white pup Mephistopheles who chewed one leg off Tom Manning's fur pants out drying in the sun, as Mrs. Manning recalls in *Igloo for the Night*.

AY's travel journal of 1930 adds one more dog yarn to this favourite theme. RCMP Sergeant Joy, whose agreeable name figures so prominently in the artist's Arctic safaris and who became Inspector Joy before the end of them, travelled on the homeward-bound *Beothic* in 1930. On Sunday, September 7th, AY's diary reads in part: "Joy told us about one of his Bache dogs, the leader or king dog. He picked up a friendship with a pup, and watched over and protected him with great devotion. When the pup was about fifteen months old, out on the trail, they were being fed one day. The king dog was in the habit of taking what he wanted, and was going to take a bone from the pup, but the pup just snarled and wouldn't give it up, and they had an awful fight. Neither won, but the pup had no more fear of him and fought him on every occasion, and in a couple of months the pup was his master. They did not like each other for some weeks. One day three other dogs tackled the leader and he was in a bad way, when up comes the pup and tore into them. And always after that when either one was in trouble the other would rush in to help him."

The little drawing, reproduced here in full size and showing a rare moment of peace in the day of several shipbound huskies, is a favourite possession of a younger Canadian artist who is himself one of our best draughtsmen. When AY saw the drawing again recently he remarked: "I got pretty good at drawing dogs, eh? No wonder; we had about fifty of them on board!"

And—is there something in the thought that artists' dogs grow to look something like artists? AY's huskies here are rather sturdy and chunky and cheerful; whereas the dogs that Varley drew during *his* Arctic voyage on the *Nascopie* in 1938, so beautifully reproduced in the book *Eskimo*, do they not have a much more melancholy, lean and lupine look . . . ?

16

PLATE 8

Eskimo dogs on board the Beothic [*1930*]

Husky dogs a y jackson

PLATES 9a and 9b
Eskimos crossing the ice at
Arctic Bay [*August 11, 1927*]

Several small 5 by 8 inch pages full of people can be found in AY's drawings from the 1927 and 1930 Arctic trips when the *Beothic* called at as many outposts as possible and often gave lifts to Eskimo families on the move. When there was no time to do an oil sketch, these rapid pencil notes were the happy result. According to Lawren Harris, reminiscing recently about the summer of 1930, "AY was drawing the whole time."

These informal visual records, supplemented by words written at the time and later, show AY's affectionate interest in the northern people: the gaily dressed, smiling Greenlanders in Godhavn, the happy settlement at Pond Inlet, the less happy places farther south where AY felt there was too much dependence on white man's clothing, food, and customs.

Some of the artist's comments show an awareness of dramatic possibilities, as in the few lines in the little unpublished journal concerning a domestic triangle at one of the posts: Eskimo husband, "an old chap near seventy, who has been a great figure in his day," newly married to a young wife, "a pretty little kid, from an Eskimo standpoint"; the latter is much admired by her stepson, "a young Eskimo who has been Sergeant Joy's companion on some of his most arduous journeys . . . fearless, energetic and resourceful. He has no wife . . . but she takes little notice of him." AY carefully recorded their actual names and thought that the situation might

18

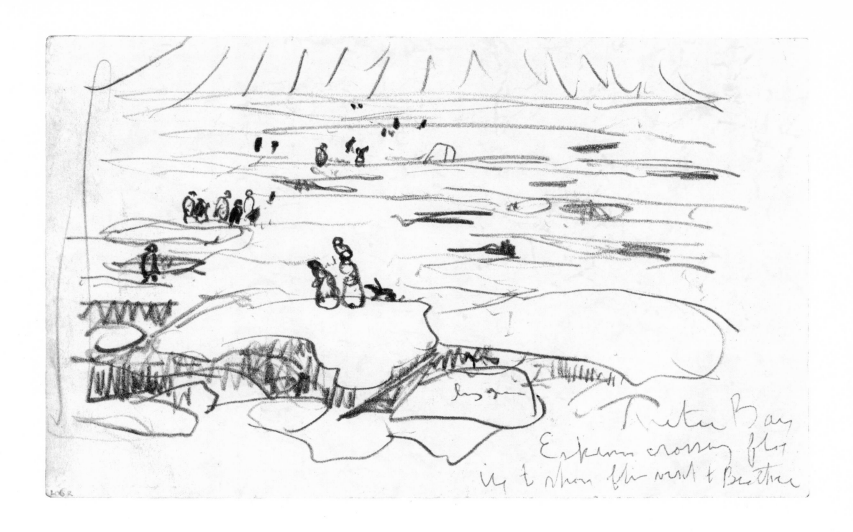

make "a fine little drama," perhaps to be put on at Hart House with Pangnirtung scenery as a backdrop—"if there was anybody to write it."

One of the liveliest episodes during the 1927 trip is described in the text for Plate 13 of *The Far North*. The pen-and-ink drawing there shows the "strange gothic-looking formations" of the coast at the entrance to Arctic Bay off Admiralty Inlet on north-west Baffin; the text goes further and can now—almost forty years later—be happily reunited with its diminutive visual counterpart drawn on August 11th, 1927 (one can guess at what speed!): "In the sheltered bay with a long curving beach and slopes above covered with moss and alpine flowers, about forty Eskimos were living.

They came out to the steamer over the ice as we were preparing to leave. When they found they were too late to come on board, they evinced the keenest disappointment.

"Their departure for the shore was dramatic—the ice was loosening. From children to grandmothers, they started jumping from floe to floe, throwing their dogs across the wider spaces. Eliza crossing the ice was nothing to the flying leaps some of these ladies took, hampered by absurd, highly coloured print dresses that reached their toes, children perched on their shoulders. They were quite unconscious of it being unusual or that Arctic Bay held the world's championship."

The mood of this heading-south-for-home drawing seems suitable for concluding—regretfully all too soon—the Eastern Arctic part of *AY's Canada*.

The light nights of northern summer are past, dangers from fog and floe-ice averted, the sturdy vessel of Canada's Arctic Patrol ploughs across the dark sea. Annual mission accomplished; men and materials (and most of the dogs) delivered to their various destinations at the far-flung outposts; one more small link forged in the long tradition of our sea-faring folk. And on board the black *Beothic* two of the Group of Seven, Harris and Jackson, have during their eight weeks with the ship netted and salted away for future use a goodly haul of drawings, oil sketches, racy tales—in their own way setting new records and broadening established traditions in Canada's cultural growth.

It is pleasant to reflect for a moment on the continuity of these traditions for seafarers and for artists in our northern regions. Though some have died with their goal unreached, many more have survived, completed their jobs, and added their findings to the final record. There is satisfaction in the thought that the same stars depicted here by AY (in a brief interval between fog and storm) once helped to guide the daredevil Norsemen steering approximately by the feather on their skipper's cap, and shone down on Martin Frobisher as he experimented with new navigating techniques. There is pride in recalling that it was on Baffin Island in 1577 that Queen Elizabeth I's enterprising gentlemen adventurers established North America's first mining company with public shareholders. They had even brought along a prefabricated wooden residence and a hundred miners-cum-soldiers-cum-seamen. Unfortunately the north and west walls of their pre-fab were lost when the *Dennis* went down in an ice-jam, and food supplies had been miscalculated, *and* the weather was filthy. ("As usual," say the old-timers.) Gallant Frobisher had to head for home with his "sea-unicorn's horn" as a gift for the Virgin Queen, who as it happened was more interested in the two hundred tons of "heavy black stone" dug from the trench that is still visible today. ("Nothing changes in the Arctic," as AY said.) Alas for the First Elizabethans—the stone was not gold but "only" iron, and Martin Frobisher had found it four centuries too soon. Would he feel gratified at seeing us continue his work today? Probably he would be excited more by our air navigation than all our old iron ore!

The *Beothic*, for all its being a mere speck when up against an iceberg, weighed a hundred and thirty-five times as much as Frobisher's *Gabriel*. And probably the Harris-Jackson expedition of 1930 brought back more memorable Arctic art than any excursion before or since; though it must be recalled with pride that the shipboard-artist tradition had also been established in Frobisher's day. Accompanying the 1577 expedition was one John White. Born between 1540 and 1550, he produced not only several fine studies of the Eskimo man, woman, and child captured and taken away to England (where they of course soon died) but also a lively watercolour of *Englishmen in a Skirmish with Eskimos*, of which the British Museum owns a contemporary copy and the Assistant Keeper of Prints and Drawings writes the following note: "The observed detail—the icefloes, the kayaks, the tents, clothes and weapons of the Eskimos—leaves little room for doubt that the artist actually witnessed this event and was not illustrating it at second hand. . . . This then becomes one of the earliest scientific graphic documents of English exploration."

Down through the centuries explorers have taken care to provide the world with visual records, and A. Y. Jackson's work in the north can take its proper place in that venerable tradition. The Group of Seven generation as a whole, including of course Tom Thomson, showed plenty of the same daredevil spirit as the earlier explorer-adventurers. Most of the Seven-plus have been willing to live dangerously, to work hard, and to travel far to reach their goals. Maybe even willing, as Master Hawkins put it in the days of Elizabeth I, "to go to Hell for the Pleasure of it"—assuming, of course, that there would be something Canadian to paint there.

PLATE 10

On board the Beothic *at night* [1930]

Safe anchorage for ships from near and far has been provided for over five hundred years in the harbour of St. John's, Newfoundland, where once upon a time the tall-masted ships of John Cabot (1497), of Jacques Cartier and the Sieur de Roberval (1542), and of Sir Humphrey Gilbert (1583) consorted with the humbler "shippes of fishers" from Devon, Normandy, Portugal and other lands. Indeed, the "Portugals" were known to be there by 1455 and according to a tradition gave St. John's its name one June 24th long ago. When Gilbert planted the flag of England on the shore in 1583, he received the "warmest reception" from those same fishing Portugals, "who above all nations did most willingly and liberally contribute wines, marmalads most fine . . . bisket, sweet oyles . . . fresh salmon, trouts, lobsters and other fresh fish brought daily."

AY reached St. John's (by air, it must be confessed, not sea) in July 1952, just three years after Newfoundland had joined Canada's fair domain as the tenth province. His mission to St. John's was a rather unusual one, as he had been commissioned to make studies and sketches of Newfoundland's capital in preparation for a canvas in the series *Cities of Canada* sponsored by the House of Seagram and subsequently exhibited across Canada as well as abroad. All the provincial capitals and Ottawa were painted by different Canadian artists. Although AY had not worked in Newfoundland previously, there seemed to be a temperamental affinity in the combination—oldest city, oldest artist.

With his headquarters in St. John's, AY spent a busy fortnight stumping up and down the steep hills that surround the magnificently located capital. He found many good subjects in the rocky headlands, the Batteries with their steep-sloping streets, and the old sections of the city, as well as at some of the accessible outports such as Portuguese Cove.

The present drawing of city and harbour, seen from Signal Hill, closely resembles the view finally selected by the sponsor for inclusion in the *Cities of Canada* series. It was "a tough subject," AY found, with so much detail in the outspread city. But in the final painting, as well as here in the drawing, he has managed to subordinate detail to general mass, stressing a few salient points of interest, such as the nobly proportioned freighter that strengthens the sharp angle of the two long diagonals which form the basic composition—a rather unusual pattern in AY's work.

This 1952 drawing was done before the erection of the imposing nine-million-dollar Confederation Building and the beautiful new Memorial University buildings which helped to alter the aspect of St. John's, capital of the fastest-changing province in Canada. In 1952 the university enrolment was somewhere around 400; it has now rocketed to well over 3,000.

22

PLATE 11

Harbour of St. John's,
Newfoundland, July 1952

July, 52   St John NF   A.Y. Jackson

The above graphic words, borrowed from James W. Bacque's excellent notes to Plate 23 of Varley-Dobbs' *Canada*, can certainly apply to AY's drawing of much the same locality, probably the Upper Battery above the harbour of St. John's, Newfoundland. If anything, the free-and-easy style of the drawing makes the houses stagger even more.

The casual arrangement of up-and-down streets, the combination of old wooden houses with angular lines set into the rugged, rounded-rocky landscape, appealed particularly to AY during his fortnight in Newfoundland in July 1952. He drew and sketched many subjects not suitable for the *Cities of Canada* commission but pleasing to his own taste. (He wishes that all the oil sketches had not been whisked away from him so fast, as there were several he wanted very much to paint up in large format.)

At the time of AY's visit the new sweepingly progressive measures introduced by Premier Joey Smallwood were only just getting up steam, so that the country AY saw was still by and large the "old Newfoundland," where most people lived pretty frugally from fishing, an only part-of-the-year employment. AY certainly liked their weatherbeaten homes, time-worn and tough, and found the rugged individualism and self-sufficiency of the Newfoundlanders to his taste. Nowadays, less than twenty years later, fishing provides a mere ten per cent of the total provincial income, the bulk now coming from power industries. Population is up nearly one-half since Confederation and the budget quadrupled between 1949 and 1965. There are over twelve hundred new schools, over sixteen hundred miles of new roads—isolation is a thing of the past. Joey, the one mainly responsible for bringing all this about, occasionally casts a nostalgic glance back upon the qualities of bygone days. "We Newfoundlanders of the older generation are antiquarians who love the past and regret to see it going—one of the prices we must pay for joining the current of modern life," Joey said (approximately) in a recent broadcast.

So perhaps there is fitting irony in the fact that the A. Y. Jackson canvas (25 by 32 inches) presented in 1962 to Premier Smallwood by the Iron Ore Company of Canada is a vast panorama of the site of the mining operations in Labrador, not a view of Joey's own colourful home corner of the world.

As the present drawing shows, around 1950 AY tended to fill the sheet of paper very full—on *both* sides—his vigorous pencil strokes pressing into the paper and causing the other side to smudge a bit. In addition he sometimes, as here, used a blue-ink ball-point pen to featherstitch his comments into the patchwork quilt of houses and rocks: "dull crim; yel 5; white sash," and so on. And for final effect he adds one of his familiar human touches: a lone wanderer, who we trust will locate the road home without too much trouble!

PLATE 12

Houses above St. John's, Newfoundland [*July 1952*]

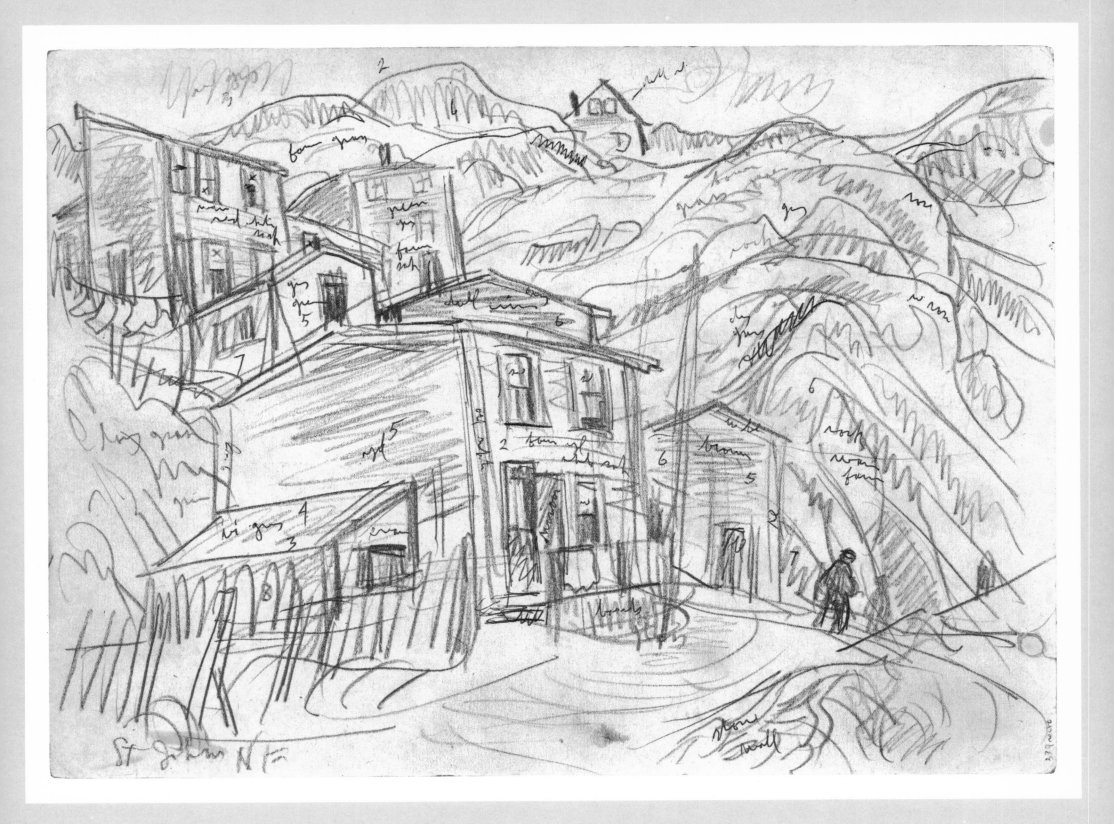

The present diminutive drawing belongs to the year 1919, just after AY had returned from four years overseas in the Canadian armed forces, ending up as an official War Artist. While he was still engaged in doing canvases for the War Records he was sent to the east coast to depict the troop transports bringing the Canadians home, most of them landing in the port of Halifax. In 1919 that venerable city on what Champlain in 1607 called its "very safe bay" still showed the scars of the terrible explosion of two years previous. This occurred when the French steamer *Mont Blanc*, carrying a deck cargo of benzine and an undercargo of three thousand tons of dynamite, on its way through the Narrows into Bedford Basin, was grazed by the Norwegian *Imo* (carrying an innocent cargo of relief goods for Belgium). Fire broke out on the *Mont Blanc* and within minutes, at exactly 9:05 on that dull grey morning of December 6th, 1917, the burning ship sent up "a big black ball, like a huge cannonball . . . then it sort of opened up and the sky was full of beautiful different-coloured ribbons. Then it all blew up," to quote one eyewitness (Mrs. William Shea, then Frances Day) who has preserved this visual memory for nearly half a century. Another survivor, the Rev. Harold T. Roe, wrote a few days after the explosion of how the *Mont Blanc* blew apart with " . . . a dull reverberating roar and a crash that defies description. In a second of time it was as though a fierce tornado had swept the city. The whole north end, practically two square miles of territory, became a burning ruin. A considerable section of the waterfront was completely shattered, and all over the city public buildings and private dwellings were wrecked and not a window intact."

In the Halifax explosion, a preview of things to come elsewhere later in the century, but all the worse for being so unexpected, eighteen hundred persons were killed outright; over three thousand were badly injured, many being blinded and deafened; and eight thousand were left homeless. A violent snowstorm soon after the explosion rendered rescue work even more difficult. Temporary barracks—wooden frames covered with beaverboard and tarpaper—were thrown together on the Commons and Exhibition Grounds, with the assistance of Army and Navy, to shelter families in blocks of twelve for the winter. Soon the sound of "K-K-Katy" and "I'm forever blowing bubbles" blared out from gramophones once again through the Maritime fog and mist. One last victim: the famous Town Clock (erected in 1803 at the foot of Citadel Hill by order of the Duke of Kent, father of the future Queen Victoria and a martinet for punctuality) remained stopped at that 9:05 for over a year, as some Haligonians may recall.

26 The drawing technique displayed here had been developed just pre-

viously by AY in war-torn Flanders, where the artist can be visualized standing close to the ragged fringe of war, jotting his rapid pencil notes in the pocket-sized notebook with thin translucent paper serrated along one long edge. Notations of tone values 1 to 10 and copious colour reminders were essential, considering the speed at which he had to work and the unavoidable time lapse before the multitude of notes could be painted up into canvases.

This little Canadian drawing also conveys the atmosphere of deathly desolation wrought by explosion and fire. Several similar notes formed the basis of the canvas, *Entrance to Halifax Harbour*, which was purchased by the British Government from the Wembley Show in 1924 for the Tate Gallery in London. The careful notes are almost poetic in their own right, for instance for the present drawing (njg 341): "cold blue grey day; flat cold dull silver. . . ." On its *verso* is a detail study of the dead tree at the right, and the words "Scheme: flat definite blue and violet greys, running to greyed lake reds. Cool ochres to brick, and touches of orange in trees and rust on boat. . . ."

It is interesting to recall that Lawren Harris at about the same time also wrote many verbal instructions into his small pencil studies—the emerging Group of Seven did its homework far from casually!

PLATE 13

Halifax, The Narrows, Bedford Basin, 1919

Halifax 1919

During his 1919 visit to Nova Scotia AY did some drawing around this nice little fishing village not far from Halifax; actually it was here he did some of the pencil studies used in the canvas *Entrance to Halifax Harbour* that later went to the Tate Gallery. This type of maritime subject is reminiscent of Arthur Lismer's work as well, and it was a pleasant coincidence for the two artist friends—both in their mid-thirties and full of vim and vigour—that their time in Halifax overlapped so that they could spend many cheerful and active hours together, helping offset the rather grey atmosphere of the conservative garrison city.

Lismer had been in Halifax since the fall of 1916, as principal of the Victoria School of Art and Design. His princely salary of $900 per annum was fortunately supplemented by commissions for canvases for the Canadian War Records (for instance, *The Olympic with Returned Soldiers*, 1918; AY did an *Olympic* too and Lismer had a *Halifax Harbour* already by 1916!). The Lismers' little rented house was at Bedford, some ten miles outside the city, and fortunately Lismer had missed the train to town on the fateful morning of the December 1917 explosion. Some of his on-the-spot drawings of its appalling devastation were published shortly after in the *Canadian Courier*.

Together Lismer and AY looked for good subjects to paint, as AY recounts in *A Painter's Country*, and both artists did canvases of the fishing village of Herring Cove. Lismer held a show of fifty-three canvases in Halifax in July 1919, and AY doubtless gave him cheerful sympathy when "scarcely one was sold," in the rather ambiguous words of John A. B. McLeish in *September Gale*. Lismer was to return many times to Nova Scotia for characteristic subjects dear to his heart—wharves with fishing gear, lobster pots, and "killicks," those home-made anchors at which AY tried his hand in our insert (njg 348r).

Recent visitors to Herring Cove say that it has changed very little since the sunny day in 1919 when this tiny drawing was done with such care. The forest fires raging nearby in May 1965 luckily missed the Cove's colourful shacks, and it is to be hoped that there will not be too much modernization by those "herring fisheries people from B.C.," mentioned in a recent radio broadcast, who have set out to spur the Nova Scotians onward to "more modern and more successful techniques." Success is such a relative matter, and for some of us who love the East Coast's ancient ways there is quite enough *success* in this evocation of the clear warm brilliance of a seaside day or—to use AY's own notations—"sky 3 blue vibrant; houses front in dark shadow same value as roofs; shed dark red, roof warm black, pink cloth on line 1; 5 blue broken, warm reflex close to shore, white boat 1."

28

PLATE 14

Herring Cove, Nova Scotia
[*1919*]

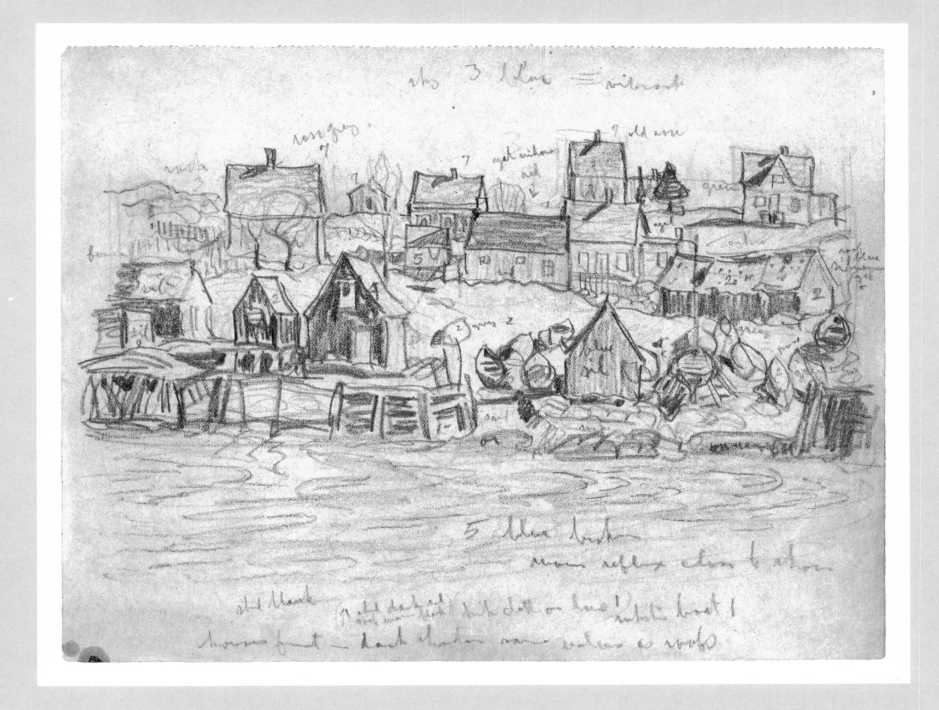

Ancient mills are usually thought of as moonlit and romantic, but AY has given a rough-and-ready, almost slap-happy treatment to this old sawmill run by water power, somewhere in the region of the many "Margarees," in behind Margaree Harbour on Cape Breton Island. This seems to be the only pencil drawing which has turned up at present that can be definitely ascribed to that delectable part of Nova Scotia. AY spent a fortnight down there "one summer before World War II," with the painters Peter Haworth and Bobs Coghill Haworth of Toronto. He was not able to stay long enough to continue with them around the northern part of the Cabot Trail and has never worked in that grandiose region.

The oil sketch of the present subject, done before the drawing, was given by AY to "a little girl down there. . . . She was studying art in New York but her work was full of inhibitions, so I made a rough sketch to show her how to tackle the thing, and let her have it after." The drawing was probably made for his own personal record, at a time when he does not seem to have done much in that medium. Its robust, casual style makes a strong contrast to the delicate small drawings he had done around Halifax about twenty years earlier.

But as long before that again, it happens, AY had paid his *very* first visit to the Maritimes—a visit he did not get around to mentioning in his autobiography but enjoys reminiscing about: "That was away back in July 1902; I would be about nineteen. I went down to Nova Scotia with Billy Ives—he's still alive. We were both apprentices in that lithographing firm in Montreal. His father was agent for a coal company on Cape Breton and we travelled all the way down to Pictou on a Norwegian coal boat and stayed for a whole month. We took our bikes down with us, and I biked all the way from Pictou to Mulgrave Harbour across from Cape Breton, and back again to Pictou, along the shore road; there were some awful hills. I'd stop to sketch, in watercolour in those days, and I'd trade my sketch with a farmer who'd put me up overnight. I never sold any of those early watercolours, I gave them all away. A couple of people still have some—old wharves and sailing boats and things like that. . . . There was a girl down there I kind of liked, but of course I never spoke to her about it. She died a couple of years later. I can still remember her name— it was Margaret."

So memories of Nova Scotia summers seem to live a long, long time. Laid between the pages of AY's scrapbook is a poem by the Maritime-born Charles G. D. Roberts. Called "In the Night Watches," it may have appealed to AY through its mood of solitude and strong sentiment.

When the little spent winds are at rest
  in the tamarack tree
In the still of the night,
And the moon in her waning is wan
  and mis-shapen,
And out on the lake
The loon floats in a glimmer of light,
And the solitude sleeps—
Then I lie in my bunk wide awake,
And my long thoughts stab me with longing,
Alone in my shack by the marshes of lone
  Margaree.

And so the most melodious of all river names in Canada brings us back full circle to the place where this small sentimental detour began!

PLATE 15

Old Mill, Cape Breton Island [*1930s*]

In the spring of 1936 AY tried the most picturesque, the most easterly—meaning the most exposed—part of the Gaspé Peninsula for his annual "early spring" (i.e. late winter!) sketching trip. This resulted in some wonderfully interesting drawings—more drawings than oil sketches, probably because the weather was so stormy, rainy and foggy that he was scarcely able to paint out of doors. A letter from Fox River, dated April 6th, 1936, towards the end of his stay, gives a vivid close-up of the artist's state of mind during that Gaspé sojourn, of which no mention whatever is made in the autobiography of 1957 (probably because he had been so mad about the weather!): "... it's a good night to write letters. The southeast wind is making the windows rattle, and a fool butterfly who got mixed in his dates is waiting for spring under the window-sill. So it isn't always the early bird that catches the worm. . . .

"It has been a lousy spring, and I have wasted a lot of time and still don't know if I am going to get anything worth while. Lost a week in that miserable little village of Gaspé, rain and fog, impassable roads, and when I finally got here the snow was all but gone. However, more came, and if it would only freeze up and the sun come out, I could find lots to paint.

"I could swap you a lobster for a salad—too much of the former and none of the latter; but it's just for a month. I am at a hotel two hundred yards from the Caribou Inn, towards the town; the Caribou is closed of course. . . . Everyone tearing round on dog sleighs; they don't seem to have anything else to do. . . .

"I don't know when I'll get home. There are a pile of panels still unmessed-up. I am the only *étranger* who ever struck the place in winter time—*le premier touriste*."

The rugged wanderer AY was not the first to feel the Gaspé's rough weather-fist. That was also mentioned by a *touriste* more *premier* than AY by four hundred and two years, in fact the very first visitor to be recorded historically in the exact spot that AY wrote about: "... being overthwart the said River [here Gaspé Basin at the tip of the peninsula] there arose againe a contrary winde, with great fogges and stormes . . . the winde became so raging that one of our ships lost an anker, and we were constrained to goe up higher into the river seven or eight leagues, into a good harborough and ground that we with our boates found out, and through the evill weather, tempest and darkenesse that was, wee stayed in the saide harborough till the five and twentieth of the moneth [which happened to be July!], not being able to put out: in the meane time wee sawe a great multitude of wilde men that were fishing for mackerels, whereof there is great store. . . ."

So the *touriste* of 1936 formed part of the travelling tradition begun by Jacques Cartier and recorded in Hakluyt's picturesque translation of the French original. The quotation is garnered from a book very dear to the Jackson family, *The Heart of Gaspé*. Written by John Mason Clarke, a geologist with the eye of an artist, this book was published in 1913, over half a century ago. Yet the Gaspé it presents, the Gaspé that was "still far from the world's thoroughfares," was much the same when depicted by AY only half that long ago. It is quite possible that there was less change in the region between the time of Cartier's visit (1534) and Clarke's (by 1913) than between Jackson's (1936) and the present—three hundred years versus thirty. So the glimpses of remote places and ancient ways that AY's drawings give can receive a new dimension of illumination, a counterpoint of eloquence, from *The Heart of Gaspé*.

The simple scene *en face*, titled only "Gaspé," may well have been done at the historic spot where New France came into being on that July day in 1534 when the first fleur-de-lys went up on the cross above the sandbar in Gaspé Bay. These sturdy old fishing vessels are the direct descendants of the generations that have anchored in the "good harborough" through the centuries.

PLATE 16

Fishing boats on the Gaspé shore [*1936*]

A.Y. Jackson Gaspé

Typical Gaspé is the snug cove of Little Fox River, with its jutting promontory and curved gravel beach strewn with indications of the inhabitants' main occupation. It lies just west of "big" Fox River, around the corner from Gaspé, on the St. Lawrence side. Here the ancient folds and troughs of the Appalachians reach their outermost north-eastern supramarine tip, with towering mountains and deep valleys forming precipitous cliffs and rounded bays that sea and storms constantly devour. All along the rugged coast, sometimes to a width of five miles, "lies a buried rock platform which the waves have carved out, a remnant of the majestic mountains which once raised their crests where the fisherman now drops his hook." An enormous volume of rock, "ground back to its primal mud," provides sustenance for myriads of fish, so that the "majestic and ragged" Gaspé coast is one of the world's richest fishing grounds.

For many, many years, centuries very likely, before there was any permanent settlement along the forbidding shore, men in small ships came annually to these rich waters for the bounteous harvest, sheltering their vessels in the small coves, rowing ashore to dry and smoke and salt their fish, then returning to distant homelands. Sometimes they made two trips a year, between June and December, reaching home well before the following Lent, the season their wares were most in demand. In 1632, a century after Cartier had laid claim to New France, there was still no French settlement on the Gaspé, though Récollet and then Jesuit missions were set up at Percé and on Bonaventure Island to minister to Micmac Indians and to visiting mariners from Catholic Europe.

The place names along this part of the coast are a fascinating reflection of what *The Heart of Gaspé* calls "an intimate side of its history," revealing the "epochs of occupation" and the resultant gloriously jumbled composite of various languages. It is fun to compare what J. M. Clarke records by 1913 with further developments (or regressions) in the half-century since, the chief source of these to hand being the well-worn Esso road map from a family visit in 1960.

The name Gaspé itself seems to have been the *Gespeg* of the Micmac Indians, meaning end or extremity (like Land's End or Finisterre), the north-east limit of that maritime tribe, the "wilde men" encountered by Cartier in 1534. On a hot July day that same year, the Baie des Chaleurs got its name—it varies between singular and plural. Clarke calls it Chaleur Bay and tells with glee of the vain attempt by Sir William Alexander to rename it Stirling Bay. Visiting seamen in the sixteenth century or earlier christened the Island of Bonne Aventure, now reduced to Bonaventure (good landmark, good shelter, good fishing) and of course the celebrated Percé Rock, whose name was transferred to the whole region. Long before Cartier got there, the Basques called Gaspé Baie à Penouil, from the sandbar peninsula on the north side, later the location of the customs and fish storage shed that once housed General Wolfe during September of 1758. According to Esso 1960, the name is gone and the "peninsula" has been eaten away into an island.

Some places were named for people: a cove south of Gaspé began as L'Anse à Bonfils, in honour of an aristocratic summer visitor to Percé, became altered to L'Anse au Beaufils (son-in-law), as it is in Esso 1960, locally anglicized to Lancy Buffy! Cap Bon Ami is on the steep forbidding beachless shore at a spot where a Monsieur Bon Ami from Jersey or Guernsey used to lower his lobster pots. French Cap d'Espoir is English Cape Despair; Italian *despera* (1546) is Latin *spei* (1660)—probably the oldest and best example in what Clarke calls this "little war." Conversely Cap-à-faim has been anglicized to Fame Point then returned in a CPR map to French as Pointe de la Renommé! A delightful development is L'Anse au Gris Fond from the muddy grey clay bottom of a cove six miles east of Fox River; this rather understandably sounded like Griffon to the English and is now L'Anse au Griffon for the French as well! A family favourite is Cap-aux-Os in Gaspé Bay, inspired by the great wave-washed skeleton of a grounded whale; this sounded like Oiseau to Captain Bayfield when he did his map, was later phoneticized to Ozo and is usually called Caboozo by the English along the coast. Plateau Island was called Plato by Bayfield; some old map called it Flat, from which the italic *Fl* was misread as Hat. A surprise is Fox River itself, because the French Rivière au Renard would indicate an animal origin as much as does Rivière du Loup further upstream, yet Clarke in his fascinating glossary of place names, says: "Probably after Chas. James Fox, 1749-1806," which would make the French the transgressors this time. However at one place in the text the author seems to assume a family name of "the Renards" who set up fishing rather late in that district! Ah well—*spes despera*—maybe Little Fox River was settled by one of the Renard children, and Rivière du Loup was named for General Wolfe!

AY's drawing, which he is presenting to the National Gallery of Canada, has something of the harbour mood of the French artist Marquet, with its firm, vivid shapes, its sturdy pier with the tide away out, its small boats for the *pesche sédentaire*, which the English rather elusively call "offshore" fishing. In the olden days Little Fox lay isolated in the shelter of its surrounding cliffs, with a covered wooden bridge over its Little Fox river; this bridge still shows in the AY canvas in the J. S. McLean collection. Now the covered part is gone and a broad highway cuts through the hill, so that before we know it we have sped onward to the River of the Big Foxes!

34

Little Fox River Gaspé
A Y Jackson

PLATE 17

The cove of Little Fox River, Gaspé [1936]

The sheet of paper on which the intimate cove of Little Fox River was recorded by AY in April 1936 reveals on its *verso* a somewhat different aspect of the Gaspé world of those days—a dignified long line of weather-beaten fish houses, formerly used either for smoke-curing the catch or for storing the precious produce after it had been dried out of doors in the sun and air, until the time came for it to be shipped away.

Fox River, with its harbour protected by bounding capes and a broad sandbar, is a great centre for fishing, although not as ancient a settlement as those further eastward down the coast. "Here is great fishing," says *The Heart of Gaspé*, elaborating with detailed and graphic descriptions the entire process of its historic development, to the accompaniment of marvellous photographs showing the splitting tables on the shore and the vast expanses of codfish drying either spread out directly on the pebbly beach, carefully kept free of sand, weeds and debris, or else lying on long stands called "flakes" built of beech pickets and covered with spruce twigs—until the coming of wire netting. The split-open fish had to be turned at least once daily so as to dry both sides. Then, before storehouses were built, the dried fish was piled in round mows thatched with birch bark held down with large stones. The ancient methods continued in use well into the twentieth century—probably until after World War II: "With the same shaped hooks and with lines rigged as now, and with the same bait, the cod was taken, and pitched from the shallops with the same shaped pew. At the splitting table built as to-day were the trancheur, decoleur and picqueur, supplied with fish from the same shaped barrow by the same shaped boy. The splitters with knives of the ancient pattern today still grasp the fish by the "ears" for decapitation, with one time-honored movement disembowel it and push the liver into the vat through a hole in the splitting table and with another cut out the backbone. The liver vat still has its wicker for the oil to drain through, and still gives off, as the livers stew in the sun, an incense too rank to rise heavenward, the special *parfumerie* of the devil, equaled only by the aroma rising from the cod heads festering in the sun's heat on the ploughed fields . . . this appalling and stupefying stench is actually agreeable to the fishermen. . . . Several thousand tons of rejectamenta are annually left to waste their sweetness on the Gaspé air."

Fishing at Fox River used to be controlled by several great fishery businesses built up by Channel Islanders after the fall of Quebec in 1759. Their drastic rules effected a stranglehold on all in their employ—which meant almost everybody in the area. The first strike in the history of the Gaspé fishing business took place in 1909 at Fox River and was only quelled when the federal government sent along two cruisers and jailed

twenty of the "insurgents." The average annual catch of one of these large companies (Fruing Co.), which had twenty-eight different stations in 1913, was estimated at three to four million codfish, "and if this is a fair figure certainly the entire Gaspé coast must afford from forty to fifty millions of cod every year. The wonder is that after these nearly three hundred years of fishing there is a cod left in all the Gulf. Perhaps no one could find a more effective illustration of the profluence of that alma mater of all life, the sea."

Nowadays the boats still go out to fish and return with plentiful catches of cod, herring, sole, mackerel, scallops and lobster for the delectation of tourists, travellers and gourmets in general—and artists who partake of the seaside bustle and activity. But the drying flakes no longer line the shore; the beaches are relatively clean and sterile; gone are the rows of fish houses. Gone is even most of that memorable, that unforgettable fishy aroma of yore. Nowadays each fisherman takes his catch into the square cement building of the co-operative and has his share weighed and recorded to his private account. All cleaning is done indoors, then the fresh catch vanishes into the deep-freeze and is moved along in due course in great freezer boxes that go from truck to train by that system sometimes called "piggy-back" but here more fittingly "fishyback."

All very modern, practical, pure, and prosaic. Not the thing to inspire AY's artistic output, except indirectly via his good digestion! It is lucky that he got there before the fish houses disappeared forever, and gave us this "historical document."

PLATE 18

Fish houses, Fox River,
Gaspé Peninsula [1936]

The manner in which AY actually reached Fox River in late March 1936 was by horse and sleigh from the village of Gaspé, "the new road straight across the mountains and pretty tough going." However it afforded him a glimpse of the high interior of Gaspé County, then as earlier largely "a heavily wooded, tenantless domain, still a place of trails and portages, as little reduced to the pursuits and demands of civilization as the interior of Patagonia."

There were no mines worked in the Gaspé in John Mason Clarke's day, nor did that learned geologist ever foresee any—proving how wrong it is to prophesy. "The fish, the lumber and the chilly farms are the sources from which happiness and contentment are here derived," the Introduction to *The Heart of Gaspé* tells us; nor had the situation changed radically even by 1936 when AY reached Fox River, "the metropolis of the south shore." It was not till later that the copper mines around Murdochville were opened and new roads broke through the interior.

The present drawing of Fox River shows the characteristic feature of its famous *barachois*, a word usually taken to mean the sandbar across the bay, but actually, according to *The Heart of Gaspé*'s Glossary: "General term applied to any water at a river mouth impounded behind a coastal sand bar . . . *Barre-cheois, barre-echuée*, the waters protected by a bar." The open passage to the outer bay is traversed by a narrow medieval-looking wooden bridge not unlike the type described by Clarke over twenty years before: "Across the mouth of Fox river runs the great sand bar joining the east and west side of the valley . . . cluttered up with cook-houses, storehouses, the drying stages and their refuse, while the little outlet of the river at the west is crossed by a simple footbridge of planks on wooden horses. The bounding hills are not high and the valley has been cut so broad that the traveler with horse must make a long detour inland and back to reach the further side of the bay; so the village really consists of two parts while the sand bar and the plank bridge wide enough only for *one abreast*, form the esplanade which binds together the social centers of the settlement."

A canvas of the exact scene of the present drawing, entitled *Fishing Village*, was donated by AY to the Relief of Leningrad project in 1943. This was Canada's homage to "the city that wouldn't die," whose three million heroic inhabitants, trapped by the Nazi army from September 8, 1941 until January 27, 1944, chose starvation and death rather than surrender. A photograph in the Montreal *Standard* for June 26, 1943, shows AY and S. M. Kudriavtsev, Secretary to the Russian Legation in Ottawa, standing in front of the works donated by Canadian artists on behalf of Leningrad. Next to AY's dark-skyed canvas is one entitled *Three Fisher-* men, also done on the Gaspé, by Betty Maw, now Mrs. Gerard Brett of Toronto, a lifelong friend of AY and all the Jacksons. Canada gave canvases (about twenty, AY recalls) and books and music manuscripts, all exhibited over here before being sent to the Soviet Union. AY wonders where they all are now. And each time he sees this drawing he says: "The old wooden bridge is gone now, and that fine old church in the background has been taken down—probably even the barachois is gone. . . ."

But at least they are recorded here in *AY's Canada* by "le premier touriste de 1936"!

PLATE 19

Old bridge and barachois,
Fox River, Gaspé
[April 1936]

Fox River

Our book proceeds upstream along the South Shore of the broad St. Lawrence as that mighty river skirts the southern edge of the Laurentian highland—river and hills that are dominant forces in the existence both of eastern Canada and of the artist Jackson who was born and has worked for the better part of a century in their sphere. We move back upstream in time as well, to the period of AY's first sojourn *en bas Québec*, in that region down-river from Quebec City that became his special domain.

The year 1921 saw AY's first visit for a couple of months of winter-spring sketching in the heart of French Canada. The South Shore, which off and on he considers his favourite place to work ("I'm never happier than when I'm sketching down the south bank of the St. Lawrence," he told Leslie F. Hannon in *Mayfair* in 1954), was favoured with full-length visits on four occasions (1921, 1927, 1935, and 1939) in one particular fifty-mile stretch from Cacouna, just below Rivière du Loup, down to Bic, just above Rimouski. Many delightful names made familiar through AY's work—St. Fabien, St. Simon, Tobin near Trois Pistoles—fit into this relatively small region. Some of AY's most distinguished canvases come from here, including several without geographic titles, such as *Winter Road, Quebec*, 1921 (C. S. Band Collection), *A Quebec Village*, 1921 (National Gallery of Canada), *A Village on the Gulf*, alias *St. Lawrence in Winter*, 1921 (F. T. Jenkins Collection), all from the Cacouna area; and two from the St. Simon-Bic area that have gone into the most homes and hands, having been used as dust jackets for two books illustrated by AY: his own autobiography, *A Painter's Country*, which uses Mrs. H. A. Dyde's canvas *Road to St. Simon* (1940), and Henry Beston's book *The St. Lawrence*, which uses a version of the National Gallery's *Quebec Village*. In both cases the horizontally striped composition is a most suitable background for titles.

The drawings for this fifty-mile strip, particularly from the 1921 and 1927 visits, are full of interesting, now historic, detail. They are all rather small in format, those for 1921 being $7\frac{5}{8}$ by 10 inches, on thin paper with serrated tops; those for 1927 being $8\frac{3}{8}$ by $10\frac{7}{8}$ inches with three loose-leaf holes along one long side, sometimes trimmed off by AY with resulting smaller measurements. Additional, much smaller notebook drawings, approximately 5 by 8 inches, were also done at those times. The relatively small size of the major drawings allows them to be reproduced here close to life-size, revealing the delicate detail which distinguishes most of them. The chapter in *A Painter's Country* entitled simply "Quebec" tells with warm sincerity the story of those early visits and it is pleasant to combine here its words and some of the actual drawings that are fresh and intimate and relatively little known.

The first included (njg 594) from that special area on the South Shore was done while AY worked about two miles west, i.e. up-river, from the village of Cacouna, boarding with the Plourde family in their old yellowish wooden house, which the present writer also knew well, having spent several summers chez Ouellet next door. Says AY of the place: "It was old settled country; the farms ran back from the highway, long and narrow, and all the houses on the highway were close together.... At first . . . I was interested in the old farm houses, in the barns and the trees."

The present rather lyric little drawing makes an interesting composition out of the clear-cut upright of the young tree balanced by the long horizontals of the straggling farm buildings and old rail fences that stretch away back, along fields ten times as long as they are wide, until they reach the shoe-box-shaped Mont Pilote (where such good blueberries grew in the summertime!). The road with its fringe of farmhouses follows the wooded rocky ridge, which parallels the River and gives protection from winter's icy winds from across the water.

This part of the country is typical of Lower Quebec. During the French régime, the seigneur was obliged to grant land to the *habitants* in return for the duty of clearing it and an additional small perpetual rent. These grants were usually four *arpents* wide (about one-seventh of a mile) and forty long (one and a half miles), which from the outset established the long narrow look. The land was redivided lengthwise among the sons so that each could have a home on the highway, with less difficult access to the parish church and the seigneurial flour mill. Such "old rural life-ways . . . [shaped] a relatively isolated, family-oriented, and self-sufficient community."

PLATE 20

Farmland west of Cacouna, near Rivière du Loup, Quebec, 1921

Cocouina 1921

A Painter's Country recounts how in March 1921 AY, sustained in part by the Plourdes' rich diet of cream and maple syrup and in part by his sturdy snowshoes, worked through the interesting aspects of the Cacouna countryside, then moved into the village itself. He persuaded his good friend Albert Robinson to join him there, which not only brightened life around the quiet little hotel but in due course resulted in what may be Robinson's most distinguished canvas, *Returning from Easter Mass*, 1922 (Art Gallery of Ontario), well known in silk screen form as well.

Quite naturally the two artist friends took a lively interest in the latewinter life of the little Lower St. Lawrence community. They absorbed the feel of the place: "... a whole parish rooted in the soil ... in the centre stands the church; alongside it, the burying-ground; close by, the *curé's* house and the *curé* himself inside it. After our parish there is another parish, and another and another, all alike; and each with its church steeple, its *curé*, its buried dead, its old soil worked by fathers and fathers' fathers, which one loves more than one's self—There you have it, this country of ours!"

This seems an appropriate place to introduce into *AY's Canada* these few words from that justly famous and beloved little work, actually written about another South Shore community nearer Quebec, but close both in time and in gentle spirit to AY's work around 1921. *Chez Nous*, by Adjutor Rivard, first appeared in French in two brochures which Clarence Gagnon enthusiastically showed to AY. The latter suggested that W. H. Blake do an English translation, and this was published by McClelland & Stewart in 1924, with end-papers and pen-and-ink illustrations by AY. All this came to pass shortly after the little Cacouna works introduced the Lower St. Lawrence phase of the artist's career.

AY's Quebec works have become so familiar to us Canadians in the course of this century that we usually simply take for granted that "Quebec looked that way in the olden days," forgetting that a thing only "looks like" something *after* someone has created an image of it and made us familiar with that image. More than any other single Canadian artist during the quarter-century from 1920 on, it has been A. Y. Jackson who has created the image of rural winter-time Quebec. It is therefore good to turn back for a moment to examine these "firsts" in his work and to rediscover *how* the image was actually created.

Here, for instance, is a diminutive drawing of surprising delicacy, a drawing in its own right, not a bit like the fine-toned but bluntly-brushed oil sketches of that same year, 1921. Here is an exquisite delineation of the heart of a French-Canadian village, aligned along the high horizon with a broad field sloping towards the foreground, ploughed furrows and

stubble emerging through the remnants of the winter snow. AY tells in *A Painter's Country* how his attention shifted during that Cacouna visit from old farm houses, barns and trees to snow shapes in their changing colour and texture. "Towards spring there was slush, and pools of water, and finally the furrowed fields appeared through the slush."

The snow-filled ruts of the carefully studied farm road, flanked by wooden fence posts in the foreground, carry the eye in and upward—as does every delicate stroke of the rolling terrain—until the entire rising movement is held and contained by the firm horizontal of the buildings across the top. It is a classical, centralized little composition in the best European tradition; it could be by Corot, if Corot could have been at Cacouna in 1921. There is a kind of fine-nerved intensity to it, such as one senses in tiny medieval silverpoint drawings. It is anything but bold, flat, or poster-like in effect, qualities which some people constantly and unobservantly associate with all Group of Seven work. AY was painting with increasing boldness in those days, but he still drew delicately, sensitively, poetically. His friend J. E. H. MacDonald was also a poet, more so in words than AY, who preserved carefully in his scrapbook a little poem by J.E.H. called "March Wind." This contains the line "The dark earth lifting through the sinking snow," which goes well with many of AY's drawings.

However we must not draw too poetical, high-faluting conclusions from all this, because AY himself never would. We need simply turn to another page of this Cacouna 1921 series to find some hilariously inept attempts to draw a horse and sleigh in motion—another first in a long, long lineage. The horse was always more in motion than the sleigh and would disappear at a gallop before AY could get it in. Those were the years when we all sang about "Horses, horses, horses." Horses were *in* for AY.

PLATE 21

Cacouna Village, with melting snow [1921]

It is interesting to observe, on the basis of the few Quebec winter drawings that can be shown within the broader scope of the present volume, how AY's choice of subject and drawing technique evolved during the 1920s, when he really got going in Canada.

On his first winter-spring sojourn around Cacouna in 1921 he strongly felt the impact and appeal of "picturesque old Quebec," as indicated in the foregoing title. His delicate, almost dainty, drawing style continued the next spring, when he and Albert Robinson stayed opposite that quaintest of all our cities, old Quebec. The following year, 1923, found AY working for several months in Baie St. Paul on the North Shore, the lovely spot discovered by Clarence Gagnon as early as 1915. Gagnon, born 1882 and therefore the exact contemporary of AY although he died so long ago (1942) that he now seems very distant, divided his time between his house in Baie St. Paul and his studio in Paris, where most of his canvases were painted up. Gagnon's subjects were the same French-Canadian village scenes that AY began to use in 1921. But Gagnon, whose *forte* was probably his fine colour illustration, clarified and idealized his subjects in a way that AY preferred not do do. Gagnon's winter canvases, as fresh and charming as if they were painted from toy models, have a certain tendency to look like delightful Christmas cards blown up in scale.

Now those years in the early 1920s happened to be exactly the time when fine Christmas cards were produced in our country, the best ever, perhaps—the excellent series by Rous and Mann comes to mind in particular. AY, like most of the younger, vigorous *and* hard-up artists of the day, gladly helped supply the Christmas card market, and Quebec-in-winter became known to the rest of the country in Christmas card style. When we add to this the fact that AY was also busy with the small-format pen-and-ink illustrations for the English edition of *Chez Nous*, it is natural that the aura of the illustrator clings to most of AY's drawings from the Baie St. Paul period. The same folk-consciousness applies to a set of dear little drawings done in the summer of 1925, when AY, in company with Marius Barbeau and the Lismer family, stayed on the Ile d'Orléans, one of the picturesque spots *par excellence* in old Quebec.

But quite early in the game AY felt the restriction of the picturesque, and wrote in January 1924 to J. E. H. MacDonald: "Here we are in the Christmas card country, at least it often looks that way. I see cards waiting to be done in two printings and a few dabs of colour put on by hand, while what I want to see are big bold compositions that will enrage the critics."

So AY soon took to the hills and the back concessions, and by March 1926 there are occasional dated drawings from more remote small spots such as St. Fidèle and La Malbaie, where Robinson was also painting in 1926. It was in early spring 1927 that AY returned to the South Shore. The year nineteen hundred twenty-seven was *annus mirabilis* for drawings, judging by what has been available for examination; some of the 1927 Arctic works have already been seen on this journey through *AY's Canada*. It may have been the congenial company of Dr. Banting, who was also with AY on his spring trip to Quebec that year, as *A Painter's Country* tells with many endearing details. More deeply, it was a good time for AY: he was breaking through into maturity as a Canadian artist.

Our first 1927 South Shore drawing is from a small place near Trois Pistoles called Tobin; "a dead little sawmill town" is all that the autobiography says of it, apart from recalling how the two painter friends got off the train to find that there was no hotel in Tobin. However by good luck a hospitable insurance agent with three charming daughters put them up, so there were no complaints. The weather grew pleasantly warm; they found plenty of subjects; AY's drawing-book with the three loose-leaf holes began to fill up with quite wonderful works in pencil.

This drawing from the Tobin area is *not* picturesque, has no illustrative appeal, could be almost anywhere along the Lower St. Lawrence—and catches the essence of that anywhereness. Sprawling across the centre in shallow diagonals is the characteristic wooden barn, broad-beamed and slightly cock-eyed; it has seen better days, but AY likes it the way it is. The composition's right-hand anchor is the settler's first little home, probably a log cabin with an added covering of vertical clapboards. It has undoubtedly produced several generations of good-sized families. To the left, at the top of the broad curve, is the later-styled, more commodious house with its nice bell roof. And out beyond is the wide expanse of *le fleuve*, the immense St. Lawrence, whose north shore over twenty miles away is concealed by a long band of fog, the little work's positive horizontal. An unromantic subject, but full of the essence of life: broad, simple, strong, and uniquely A. Y. J.

"I suppose I get bored by making just nice sketches," AY wrote from another spot on the South Shore, a good deal later. His statement can serve, along with the title chosen for our text, to conclude this brief glance at his style in its evolution: "I want an organization, horizontals, verticals and oblique lines. Colour harmony does not interest me much, nor does getting an effect...."

These are sober, basic essentials. Incidentals can have more charm—as does, for instance, the glimpse of sleeping Tobin's winter shore that forms the *verso* of the same drawing—but it is good to have AY's own essentials to keep in mind.

PLATE 22

Farm at Tobin, near Trois Pistoles, Quebec [1927]

In its present state the drawing creates the extraordinary effect of being a dream—full of intensive detail—looming up out of a fog. This is because at some stage AY erased the notes that covered the margins. After the present writer had pored over all this fine pencil detail ("Ça doit prendre beaucoup de patience!" as our little onlookers down the River always say in compliment) there was a chance to ask AY: "Did you actually make this whole careful drawing before you even *started* to paint your oil sketch, or didn't you paint one that day?" To which to my absolute astonishment AY answered: "Why no, I did this *after* the oil sketch; that's how I did nearly all those careful drawings—after I had caught the subject in paint first. The drawing was to help me when I painted the canvas later." (This noteworthy practice has been mentioned in the Foreword.)

The actual location of this dream of a difficult road that leads up an endless hill is four or five miles down-river from Tobin, towards St. Fabien and fabulous Bic. On the river side runs the rocky rounded ridge well known to us from such canvases as *The Road to St. Simon*, 1940 (Mrs. H. A. Dyde), *The Road to Bic*, by 1939 (Mr. and Mrs. Sandy Somerville), and many sketches. To the south, away from the River, near St. Simon, this little side road mounts the long hill to St. Mathieu. Banting and Jackson passed that way on their 1927 trip. A later drawing (probably

1935) from about the same spot shows the CNR tracks. It lacks the ivory-carved delicacy of the earlier work.

We can reconstruct the sequence of events of that mild, lightly-clouded early spring day forty or so years ago. The sketch in oils on the wood panel 8½ by 10½ inches (*where is it now?*) was done to catch the play of veiled sunlight on sodden snow and half-dried shingle—quickly, before the light changed too much. Then out came the sketchbook and pencil to capture and keep the fine detail of the sharp angles of the little home set offside against the series of rising ridges, each modelled by its pleated furrows, with the road telescoping wildly straight up the middle of the composition. What a tour de force! The lacy arabesques of snow in the left foreground are offset by the spiky fence and the round hump of the old bake-oven to the right. Then every available inch along the margins was filled with meticulous analysis of relative values: light-dark, warm-cool; and maybe a note for a spot of human interest to be added later in the canvas. Then away with the notebook into the old grey sail-cloth bag alongside sketchbox and oil tubes, there to acquire a rather oily patina. The next appearance of the drawing will be when it is tacked onto the top of the easel at home in the studio, in preparation for the canvas. And perhaps as wonderful as anything else—the little in-betweener, the marks of the plain 3-B graphite pencil on the scrap of paper with three holes at the top, now appears in public on its own as an important element in *AY's Canada*!

46

PLATE 23

The road from St. Simon to St. Mathieu [*1927*]

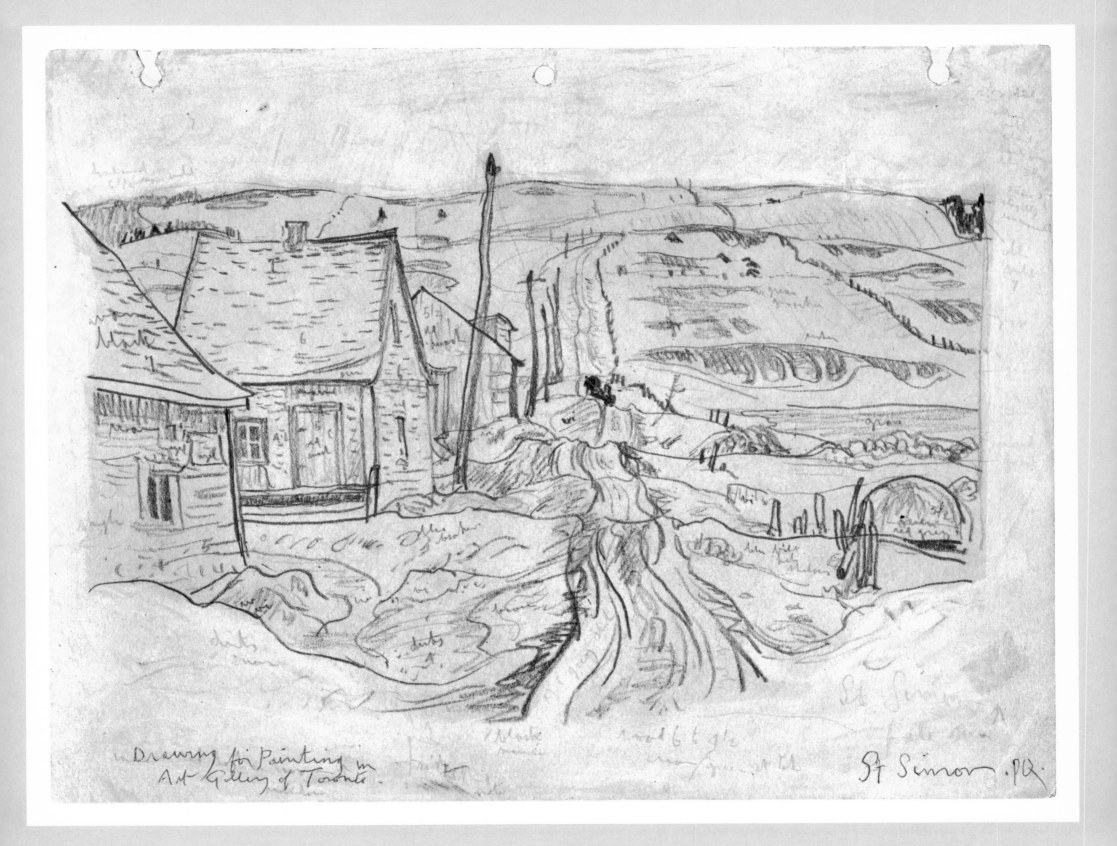

"Drawing for Painting in
Art Gallery of Toronto."

St Simon .PQ.

The farthest point reached by AY and Dr. Fred Banting on their winter-spring sketching trip down the St. Lawrence in 1927 was Bic. Here they stayed only a few days, working around the village with its rather ornate church (built in 1892 after fire had destroyed the first 1840 church) and tramping out into the country that still lay blanketed in snow, to judge by this grey-day drawing. With its wooded hills filled in for dark contrast, and its explicit colour directions—"islands in back violet black; nearer islands vi brown; river green grey; sky yel grey with blue slate grey"— it affirms the sombre mood of W. H. Blake's words above from his translation of *Chez Nous.*

AY is here looking downstream towards Bic, with a glimpse of the St. Lawrence on his left and the village hidden behind some of those fantastic bumps of Bic, the sudden outcrops of rock that form the characteristic razor-backed humps of nearly all the hills and islands along the South Shore east of Ste. Anne de la Pocatière, reaching their climax at Bic with its beautiful bay and rich history.

Once upon a time most of this land was covered with great forests of pine and spruce. The first *habitants* settled at the projecting Cap l'Orignal (Moose Point) towards the end of the 1700s. In 1845 the Seigneur Campbell sold rights to Les Prices Broders (*sic* down there, with -s on Price but not pronounced, and the -ers pronounced as in French -*eur*) to erect a sawmill and to *bûcher du pin* on Bic Point. Down crashed the primeval forest; a bigger quai was built for lumber transport, and a rather necessary lighthouse, the famous *phare du Bic,* begun 1842, was finished by 1844 with imported stone. (Why *imported,* one wonders? The locals down there call it *pierre d'Italie!*) Work on the Intercolonial Railway began there in 1869, and by 1873 the daily train rumbled through the steep cuts as it does today, along with trucks, buses and innumerable motorists, all bound for Rimouski.

There is a blood-freezing tale (called *légende* down there so undoubtedly having historic elements) which seems to suit the sullen-skyed loneliness of this little drawing. It concerns the Isle of the Massacre and was kindly sent to me by helpful residents of Bic (Mlle Marie-Rose filled a whole green booklet!). This tale is "probably the oldest of the Indian legends of Canada, related by Donna Conna to Jacques Cartier on his first ascent of the St. Lawrence in 1535. The Micmac Indians lived in Bic, very peace-
(continued)

PLATE 24

The road to Bic
[*March 1927*]

fully. When the wild Iroquois were sighted in their war canoes, the old and young of the Micmacs [about two hundred, says one source] took shelter in the cave on Bic Island, going out there at low tide, while some of the young men went for help. But the Iroquois found the marks of their feet in the sand at the water's edge and knew where they were and waited till the tide was low again, and went to the cave and smoked them out and slew them all. The water in the bay was red with blood, and for a long time after, human bones lay scattered on the island. But there is no large cave there now and it isn't very interesting any more—a pity!"

Well, yes, it is all rather a pity! Very likely it is the famous Isle of the Massacre that can be seen in the background of the drawing opposite.

But we choose to end on a happier note, having come across a delightful description of the famous island by an observant lady who fortunately did not learn about the blood-bath of long ago. The day on which she wrote down her observations was August 6, 1832, almost a century before AY got there and twelve years before Les Prices Broders began to fell the white pine. She was journeying to Canada with her newly-wed husband on the brig *Laurel*, and although her journal was at first published anonymously under the modest subtitle "Letters from the Wife of an Emigrant Officer," we know her and love her as our Mrs. Traill, author of *The Backwoods of Canada*. "This morning we anchored off the Isle of Bic, a pretty low island, covered with trees and looking very pleasant. I felt a longing desire to set my foot on Canadian ground, and must own I was a little disappointed when the captain advised me to remain on board, and not attempt to make one of the party that were preparing to go on shore:

my husband seconded the captain's wish, so I contented myself with leaning over the ship's side and feasting my eyes on the rich masses of foliage as they waved to and fro with the slight breeze that agitated them. I had soon reason to be thankful that I had not followed my own wayward will, for the afternoon proved foggy, and on the return of the boat I learned that the ground was swampy just where the party landed, and they sunk over their ankles in water. They reported the island to be covered with a most luxuriant growth of red clover, tall trees, low shrubs, and an abundance of wild flowers.

"That I might not regret not accompanying him, my husband brought me a delightful bouquet, which he had selected for me. Among the flowers were fragrant red roses, resembling those we call Scotch burnet-leaved, with smooth shining leaves and few if any thorns; the blue flower called Pulmonaria or Lungwort, which I gathered in the Highlands; a sweat pea, with red blossoms and wreaths of lovely pale green foliage; a white orchid, the smell of which was quite delicious. Besides these were several small white and yellow flowers, with which I was totally unacquainted. The steward furnished me with a china jar and fresh water, so that I shall have the pleasure of a nosegay during the rest of the voyage. The sailors had not forgotten a green bough or two to adorn the ship, and the bird-cage was soon as bowery as leaves could make it."

What a symphonic sequence of contrasts—the frightful bloodbath of Indian legend that reddened the soil of Bic Island; the red roses for Mrs. Traill on her fair summer's day; and finally the grim but beautiful March morning when AY paid his grey-day visit.

It gives very special pleasure to introduce this place with the delightful name as the focal point, the hearth, the heart, around which will be arranged the next little group of drawings from yet another area of A. Y. Jackson's activity over a goodly number of years.

St. Jean Port Joli (olden days with a -y) lies on the South Shore of the St. Lawrence, about sixty miles down from Québec-Lévis and about twenty miles from Baie St. Paul across the river. Our drawing shows, to the left, a rather unorthodox angle (none of that post-cardy *pittoresque*, remember!) of the celebrated parish church with its two fine bell turrets; to the right, the convent school with *its* little belfry; in the foreground a glimpse of a typical village yard in late-winter *déshabille*.

This is another of the drawings made on that fruitful, happy expedition of 1927, when AY came from Toronto in company with his good friend Dr. Banting for winter-spring sketching in St. Jean Port Joli, Bic and Tobin. It was in the first-named that Banting crouched behind the fence for shelter from the ferocious March wind ("straight off the Labrador," they say in those parts) and uttered the famous phrase which AY delights to recall: "And I thought this was a sissy game!"

A wealth, a veritable goldmine, of further sources could easily make this the best-documented AY drawing ever: firstly, because the area around St. Jean Port Joli happens to be the warm heart-centre of that region of the Lower St. Lawrence known intimately to *les Jacksons* in general from *almost* 1927 on; secondly, because there is a wonderful book about the parish, usually referred to simply as *Ma Paroisse*, written by a native son, Gérard Ouellet, and published in 1946, with 350 big pages full of absorbing *informations* and ancient illustrations.

It is challenging as well as à propos, to start out scientifically from the drawing itself and to see how far we can go. It was obviously made from an upstairs window. Was AY indoors keeping warm while Banting crouched behind the fence? Hardly likely; AY was probably filling in time before breakfast. . . . From the general location, the upstairs window must be in the Castel-aux-Falaises (AY has confirmed this), St. Jean's time-honoured first hotel, formerly the residence of Dr. Salluste Roy (died 1886). This popular, though non-practising, medico-philosopher was a good friend of the parish's most illustrious son, Philippe Aubert de Gaspé (1786/1871), "Seigneur de Saint-Jean Port-Joly, la Pocatière, etc." and author of the great historical novel *Les Anciens Canadiens*. That "véritable épopée" was written when de Gaspé was seventy-six, and published in book form in 1863.

Although born in Quebec City, Philippe Aubert de Gaspé spent the greater part of each year from 1841 onward in his manor house at the west end of St. Jean parish, towards Trois Saumons where the seigneurial mill was built to benefit from the plentiful waterpower from deep Lac des Trois Saumons high in the hills to the south. The manor house was the second one, built after the first had perished in the "promenade aux flambeaux," the torchlight parade, as local wits refer to the burning by the English army in 1759. The seigneury itself had been established in 1677 and acquired nine years later by Charles Aubert, Quebec City's wealthiest merchant, who subsequently added de Gaspé to his name. Heirs of the family still have some connections with the district, though the land passed long since into more plebeian (likewise more capable) hands. The second manor house in turn burned to the ground one April evening in 1909 (faulty chimney), leaving nothing behind but the old bake-oven and its own image on variously coloured hooked rag rugs in the neighbourhood. Seigneur Philippe Aubert de Gaspé was the last of his line to be buried near the seigneurial pew in the venerable church, after a memorable funeral attended by half Quebec.

Erected in 1779 and dedicated to St. John the Baptist, the church of St. Jean Port Joli is considered one of the most beautiful in all French Canada. "My jewel"—"le bijou de ma diocèse," Cardinal Bégin called it in 1917, while the late, great Ramsay Traquair, professor of architecture at McGill, termed it "l'une des mieux pyramidées de la province." An especially favourable aspect of the church is from the east, as in our drawing, although here the elegantly proportioned sacristy and winter chapel attached to the chancel end are concealed.

Ma Paroisse is full of fascinating detail on the manner of the church's construction, and on the contributions of the parishioners, who worked in relays (*corvées*) to bring the beautiful rosy, tan or grey stone from the fields and lumber from the sawmill, and to prepare the lime at the two kilns erected nearby. All items of expense have been recorded; for instance on February 4, 1781, the record shows "19 portugaises" drawn from the strong-box to pay for 700 windowpanes, 32 pounds of putty and 15,500 roofing tacks. Monsieur Jean Michon received 75 piastres "pour la façon du mur," presumably the tailoring of the field stone, whereas the first church bell cost 110 piastres and was later replaced by three even more expensive. In 1794 the contract was signed for the noted master sculptor, Jean Baillargé, then seventy-one years old, to carve and gild the altar and reredos, aided by his son Pierre Florent. The work was completed in 1797 at a cost of 5,994 livres. By 1815 the parish had grown so large that the church had to be extended thirty feet at the west end; also the stone sacristy was added to the east end, and the present main bell-tower set in place. The extension meant redecorating the barrel-vaulted ceiling of both

(continued)

nave and chancel; this was done most elegantly and delicately (for 1,250 livres) by Chrysostôme Perrault (died 1827), a native of St. Jean Port Joli. The first pipe organ, a Mitchell, cost $800 in 1883; it was replaced by a Casavant from St. Hyacinthe in 1943 (for $5,050, with some of the old pipes in for sentiment). In 1937 a new pulpit was carved by the Bourgault brothers Médard and Jean-Julien, also sons of the parish.

These details, selected from among many, show how the parishioners of St. Jean, for all that they always seem to have had a reputation for being "des turbulents" with a penchant for racing their horses of a Sunday after mass and for feuding with their curé, none the less handed over their hard-earned piastres to embellish their fine church. There certainly is proof that this is "une paroisse qui respire l'aisance," a comfortable, well-heeled parish. It is significant that there has been almost no change in the number of its parishioners for almost a century: the figures in *Ma Paroisse* stand at about 2,300 souls (345 or so families) from 1875 up to 1945. But of course it must be taken into consideration that several younger parishes to the south broke away from the original St. Jean parish, including St. Aubert, named in honour of the seigneurial family.

It is impossible to resist giving a few choice bits about the memorable curés of St. Jean Port Joli, whose life and work centred round the beautiful edifice in our drawing. Honour of first place goes to the greatest character of them all—l'Abbé François Boissonnault (1775/1854), who lived forty years in St. Jean parish, twenty-nine of them as curé (he stayed on after and built a big house for his cousins and his aunts). Monsieur Boissonnault was "un curé volumineux" and "un homme de poids," with his triple chin and his "appétit pantagruélien." He had a curve cut out of his dining-room table to accommodate his ample paunch and one New Year's Day he and his cook consumed two whole roast turkeys—one apiece. Monsieur Boissonnault's temper matched his appetite and he was often at logger-heads with his parishioners. On one occasion he was being conveyed by carriage by his *marguilleur* (church warden), Bénoni Bourgault, who became angry and said to the curé, obviously very curtly: "Débarque!" But Monsieur le curé remained immovable. "Débarque!" quoth Bénoni once again. But the curé, he stayed put. So Bénoni débarqued himself, unhitched the horse, and marched away with it. . . . On another occasion the curé got tired of waiting for a tardy funeral party to arrive with the deceased, so he went ahead with the funeral service, which was just terminating when the mourners arrived with the coffin. Monsieur Boissonnault was so voluminous that he had trouble leaving the church by the central aisle in winter, on account of the bulky raiment worn by the women of the parish: "les créatures" stood in the aisles for church service in those days while the men sat in the pews.

Another curé to mention: Monsieur Panet, a strict Jansenist, who had a draw-bridge (*un pont-lévis*) built in front of his presbytery door so that he could be left in peace after sundown. . . . And the absent-minded curé who had another curé's precious otter-skin winter cap made down to fit him, having taken the wrong cap after a meeting.

But the curé who best of all deserves to be remembered, happily named Monsieur Lachance, is the one who saved the famous old church from destruction. This was as recently as 1919, when much-needed repair work was assessed at $35,000 and one strong faction in the parish (*favoured by the Bishop, Monseigneur Roy, two years after the Cardinal had talked about his "jewel"!*) voted for demolition and for building a new church. But Monsieur le curé Lachance would not hear of it. He practically barricaded himself in, he talked and talked and finally out-talked and out-wore the others. It took him four years, but eventually the old church was restored, glorious vault, altar and all, and for only $14,000 as it turned out. Assuredly *le bon Dieu* had a hand in that deal!

So the church of St. Jean was triumphantly awaiting AY's arrival five years later in 1927. AY arrived only two years after electricity came to that part of Quebec; only eight years after the very first airplane had flown over St. Jean Port Joli (1919); only twenty-one years after the very first motor car had rolled sedately along the nice shady village street, raising a cloud of dust and scaring the horses, a harbinger of approaching uglification such as the widening of the road that took the great old leafy trees and several fine old houses at the curve by the church.

One more date is needed: it was on August 18, 1903, that the entire village turned out at the railway station to welcome the first teaching Sisters of the Order of St. Joseph de Saint-Vallier (founded in 1683 by Quebec's great Bishop of that name), recently arrived from France and soon established in the building to the right in AY's drawing. On their first evening in St. Jean the eleven Sisters were given a hearty banquet followed by fireworks—a warm welcome for a warm summer evening.

It scarcely seems necessary to mention the renown of St. Jean Port Joli as centre for the local arts and handicrafts. When AY got there, Médard Bourgault had already been working for seven years in his modest workshop behind his house, while that old character Servule Dumas, king of the beggars or *quêteux*, who excelled as much at *discours politiques* as at concocting *billets doux* for shy lovers, had been serving for years as model for the figurines of Médard's brother André. Eugène Leclerc was already famous for his miniature sailing ships in bottles, and the busy fingers of Madame Edmond Chamard, Madame Joseph Chouinard, and others were weaving in local linen and wool. There were dozens of charming, witty Lavallées around, although no direct descendants of Calixa Lavallée, whose *O Canada, terre de nos aïeux* sounds even better in French than in English.

And so we take our last glance (for now) at this dear place, and note in farewell that those two rooster weather-vanes "disappeared" when the church's roof of shingles was replaced (in 1936) by one of prosaic metal. But the weather-vanes have a permanent memory-place in *Ma Paroisse;* and here, in AY's drawing.

PLATE 25

St. Jean Port Joli, County L'Islet, Quebec, church and convent school [1927]

52

The region in behind St. Jean Port Joli on the South Shore was visited many times by AY after he discovered it in the twenties. When the villages on the main highway paralleling the St. Lawrence became too popular with *les touristes* he explored the quieter unspoiled little places on the back concessions of L'Islet County, in particular the agreeable angle formed by the *quatrième rang*, on which St. Aubert is located, and la Route Elgin. Laid out at the time of the Governor-General who had such good rapport with the Canadiens, Elgin Road runs straight south (and uphill) to the border of Maine, some sixty miles. This region has been the summer haunt of *les Jacksons* since the early 1930s and the H. A. C. Jackson home, "Patly Hill," has often been AY's headquarters for spring and fall sketching, as well as for pleasant summer visits, "with the vast panorama of the north land spreading out before you."

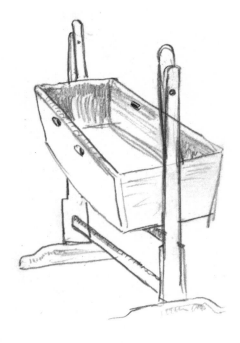

The village of Ste. Louise lies in the plain a mile or so east of Elgin Road, with nice humped hills close by. AY may first have seen it from the train in 1927, and it has long been a favourite, revisited many times for long periods, "to paint old barns, old sleighs, manure piles and such things," as he wrote when planning a visit in March 1940. On the 25th of that month he wrote rather disconsolately from the little hotel in Ste. Louise: " . . . this is the third day of the blizzard [illustrated by a tiny "blizzarded" horse and sleigh] and I have done no work at all. I figured on an early spring, as winter started early and has been very streaky.

"The church at Ste. Louise is good 1857, but the barns are mostly 1938, not so good. Why is it some things like barns, cheese, and whisky are only good when they are old, while fish and tomatoes and beer ain't so good. . . ."

That momentary mood applies nicely to this study of the old house in Ste. Louise, of interest for its architectural and archaeological detail. The manner of construction of the roof, with a framework of solid beams covered first by vertical planks and then by tough cedar slab shingles on both roof and gable ends, shows clearly in our drawing. These gables may slant in a trifle, but not enough for the small windows in them to project as dormers. Remains of well-fashioned pedimented window frames can be seen, and a handsome lintel over the door. Home-braided rugs and striped rag *catalogne* are hung to dry on the garden fence. Many a good piece of weaving and rug-making has come from the Ste. Louise district.

This house looks old enough to outdate the parish church of Ste. Louise (1857), which was established long after hardy pioneers had settled in the district. The old house has obviously seen better days, but just the same it keeps its sturdy good cheer, perhaps thinking back with satisfaction to the generations of families it has brought forth and sent into the world.

54

PLATE 26

Old house, Ste. Louise, Quebec [late 1920s]

St Louis Ry
A Y Jackson

The subject of the present drawing—the village of St. Onésime perched on its bumpy ridge high to the south-east behind Ste. Louise—is a long way indeed from the cosy little hotel back in Ste. Louise village. Now there was certainly nobody in those wartime days to drive AY around by car, *ergo*, he must have got there on his own sturdy shanks' mare!

When proof was sought from the horse's mouth, so to speak, and AY was asked to think back for a moment, he sat frowning at the drawing for a while, letting his mind range over a quarter of a century or so, and *remembered* the day he did this drawing: "It was a fine day for a hike so I walked from Ste. Louise up to St. Onésime. I made two pencil drawings, and a sketch too, I guess. Then I walked back down to Ste. Anne de la Pocatière on the CNR tracks one station east of Ste. Louise, to take the train back. But I found out that I would have to wait about three hours for the train, so I walked back to Ste. Louise. . . . I guess it would be around seventeen miles altogether, I forget. But the road was full of slush and mud by afternoon, I haven't forgotten that!

"I was back there around St. Onésime in June 1965, and Lordy, what a change—all broad paved roads now, not nearly as interesting. This last time I did a couple of summer sketches, everything green. I guess I'm not as tough as I used to be—we've all got tenderized. But this old St. Onésime drawing is good and tough. . . . "

April 9, 1940—Ste. Louise, L'Islet, Quebec.

. . . It's a black night out, and the rain is pattering down on the snow, making slush and mud puddles. It isn't a first class spring—you know: bright shining days, with blue snow shadows, and old tough drifts defying the sun to melt them. You have pictures in your mind, but you find it is always different to what you expect. Sometimes it is better in reality but not often.

. . . I like Ste. Louise because it is just a typical little French Canadian village. The church is good, without it the village would be nothing. The people are nice, they have not been spoiled by tourists, and the little hotel is cosy. I have a big room with two windows and it is clean, spotless, so I am sticking round. But I want sunlight . . . nearly all the sunny days have been accompanied by cold sharp winds which is no fun.

Ste. Louise, Co. L'Islet, Quebec. March 25th [1940]

I have not been very far afield, the weather has not been propitious. Probably old age is getting in its dirty work. I don't like sketching with frozen hands, with snow drifting round in my box. . . .

Tell Aunty Kay to send me down a studio tube of Raw Sienna, mine has gone gummy. Eaton's should have it. Still the blizzard rages. . . .

PLATE 27

Village of St. Onésime, Quebec [1942]

St Onesime
Que

Here is an interesting situation. This little drawing on manila paper, probably from 1942 or else 1940, was originally considered too unexciting for *AY's Canada*. When AY wrote from Ste. Louise he himself admitted that most of the country was too unaccented: "pas assez accidenté," he put it. But it was the very simplicity of the place that had its appeal both to him and to those who saw his work from there. This includes some quite illustrious persons, it now turns out.

On going through AY's scrapbook I came across a newspaper clipping with the illustration of a winter scene sketch "recently acquired by Her Majesty Queen Elizabeth." Being in the 1940s this would be the present Queen Mother Elizabeth. According to the Montreal *Gazette*, Saturday, November 4, 1944, the subject was "unidentified as to precise location." But to my great pleasure I could be very precise about it, since I own the drawing, given me in 1953 by AY before he left Toronto. The sketch and drawing represent the snowy, wind-blown fields south-west of Ste. Louise in L'Islet County, about four miles from where we live in summer.

Now AY's scrapbook full of treasures has produced a letter that refers to the event. Headed "Office of the High Commissioner for the United Kingdom/Earnscliffe/Ottawa/25th September, 1944," it reads in Malcolm MacDonald's own hand:

Dear Père Raquette:

You will probably remember that I let you into a secret some time ago, to the effect that the Queen had got one of your sketches. She has now said that she would be very happy to agree to a newspaper announcement about this. . . . I hope that you will be pleased about this. Personally I think it is a very fitting recognition of Canadian painting in general and your painting in particular. . . . Incidentally, whenever I see the Queen she tells me what great pleasure the picture gives her. I know she is sincere in saying this because she keeps it in her own sitting-room, and often it is standing on the desk where she works. . . .

When next I am coming to Toronto I shall drop you a line in the hopes of finding you free for an hour's gossip and enjoyment in your studio.

Yours very sincerely,
(signed) Malcolm MacDonald

PLATE 28
Snowy fields near Ste. Louise, Quebec [1942]

The same climatic conditions that AY likes for his early spring sketching—cold nights that stiffen up the last of winter's snow in interesting shapes, and warm days with brilliant sunshine—are of course also the perfect weather for Maple Sugar Time in eastern Canada, when the wonderful sap of *Acer saccharum* stirs and rises and runs.

It is pleasant to recall that the maple sugar tradition is older than any of our white race here in North America, justifying all the more our present use of the maple leaf symbol. It was the Indians who discovered how to extract sap from the "wounded maple" during the Sugar Month, to boil it in pottery vessels and to store the precious product, *sinzipikwat*, in boxes of birch bark for later use and trade. Blodwen Davies' book *Quebec: Portrait of a Province* gives fine tidbits of lore in the chapter "The Sugar Maple Country," including the fact that maple sugar was not made by the French settlers in America until the start of the eighteenth century, when the British blockade kept the supply ships from landing. It was the energetic Madame Agathe de Repentigny who adopted the Indian sugar-making methods for the colonists and who reported a few years later to the king of France that thirty thousand pounds of maple sugar could be made annually on the Island of Montreal alone.

In L'Islet County, centre of our present little group of drawings, the hillsides and ridges that rise behind Ste. Louise to St. Onésime, and from St. Aubert up to St. Damase, have large sections of beautiful open hardwood maple. Observing the seasonal changes on what we summertimers always call the Côte d'Erable (Maple Hill), south of the Jackson domicile at St. Aubert, is a happy daily pastime. Each of our farmer neighbours has his good-sized sugar bush and his own shanty with well-stocked woodpile. Each shanty has its own shape and character: that of the Zéphirin Dubés on Côte d'Erable, for instance, is different from that of the Josaphat Pelletiers next along the ridge. A friendly rivalry exists in regard to both quality and quantity of the delicious products, so that *les Jacksons* and friends are often called in as tasters.

AY spent several spring seasons in this St. Aubert district in the early 1940s and made the rounds of the sugar shanties; more for art than for the stomach's sake, of course! Sometimes, especially as the season got warmer, he was accompanied on his rambles by his eldest brother Harry, whose eldest daughter is the present writer. Here is part of H. A. C. Jackson's journal for May 7, 1945, after the joyful exclamation in the margin "*The war is over!*": "... We enjoyed every minute of our walk to Pinguet [about five miles] over this picturesque rolling country. The weather became so foggy at times that it was hard to see any distance ahead. A.Y. stopped and made a pencil sketch of an old sugar house near the ancient little wooden church with the strange big cross on it. [The French Protestant church from the time of "Father" Chiniquy. The cross was carved by André Chodat.] Then we both went down to the little tarn and ate our lunches, after which AY wandered off to sketch and I to fish. ..."

The drawing of that day in May 1945 does not seem to be around, so the one here has been chosen because "it sits well on the page," in AY's words. On another occasion at St. Aubert, in 1942, he wrote in a letter: "I have used up all my panels, but will make some pencil notes. ... Peter [the Jacksons' cocker spaniel] goes sketching with me and knows as much about art now as Morgan Powell. ..."

In her book, the late Blodwen Davies has described the vast scientific cooperative enterprise for maple syrup and sugar making, begun in 1925 and centred in Plessisville on the South Shore near Quebec City. At the date of her writing (1951) she stated that twenty thousand people were engaged in this cooperative, producing "well over two million gallons a year," while Quebec as a whole produced between eighty and ninety per cent of all commercially handled maple products in Canada. In a "Farm Broadcast" on March 18, 1966, Arthur Phelps put Ontario's 1955 output at 547,000 gallons of maple syrup, which by 1964 had *sunk* to 165,000 gallons, owing largely to the cost of mechanizing the industry; "miles and miles of plastic tubing," said Arthur Phelps in disgust.

So we had better treasure the existing records of bygone days, the fine old hand-carved moulds for maple sugar candy collected by Marius Barbeau in the twenties and thirties on the Ile d'Orléans and in his native County Beauce not far from Plessisville; the drawings and paintings by AY and many other good artists that show the old-fashioned method, with driver, horse and sleigh making the rounds of the maple trees on sunny nippy spring days smelling of hardwood smoke from the sugar shanty. There will always be rugged individualists who will make syrup and sugar for their own use and pleasure (one friend of Arthur Phelps figured it cost him about $15 a gallon); and there will probably always be ersatz sleigh-rides out to woodland shanties on April Sunday afternoons, when the weather is good, for sugaring-off parties. Alongside such ritual reminders of the past we treasure our visual souvenirs that "sit well on the page."

PLATE 29

Sugar shanty, St. Aubert,
County L'Islet [early 1940s]

Sugar Shanty
St Aubert Cry
a y Jackson

If we travel by car or bus, up-river from Montmagny on the South Shore of the St. Lawrence, along the concession road south of the Canadian National Railway line, we pass through the village of St. Pierre de Montmagny. Here AY worked for a while in the spring of 1942. He and his friend the late Randolph Hewton boarded at the little railway hotel, Hotel Collin. A quarter-century later, the neat black-and-white hotel signboard which AY lettered for the proprietor is very likely still in place, visible from the local train when it stops at St. Pierre station. "I did a good job and gave it two coats of my best paint," says AY. "I guess you could call it an important late example of my commercial art work, only of course I did it free."

During that visit, on March 29, 1942, AY wrote one of his always welcomed spring sketching letters, using the Hotel Collin paper which was patriotically stamped with a red V for Victory, plus dot-dot-dot-dash. Part of that letter makes a good accompaniment for the drawing of St. Pierre village shown here: "Sunday morning and I am taking it easy, though the sun is shining and I should be out sketching. This place is about half way between Lévis and St. Aubert. Not very exciting country—flat, treeless, and not very picturesque as far as houses and barns go. The village of St. Pierre is a mile and a half away from the hotel, which is beside the station. Nice little burg, one of the few unspoiled villages in Quebec; nice old parish church. It's a poor little place, humble little houses that contrast with the big substantial farm houses that one finds all over the district.

"... There is a stream runs through the flat land, which breaks it up, and while it is still frozen up it makes nice lines of movement. You still need snowshoes to get about. The snow holds you in the morning but by noon it softens up and you go through up to your seat.

"It is very different from St. Tite, where everything was within a few hundred yards. However we are comfortable and the people are nice, and spring will come along sometime."

By 1942 AY's drawing style had developed a casual, robust, full-bodied character which is well exemplified in this drawing. It shows part of the village, and the church from its north-east corner. A somewhat different view, with the church seen straight along its north side, is represented in the oil sketch *Grey Day, St. Pierre, Montmagny*, 1942, in the collection of Mrs. J. S. McLean of Toronto; this was No. 223 in the 1953 A. Y. Jackson retrospective exhibition.

The *verso* side of the present drawing (njg 359) shows the curving "nice lines of movement" of the frozen stream mentioned in the letter, possibly a tributary of the Rivière du Sud near Montmagny.

62

PLATE 30

St. Pierre, County Montmagny, Quebec
[*1942*]

This sturdy rendering of a typical old French-Canadian stone house at St. Michel, about twenty miles downstream from Lévis, was likely done in the fall of 1929, on a trip AY took by car with Lawren Harris along the South Shore of the St. Lawrence—the trip that produced Lawren's stunning canvas of the lighthouse at Father Point. There are a few AY drawings in this odd size of approximately 7⅝ by 11 inches, obtained by folding and tearing a larger sheet of good solid drawing paper and then pressing the long side into the three-ringed loose-leaf holder, creating the home-made look that is also found in some Arctic drawings of the following year, 1930.

The old house here has likewise the firm home-made look characteristic of many ancient structures in that beautiful district just below Quebec City where the St. Lawrence widens into two broad arms to embrace the fair Ile d'Orléans. The owner of the old house in St. Michel, sitting before his front door on that little bench (likewise home-made), could look north across the island's fertile curve and see the distant peaks of the Laurentides behind Ste. Anne de Beaupré on the North Shore.

This is the country that AY's old friend the noted anthropologist and folk-lorist Marius Barbeau came from and knows so well. He was born in Ste. Marie de Beauce, south of St. Michel about thirty miles as the crow flies, in 1883, one year after AY's own birth date. "Compared to him I am a mere boy!" has been Barbeau's boast for a long time. His maternal ancestors, the Morencys, lived on the Ile d'Orléans in a house much like the Ste. Famille *maison bloc* in our vignette (njg 474r). Such a dwelling is the oldest type, where kith and kine dwelt amicably (and in winter more warmly) under one roof. This little Ile d'Orléans drawing was made in 1925, four years before the St. Michel one, when AY and Barbeau and the Lismer family paid a delightful summer visit there.

The many fruitful experiences in *ancien Québec* resulted not only in many of Marius Barbeau's fine books and excellent full-page articles in *La Presse*, but in the preservation for posterity of fine wood carvings and other objects, some of which have reached Ottawa and Toronto. It was AY who prompted the Toronto Art Gallery (as it was then) to acquire, for the lordly sum of $75, the "admirable angel" carved from a block of wood four feet high by Master Louis Jobin in Ste. Anne de Beaupré. (AY and Marius had spotted it during their summer visit of 1925.) In November of that year AY wrote in *The Canadian Bookman*, to whose section "In the Realm of Art," conducted by Bess Housser, he was a frequent contributor: "This is possibly the first recognition that has been given to the Quebec wood carvers by an art gallery. . . .

"In many of the figures there is a certain rude vigor that is in harmony with the early architecture. They both grow out of the soil. . . .

"It is to be hoped that . . . before we go poking all over the earth for other people's antiques we might first see what there is at home."

The St. Michel house in our drawing here does indeed seem to "grow out of the soil," and represents perhaps the finest type of stone house from the olden days. Its heavy rectangular walls are of field stone embedded in rough plaster and then whitewashed. Its shingled, bell-cast roof is steep-pitched and slopes in on all four sides, as can be seen by the typically tiny projecting dormer windows (four in front, one on each end), whereas the old house at Ste. Louise (Plate 26) had vertical triangular gable ends. Our title for the St. Michel house comes very fittingly from Adjutor Rivard: "Perhaps other houses made a braver show, but not one was pleasanter for the eye to rest upon. Its four stout walls, solidly laid, soundly knit, gave an air of secure repose. The stones were old, but every spring they donned a new dress of whitewash, and the whole parish could not boast a house more shining white. . . . " The beloved old home described thus in *Chez Nous* also belongs (or belonged), if I am not mistaken, to this district on the South Shore, near Plessisville. And there is likewise an agreeable affinity in the trio Barbeau, Rivard and AY: the first two interpreting their native corner of old Quebec, and Jackson benefiting so greatly from his contact and explorations with Barbeau and then providing the fine little illustrations for *Chez Nous*.

The broad modern highway along the St. Lawrence has taken away much of St. Michel's ancient character, and the bridge built about 1936 across to the Ile d'Orléans has made it almost too accessible to the outside world. The disappearance of the stout old stone houses is due more to the encroachment of modern times than to any fault in their construction. As Marius Barbeau writes in *Quebec, Where Ancient France Lingers:* "Winter blasts and summer storms hold no terrors for them, for their massive stone houses have stood the test of time for more than two hundred years."

PLATE 31
Old house near St. Michel, Quebec [1929]

At this stage, having already worked our curving way happily up the South Shore of the St. Lawrence, almost to the threshold of Quebec City, we must not forget that there is an equally important North Shore in AY's life. So we backtrack a little and leap from St. Michel on the gentle south bank straight northward as the snow goose flies, over to where St. Joachim lies at the foot of the mighty headland to which Champlain gave the telling name of Cap Tourmente.

The stretch of eighty miles or so north-eastward from St. Joachim, either along the shoreline past Petite Rivière and Maillard to Baie St. Paul, or up over the high plateau where St. Féreol and St. Tite des Caps are located in County Montmorency with the magnificent Laurentians to the north, and eastward from there into County Charlevoix, encloses another favourite region for AY's winter-spring sketching expeditions during the years from 1923 onward.

The village of St. Tite des Caps takes place of honour in our present North Shore group of drawings. AY knew it well from the early 1930s on, and spent a month to six weeks there in 1937, 1941, and 1946, calling it, "One of the places we loved to paint.... It was not one of the old villages, but it lay in a hollow encircled by hills, and we could look down on it from several directions. The snow lingered there when it had gone in most other places."

There was never-failing hospitality in the old Hotel Tremblay in St. Tite, warmly remembered in the autobiography and in the colour movie *Canadian Landscape*. (Filmed there largely in early spring 1941 by the Crawleys, and issued in 1942, this was the first of their series of valuable films on Canadian artists.) Perhaps the happiest of all the stays at St. Tite was in 1937, when AY wrote the following letter, dated April 12, 1937, to his niece in faraway Weimar, Germany:

Hi, Old Timer!

Not a creature is stirring, because it's 10.30 p.m. which is a dreadful hour to be up at St. Tite. I came down here on St. Patrick's Day with Dr. Banting, and he had two good weeks—lots of snow and sunshine and cold, and he worked from 7 a.m. till sunset. It's a good thing to be the son of a farmer.

The Tremblays were expecting me when I arrived, just had a feeling I was coming, and they were very pleased, from the material side too. It's nice to feel you are a kind of godsend to people; they make nothing in the winter time, and have all their poor relatives come to visit them....

Have seven more panels to mess up, and expect to leave this week.... The snow is getting mushy for snowshoeing, but you can't get far without

them. Going strong on pea soup, wild strawberry jam, etc. but too much fried stuff and no greens—however they are the kindest souls in the world....

I'm not going to the Coronation, trop de monde. I sold a picture to the National Gallery at Cape Town, I must be pretty punk.*

Well, happy days, kid—

ever your old Unk XXXxxx

Four years after that letter was written, AY was back at St. Tite des Caps, but with a sad difference. Like Tom Thomson, Fred Banting had died at the height of his career. On February 21, 1941, Sir Frederick Banting's plane crashed over Mulgrave Harbour, Newfoundland, while on a duty flight. And so AY lost the second of his great friends and sketching companions. Many pages of clippings in the artist's scrapbook bear witness to the weight of that further tragedy in AY's life. On March 27, 1941, he wrote once again from St. Tite des Caps: "The last time I was here was with Fred Banting and we had a very happy time together. He was quite the greatest man in Canada and yet seemed so completely unconscious of it. He intended to spend practically all his time painting when the war ended."

Two years after Banting's death a memorial exhibition of his paintings was held at Hart House in Toronto and AY published his little book *Banting as an Artist* in memory of the friend whose portrait photograph hangs in his studio to this day.

The scene portrayed in this wonderful, battered drawing of 1941, with its loose-leaf holes ripped open, its thumbtack marks, its oil stains covered over (by AY) with poster paint as if it too had been through the war, has now entered literally millions of homes all over the world as UNICEF's greeting card for 1966, "Village in the Snow." Made from the canvas of 1942, the colour reproduction differs from our original drawing here by playing up the rising background and the heaven-pointing spire of St. Tite's nice old church, while at the same time simplifying the detail of the road sides and adding a small sleigh for warm human interest.

The Art Gallery of Ontario has another St. Tite des Caps drawing, (njg 374, $7\frac{3}{4}$ by $10\frac{1}{2}$ inches) probably earlier than the drawing here. It also shows a typically splendid sweep of the plateau country, with the village tucked more into its hollow, and masses of marginal notes all around it.

*The South African government later cancelled this purchase, and the handsome canvas *Winter in Quebec, St. Urbain*, 1933, went to the Art Gallery of Wellington, New Zealand—much to AY's satisfaction. It is reproduced in the large Phaidon Press 1945 edition of *Canadian Painters* as plate 53, incorrectly credited as being in Dunedin, New Zealand.

PLATE 32

The village of St. Tite des Caps, County Montmorency, Quebec [1941]

This drawing of about 1930 shows one of the North Shore's most celebrated (and nowadays most colour-photographed) vistas, looking up-river from Les Eboulements into the wide stretch of Baie St. Paul, beyond which the steep shoreline hills carry today's highway upwards and across the plateau to St. Tite des Caps and on to Quebec, about sixty miles away. The strange name *Eboulements* or "landslide" comes from the terrible time in 1663 when for seven months the worst earthquakes on record rocked the district, causing the whole face of the cliff, on which already several *habitant* farms were located, to fall into the sea. The masses of fallen debris formed the lower level on which St. Joseph de la Rive is now located. The name Côte-de-la-Misère (approximately Misery Mountain), which Marius Barbeau in 1917 calls the steep road between Baie St. Paul and Les Eboulements, may stem from that early disaster or equally well from the difficulty of ascent! The little bay and the quay from which the ferry leaves for the Ile aux Coudres are visible in this drawing; the island lies out of sight on our left. The deepest river channel for ocean vessels runs between the Ile aux Coudres and the foreground shore of our drawing.

AY's skilfully foreshortened vista here shows part of the country that W. H. Blake drove through on a memorable sleigh-ride all the way from La Malbaie to Quebec City, in sub-zero weather between Christmas and New Year's. Blake made his jaunt back in the first decade of this century and AY got there, perhaps less than twenty years later, to find much the same driving conditions as Blake described. The chapter "A Christmas Jaunt," in that gem of a book, *Brown Waters*, tells vividly about that eventful ride, and incidentally pays the best imaginable tribute to the true hero of Quebec's past—the horse: "With heavy robes and hot bricks wrapped in sacking the tiny *cariole* was very comfortable, though the north wind blew fiercely, snatching away one's breath with its violence, and driving the fine hard snow like a sand-blast against the face. . . . The easterly and westerly roads, wherever exposed, were drifted fence high with hard packed snow, through which only an experienced horse could force a way. A town-trained animal would have gone wild with fear, and exhausted itself with futile plunging and struggling in a few hundred yards, but to steady-going old Coq, whose patient soul is imbued with his master's philosophy that 'nous sommes dans la vie pour rencontrer des obstacles,' this was all in the day's work.

". . . It was a stormy passage, where a sleigh with high runners would have been capsized a dozen times, but the craft of the country is built so that after sinking but a little distance it rests on the bottom and can weather almost anything in the way of drifts."

W. H. Blake's sleigh ascended the great hill in the background of AY's drawing: "Eight o'clock the next morning saw us climbing away from sea level behind a clever tandem. It was pretty to see the teamwork as for two hours we mounted the long hills. The shaft horse never made the mistake of putting in weight until his mate had tightened the traces, and never failed at that precise instant to move forward; on the descents the leader cantered free, keeping neatly out of his companion's way. As with many halts we worked up from one raised-beach plateau to another, there were ever-widening views of the valley we had left, the northern mountains through which the St. Urbain road finds a difficult passage, the heights of Les Eboulements, the St. Lawrence and Isle aux Coudres far beneath us, half hidden in ragged vapours gilded by the heatless beams of the low sun."

AY's visits to the Lower St. Lawrence were of course usually later in the winter season and less extensive than W. H. Blake's Christmas jaunt, but travel by horse and sleigh was most natural and enjoyable for the artist as well, as hundreds of visual records show. The scene of this present dynamic drawing, modified into a summer aspect, was used for the end-papers of Henry Beston's book *The St. Lawrence*. The canvas ("a very nice one," AY always states), for which this drawing notes on the *verso* "red violet looming through blue," belongs to Mrs. Elise Kingman Bacon.

68

PLATE 33

The coast at Les Eboulements, looking towards Baie St. Paul, County Charlevoix [c. 1930]

les Eboulements

A.Y. Jackson

Les Eboulements

The terrain that perhaps more than any other combines the characteristics of intimacy and grandeur mentioned above by AY in a letter of 1946, lies within the compass of Quebec's Charlevoix County, all within a hundred-mile drive of Quebec City—magnificence not being commensurate with mileage.

Baie St. Paul, the county centre, has already been mentioned as seasonal headquarters of most of the snow-painting artists of our land—Clarence Gagnon, Albert Robinson, Edwin Holgate, Fred Hutchison and Randolph Hewton, as well as A. Y. Jackson. Arthur Lismer, George and Kay Pepper, Mabel May and others have likewise been occasional visitors. Indeed, today the painter René Richard lives in Clarence Gagnon's old house there, and Jean Paul Lemieux uses the ancient stone mill on nearby Ile aux Coudres. From Baie St. Paul two main artist trails have run east and north, the former closer to the River, passing through villages once accessible only by boat—Les Eboulements, Ste. Irénée, La Malbaie, and beyond that towards the mouth of the Saguenay through St. Fidèle, Port au Persil and St. Siméon, which faces Rivière du Loup and Cacouna on the South Shore. The other artist trail, along a more ancient road, runs inland, north from Baie St. Paul up the glorious valley of the Rivière du Gouffre (River of the Whirlpool) towards St. Urbain, near which the hospitable log cabin of the Peppers has been located these many years. The trail then branches eastward, past St. Hilarion and Ste. Agnès, to the Malbaie or Murray River, whose double name stems from the two ancient seigneuries, one on its western and one on its eastern bank respectively.

Aspects of both grandiose and intimate nature abound along both these routes. The intimate is chiefly in the little villages of which our book selects one or two examples out of many; the grandeur in vistas such as the preceding coastal panorama from Les Eboulements and the present terrain rolling nobly towards the Laurentide highland in behind St. Urbain. William Hume Blake, the felicitous translator whom we have already met, spent months in this region every year during the half-century from 1875 onwards. His body rests in the little Protestant graveyard on the bank of the Malbaie River, beneath an epitaph combining English and French, as he so eloquently did during his lifetime. Well over fifty years ago he described the country in *Brown Waters:* "The true range of the Laurentians is distant from the shore of the St. Lawrence some twenty miles. . . . The nearer and gentler slopes shut out the great mountain masses that march sou'-west and nor'-east from Quebec to the Saguenay, so that one who does not go out to seek for them might easily be ignorant of their existence. . . .

"As to the heights of these mountains one searches in vain for authentic figures. Eboulements and Ste. Anne, both near the shore of the St. Lawrence, rise over two thousand five hundred feet, and one peak in the valley of the Gouffre is credited with a height of three thousand two hundred feet, but these elevations are greatly exceeded as one journeys inland. Observations with several aneroids show that the St. Urbain road, the only highway that crosses the mountains, is three thousand feet above the sea at a point some thirty-five miles from Baie St. Paul, while the surrounding hills might be credited with another fifteen hundred feet. . . .

"The outlines of these ancient hills have been flattened and rounded by the age-long grinding and chiselling of glaciers, which have also built up huge moraines, and strewn the country with boulders. . . ."

The quotation is taken from Blake's essay on the Laurentide National Park, in the establishment of which in 1895 he played a major part. Now about four thousand square miles in extent, with over fifteen hundred lakes, this provincial park is one of Canada's greatest game preserves. It is interesting to note that at the time Blake wrote, the St. Urbain road, shown here in AY's drawing, was still the only land route to the Lake St. John area, and it was over this old road, skirting the eastern boundary of the Park in exhaustingly steep gradients, that thousands of settlers moved northward. Long before their day, before 1700 in fact, the Gouffre valley had been cleared of the grand primeval red pine timber up to the edge of the Laurentian highland, the felled trees becoming masts for the navy of France.

AY has given many interpretations of this magnificent highland beyond St. Urbain. There are several versions of this particular vast stretch, with its characteristic hump of a small hill in the centre. A closer aspect of the same humped hill, with a grandly muddy late-spring road, changed owners several times and was acquired in 1957 by the Elsie Perrin Memorial Art Museum in London, Ontario. This canvas, 21 by 26 inches and dated *circa* 1936 (njg 982), was initially called *Road, Charlevoix* but has somehow, rather understandably, slid into *The Road to Charlevoix*. There is no actual town called Charlevoix, alas; that lovely name evokes a memory land. The old road curves off grandly towards a place no one can reach. In AY's earthier terms: "They've taken all the kinks out of the road and straightened the whole thing, ruined it. All those nice old wooden fences are gone, and now the road is ploughed all winter and the cars roar past a mile a minute. I tried a sketch there a couple of years ago; it was a dud."

PLATE 34

*The old road northward
from St. Urbain* [early 1930s]

70

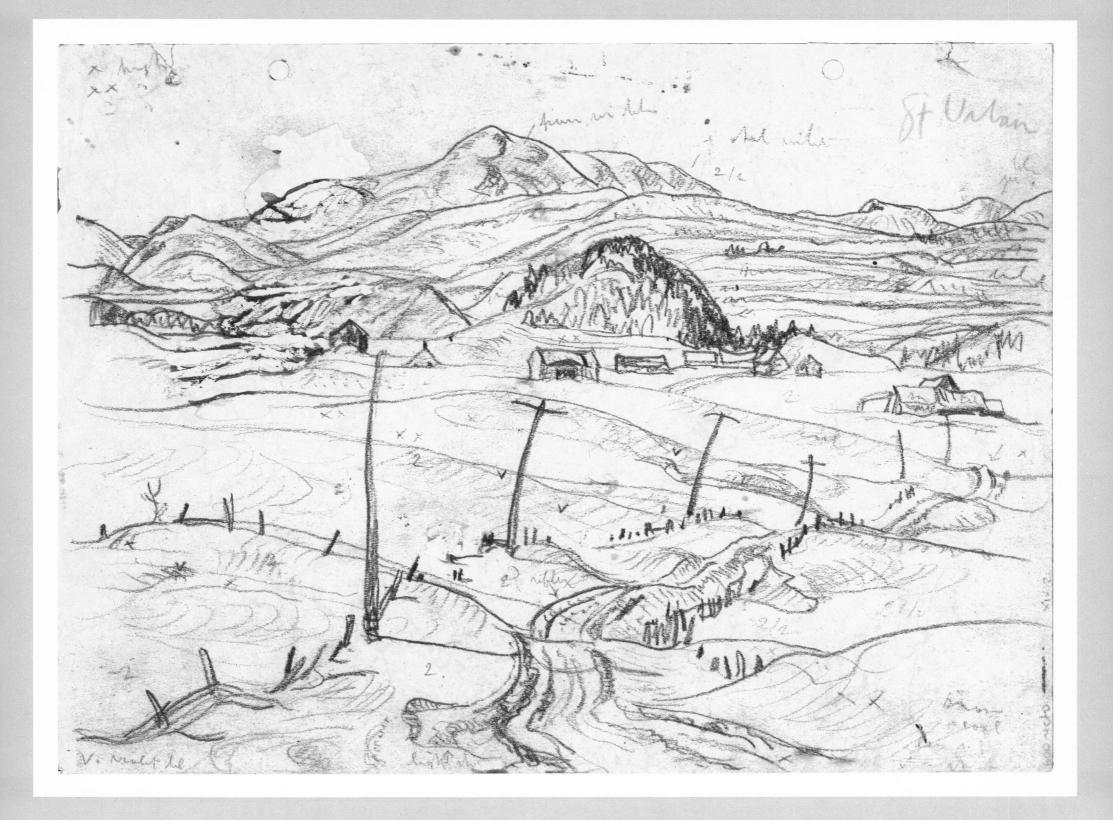

This little village of long ago has an anonymous anywhere look, but AY says it is a place he walked to from St. Urbain when he was staying there with Randolph Hewton. (Strange that the name of St. Urbain, where AY worked so often, is not mentioned in *A Painter's Country*.) "There was a hill that must have been about twenty-four hundred feet high. Hewton tried to get up it in the morning, and came back and said: 'There's no end to that hill!' But I got up it in the afternoon and made a sketch and a drawing, and a canvas later—it's out in Vancouver now. . . . Hewton and I were both old soldiers, so when I got back to St. Urbain in the late afternoon I told him that the 60th had to finish up what the 24th fell down on . . . ."

This tale of toughness calls to mind a remark by the late Pearl McCarthy, long-time art editor for *The Globe and Mail* of Toronto, when she reported that "Spring must be here—A. Y. Jackson is back!" with a crop of forty sketches she had not yet seen. "One reason why nobody can prophesy on the Jackson sketches is said to be that he so outwalks anybody who might accompany him that the companion is in danger of getting pneumonia from the violent exercise followed by sketching in the snows."

Since one good yarn deserves another, here is the way that AY likes to refer to the three churches of St. Urbain: "The oldest one [probably about 1837] was known to Gagnon in the mid-twenties, before I ever got to St. Urbain. He said it was a fine little old church, but the curé wanted a new one, so when the old one got a little crack in it he had them tear it down. The second one was the one I did so often, not bad either. But then fire destroyed more than half the village in the late 1930s, and now they have a thing made out of plywood with a spire like a toothpick, and the village is all square wooden boxes with false brick fronts. And not one nice old barn with thatched roof is left."

And last of all, the source of the title about the little street with little houses which seemed to fit this drawing: it comes from *The Village of Viger*, by Duncan Campbell Scott. Duncan Campbell Scott was born in 1862, twenty years before AY, in the generation of W. H. Blake and Adjutor Rivard. *The Village of Viger* has at first reading a rather sentimental effect, with its "Rue Alfred de Musset" and its little visiting milliner from the big city whose lights gleam on the far horizon. But behind the sentiment is a sharp awareness of the psychic mechanisms that make Viger tick, namely strong characters and competing personalities, rivalries and feuds. No doubt that is what also makes AY's little anonymous village tick in its unsentimental way!

72

PLATE 35

*Village up behind
St. Urbain, County
Charlevoix* [*1930*]

One of the North Shore Quebec villages to which fond memories attach, both for AY and for those of his friends and relatives who have visited and sketched there, is the little town with the delightful name of St. Hilarion, on the inland road (now Route 15A) from Baie St. Paul to La Malbaie.

"St. Hilarion is like one of the Italian hill towns; the country around is cleared of trees, and the town stands on the top of a hill," wrote AY in his autobiography. The village's complete visibility for twenty or so miles all around made all the more touching the concern of old Monsieur Tremblay, at whose son's house AY stayed, that the artist might not be able to find his way back from his day's sketching in the field. Some of the rest of us remember trying to find a place to sketch where we would *not* be discovered, pursued and surrounded by all the kids of St. Hilarion. No matter how far away we got they always found us. Probably they had been encouraged in their art interests by Arthur Lismer when he and AY worked there together. (Lismer's fine panorama *Quebec Village*, 1926, 52 by 63 inches, now at Queen's University, Kingston, was one result of the trip he, Barbeau and AY made to the district in the summer of 1925.)

There are also marvellous little drawings that both Lismer and AY made of the interior at the François Tremblays, opposite the church. A quite elegant little pen-and-ink of AY's bedroom can be found on page 65 of Beston's *The St. Lawrence*, showing the spool bed with patchwork quilt, hand-carved wash stand with old oil lamp, round braided rug, and best of all, the ancient, home-made rocking chair, its rockers worn flat by long use. This same chair (with a new coat of paint) still graces the country bedroom of the present writer. And, as *A Painter's Country* tells with warm affection, Grandpère Tremblay's own old rocking chair (njg 612), shown here with our text, came eventually after the old man's death to be one of AY's "favourite possessions," in which he sat to write his memoirs. Along with other French-Canadian mementos it still lends its homely tone to the Jackson studio and has been sat in by generations of visitors who agree with AY's words: "There was something about these associations that touched the heart."

Assuming, as we have been doing all along, that different sizes of drawing paper probably indicate different dates of drawing, our main drawing here may well be from a visit to St. Hilarion in the thirties, possibly 1933. "Mon pays, c'est l'hiver," suits AY as well as many other Canadians. The snow lay longer around St. Hilarion than out near the coast of the St. Lawrence, so AY often visited up there towards the end of the spring sketching season. One of his canvases, entitled simply *St. Hilarion*, drew especially favourable attention in a long article by Emile Venne in *La Renaissance*, November 23, 1935, on the occasion of AY's

exhibition of forty canvases and oil sketches at the Scott Gallery on Drummond Street in Montreal: ". . . voici un tableau qui atteint à l'expression typique et de nos villages et de nos hivers. C'est le village dans son pays de neige. . . . Un fond de montagnes ondoyantes. Les petites maisons de bois se pressent autour d'un candide clocher. . . ."

This appealing epithet *candide* (which in Latin means "light" but not "shining") recalls other fond memories of St. Hilarion recorded in the small diary kept by AY's niece and a friend during the summer of 1934: "We had a quick visit in St. Urbain where we found Kay Pepper painting in a cabbage patch, then back to St. Hilarion, where we are now installed in comfort, in fact in French-Canadian grandeur at the home of the François Tremblays—we are following close on AY's trail! . . ."

Then after a few days: "Monsieur le Curé has asked us two "artists" to touch up with our oil paints a group of plaster saints in the church; they were damaged in a fire—church artists! What will mon oncle say!!"

And at the end of our visit: "Our expenses at the Tremblays: 6 nuits @ 25¢ is $1.50; 10 repas @ 25¢ is $2.50; 3 pounds of maple sugar is 25¢."

In fact nothing went above 25¢ except the old rocking chair, which was $2, probably including shipping charges. No wonder we all loved St. Hilarion and its candid spire!

PLATE 36

St. Hilarion, County Charlevoix [*c. 1933*]

AY's lifelong attachment to barns is so self-evident as seemingly to require little comment. Big long barns, little low barns, barns with thatched roofs, barns with shingled gable ends; the painterly *Red Barn*, with rich cadmium red roof set off by shining whitewashed walls and deep cerulean sky; the sturdily sculpturesque group of the Ontario Art Gallery's grey weather-beaten *Barns* (whose surprisingly delicate little drawing was done near La Malbaie in 1926); here on the facing page this long elegant old edifice, with a slight sway to its beam—AY liked, sketched, drew, painted them all. Yet he did not, does not, like *all* barns, not by any means. Not even any *old* barn. There has to be something special about each barn he honours with permanency in his work.

It is probably no accident, for instance, that two of the Quebec counties where AY painted many—perhaps most—of his barns were the very counties (L'Islet and Charlevoix) noted in general for their regionally distinctive barns. Not that AY checked all that before setting out; it was simply his good instinct for good barns that led him to the best.

A propos this barn theme, a whole monograph devoted to Quebec's barns, *Les granges du Québec, du XVIIe au XIXe siècle*, by R.-L. Séguin, was published recently by the National Museum of Canada with sixty plates containing ninety-four examples, some of them actually recognizable in works by AY. One sees in Séguin's book how heritage combined with adjustment to climate in favouring the steep-pitched roof brought from the French provinces bordering the English Channel; in discarding walls of stone which frosted heavily in our winter clime in favour of wood construction with its superior ventilation; in evolving the Canadian version of the two-storied or banked barn, with its relatively smaller area of roofing. Roofing materials, for their part, progressed from the earliest bark strips in Indian style to copious use of thatch, to planking, shingle, and finally sheet metal.

Wealthy L'Islet County developed not only the Quebec version of the banked barn (which will appear again when we reach Ontario) but likewise the mansard-roof barn, often with a charming little cupola and perhaps a horse or rooster weathervane. L'Islet was also a main centre for the *batteuse à vent*, a sort of wooden windmill used in threshing.

According to M. Séguin's book, however, it is Charlevoix County on the North Shore that has retained more special ancient features than anywhere else, including the thatched roof. Each parish formerly had two or three professional thatchers permanently employed. A good ten-inch thatch would last up to seventy years. Around conservative St. Urbain, in behind Baie St. Paul, the use of thatch survived until the 1930s, and the passing of the good old barns there was lamented by AY. By 1960,

according to M. Séguin, there remained scarcely a dozen in Quebec.

Back in 1825 the general use of thatch had begun to yield to that of the split cedar shingle, which also lasted well and was especially resistant to salt-water winds. The barn of wood with shingled roof pleased AY too, since it tended to follow the contour of the land it was built on, adjusting to the humps and curves as it mellowed and settled a bit under the weight of winter snows. It was often made longer by additions, as needed, and its lines acquired the kind of rhythm AY likes—a long horizontal roll, with perhaps a slight hump in the centre; a living line, a Laurentian line. Such barns weathered well, painted or not. The shingles turned to silver and were patched with tin which turned a rusty red; the whole mass relaxed into the hills and hollows, the furrows and snowdrifts; with old age came dignity.

St. Tite des Caps just over the hill from Charlevoix County provided the noble old King Lear of a barn shown here. Its handsome, dark-skyed canvas, titled *April, St. Tite des Caps*, was acquired in 1935 by H. S. Southam of Ottawa, along with other works from the Jackson show at the Scott Gallery in Montreal. AY does not know its present whereabouts. This particular canvas was singled out by Emile Venne in *La Renaissance* as being among the show's "oeuvres puissantes." His analysis fits the drawing as well: ". . . au centre, une vieille grange aux formes sinueuses semble résister avec ténacité à l'assaut de monstrueuses dunes de neige. Ces tableaux expriment plus que l'hiver, et plus qu'un pays; ils atteignent l'expression d'une profonde pensée. Volonté de durer. Monsieur Jackson a compris, il a du moins exprimé cette véritable poésie de chez nous. Nos maisons de bois, comme des campements provisoires, un coup de vent pourrait les emporter, penserait-on. Vient la tempête, l'hiver, elles se concentrent sur elles-mêmes, se recroquevillent, s'accrochent au sol par tous les moyens. On veut durer."

They want to last . . . but alas, nothing lasts forever, except maybe the Laurentian hills. By the mid-thirties AY was beginning to worry about the disappearance of his barns; the old-timers were being ousted by stiffly rectangular hard-edged nonentities with shiny laudably fireproof tin roofs and asbestos-shingled walls which he refused even to look at. "Barns are getting scarce," he wrote plaintively from St. Tite on April 12, 1937; "I'm going to make some models, and get a few pounds of salt for snow, and do them in the studio."

By now, a generation later, the independent family farm itself is threatened with extinction, being "uneconomic" to run. Larger-geared enterprise seems to be taking over. The "volonté de durer" will undergo its inevitable transformation.

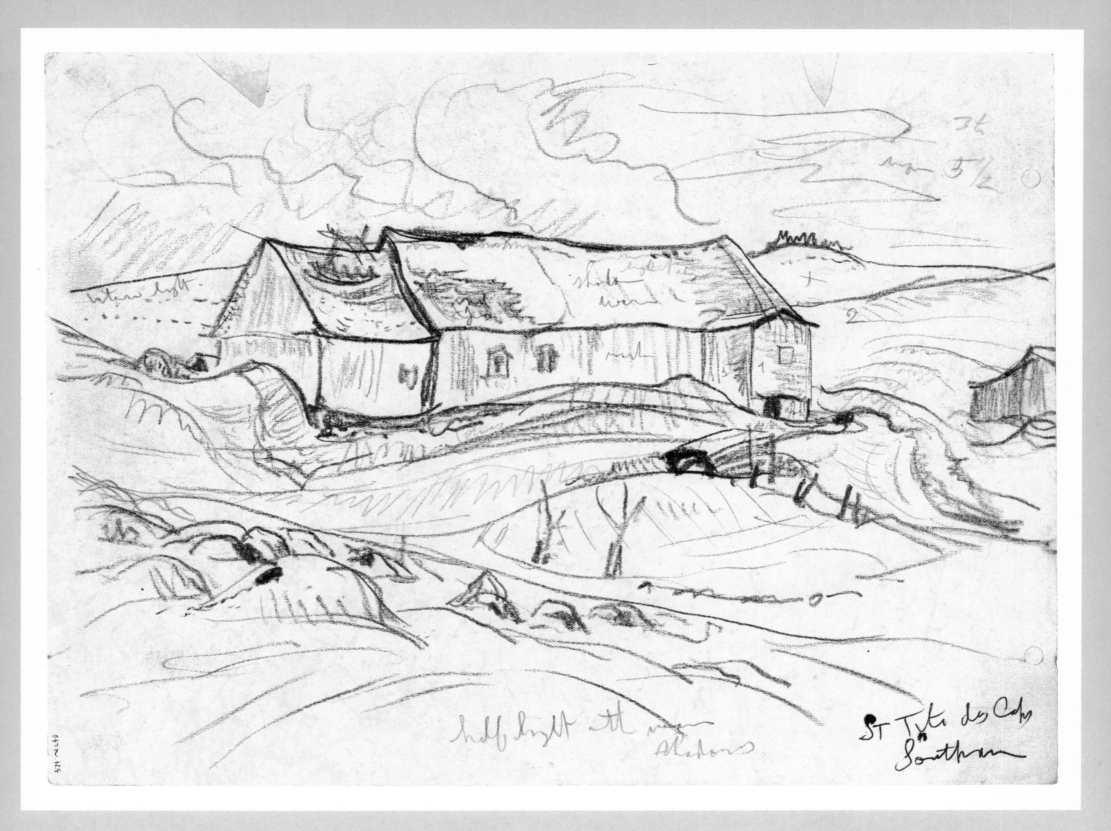

PLATE 37

Old barn, St. Tite des Caps, April [mid-1930s]

So a farewell to old rural Quebec; but better expressed for AY with a bang than a whimper. This positively last Lower St. Lawrence appearance helps to show the bang with which the Machine Age hit St. Tite des Caps sometime in the early 1940s. AY reminisces: "I stood out in the middle of the main street to do this one, looking towards the Hotel Tremblay—that was the old hotel—ramshackle, creaky, but what a friendly place! It burned down in 1945. I couldn't paint standing out there—too much traffic by then, so I just drew. That old sleigh there—it looks as if it's been put in the junk heap, and the new automobile is right in the middle of the picture. I left the "S" off the SHELL sign on purpose. I even left it off the sketch I painted afterwards from the drawing."

Around the margins of AY's notebook studies of horses, sleighs, and buggies—no two the same—are verbal details and abbreviations that are fun to read: "yell horse, old vermilion collar; old wood unpainted; red and black checked dress, peacock blue sleigh," or "warm rose, red edge, rose grey; black horse, red tassel, pink muffler;" or simply "Plug;" or finally "dirty yel; striped blanket faded red; dark figure, warm [or worn?] chocolate."

AY never achieved the agility of a Krieghoff (1815/1871) or an Henri Julien (1852/1908) in depicting the wonderful world of horses, *le cortège joyeux* of the olden days. But he saw many of the sights those artists saw; nor was the winter world in the early twenties so very different from back in 1795, when on a snappy bright February morning Governor Simcoe's lady set out from Quebec City to drive all the way to Montreal in her *dormeuse*: "the head of Seal Skin lined with Baize, a large Bear or Buffalo skin in front, which may be unhooked . . . a low seat, and a feather bed to keep one's feet warm. . . . We changed post horses every three miles. . . ."

And AY could appreciate the enthusiasm with which W. H. Blake described his Christmas sleigh ride through St. Tite des Caps and down the great hill behind Cap Tourmente to St. Joachim on the way to Quebec City: "The rush down steep, winding hills to the St. Lawrence was a mad and exhilarating progress, giving scant time for speculation on the upshot should a cantering horse lose his footing or take a curve too sharply. No motor car in its best flight could so fill the imagination with the idea of swift and rhythmic motion—of sheer space-annihilating speed. Dull mechanical devices are uninspiring beside the strenuous, free action of the living creature. If this be deplorable conservatism, then pray range us with those who are hopelessly and happily unprogressive."

But progress had to come, and AY looked on as sleighs were replaced by snowmobiles, and as snowmobiles were outdated by the big power plows until finally cars replaced sleighs for keeps.

"*St. Tite des Caps, March 27, 1941:* Back in the old Tremblay Hotel again. . . . Came up from St. Joachim in a snowmobile, which is just a symbol of the change that is going on all over Quebec. However, I wish they would give the old barns a rest and concentrate on toilets and baths."

"*March 29th, 1946:* We are going modern—snowmobiles all over the place; new houses, and the old ones done over in tin, imitation brick, and other artist-proof abominations. The village is humming with industry; it used to be such a sleepy old place in winter. A lot of nice little corners where I used to be sure of a sketch have disappeared."

While AY deplored the inevitability of change he was not the one to give up on his native Quebec countryside. On the same date as the excerpt above, he expanded his thoughts in an article entitled "A Changing Paradise," for the Toronto *News*. ". . . The old clapboard and shingles which took on such subtle colour in weathering are no more. But the hills and fields and the creek that becomes a wild river in the spring, and the snow that piles up in big drifts have not changed; and the weather and the endless effects of light that plays over the country are all still here to stir the imagination; and so, while one regrets the passing of things that are beautiful in themselves, the artist is not dependent on old houses and barns. The old and the new are all grist to the artist's mill. There are colours and forms, and lines of movement and varying effects of light, and if there is less ready-made stuff then it is up to the artist not only to observe but to emphasize and create and to give his own interpretation to what he sees."

So the conclusion is positive after all. Paradise has merely changed. The "S" can go back onto HELL. The mountains are still there, the spring and the sun and "the dark earth lifting through the sinking snow." If there is anything to the concept that the soul-waves of a person continue to swirl around a place that meant much to him, then around the Laurentian regions there will always be a stocky little ghost on bear-paw snowshoes, with a cheerful ruddy face and keen eyes noting the subtleties of silvered shingles that vanished long ago, of "the parish rooted in the soil," of the "old vermilion sleigh" and the "yell horse."

PLATE 38

Street scene in St. Tite des Caps, Quebec [early 1940s]

We now actually come to some cities as we move westward through AY's Canada! Our first encounter is one of the country's most famous city views, which tempted artists as early as 1709, when Jean Baptiste Decouagne made the lively panorama that graces the title page of Marius Barbeau's *Quebec, Where Ancient France Lingers*. Among many others who painted the city we can recall Thomas Davies around 1787, Mrs. Chaplin and W. H. Bartlett about 1840 and J. W. Morrice a decade or so before AY's entrance on the scene. AY arrived in company with his good friend Albert Robinson in 1922, the year after they had been at Cacouna further downstream. Characteristically they chose to stay at a distance, with the city forming a background for plenty of foreground landscape, or rather water-and-icescape. ". . . Robinson and I went to Bienville, a small village just below Quebec on the south shore. In March when the snow was melting, when the roads were covered with slush and the ice was going up and down the river with the tides, it was a fascinating place to paint. . . . One of our favourite sketching locations was on the Canadian National tracks beside the river, where we could look across to Quebec, with the ice drifting up and down in the foreground."

The drawings from that 1922 visit are almost as small and delicate as earlier ones from Europe and as those of the previous year from Cacouna. They seem a good deal closer to the topographical tradition of the eighteenth and nineteenth centuries than to AY's later, more vigorous style. It is rather nice to see him at first fit into the old tradition before forging ahead on his own.

The soundly composed drawing here, small enough in format to be reproduced full size, looks as if its semi-translucent paper had been out in a spring rainstorm. It was utilized almost twenty years after its creation, in a much less effective ink-wash technique, for the two-page spread in Henry Beston's book *The St. Lawrence*. The Quebec skyline of AY's 1922 drawing lacks (quite happily) the one skyscraper that went up in the 1930s, the Price Building (possibly connected with our old friends Les Prices Broders?). AY has wisely played down the towering form of the Canadian Pacific Railway's Chateau Frontenac. The characteristic Citadel and wall fortifications were installed in 1830 or so; accordingly the silhouette of the handsome city would not have looked so very different than it does in AY's drawing when Mrs. Anna Jameson arrived in 1836 and made the note in her journal about "Quebec who sits bristling defiance on the summit of her rocky height."

PLATE 39

Quebec with the Citadel and Plains of Abraham, seen from the South Shore [1922]

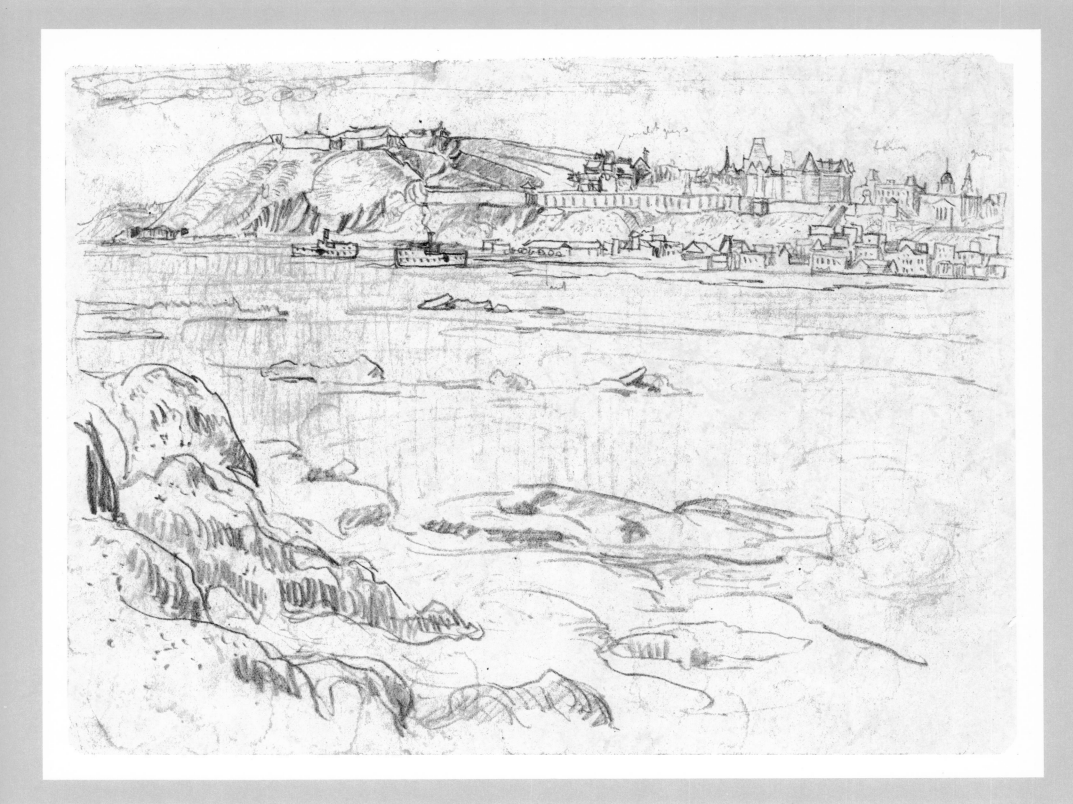

Canada's most prestigious city presents a different face to each visitor who undertakes to describe her, verbally or visually. This includes A. Y. Jackson, who made major visits to Quebec and vicinity in 1922 and 1934, as well as occasional briefer sojourns when passing along the St. Lawrence. Samples of his two main Quebec City visits follow in sequence here for contrast—the "bristling" 1922 profile and the larger, later drawing of the town street indeed covered with snow.

It is only appropriate to provide some historical background for this intriguing, many-faceted subject. Our title was established away back in 1791. "At 7 I looked out of the Cabbin window and saw the Town covered with Snow & it rained the whole day. I was not disposed to leave the Ship to enter so dismal looking a Town." Thus wrote the elegant Mrs. Simcoe on November 11, 1791, after a voyage of forty-seven days during most of which the deck of her leaky "Cabbin" was so awash that she went about in wooden clogs. En route to join her husband, Colonel John Graves Simcoe, newly appointed first Governor of Upper Canada, Mrs. Simcoe had perforce to disembark that same evening and venture upon some of the town's gourmet surprises: "I met with fine partridges and excellent Apples called Roseaux, pink throughout, and they had a flavour of strawberries—a very early apple and they do not keep." In the course of her five years in Canada Mrs. Simcoe spent several months in Quebec City, with her own Establishment, including "a covered Carriole, a Horse, a Cow & a Cat & a Canadian Driver." Moreover she admitted that she "liked excessively" the big parties at the Château St. Louis, headquarters of Lord and Lady Dorchester.

Forty years later, a quite different type of English lady wrote: "At ten last night, August 15th, the lights of Quebec were seen gleaming through the distance like a coronet of stars above the waters." This was our much-loved Mrs. Traill, who reached Quebec in 1832 as the bride of an "emigrant officer," having made the voyage in the state cabin of a rum-loaded freighter for the high price of £15. Mrs. Traill was bitterly disappointed not to be allowed ashore on account of the cholera epidemic raging in the city. Her book *The Backwoods of Canada* (my edition the Second, 1836, pages 22 ff.) gives wonderful details of the *twelve* ferries plying between Quebec and Lévis, "comical-looking machines" with side paddles moved by four horses aboard each ferry.

Four years later came another writing lady, Mrs. Anna Jameson, who visited the Canadas in 1836/1837, ostensibly for reconciliation with her husband, Attorney-General of Upper Canada, but more likely in order to gather material for one of her many books. Presumably the "bristling defiance" noted by Mrs. Jameson was more against les Américains than les Anglais, at that stage!

But let us allow the gentlemen the word after our three ladies. In May 1842 Charles Dickens stood gazing from the "giddy heights" of Dufferin Terrace and exclaimed over "this Gibraltar of America . . . its citadel suspended, as it were, in the air; its picturesque steep streets and frowning gateways; and the splendid views which burst upon the eye at every turn. . . ." Almost a century later his words were quoted by W. P. Percival in *The Lure of Quebec.* This well-composed, richly illustrated and most informative book pays its homage in the Introduction thus: "Probably no city on earth stands so nobly on such a stately headland."

Dr. Percival's book belongs to the period when AY did most of his Quebec City drawings. To the same decade belong two other contrasting views of the city by writers more closely connected with AY himself. On the one hand we have our own well-loved Marius Barbeau describing his Quebec in 1936 as " . . . a quaint oasis in the midst of man-made uniformity . . . the citadel, the ramparts and spires . . . were those of a fairy tale . . . the people . . . enjoy themselves and are strangely youthful. A holiday spirit pervades the place. A romantic atmosphere. . . ."

But in 1941, only five years later, the New Englander Henry Beston

(continued)

PLATE 40

Quebec City, Rue St. Gabriel, corner Côte Ste. Geneviève [c. 1934]

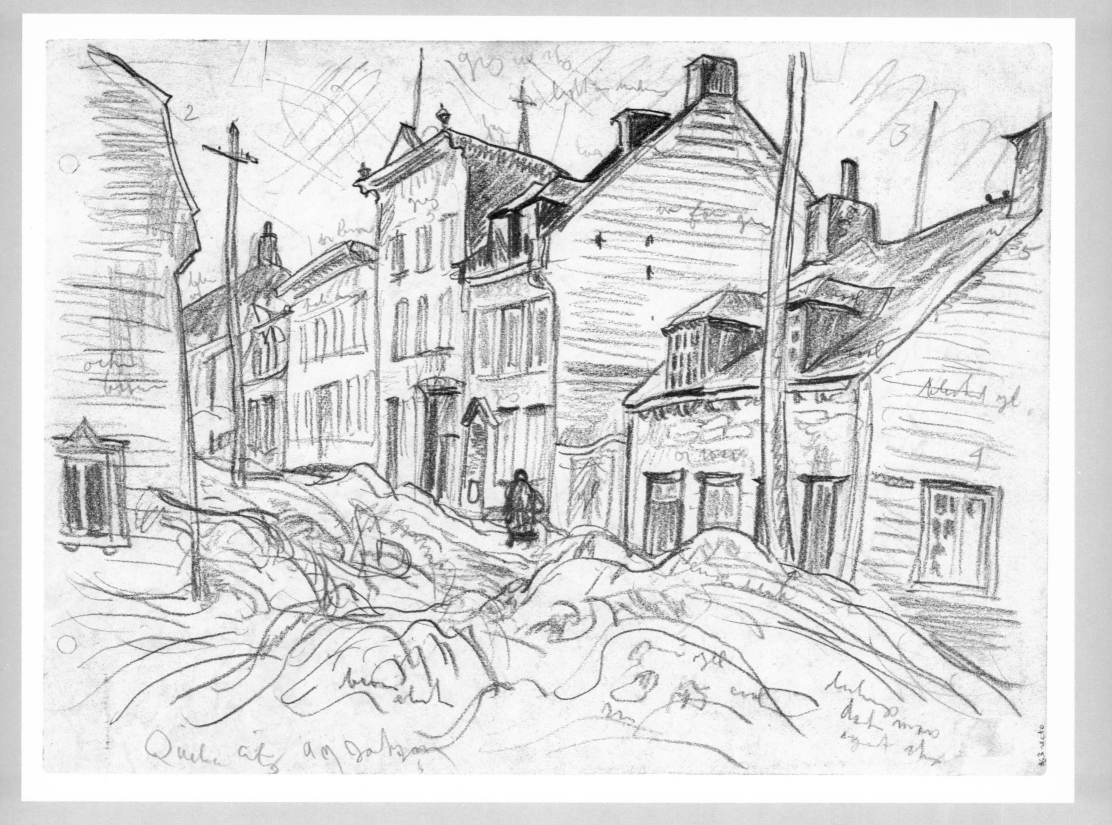

writes in the chapter "The City on the Rock" of *The St. Lawrence:* " . . . The *ancien régime* has melted like the snow. The clock of architectural time on the rock stands at the mood of 1830. What the core of old Quebec really recalls, under its modernity and its guidebooks, is a French provincial town of the time of Louis Philippe which has managed to get itself enclosed in a British military wall. What has been added of earliest Victorian England has merely strengthened the effect. These older streets with their grim façades and serious doorways are not backgrounds for eighteenth century wigs and brocades. They are meant to frame groups of such handsome young women in hooded bonnets and uglily-quaint puffed sleeves as one sees in the portraits of Ingres or might read of in Balzac. . . . There is little of what the French call *riant* about Quebec. It is a place *forte* in character as well as in natural appearance, a kind of fortress of the courage and tenacity of man facing on the one hand the intermittent human enemy and on the other the timeless weight of nature and the sure, recurrent savagery of winter and the cold."

And now AY: what faces did Quebec turn towards him? One could almost say one young face, one old. There could scarcely be greater difference between the aspect of 1922 and that of a dozen years later, a stretch short in time but great in change for AY. All available drawing records for March 1922 show Quebec City from across the River on the South Shore, where AY and his friend Albert Robinson stayed at a small place between Lévis and Lauzon, boarding in the haphazard household of an agreeable widow with a lively family. Fine small drawings ($7\frac{3}{8}$ by $9\frac{7}{8}$ inches) reveal the grandiose vista of the beautiful city in the background, while interesting ice shapes in the tidal river take up most of the foreground. The detailed representation in these drawings links AY with earlier travellers to Quebec; like his Cacouna works of the year before, these are more delicate and linear than the robust little oil sketches they accompany. Works of Frenchmen such as Corot and Ingres come to mind, perhaps not so strangely, since AY was in France until 1919.

Then in 1934 comes the wonderful set of strong drawings in rich soft graphite pencil, using the later, larger, 9 by 12 inch paper. Located so far are fourteen 1934 Quebec City drawings on eight sheets of paper, i.e. all but two have both a *recto* and a *verso* side. They all have two looseleaf holes in the shorter end and two more pushed into the long top, making a handy identification mark for this vintage year. Once enough opportunity has been given for additional Quebec drawings to turn up, I hope to publish them all in a separate sequence. As a group they are unique to AY's career in two ways: as pure drawings, and as a city series. They belong to the artist's most vigorous drawing years, and bring close-up views of a city that has changed more than can be believed possible.

It seems that one March AY spent about a week in Quebec City before proceeding down-river to his usual haunts. The drawings are not dated

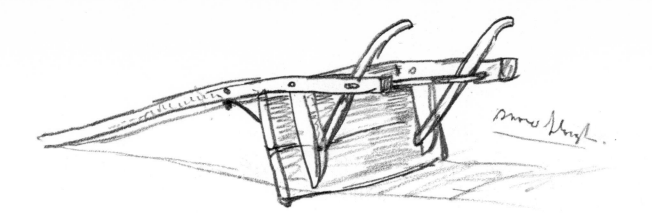

but one was painted up as a canvas and exhibited by fall 1935, so 1934 is likely the year, since AY was elsewhere in March 1935. He stayed in Quebec at some pension whose name rather understandably eludes him after the interim of over thirty years. "But I do remember that there was a great big fall of snow while I was there, and the snow drifted into wonderful shapes in the streets and lay there for days. I went around making drawings all over the place—only drawings, I don't remember doing any painting until afterwards when I made a couple of canvases from the drawings." One of the canvases (21 by 26 inches) is in the Montreal Museum of Fine Arts, where it is called *Street in Quebec;* it is given as Number 58 "painted about 1935" in the catalogue of the 1953 Jackson retrospective; its drawing is njg 366 *verso* and it actually represents Canoterie Hill. The other canvas, according to AY "looked something like a Morrice and used to be in the H. S. Southam collection—present whereabouts unknown. It was more open, with a horse and sleigh in front."

So this is a whole set of pure drawings done, not before or after an oil sketch, but in order to record good subjects. This helps to explain their vigorous use of black areas and their rollicking pencil rhythms. Obviously AY stood on street corners or in doorways, wherever it suited him, and made compositions of the marvellous old place to his heart's content. No panoramic splendour this time, nor any stress of the historic, nor of the particularly picturesque, though that was hard to avoid! Only one drawing bears a street name—Rue St. Vallier (njg 145)—the rest are simply Quebec. But of course some scholarly epigones cannot rest content with that kind of simplicity, and the following shows the ironic twist of our recent research. Until recently we (meaning AYJ and NJG) had been titling the present drawing *Montcalm's House,* after the nice little old house to the right in the drawing. The name "Maison de Montcalm" is touristically applied to the A.D. 1677 house at 36 Rue St. Louis, one of muchburned and rebuilt Quebec's oldest edifices. Everybody knows that it is "not really" Montcalm's house, which is the tall gracious *Candiac* over on Rue des Remparts. Dr. Percival says it is doubtful whether General

Montcalm ever even entered Number 36, but most of today's photo takers are not too worried by that fact! Anyway, Blodwen Davies provides another interesting occupant to replace the missing Montcalm: our old friend Sieur Philippe Aubert de Gaspé, who lived at Number 36 Rue St. Louis for a time.

In the research for the present work, a careful comparison of our drawing here with illustrations of 36 Rue St. Louis and its adjacent buildings showed that our drawing is not even the *soi-disant* Maison de Montcalm. Dr. and Mrs. B. T. Denis, the kind and energetic friends in Quebec City who walked miles, our photos and their street map in hand, sent the following surprising information on poor but beautiful njg 363 *recto:* It is (or *was,* one is tempted to say) on the Rue St. Gabriel looking up from the Côte Ste. Geneviève, in neither the Lower nor the Upper Town but well outside the old walled city to its west, off the Boulevard Ste. Foy. The church spire tip just visible is that of St. Jean Baptiste Church. And—here is perhaps the strangest part—everything on the street has been changed since this drawing was made, except the "house with the flowerpots on the roof" and the "still recognizable" house on the left. So the *soi-disant soi-disant* Maison de Montcalm is gone in any case. AY's drawing may well be the sole record of it.

One suspects of course that back in 1934 AY didn't much mind whether Montcalm lived there or not; indeed if he had, AY would probably have moved along to draw another house. What AY was enjoying was all that lovely snow that "covered the town." Not for him Mrs. Simcoe's dim view, nor Mr. Beston's "recurrent savagery of winter and the cold." AY likes cold and loves snow. How well we can tailor our dear old limerick to him:

There once was [A. Y.] in Quebec
Who fell into snow to his neck;
When asked: "Are you friz?"
He replied: "Yes I is,
But we don't call this *cold* in Quebec!"

This is another of the vigorous pencil drawings, fourteen or more, that AY did during one snowy March week in old Quebec. We can picture him stumping sturdily all over Lower Town, Upper Town and out beyond the city walls, getting the spirit, the feel or even more accurately the guts of the place. It is interesting to observe how much more gutsy a drawing can be than a photograph of the same subject. In Peter Varley's *Canada*, for instance, all his Quebec city streets are nicely angled and neatly titled so we know exactly where we are, yet AY's untitled compositions of casual, sometimes even scruffy corners and snow-tracked streets are probably closer to the way Quebec has actually looked for most of its three hundred and fifty years.

Most of the drawings include a small human figure or two, little black *bonhommes* working their way through the snow, and AY's views are those of the man in the street, the real old Quebecker, not of a touring culture cultivator. AY probably knew, vaguely, that of Quebec's 400,000 inhabitants about 25,000 have English as their mother tongue but that all can speak French. He would be conscious of the fact, visually, that Quebec has forty convents and fifty churches (though only one English Catholic church, St. Patrick's) but he put into his drawings only the tip of the spire of a couple, one of which we can see here. AY tramped miles through Quebec, but as he passed Number 57 Grande Allée was he aware that it was the site of the home of "la belle de Québec," the beauteous Miss Mary Simpson? Horatio Nelson, then Captain of *HMS Albermarle*, felt such consuming passion for that lovely lady that he would have given up his commission and stayed in Canada to wed her had not England, in the guise of his junior officers, persuaded him to do his duty elsewhere. AY may not even have tipped his hat as he passed 295 Grande Allée, the only house with bell-cast eaves remaining in Quebec City and once the home of Cornelius Krieghoff to boot.

Finally in this artful parade of facts AY may not have bothered to read up on, but which are nice to know, must be included a note that although the great Molière was a bosom friend of Samuel de Champlain, it was *Le Cid*, by the more serious Corneille, that became in 1646 the first play ever produced in North America. However AY *did* get to a theatrical performance during his stay in Quebec. He reminisces: "It was a wonderful sort of cabaret place in a cellar, where they put on bilingual plays that were terribly funny. The audience took part in them too, and nobody seemed to care which language they spoke. There was one part where a chap was asked about his acting experience, if he'd ever been in an English play, and he answered: 'Mais oui, bien certain, j'étais un bloodhound dans *Oncle Tom's Cabane!*'"

This bloodhound reminds us of all the active tracking and tracing that was done to locate the curving street corner with its typical mixture of styles, shapes and sizes represented in the present drawing. On leafing through Pierre Berton's *Remember Yesterday*, and putting our Sherlock Holmesian magnifying glass to the splendid old Notman photograph of the 1902 view from Dufferin Terrace—lo and behold! there is AY's corner, down in Lower Town, just below the left side of the terrace parasol. There is the same house with the steep roof to the left, the same mansard roof in the centre (with even the same deep shadow between them), and finally the inevitable, helpful glimpse of a church spire which is that of Quebec's oldest church, Notre Dame des Victoires. Further sleuthing by our capable Quebec assistants produced the information that this is the corner of Rue Notre Dame and Place Champlain; that the house to the left is now an antique furniture shop; and that the queer, half-finished look of some ancient houses is due to the fact that "after the 1866 fire the authorities lifted the municipal taxes to allow the people to rebuild, until that time that their house should be finished—so some are still not finished! That is the reason for those half-houses you find in Lower Town." (This tidbit came from M. Morisset, the Director of Quebec's Provincial Museum.) So all this pleasurable tracking-about in bloodhound style perhaps justifies the choice of title for this old drawing.

PLATE 41

Corner of Rue Notre Dame and Place Champlain, Lower Town, Quebec City [1934]

One of the most endearing angles of Quebec's face can be seen from above, from an upstairs window, and preferably in winter. Each renewed acquaintance with Quebec City brings yet another revealing glimpse, such as from a window in the Hotel St. Louis over towards the Château, across the roof of the handsome old building that once was the Duke of Kent's town house; or down into the courtyard of Le Petit Séminaire, where black shovels are stuck into a big pile of white snow, as in Claude Picher's unforgettable photograph in the Quebec Number of *Canadian Art*. Almost a century before AY did his set of Quebec City drawings, an English lady artist of great talent, Mrs. M. M. Chaplin, delicately drew a whole sketchbook full of delightful vistas in and around the fascinating city, some of them from her own window near the Convent of the Ursulines.

AY's view over the rooftops is a far cry in technique from Mrs. Chaplin's trim little world, yet the subject matter is quite close. One can't help wondering exactly where he was when he did this fascinating detailed study. (It is referred to locally as "More Icicles," the comment added in ink to the original pencil rendering.) If he was sketching from his hotel window, he might have been staying at the old Hotel Victoria on Rue St. Jean, looking across to where St. Patrick's lies hidden among small streets. The dormer windows look like those on *Candiac*, Montcalm's "real" house on Rue des Remparts, yet, as Dr. Percival's book shows so nicely, that wall and chimney to the left are exactly like those alongside La Maison McKenna, which has the old University in behind it. . . . It is rather fitting, however, to end our views of Quebec with a subject that could be several places in the city. Perhaps it no longer exists today, except here in AY's drawing. Let it stay semi-anonymous. There can be no doubt whatever about its Quebecness.

In 1941 AY was back in the Quebec area, preparing illustrations for Henry Beston's book on the St. Lawrence River and being hampered by wartime restrictions. It is a pity that none of these earlier street scenes were used for the book instead of that rather conventional panorama with Château *et al*. But in the Beston book there is a pen-and-ink version of our final vignette for Quebec, a nice feathery little summer drawing of Pointe Lévis across the river, with a characteristic combination of ship, church and steep hill topped by its convent.

As we turn our own face away from the many faces of that part of Canada which sometimes bristles in its Quebecness, we can take with us some meaningful words uttered by AY himself during those same years, and recorded for the *Toronto Daily Star* by the Toronto critic Augustus Bridle. The latter visited AY's studio in May 1939 to talk over the Canadian pictures at the New York World's Fair and manoeuvred the artist into fruitful conversation about his favourite parts of Canada. "He likes Quebec" is one section of the caption, and further on we read: "I always like Quebec . . . partly because the French-Canadian so ardently loves his own 'pays'. It's his one great passion; more to him than England can ever be; far more than France, of which he retains only the language, the folksongs and the customs [Is by any chance a word missing here, such as 'legal' customs?]. Canada to him is the one land of hope and glory. It makes him sing for joy. That's why, nationally [*sic*, maybe 'naturally'?], I like to paint Quebec, where I was born."

PLATE 42

Quebec City rooftops in winter [*1934*]

Up-river from Quebec City, south of the St. Lawrence between Lévis and Montreal, many favourite place names have been collected by the Jackson clan during annual summer migrations: names like St. Agapit and Ste. Anastasie, St. Télésphore and St. Polycarpe, and—a recent addition from a bit further west—Salaberry de Valleyfield. But the place name that suggests the essence of that part of the world perhaps best of all is St. Hyacinthe, known throughout the land for its superlative Casavant organs, and to many as the home of Gratien Gélinas' unforgettable non-hero, Tit-Coq.

St. Hyacinthe on the Yamaska has been AY's stamping-ground as well, as the present drawing shows. He went there originally for what some people might consider an unusual reason, but was for AY an utterly reasonable reason: he was on the track of "some good old barns." He had noticed them from the CNR train as he passed that way some time back in the late 1930s, so on his next trip he simply got off the train at St. Hyacinthe, parked his suitcase at the hotel nearest the railway station and walked back along the tracks ("about four or five miles") until he came to his barns. He remembers making several pencil studies, an oil sketch, and later a canvas of the subject. The town appealed to him as well, so he spent three or four days working around it.

The present drawing captures the feeling of a typically Eastern Canadian day sometime between winter and spring, in a typically Eastern Canadian place somewhere between town and city. The place has not yet felt the war boom of the 1940s. It has a rather old-fashioned look, with its water tower, its old brick factory and chimneys. It's a bit ramshackle, yet nice, its river filled with AY ice, and plenty of AY notes conveying the mood of the day still more: "old brick, black brick, black smoke; vi black, sil greys, ice, ice, ice. . . ."

This drawing was chosen for our book completely on its own merits as "good AY" and valuable Canadiana. But there was also something tantalizing about the now-deleted question mark, obviously added later, that AY had placed after the name of St. Hyacinthe. It became rather a challenge to find out if this really was St. Hyacinthe, and if time had made very much change in the place with the poetical name. The combination and particular arrangement in this drawing of the twin spires, the river, and the old water tower (providing it was still there), made good landmarks to work from. So on a beautiful June day not long ago we followed the winding course of the charming Yamaska right into the heart of St. Hyacinthe, along a curving street of elegant nineteenth-century town houses frilled with fresh paint and flanked by fragrant lilac and honeysuckle and neat-bedded tulips blooming late. Not an AY season, to be sure. As we

got into the older part of the town, which seemed still intact and very well maintained, there was the old water tower; there, considerably added to, was the old brick factory close to the bank of the Yamaska, where many small trees still stood. We turned on to Rue Mondor, drove down to the river's edge and stopped right in the middle of the drawing, so to speak.

The first person we talked to was a nice elderly lady at work in her garden; her name was Madame Beauregard and she said the old factory was "une grosse shop de chaussures"—a big shoe factory. The next person we talked to was Monsieur J. P. Héroux, whose father owned the shed on the left, now being rebuilt. Monsieur Héroux said that the Coté family, which had built the shoe factory in 1897, still owned it (J. A. & M. Coté Ltée) and that the twin spires belonged to the Cathedral of St. Hyacinthe. The chimney stack to the left was gone, but church spires and water tower were right where they should be, and always had been.

As we drove from the town the noon bell tolled from the Cathedral as it had been doing every single day—eleven thousand times or more—since AY was there. The notaries Messieurs L'Heureux et L'Heureux could be seen heading home for lunch; many secretaries and schoolgirls really did have hyacinthine locks. All in all, Time had been kind to St. Hyacinthe, and it could even offer new nice names—Madame Kind Glance and the lawyers Happy & Happy—to add to our list of favourites.

PLATE 43

St. Hyacinthe on the Yamaska River [late 1930s]

Here is a very special city heart-beat, since it nourished AY himself. Not that he was born on this actual street, but his grandfather Henry Fletcher Joseph Jackson did own property somewhere on its north side back in the 1850s. The street is, of course, the venerable St. Paul Street in Montreal's *Vieux Quartier*, now hauled back from the very brink of destruction by almost a miracle and resuscitated as a major attraction for Expo 67.

It was within a few blocks of here, and at the turn of the century, that the teenager AY worked as a lithographer's apprentice and sketched in watercolour around the harbour. But soon the close home-town ties were cut, first through years of study and work in Chicago and Europe, then through the definitive move to Toronto in 1913, there being at that time no generous Dr. MacCallum for young artists in Montreal, no Lawren Harris with his Studio Building. Montreal continued to be the home of most of AY's kith and kin. He visited there annually, held occasional exhibitions, and continued to supply certain art dealers with his works, but Toronto with its Studio Building on the edge of Ramsden Park became his real home until the 1954 move to the Ottawa district.

The only Montreal subjects AY touched after 1910 or so are represented by the few drawings done in 1941 for *The St. Lawrence*, including the present drawing that was done from the corner of Place Jacques Cartier, better known as Bonsecours Marketplace, and St. Paul Street, looking eastward along the latter. The old eighteenth-century house to the extreme left of the drawing, i.e. on the north-east corner, still retaining its original typical tin roof (against fire) and one of its characteristic pierced iron shutters (against fire, prowlers and "unhealthy night air"), was recently rescued in the nick of time from demolition to make additional parking space for visitors to the nearby Château de Ramezay. The house has become the headquarters of the Jacques Viger Commission, the Old City's champion and saviour since 1962 (backed by city funds; *Dieu et Drapeau merci*). Above its steep roof, in the drawing's upper left corner, projects the bold roofline of the famous old Hotel Rasco, built in 1835 and described by travellers of the time as "one of the finest hotels in North America," with accommodation for 150 guests and a luxurious dining room where the *beau monde* of the city foregathered amidst the red plush and polished wood and mirrors.

The graceful spire just left of the drawing's centre is of course Montreal's celebrated Notre Dame de Bon Secours, the Sailors' Church, on the site of Ville Marie's first chapel erected for Marguerite de Bourgeoys in 1642. Next, on the south side of St. Paul Street, can be seen the beautiful neoclassical Bonsecours Market building, complete with its dome which was destroyed by fire in 1947, just six years after this drawing was made. The dome has recently been rebuilt at municipal expense, the entire edifice being now restored to almost startling freshness. Let a well-qualified voice describe it for us: "Even at the time of its construction (begun in 1845) the Bon-Secours Market was regarded as a striking piece of architecture, with its vast assembly halls, its finely proportioned dome, and the imposing Doric porch with its cast iron pillars. . . . It was to this building that the government of the two Canadas moved after the Tories burned down the Parliament house on Youville Square in 1849. The market building also housed Montreal's municipal government until the present City Hall was completed in 1877. The designer of the Bon-Secours Market, William Footner, was criticized for his extravagance (the cost was more than seventy thousand pounds sterling) but he refused to compromise his design. For some seventy-five years the building was one of the principal centres of activity in the city, but as the automobile and motor-truck replaced the horse and wagon, the market became less and less functional in the modern sense of speed and efficiency, and its importance dwindled. In the spring of 1964 the city government announced a program of restoration for the building at a cost of $1,400,000, a project which demonstrates the government's determination to redevelop Old Montreal within its existing framework."

The author of the above, and the source of so much useful information about St. Paul Street and Old Montreal as a whole, is naturally none other than Eric McLean, author of the excellent book *Montreal*, and prime mover in the rehabilitation of the *Vieux Quartier*. It was he who recognized at first glance the projecting roofline of the Hotel Rasco in this AY drawing from a quarter-century back. The courageous restoration by Eric McLean of the Louis Joseph Papineau house on Rue de Bonsecours has set a handsome example to other Montrealers, including the noted architect Fred Lebensold whose enthusiastic opinion of St. Paul Street gave us our title.

The dramatic Plate Number 53 in *Montreal* shows that by 1963 a sad tangle of rubble is obviously all that remains of the small steep-roofed house with the lone upper dormer towards the right of AY's drawing, where the south side of St. Paul Street is intact. Perhaps the old house collapsed after 1941. More likely it fell victim to the urge of property owners to avoid taxation by razing their buildings, leaving a gaping hole like a missing tooth in the smile of the ancient street. Perhaps this AY drawing may provide a model for future restoration of that particular gap? Who knows. Rise again in glory, Old Montreal!

PLATE 44
St. Paul Street, Montreal [1941]

The journey so far through *AY's Canada* has tended to be fairly specific as to locality, reconstructing how, on a certain day of a certain year, the artist stood on a certain shoreline or a certain street corner and looked in a certain direction at a certain mountain top or a certain roofline. But local detail must not be allowed to outweigh the importance of the myriad unnamed corners of Canada towards which the weather-tanned face of our AY (somewhere referred to as "the ruddy old Daddy of Canadian landscape") has been turned in interest. It is good to introduce a more general perspective by presenting, from time to time, subjects that can be found almost-anywhere in wide stretches of our country. This drawing of a field, a fence, and a bit of bush requires no data regarding place and time. It is simply "our part of the world," with its old cedar rail fence, its snowy rough terrain, its suggestion of the crispness of a bright winter's day.

AY has often related how he only became fully aware of his own country as potential material for artists *after* he had been away from it for several years, training his eye to perceive and his hand to carry out his wishes by practising, so to speak, with foreign materials. It was in 1910, after two and a half years in Europe, that AY saw with fresh eyes that ". . . the clear crisp air and sharp shadows of my native country . . . were exciting. It was good country to paint, with its snake fences and weathered barns, the pasture fields that had never been under the plough, the boulders too big to remove, the ground all bumps and hollows. . . ."

In depicting this kind of country at that date, AY was certainly a pioneer. Perhaps the artist felt drawn by some atavistic compulsion towards subjects which had been given their characteristic shape by the hands of an earlier generation of pioneers—bits of bushland cleared, fences built from the materials at hand. How many pioneers before AY not only endured but sometimes even enjoyed the extremes of our Canadian climate. Here is Mrs. Traill in *The Backwoods of Canada* up behind Peterborough on March 14, 1843, in Letter XIII, concerning "Health enjoyed in the rigour of Winter" a century and a quarter ago: "You say you fear the rigours of the Canadian winter will kill me. I never enjoyed better health, nor so good, as since it commenced. There is a degree of spirit and vigour infused into one's blood by the purity of the air that is quite exhilarating. The very snow seems whiter and more beautiful than it does in our damp vapoury climate. During a keen bright winter's day you will often perceive the air filled with minute frozen particles, which are quite dry, and slightly prickle your face like needle-points, while the sky is blue and bright above you. . . . There is almost a trance-like stillness in the air during our frosty nights. . . ."

So Mrs. Traill liked Canada's winter, but she thought less highly of what she called our "zig-zag fences of split timber," adding "these fences are very offensive to my eye. I look in vain for the rich hedgerows of my native country. . . . The settlers, however, invariably adopt whatever plan saves time, labour, and money. The great law of expediency is strictly observed;—it is borne [*sic*] of necessity."

We may rest assured that the energetic Mrs. Traill soon had a nice "wattled fence" around her own little Ontario garden, with wild vines around the "stoup" in front of her log cabin. For AY, however, the native country was this same un-hedged-in Canada with its snake fences "straggling over the untidy ground. Not a collie dog nor a little lamb in sight," as he remarked comfortably to Leslie Hannon, reminiscing for *Mayfair* in 1954. . . . East, West, Home's best!

PLATE 45

Corner of a field with cedar rail fence [*1930s or 1940s*]

94

Old fences, old barns—AY loves them both. In earlier days he thought nothing of shoving a lunch of cheese and raisins into his pocket and setting out on a thirty- or forty-mile hike into the countryside in search of good examples to study. This predilection led him later to do this pure drawing, never painted up, as a careful rendering of intricate shapes. He was no doubt on one of his many visits to friends who live in the Caledon area of Ontario, some forty miles north-west of Toronto.

Like the rail fence of the foregoing page, this fence is another relic of pioneer days in Upper Canada, in appearance perhaps the most fantastic in all the land. Yet nothing could be more "expedient," to borrow Mrs. Traill's expression, than to use the solid stumps wrenched from the soil, upended so that the tough roots form an almost indestructible barricade. Today, as you roll along the Macdonald-Cartier Freeway, Route 401, west of Toronto, with the sound of jets zooming overhead towards Malton, you may still see vestiges of those days of yore, black with age, but probably as effective as ever in keeping the cattle where they belong.

The old barn asleep here behind its formidable thorny hedge has the characteristics of the banked barn, a tall structure in which the hayloft is over the stable so that the hay and grain stored in the upper level will help insulate the stable below from winter's cold and summer's heat. The roof is smaller and easier to maintain than that of the spread-out type of barn or that of two separate buildings, and feed is handy for the cattle in inclement weather. The hayloft is reached from outside, either by banking the building into a hillside in split-level fashion, or, in flatter terrain, by constructing a solid earth ramp to the upper level, where a wooden bridge usually makes the final connection. The large doorway of the upper level is often turned towards the prevailing wind so that the snow is blown away from the entrance to the stable tucked in under the heavy ramp.

The banked barn seems to have originated in alpine Europe (Switzerland and Southern Germany), and to have become customary first in Pennsylvania and then all along the eastern seaboard, whence it came to Canada, possibly appearing first in Upper Canada with the United Empire Loyalists. R.-L. Séguin's book on the Quebec barns indicates that the adaptations of the style for use in Quebec took place in the latter half of the nineteenth century. In a charming illustration taken from Eric Sloane's *American Barns and Covered Bridges* and shown by Séguin on page 40, the text reads: "In Pennsylvania the Barns are 'banked a'hill', stone to Weather . . . and Wood on the Southern side." In AY's pencil sketch the ramp to the tall barn's upper level must be on the side not visible to the artist, with the stable doors below it.

Not far from the Caledon district where this drawing was made, in a lovely hilly woodland near the village of Kleinburg; Robert and Signe McMichael in the mid 1950s set up their flourishing collection of Group of Seven works. The collection has been turned over to the Ontario government and opened to the public, in surroundings which also hark back to materials and forms of early days—good weathered pine and cedar plank walls, rescued from a score of ancient abandoned barns like the one in AY's drawing, and many other relics of the pioneer past of Ontario.

This might be a good point to remind ourselves that many of AY's own ancestors lived in south-western Ontario. In 1834 his maternal grandfather, Alexander Young from Kelso, Roxborough, Scotland, settled in Dumfries Township and in due course was schoolmaster in Galt, St. Thomas and Berlin (renamed Kitchener during World War I). His wife, Ann Keachie, was born near Paris, Ontario, of Scottish Empire Loyalist stock. Their daughter Georgina Young was AY's dear and gallant little mother.

Alexander Young was a keen botanist, and specimens of Ontario plants collected by him were eventually presented to the Natural History Society of Montreal. In honour of the elder "AY," many of whose interests were passed on to his grandsons, we present in vignette form this little drawing of the regal mullein (njg 892), made by our "AY."

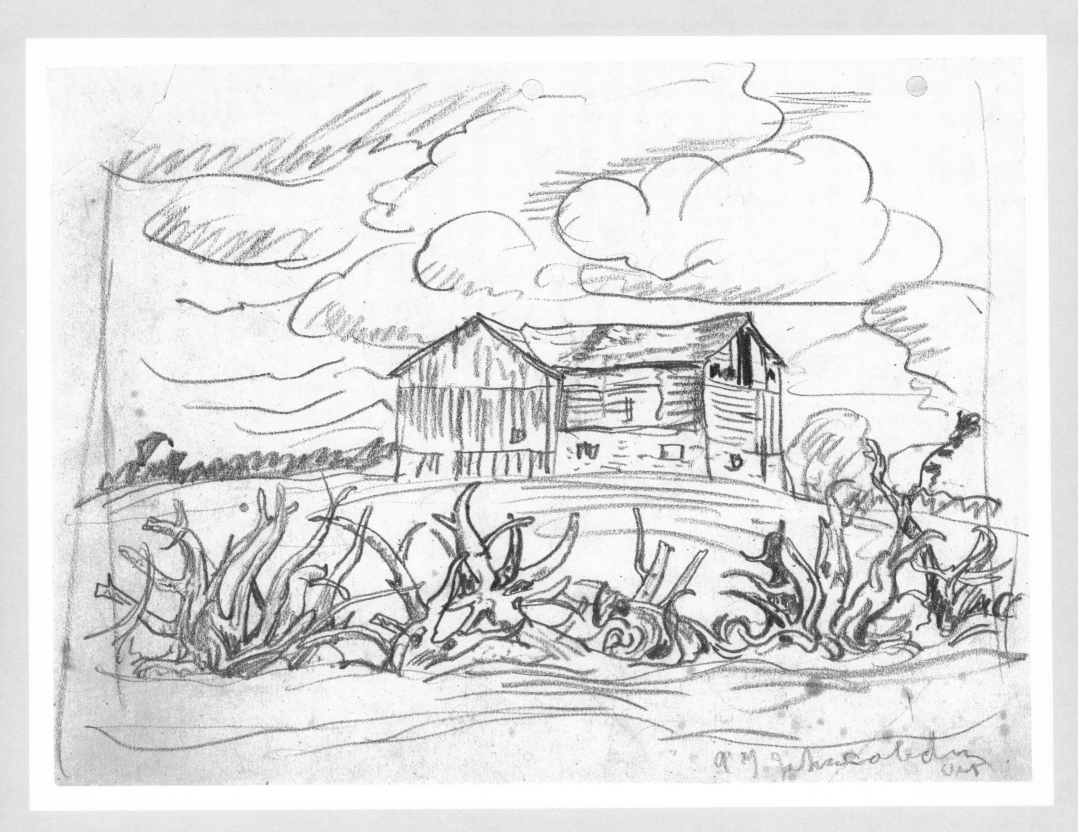

PLATE 46

Old barn and root fence near Caledon, Ontario [1930s]

A part of Ontario that has retained many features of early days, and has provided AY with plenty of good subjects, is the hilly, rocky, wooded, river-and-lake-filled area north of Madoc and Marmora, familiar names in Ontario's early mining history. Algonquin Park lies to the north-west of this region, which is usually referred to as the Madawaska Valley. AY has worked the area for many years, using either Lake Clear or Combermere as headquarters and driving with friends "Dr. Bob" Starrs or Ralph Burton to find good sketching spots. He likes it both in spring and fall.

The present drawing was done around 1938, AY believes. It depicts part of the little town of Maynooth, located fifteen miles up from Bancroft and about eighteen south-west of Combermere, in long narrow Hastings County whose administrative seat is Belleville, away down south on the Bay of Quinte. Maynooth was once an important crossroad point for the Old Hastings Road and the Peterson Road. Many of the early settlers came from famine-stricken Ireland, entering by way of Pembroke, to the east on the Ottawa River, in the days when rivers provided the best means for getting through the wilderness with one's household possessions, not to mention taking out logs.

Most of the above information and a good deal more is contained in a nice little book, *McClure Heritage*, published in 1966 by Darius King Card of nearby Lake St. Peter, a native of the area and exactly the same age as AY. An ancestor of the same distinctive name obtained the deed to his lot in 1869 and in due course set up a sawmill, which among other things made spinning wheels. Darius the First and a neighbour both had a six-by-eight-foot loom in their log cabins for weaving the local wool.

In the decade before the settlers started clearing the rocky land for farming, and burning the hardwood for potash, the area had been denuded of its magnificent primeval stands of white pine. The first local cutting licence for 444 square miles was issued in 1850 to two Conroy brothers, who during the 1860s had camps just north of Maynooth, often employing a hundred men per camp. The lumberjacks ate and slept in the camboose type of shanty (French *cambuse* means "a provision room on a ship") built of rough logs, approximately thirty-five by fifty feet square, with an earth floor and no window other than a six-foot hole cut in the roof to let out the smoke from the central open fireplace—the actual "camboose"—a log frame ten feet square and two feet high, lined with stones and filled with sand. A fire burned at all times in its centre. Huge iron pots were suspended by chains over the fire or buried in the hot sand to bake the beans and the bread. The shantymen walked to and from their place of work, slept, sat and ate in their two tiers of bunks, there being no tables, chairs, lamps or other niceties until the following century. Con-

sidering the cramped conditions at the camp, we can imagine how Maynooth must have swung on a Saturday night when the lumberjacks hit town!

The very first farmland was cleared to grow potatoes for the hungry shantymen, and hay and oats for the horses that hauled the logs to the rivers. Roads were so primitive that it took a team of horses with a thousand-pound load from Monday morning to the following Saturday night to get to Belleville and back—a round trip of about 160 miles by today's reckoning. In course of time the settlers found that wood was the best crop produced in that rocky terrain, and many sawmills sprang up, to be abandoned when their day was done, or when fire burned out the district.

Within the pre-Cambrian crust lie mineral treasures untold (still six billion tons of iron reserves in Ontario alone!) so that some of the Maynooth men found employment in the small iron mines, of which over forty flourished in eastern Ontario until 1890 or so, when they could not compete with British imports. There was work for a while after uranium was found near Bancroft in 1950, but that has stopped again. Nowadays some Maynooth men drive as far as Oshawa to work at General Motors.

Perhaps the most successful lines of occupation today are connected with the summer visitors and sportsmen. Many of the abandoned farms have been bought up by "hunting clubs or by city dwellers anticipating retirement." The old grassy lumber trails suit the birdwatchers to a *T*; the old abandoned mines lure the amateur geologists and rock hounds (there is an active mineral club at Bancroft). The country has kept its beauty through it all. Little summer art schools flourish and also have their day; artists come and go . . . .

Wood having been the handiest commodity all along, we find plenty of it in the local churches, as our drawing shows. The first church in Maynooth was put up by Roman Catholics between 1864 and 1878, closely followed by the Methodists' Grace Church, still in use as the Orange Lodge. In this town of something over three hundred inhabitants, plus around two hundred on the neighbouring farms, there is furthermore an Anglican church and a Lutheran church not far away. A photograph of Maynooth in the early days, on page 22 of *McClure Heritage*, shows the striking tower and roof of the church of our drawing, at present the United Church. Since the drawing was made, it has, in AY's words, been "all fixed up etc. with white paint." But AY enjoyed doing it as it looked in the thirties, full of years and character and dignity. He says he gave a drawing similar to this, but with a horse and buggy in it, to a local Anglican clergyman; we hope it turns up again some day.

PLATE 47
Maynooth, Ontario [c. 1938]

Surely rather exceptional in AY's work in both subject matter and mood, is this suave, idyllic little drawing of the venerable Anglican church of St. Thomas at Frankville, in the early-settled part of Ontario along the Upper St. Lawrence River. The town of Frankville lies some fifteen or twenty miles north of Brockville, in a quiet backwater that AY has found pleasantly paintable. For a decade or so around 1930, as he tells in his autobiography, he paid an annual September visit to the summer colony of artist friends—Prudence Heward and Sarah Robertson of Montreal and the Eliots of Ottawa—at Fernbank on the River just up from Brockville. The present drawing was no doubt made on one of the many pleasant expeditions for sketching and picnicking around the countryside.

The Frankville district seems full of historic interest and of characters both past and present. There is, as a starter, Mrs. Louise McKinney, who was born in the parish and went on to become the first woman Member of Parliament in the British Empire, a member of our Senate, and one of the founders of the Women's Christian Temperance Union—all of which we learn from the historic marker outside the tiny log cabin in which the local Kitley Historic Association has its very active being. The old log cabin was the pioneer home of Joseph and Sarah Montgomery, and was moved in 1963 to its present site, as the founder and president of the Association, Mr. Don Strikefoot, related with racy expressiveness. "We don't have any funds, so everybody does things for us for nothing. Bundridge Construction moved the house for us from two miles down the road to this little piece of land, which we got free. I rode on top of the roof to keep telephone wires out of the way. At one place there were about twelve wires to move all at the same time and I durned near fell off that roof. . . . All the people around here have brought in their cast-off furniture from the olden days, and homemade wooden farm implements, and old christening dresses and such stuff. The only thing we've had to *pay* for so far is this two-storey iron stove. Isn't it a beauty? I discovered it under an old blanket on one of the backroads in behind Numogate and got it for only ten dollars. We had a big do here the other day, with floats and bands and races and contests and a beauty queen—and we sold five hundred and eighty barbecued chickens."

Mr. Strikefoot's profession is home maintenance and he was able to tell a good deal about the church of St. Thomas, which is referred to locally simply as "the stone church." "I had the job of painting its roof, though I'm not an Anglican, but my friends told me I wasn't likely to fall off such a holy place and break my neck. The old pointed steeple in this photo of your uncle's drawing got blown down in a storm a few years ago and they've put up a heavier four-corner cap on the tower."

At the crossroads in Frankville is a nice green road sign bearing the appetizing name "Plum Hollow." Harry Walker, the Ottawa Valley's popular historian, tells the tale of "The Witch of Plum Hollow." "Far off the beaten ways of men runs the road of Plum Hollow, a forgotten pioneer village. The old road is now a concession line. But in a vanished age of crinolines and homespun the road to Plum Hollow was a well-travelled turnpike. On Sundays particularly, it conveyed a continuous traffic of troubled humanity of all classes and conditions, journeying to consult the 'Witch of Plum Hollow'—Mother Barnes—in her log cabin . . . that brooded in the shadow of a mighty oak . . . there to seek the solution to some enigma of life—or death—or maybe only a lost cow or a faithless lover!"

Some pleasurable research made recently helped to locate the old ruined log cabin where Mother Barnes once lived with her numerous progeny—she brought up three adopted children along with her own ten! Apparently her neighbours were most indignant when she was referred to as a "witch." She was a respectable and respected granny who lived to be ninety and left sixty-eight living descendants. She was born Jane Elizabeth Martin in County Cork in 1800, seventh daughter of a seventh daughter (which gives us food for thought, of course). She came of a gentle family with some Spanish gypsy blood; that also just *happens*. Instead of marrying the colonel to whom she was affianced, she eloped at twenty with a more attractive army sergeant "from Canada," says our source. She was a widow at twenty-seven, with one son, and later married David Barnes of Connecticut, a shoemaker by trade. She came with him in 1843 (sixteen years before Frankville's St. Thomas was built) to take up land in the all-Quaker community at Sheldon's Corners, in whose ancient burying ground she lies "among the Knapps and Whitmores and Yates and Tackaberrys"—names still to be seen today on many a rural mailbox around Plum Hollow. Mother Barnes really seems to have had a keen sixth sense for locating lost objects (including corpses). People came to consult her from far and wide, even across the border. Even Sir John A. consulted her (perhaps about a lost election?).

As Harry Walker says, it is a pity that Mother Barnes' old log cabin on the pretty maple-lined road from Plum Hollow to Lake Eloida is not being preserved for interested visitors to enjoy. Perhaps the Historical Association of Kitley Township not so far away can salvage some souvenirs from around the grass-choked, once-famous doorsill—a lucky horseshoe or some ancient shards of the teapot and teacup that played their part in her consultations.

A place full of characters and colour, though drawn so gently here.

Sept 1932

St Thomas Church
Frankville Built 1859

PLATE 48

The church of St. Thomas, 1859, at Frankville, Ontario, September 1932

What could contrast more radically with the British mildness of old-settled Southern Ontario's church of St. Thomas, Frankville, on a gentle summer day—or for that matter with the late nineteenth-century garish grandeur of Casa Loma in Toronto (of which rather understandably there is no AY drawing)—than this energetic wintry rendering of the best known shack in all Canada? The perspective of our drawing shows that AY was looking down from one of the second-floor windows at the back of Toronto's Studio Building where the Shack used to sit tucked in against the hillside of the Ravine. For many long, happy, fruitful years this was a sight very familiar to A.Y. Jackson as to other Torontonians—but the man whose name the shack still bears had only a couple of short winters to use it.

So much has been recounted and repeated about Tom Thomson's Shack in publications and interviews through the past half century that it is tempting to review here, affectionately but objectively, some of the actual facts and figures about the dear place, and to compare them with the flourishing legend which recalls things maybe not exactly in the way they actually happened, but in the way they *should* have happened. This is not the place for a complete thesis, and what stands here opposite AY's drawing can be taken as a casual running commentary on this absorbing subject.

Having just said that we want actual facts and figures, we must start off modestly by admitting some uncertainty as to exactly *when* the Shack came into existence. It stood there, deserted, before the erection of the Studio Building. AY recalls that it was originally a cabinet-maker's establishment; he was once visited by the former owner's grandson but cannot lay his mental finger on the name. Lawren Harris recalled in 1964: "There was a dilapidated old shack on the back of the property which was built in the days when that part of Toronto was the town of Yorkville." Thoreau MacDonald remembers it from his boyhood days, before the Studio Building went up.

Now come some very specific figures. By happy good luck, the big old purple-covered cash book that once was Lawren Harris' account book for the Studio Building was given to the present writer many years ago. All the used pages in front had already been cut out, but *one* page full of figures was overlooked at the back of the book and here, at the foot of it, is revealed exactly what work done on the Shack cost the two men responsible for erecting the Studio Building itself. In Lawren Harris' firm handwriting stands the entry:

shack

Dr. MacCallum	62.45
Lawren Harris	113.57
	176.02

It is a pity that the costs for the work on the Shack are not itemized, nor any date given. The construction and upkeep costs for Toronto's Casa Loma are not available either at the moment, but it is safe to wager that from even a purely financial standpoint, quite apart from any concern with art, the money spent on the Shack was probably the best interest-bearing investment ever made in the first century of our fair Dominion's history.

Pursuing other pertinent facts and dates: AY and Tom Thomson first met in November 1913, AY having just arrived in Toronto from Georgian Bay, Thomson from Algonquin Park, each laden with sketches. AY had first visited Georgian Bay in 1910; 1913 was his second, more important visit. The moment we seek to establish the date of Tom Thomson's first visit to Algonquin Park, we can sense how fact and legend face up sharply against each other, bristling. Perhaps the major impetus for the legend is the sentence: "For a dozen or more years he had lived in his north country, being much alone . . . ." These words were published in 1926, nine years after Thomson's death, on page 116 of *A Canadian Art Movement* by Fred B. Housser—an excellent pioneer work on the emerging Group of Seven, and beautifully printed, with AY's lovely starry-night and campfire scene on the dust jacket. But for our present purpose we would wish for more specific details on when those "dozen or more years" had been, for if they were at the end of Thomson's life he would have been steadily in the wilds from about 1905, just after his four-year sojourn in Seattle, and this was not the case. Unless further documentary evidence can be produced to prove it otherwise, Thomson first reached the Algonquin Park area in the spring of 1912. Indeed, according to the late Miss Blodwen Davies' book on Thomson, this was his first extensive visit to the wilderness in years, incredible as that seems. The trip in May 1912 in company with H. B. (Ben) Jackson of Grip Ltd., was devoted more to fishing and canoeing than to sketching or as Miss Davies says, in "making notes and casual studies, for the passion for paint was not yet on him." A letter from Thomson recently examined, dated Toronto, October 17, and postmarked 1912, shows clearly that even on the longer canoe trip with W. S. Broadhead (whose address he was using at time of writing) Thomson's main interest was in the "many good snapshots of game, mostly moose" which they got up in the Mississagi area. He makes brief mention of "some sketches" but it is the loss of nearly "14 dozen" rolls of film when their canoe was swamped that he regrets. (All that film is never mentioned in the two books on Thomson written by Blodwen Davies and R. H. Hubbard!)

The following year, 1913, was, according to Miss Davies' book, Thomson's first real sketching visit in Algonquin Park, and the year when he enquired from the forest ranger Mark Robinson about the *possibility*

(continued)

PLATE 49

Tom Thomson's shack behind the Studio Building, Toronto [*late 1930s*]

of doing some guiding there, no doubt in order to eke out the $200 he had been paid for his first canvas, *Northern Lake*, 1913. It would therefore seem that at that stage, 1912/1913, four years before his death, Thomson was *not* an old hand at guiding in Algonquin Park. The legend sees him there *years* before he met AY in the fall of 1913, and likewise as a young man at the time of that first meeting. AY in his seventies recalls, in *A Painter's Country*: "One day Dr. MacCallum brought to Harris' studio [at that time atop the Bank of Commerce at Bloor and Yonge] a shy young fellow by the name of Tom Thomson . . . ." Actually, in November 1913 AY had just turned thirty-one and Thomson, born August 4, 1877, was thirty-six and AY's senior by five years. But Thomson would be wonderfully fit after his months in the wilds, and always looked young for his age. He has remained that way in AY's living memory as in everybody else's, while the rest of us grow older and older. Thomson would have been ninety for Canada's Centennial.

AY's first written and published impression of Tom Thomson was set down in November 1918, exactly five years after that very first meeting. AY had meanwhile been wounded in Flanders, engaged in War Records work and sent back to Canada to prepare equipment and art materials for being sent to Siberia. (We remember all those tubes of white paint for snow—how he would have enjoyed that trip!) It is interesting to see what he said at that early stage about Thomson, who had been dead less than sixteen months. AY's statements are contained in the foreword for "An Exhibition of Paintings by the Late Tom Thomson," a showing of sixty-six works held in Montreal at the Arts Club from March 1st to 21st, 1919. (By that time AY himself was down in Halifax.) He recalls the first meeting in November 1913: "He had a few dozen sketches that were not remarkable, except that they showed great knowledge of the country and were very faithful and painstaking. One felt that he would not move a branch or change the contour of a hill, however much the composition demanded it. His sketches were also surprisingly sombre and dead in colour, and were also peculiar in composition, in that many of them were of an upright panel shape, showing a low shore line and a big sky. The country in them always seemed to be viewed extensively. There were no gay little rapids or wood interiors, or patterned rocks, but only the opposite shore of lakes, far hills, or wide stretches of country." In another source, probably a radio broadcast given on some fairly early anniversary of Tom Thomson's death, AY formulated his perceptive first impression of his friend: "You liked Thomson right away, a quiet friendly chap, something of the Indian in his bearing, a kind of indolence that changed to sudden alertness and quick movement when the occasion arose. Modest about his

(continued)

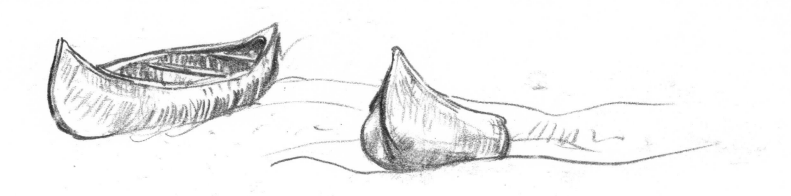

painting efforts, the idea of being an artist by profession he did not take very seriously." But by the end of December of that year, 1913, as the Studio Building neared completion, Thomson had been persuaded by his friends, including Dr. MacCallum, to give up his commercial art job at Grip Limited and to paint full time. In January 1914, "while workmen were still all over the place," Jackson and Thomson moved into the first studio to be finished, Number One, on the ground floor at the end away from Yonge Street. Payment of the rent of $22 a month they split, each using some of the $25 apiece with which Dr. MacCallum occasionally bought their sketches.

They had less than two months painting together during that stage. Judging by canvases exhibited in the Ontario Society of Art's spring show, 1914, Thomson had been working at *Morning Cloud* and the almost monochromatic but intensely striking *Moonlight*, while AY showed two Georgian Bay canvases and two Assisi works brought from Italy.

In late February 1914 AY went off alone to Algonquin Park to sketch, inspired by the enthusiasm of Thomson who, AY tells us, stayed struggling over his canvases in Studio One. AY arrived at Canoe Lake Station "one moonlight night with the temperature around forty below zero," according to our 1918 source. (By the 1930s it was 43° below; by the 1957 autobiography it had gone down two more degrees!) ". . . the only roads a few snowshoe tracks. Down the lake straight as an arrow ran the track of Bud Callaghan, park ranger." There is no mention of Thomson joining him that time, although J. W. Beatty and J. E. H. MacDonald did so later.

By the time AY got back to Toronto that spring, in the words of his radio broadcast, "Tom was packing up to leave for Algonquin Park, not to return until November. With him went Arthur Lismer for several weeks sketching." The summer of 1914 AY and J. W. Beatty spent in the Rocky Mountains on a painting commission, of which more in later context. In late September AY hurried by railway direct to Canoe Lake, not bothering to stop in Toronto, and joined Tom Thomson *for their only sketching trip together*—that unforgettable sojourn in Algonquin Park that in the legend stretches out timelessly through many seasons; and rightly so, considering its evocative impact. The 1918 text states factually: "We worked together about six weeks. He was making great progress. No longer handicapped by literal representation, he was transposing, eliminating, designing, experimenting, finding happy colour motifs amid tangle and confusion, revelling in paint, and intensely interested. Full of restless energy, the amount of work he did was incredible. There were long canoe trips, and we were up and out fishing at dawn. He seemed to require no sleep." To return the compliment Jackson paid Thomson, here is a brief extract from the latter's letter of October 6, 1914, to Dr. MacCallum: "Jackson & myself are having a fine time and seem to have about the same habits about camping and can always find sketching near the same place so everything is O.K. Alex has made some fine sketches here."

On that wonderful camping trip together, AY saw Thomson in his natural element and observed his nature well. The 1918 source—earliest, closest, and perhaps best—can be set down here again to nourish both factual memory and legend: "He was modest, over-sensitive, almost naive in his outlook, a pal to every man who came along—lumberjack, trapper, or artist. Camping, he was not happy unless he was doing three-quarters

(continued)

of the work. Careless of money, he left it lying about in the bottom of his canoe or tent, equally happy when he caught a big trout, when his bannock turned out well, or when he brought back a gorgeous sketch: a poet, a philosopher, and a good friend."

In late autumn 1914, after the last leaf had fallen in Algonquin Park, the two artists returned to Toronto and Studio One. In the course of the *first week* after he got back, AY painted up his canvas *The Red Maple*, his richest work to date, a glowing tribute to a good friendship. AY cannot now recall exactly what Tom was working on during their last studio time together. It would be nice to think it was the wonderful *Northern River*, exhibited the following spring in the O.S.A. show, worked up, says AY, not from a sketch nor from the part of the Park they had been in together, but "from something Tom had seen further north."

Meanwhile AY himself was reached by the tentacles of World War I and just before Christmas 1914 he left for Montreal, then by May 1915 for training camp at Valcartier, and finally overseas. He never saw Thomson again. All in all, they had had at most only fifteen weeks in which to work together. The poignant brevity of the time adds to the intensity of the contact. How vividly we can conjure up what AY expresses so well forty long years later: "When I remember back to before World War I, to early spring days in northern Ontario, skimming silently along a brooding lake with Tom Thomson—ah, you can have all your marble cities..."

Now let us focus specifically on that Shack, once again conscious of the relativity of time, both in general and in regard to Tom Thomson's occupancy. The way Lawren Harris recalls it in the fine little 1964 *Story of the Group of Seven*, based largely on a lecture of 1947, Thomson did not paint in the Studio Building at all, but used *only* the Shack: "MacDonald, Jackson and I had studios . . . . We tried to induce Tom Thomson to join us. Thomson loved the north . . . . He lived through the winter in town with the sole idea of making enough money so he could go north as soon as the ice broke in the rivers and lakes. Tom did not want a studio in the building . . . . We fixed [the Shack] up, put down a new floor, made the roof watertight, built in a studio window, put in a stove and electric light. Tom made himself a bunk, shelves, a table, and an easel, and lived in that place as he would in a cabin in the north . . . ." But as AY recalls it, in 1914 the Shack was used only by workmen on the Studio Building for storing their tools. *A Painter's Country* indicates that after AY left in December 1914, Thomson could not afford Studio One alone and moved into the Shack. Finally, the late Blodwen Davies tells how, after AY's departure, Frank Carmichael of Orillia moved into Studio One *with Thomson*, and there "they worked and cheerfully contrived their very economical way through the winter"—the winter being 1914/1915. This has such a prosaic, business-like sound that it rings very true. AY cannot recall ever even meeting Carmichael until after the war,

for the simple reason that Carmichael went abroad to study in September 1913, before AY got there, returned to Orillia in the fall of 1914 and to Toronto only after New Year 1915, after AY had left. Carmichael worked in Toronto until his death in 1945, ten years after Miss Davies' book on Thomson came out, and she doubtless got her information at firsthand.

According to Miss Davies' chapter on the Shack, it did not become Thomson's winter abode until the fall of 1915, when he returned from the Park to find that Carmichael had married and left Studio One, which was already occupied by someone else. AY indicates that this was Marion Long, and recalls that Thomson paid $1 a month for use of the Shack. Several authors agree that Lismer shared the Shack with Thomson for a few months, using it as a studio. Miss Davies adds that "that winter the shack was the focus of a good deal of interest and attention . . . Lismer, Harris, MacDonald, Varley . . . Carmichael and several others . . . frequently dropping into the shack to share Thomson's beans or mulligan . . . ." This time it is the legend of Thomson the lonely worker that rather suffers. In any case, it was the mid-winter months of 1915/1916 and 1916/1917 that he worked there, in all probability not more than eight months. But in that brief time, under that modest, snow-covered roof as we see it in our drawing here, the last great glorious canvases came into being—*Petawawa Gorges*, *The Jackpine*, *The Drive*, *The West Wind*, while in the corners the multitude of 8 by 10 inch sketches lay like heaps of jewels.

In the place of honour in AY's scrapbook, right inside the front cover, is a photostat of Thomson's last letter, dated July 7, 1917, from Mowat Lodge in the Park, in which he tells Dr. MacCallum how bad the black flies have been, but that the heat is killing them off; how he will send down his "winter sketches" (i.e. March to June 1917) to be spread out in the Shack to dry; and how he looks forward to get back to his sketching "in a day or two." Those simple words still cause a dreadful pang. By the afternoon of the next day Thomson was dead, and the promise of all that genius was lost forever.

With Thomson gone, the Shack was used a bit by Varley and others but gradually fell into disrepair. The wall against the hillside began to cave in, the roof leaked and the whole threatened to become derelict when, in AY's words from the happier 1930s: ". . . a prospector with the same careless, friendly outlook on life that Thomson had, found it, and now it is snug and tight again, and Keith McIver and his dog, Brownie, live in it when the northland is too deep in snow for them to prospect." With AY's friend the late, dear Keith McIver, began the old Shack's new

happy phase, which lasted until the mid-fifties. This was its heyday as meeting place for artists and their many notable visitors, such as Malcolm MacDonald, then British High Commissioner to Canada, several Governors General, famous visiting musicians, writers, and artists, too many to name here. This was the period when the Shack was decorated with various vivid murals, including the lady *au naturel* entitled "Hell Rosa" of AY's autobiography. He took breakfast and lunch there with Keith most days, and occasionally dinner. For *Maclean's Magazine* in 1956 he wrote up as his "most memorable meal" one to which were invited Wyndham Lewis and his wife, and a couple of other friends: "not a banquet but steaks grilled over a coal fire, which McIver could do to perfection. Over a bottle of good Scotch, Lewis, usually reserved, got in a reminiscing mood and talked of his experiences with writers and artists we had heard much about [Augustus John, James Joyce, Ezra Pound are mentioned elsewhere by AY.]. He spoke with a slight drawl, his remarks punctuated with sharp critical comments. He enjoyed himself and we were greatly entertained."

At the smaller end of the Shack, to the right in this drawing, lived another grand character, whose modest shingle read simply "Walter— Cabinet Maker." Walter Adamovitch hailed from Russian Poland and was until his death in 1945 "an integral part of the little colony of artists there," as AY wrote in his warm tribute "Portrait of an Artist" which appeared in the Toronto *News* of January 27, 1945. Walter was a true craftsman who made not only book cases and sketch boxes but also violins, one of which in Depression days he traded for music lessons for three of his children. During the Aid to Russia Campaign in World War II, Walter's contributions of a violin and dresser brought $200 to the fund.

Time marches on, as we know, and usually downhill for buildings made of wood. In the 1950s Keith McIver and his wife moved to their farm near Palgrave. In 1955 AY, last resident Group of Sevener, pulled out of his old base in the Studio Building. Not very long thereafter the old Shack left too. By a happier turn of fortune's wheel, the venerable shell which had hatched such a remarkable brood was given a new old-age home. Set up in sylvan green surroundings at the McMichaels' place at Kleinburg (which was taken over and formally opened by the government of Ontario on July 8, 1966, the forty-ninth anniversary of Tom Thomson's untimely death), the old Shack lives on as a cherished relic of the past, once again close to many of the treasures it had sheltered long ago. The McMichael Conservation Collection of Art also boasts a drawing (njg 947) of the Shack in its old setting. It is similar to our "historic document" here, but not quite as tough.

The hearty, healthy existence suggested by the present theme may well represent heaven for more people in Ontario—not all of them Ontarians either—than in any other province or part of Canada. The Ontario ideal of heaven is two tough tents on a granite island under the blaze of sun or the shimmer of starlight, standing firm in west wind and rain squall, an abode for the gods and the heroes of our own particular breed.

AY, born in Canada's most civilized city and not in Ontario, adjusted to the latter's ideal with the greatest ease and at every opportunity, nowhere more happily than on Georgian Bay where he has so often camped. The present drawing was made on one of his several camping sojourns on the Western Islands outside Go Home Bay. AY's autobiography, his many talks, and of course his personal letters are full of warm tributes to The Bay in its many moods and to the joys of camping in general. First the source of our title: "Georgian Bay has been one of my happy hunting grounds for camping and fishing at all seasons, and in all kinds of weathers." Then from a personal letter dated July 16th, probably 1931, which records happy days with the Williams' at Wawbec: "The summer has been a beauty so far . . . you know—sunshine, warm rocks to lie on, water soft and gently lapping on the rocky shore. When the primitive instincts come to the surface you go out and kill a water snake, then take two girls out canoeing . . . .

"I am not working, for fear of making the unemployment situation more acute, but about the first of August I will be going to my cousins the Erichsen Browns at Go Home Bay ten miles west of here, and will probably get out my little paints and make 'a pine tree on a rock'. Just now I am reading Powys' *In Defence of Sensuality*—it would probably be duck soup to you. I'm better at portaging canoes. . . .

"Well sich is life, kid, to an unsophisticated old painter. . . ."

Another time we see a different mood as AY growls: "Dirty Monday, rain all day, tough summer for painting, dull and foggy half the time. . . ." And in conclusion, a passage recalling the classic combination of camping and sketching in the Ontario wilds with his classic partner, Tom Thomson, back in 1914: "We sketched on small birch panels, always with the idea that the sketch was a motif for bigger compositions later on. The difficulty of carrying canvases around by canoe and living in tents has led many Canadian painters to work this way. In the evening around the campfire we discussed the day's work while we cooked good husky meals—no canned stuff. Tom was an expert on bannock and flap-jack and I specialized on doughnuts, and of course we had fish, which Thomson seldom failed to catch."

The tents in this lively drawing have seen good wear through the years.

They stand as symbols for many an expedition with many a good companion: the energetic Dr. MacCallum—AY has "many memories of long canoe trips and rough portages with him, and of campfires on delectable islands"; Lawren Harris, the epitome of enterprise and enthusiasm; Keith McIver, quiet and capable; Barker Fairley of the University of Toronto; Frank Erichsen Brown, keen amateur painter, whose grandmother was sister of our ancestor Alexander Young and whose daughters are Isabel LeBordais and the late Gwethalyn Graham, devotees of Georgian Bay from childhood on.

Whenever AY sees this wild drawing of the two tents in which he and our late Cousin Frank camped on one of the Western Islands (tall Frank in the tall teepee) AY chuckles because he remembers the big boulder, unseen but not unfelt, inside his smaller tent on the right: "There was hardly a level inch of ground on that little granite island to pitch my tent on, and of course no soil to hold the tent pegs firm. So I simply put it up around a big boulder and wrapped the guy ropes around a couple of logs at the side. Then I curled up around the boulder and went to sleep. . . ."

Well, lusty laughter still rings from around many a campfire's nightly gleam; tall tales are still told about the big ones that got away; sketchers still compare and discuss their products of the day; water laps against the rocky shore; and overhead the aurora dances. All this is at the heart of AY's Canada.

108

Winter Jahr

With the motif of the wind-swept pine on the wave-beaten shore we reach the storm centre of the Group of Seven in its initial years, and the early great canvases rise to mind in all their pristine splendour.

First in time, first in many ways, comes Tom Thomson's very first canvas, *A Northern Lake*, 1913, finished in time for a spring exhibition in 1913, therefore from a sketch of 1912; sold immediately, to the Ontario Board of Education, it now hangs in the office of the Premier of Ontario. The $200 received by Thomson meant very solid encouragement, needless to say. With its trees placed close to either side and in its centre the open lake and empty sky, this firm, sombre work creates the impression of a stage set for action—not exactly empty, but rather waiting and ready, unlike anything the country had produced before. . . . Then, at the latter end of Thomson's tragically short career, his last canvas, *The West Wind*, 1917, lets the harp-shaped pine intone a grand melancholy dirge.

But back to the beginning, and enter AY with *Land of the Leaning Pine*, also 1913 but later than the "first" by Thomson whom AY had not yet met when his canvas was painted out of doors at Georgian Bay. Next, for J. E. H. MacDonald we bring on *The Elements*, 1916, reproduced on the cover of E. R. Hunter's book on MacDonald, with the embattled old pine tree against the gorgeous stormy sky. Glinting waves and a splash of scarlet campfire provide the other elements. This work became the literal storm-centre for attacks on the group not yet named Seven.

Next enter Varley's beautiful *Stormy Weather, Georgian Bay*, 1920, and Lismer's powerful *September Gale*, 1921, painted within a hundred feet of each other on MacCallum's Island, and, according to AY, forming with Thomson's *West Wind* "three of the finest paintings ever done in Canada." There can never again be such a unified upthrust of national genius in our visual arts, mainly because subsequent movements, strong in themselves, are no longer specifically Canadian but a segment of the international scene. The grand abstract swing in art belongs to the world at large.

The Group of Seven has it the Canadian way, and its subject matter is of course an unbeatable trump card in popular appeal. So is the particular blend of picturesque and varied characters brought together in the Group by chance, and *wanting* to be together in the strength of their union: the incomparable Tom Thomson, voice of the wilderness too soon stilled; Lawren Harris, the centripetal force, taut as a spring, generous with ideas and with other wealth; J. E. H. MacDonald, the one they all loved, their poet-philosopher, "who made us see," as AY expressed it, "that if we didn't do something with this big pre-Cambrian country we had no spirit at all"; Arthur Lismer, the wise and witty, whose insight influenced the entire art education of our country and who as artist was "the one who

took fullest possession of Georgian Bay," according to AY; F. H. Varley, the maverick master of all in subtlety.

And in the middle of the heap, our AY. What was his special contribution to the grand combination they formed with such spectacular solidarity? AY is in character as in physique the most rugged and rambunctious of them all, the one who liked best to wade in and face the fight, who has always revelled in stormy weather and squalls, be it on Georgian Bay or elsewhere. "After blowing from all directions, the wind struck from the north-east. There was a blast and a squall of rain, and down came my tent," he tells with relish in *A Painter's Country*. And as for the other kind of squall, there are whole pages in AY's large scrapbook devoted indeed to scraps: the Hot Mush School controversy; the tilts with the Academy; the 1927/1928 feud with art critics of Montreal, which AY referred to as "Canada's most bigoted city," to which one Montreal paper riposted, perhaps not entirely without justification, "Who Bit Mr. Jackson?"

All in all, AY has always enjoyed braving stormy elements both human and "natural." That is one reason he loves Georgian Bay as a grandiose elemental stage where he has made an appearance almost every year since he discovered it in 1910, when "fate took over," as he expressed it recently to a gathering of members of the Georgian Bay Association. The most fateful and famous meeting in AY's life took place on Georgian Bay in the fall of 1913, when Dr. MacCallum offered to set him up financially for a year so that he would not have to emigrate to the United States. The elation over this act of faith opened creative well-springs in the artist and became bound up with his feeling for that part of the world which he finds "every bit as exciting today."

The drawing here was carefully selected for the multiple purpose of our book. First of all, it typifies the Georgian Bay country, "in outward appearance pretty much as it had been when Champlain passed through its thousands of rocky islands three hundred years before." Then it belongs to the magnificent, the unforgettable "blasted pine" tradition which we associate particularly with the Group of Seven. Finally it is a good symbol for tough, dynamic AY himself, the rugged recipient of many a storm lashing as well as plenty of sunshine. AY and this country go well together. Let his old friend Arthur Lismer have the final word, selected to fit the present context from his admirable Introduction for the catalogue of the 1953 A. Y. Jackson Retrospective Exhibition: "His symbols are inventive and full of meaning. . . . There is something cosmic in his interpretation of the movement of earth and sky and weather forms . . . but he never pushes the medium to extravagant expression. Always it seems that he grasps the fundamental unity of spirit and technique. . . ."

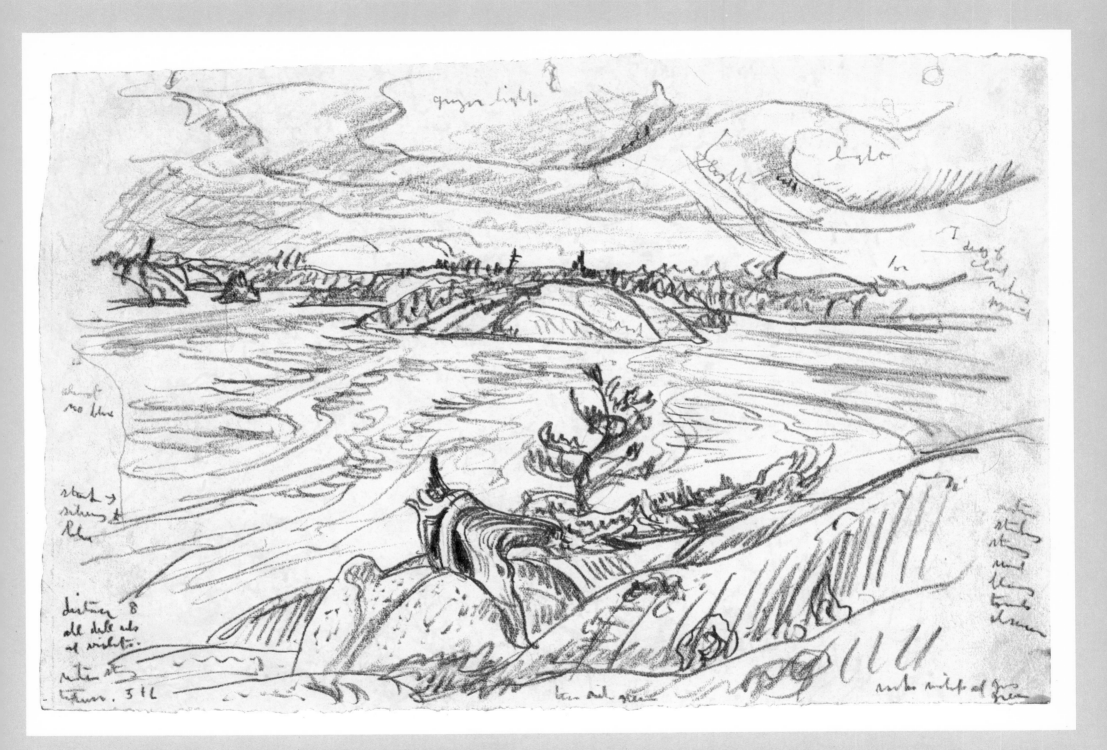

PLATE 51
Windy day, Georgian Bay [*mid-1920s*]

The final words of the preceding text become an appropriate title for a few remarks on the present drawing; not that this one requires any special interpretation to those who prefer to watch AY's drawings unfold without verbal assistance. The other side of this untitled work is marked "Go Home River," so it is likely that this one as well belongs to the area about which AY wrote in his autobiography: "Paddling around the islands and exploring intricate channels and bays that cut into the mainland provided me with much material." The present drawing lends itself well to a spot of art-historical analysis on the basis of what Lismer called "the fundamental unity of spirit and technique," not forgetting of course that the subject matter is also part of that unity.

In subject this is a characteristic quiet corner anywhere in our northland: a stretch of shoreline in solid pre-Cambrian granite which ages of ice have gouged into ridges and furrows. A suggestion of wooded shore indicates the background, a couple of bone-dry skeletons of conifers complete the foreground. Rocks, trees, and water—nothing could be more typical.

But look at the way they are arranged by this artist AY! The shoreline to the left works its way into the distance in a repeated rhythm of rising curves and horizontals, each ridge strongly modelled, so that the entire foreshortened complex acquires both depth and texture. The woodland frieze along the high horizon is on the contrary treated in a few summary lines which serve to contain the composition at the top. To the right it is supported by a clear-cut, light-weight, sinewy diagonal of spiky tree forms, past which our eye slides into the picture. The water is quiet but without reflection, except a trifle in the left foreground; it offers peaceful relief to all the thrusting shapes. It is hard to conceive of a more interesting placing of the "simple" elements tree-rock-water.

It is also hard to imagine a medium or tool with which to tackle such a subject that would be better than the plain 5B graphite pencil, sensitively varied in stroke from finest point to rich, dark slash. Even the placing of the written words concerning "greys and red browns, water grey, slightly blue at top, trees vi grey," helps to fill the lower right corner and close the composition. The amount of colour detail also suggests that this particular subject was first drawn in pencil and not painted on the spot. One wonders in any case how oil paint could ever attain the sparse linear elegance achieved here by the pencil. The favouring of diagonals and the elaborate linear interlacing of the forms of nature evince the same ease and delight with which Celtic and Nordic devotional masterpieces of long ago were embellished.

We can visualize AY in his canoe, paddling silently along this intimate and secret shore, his eye ranging over every inch and angle of it until he finds just what he wants. Flexible canoe, flexible pencil, experienced eye and hand—and here is the spirit of our northland caught, comprehended and conveyed.

Arthur Lismer, thinking back over his years of working alongside AY, wrote in 1953: "His attitude toward the Canadian environment was that of a Northerner—born to explore the meaning of mountains, streams, woodlands, and lakes, and come to terms with them. Such is the nature of the English and Celtic strain and of Northern art. . . .

". . . Jackson's [works] . . . are easy to look at, disarming at first in their simplicity. In the hands of a lesser [artist] they could be commonplace, but they also invite participation in the subtleties of his execution, of his thoughtful composition, and in the definitive mood. He gives the impression of an [artist] born to create backgrounds for others to occupy with any style, modern or otherwise, that the onlooker wishes, or is capable of projecting into them. He has the true pioneer touch of setting the stage for the spectator to dream his own convictions and to imagine other things. This is the time and space quality of his work."

PLATE 52

Rocks, trees and water,
Georgian Bay [late 1930s]

Having had Arthur Lismer carry the torch for AY in the central Georgian Bay area, we now move towards the north again. We enter into "a grander, more sombre country of rolling hills covered with hardwood forests," the special domain of J. E. H. MacDonald "in the joyous young days when the Group of Seven was discovering Canada in the Ontario wilderness," as Robert Ayre expressed it nostalgically in his article "The Magic Is Still There," on the occasion of the beautiful J. E. H. MacDonald exhibition in Toronto and Ottawa in the winter of 1965/1966. Needless to say, this show was visited whenever possible by AY who could be seen basking in the glorious reminders of "MacDonald's country."

If we follow the pleasant route by car up the Bruce Peninsula to Tobermory, take the ferry across the entrance of Georgian Bay to Manitoulin Island, and cross from Little Current northward into the region up towards Espanola, we will have reached another favourite part of AY's Canada. The term "Algoma" seems to apply rather loosely to a vast area stretching from south of Sudbury (Algoma East) westward across to the region above Sault Ste. Marie, where the Central Algoma Railway ambles off towards the North Pole, more or less. AY has worked over much of the Algoma district, as a few drawings can bear present witness.

It was probably in the early 1930s that he began to visit the country in behind McGregor Bay, with its hill-bound lakes rejoicing in names such as Nellie, Grace and Gem. Sometimes he camped with his friend, the mining prospector Keith McIver; sometimes alone. In May 1938, for instance, he wrote that he was going up "to find some early spring, . . . camping by myself," adding later, "the blackflies gave me a great welcome!" The present drawing, dated simply "May 23rd," most probably belongs to that year, and must have been done from a hilltop near Grace Lake, looking down towards an arm of Georgian Bay, on whose shore the settler's tiny shack helps give scale to the immensity of the landscape.

This country, with its vast receding stretches of long-rolling forms, is the type that J. E. H. MacDonald and AY have both loved to tackle. Without attempting too erudite a comparison, especially since this is a little 9 by 12 inch drawing, and MacDonald's subjects are best known to us as panoplies of colour 48 by 60 inches or more in size, we can perhaps none the less sense a basic difference in the way the two artists looked— or would look—at the same subject. MacDonald was very conscious of how nature's patterns are to be perceived and transformed by the artist. "A picture is a perfected enclosure of space seen with heightened vision," he stated in his 1929 lecture on the "Relation of Poetry to Painting." In handling AY's theme here, JEH would indeed probably have enclosed the space more; he would have built up his background more as part of the

picture plane and not let it melt away almost into infinity, as AY seems to do here. In the text to the exemplary catalogue of the MacDonald show, Nancy Robertson notes how her artist in the Algoma period softens "the remoteness of the scenes . . . simple masses . . . and long simple lines create a sense of space and distance, the colour transforming what otherwise would be an atmosphere of emptiness to one of magnificent solitude."

Perhaps it is the very emptiness of the wilderness which AY *wants* to express in this drawing of innumerable receding forms pencilled in with infinite delicacy and only slightly balanced by the diagonal tree that is so far to the right it practically becomes part of the frame. "How immense it all is!" AY seems to be saying. And then comes the tiny touch that is typically Jacksonian and would probably never have occurred to his gentle, idealistic friend Jim MacDonald. AY's eagle eye notices in the midst of the great open spaces the diminutive homestead of a young acquaintance of aristocratic background who made an unsuccessful attempt to settle in our northland and then headed back to a softer berth in old Europe. So AY titles his vast panorama "Max Hausser's Farm"; and leaves us to draw our own conclusions!

It is pleasant to recall how Jackson and MacDonald shared their enthusiasms and experiences. According to Nancy Robertson's admirable biographical notes, MacDonald seems to have been the first of any of the later Group of Seven to reach the area around Algonquin Park. In 1909 he was sketching near Burk's Falls on the Magnetawan River just west of the Park. Perhaps it was he who helped send Tom Thomson (1912), who in turn sent A. Y. Jackson (1914), in the direction of Canoe Lake. That same spring of 1914 MacDonald joined AY in Algonquin Park for spring sketching. AY thinks back fondly to how he helped the more delicate MacDonald get around in the bush. "I paddled Jim to that spot in that red canoe," he remarked recently, on seeing one of MacDonald's subjects, *Beaver Dam*, from further west in Algoma. It was AY who persuaded his friend to switch from the dull grey millboard sketch panels to the much lighter, more alive little panels of birchwood that became the stock-in-trade of the Group.

It was to J. E. H. MacDonald that AY dedicated his autobiography, *A Painter's Country*, in 1957, a quarter century after his friend's death. And a final nice touch for our modest tribute to that incandescent spirit in its fragile frame is the discovery, also thanks to the MacDonald Exhibition Notes, that the artist's very last sketching trip, in September 1931, only two months before the first of the strokes that proved fatal the following year, was to McGregor Bay—the very region in which AY later pencilled the present panorama.

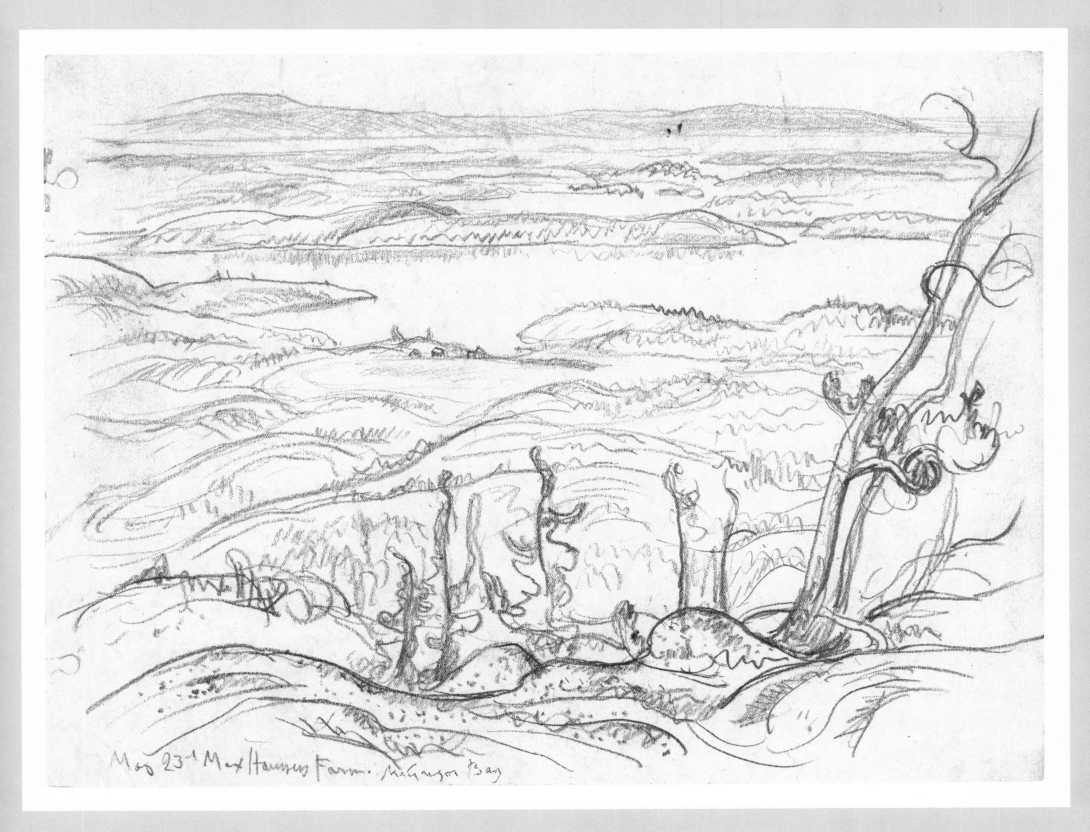

May 23rd Max Hausser's Farm. McGregor Bay

PLATE 53

Max Hausser's farm, McGregor Bay, Ontario, May 23, 1938

Algoma has given its artists not only the great open vistas of land, water, and sky, but also what Nancy Robertson calls "the closed intimate nooks" likewise dear to J. E. H. MacDonald's heart, and one of which AY portrays with almost Oriental virtuosity in this little *Lake in the La Cloche Hills*.

The beautiful wild region north of Manitoulin Island has long been known to discerning visitors. A whole century before AY got there, the intrepid Mrs. Anna Jameson, coming *en bateau* from Sault Ste. Marie in August 1837, described the La Cloche area: " . . . we perceived in the east the high ridge called the mountains of La Cloche. They are really respectable hills in this level country, but hardly mountains: they are all of limestone, and partially clothed in wood. All this coast is very rocky and barren; but is said to be rich in mineral productions. . . . La Cloche . . . derives its name from a large rock, which they say, being struck, vibrates like a bell . . . the Indians regard the spot as sacred and enchanted. . . ."

Something of ancient nature-magic and enchantment is conveyed in this pencil sketch. AY has always loved mountain lakes, which he often describes as "glorious." One of his letters, written when the day's work was over, tells how "the lake is like a sheet of glass and the moon which has just risen over the hills, is sending a big silver shimmer over the water and straight into the tent."

There is another letter, written not far from the present scene while AY was camping on the shore of Grace Lake. It conveys in words some of the sense of solitude that feeds the creative soul, and expresses at the same time a warm appreciation of the small things that help make up everyday life: the double aspect of the essence of our artist's personality. The letter is postmarked "Willisville" (which had nine inhabitants, according to AY) and stamped October 25, 1933: "Grace Lake, no post office, no nothing. Oct. 22nd."

Dear Naomi:

Unky Punk [the niece's childhood name that has stuck] is in his tent, with a tin pail full of cinders to keep him warm and a little candle to give him light, and some balsam boughs to sit on. Outside his tent the fire is crackling, it's a nice sound, you never feel quite alone with it.

It's a large marble fire-place: these hills are all made of it, and it burns in any kind of weather, particularly when it is pouring rain. It eats up rain like coal oil—you just put some red pine on and it roars. If it roars too much you feed it green poplar and it goes slower. If you want nice red embers to put in the tin pail you give it maple.

I'm all alone, but a friend named McIver is four miles away, working on some mining claims, and every few days just about dusk he blows in and spends the night. He generally brings some of his home-made bread or a pie. He's a prince. He hacks down the forests and blows up the rocks with dynamite, and rushes canoes over portages, he's some boy.

I merely make sketches. I have a box full of them. It's been hard work getting them with so much rain and cold wind. Grace Lake is surrounded with big rocky hills. There are several little islands in it. Your Dad would love to spend a summer here. There is one little lake right up on top of the hills, with muskeg all around it, just full of pitcher plants.

I believe there are wolves and bears around, but they mind their own business, just like me. The mice are much more dangerous—I have to keep my grub hung up on the ridge pole of the tent. I feel them running over my sleeping bag at night, and I turn my flashlight on them and they go like hell.

Well, such is life at Grace Lake, my dear. . . .

PLATE 54

Lake in the La Cloche Hills, Ontario [c. 1930s]

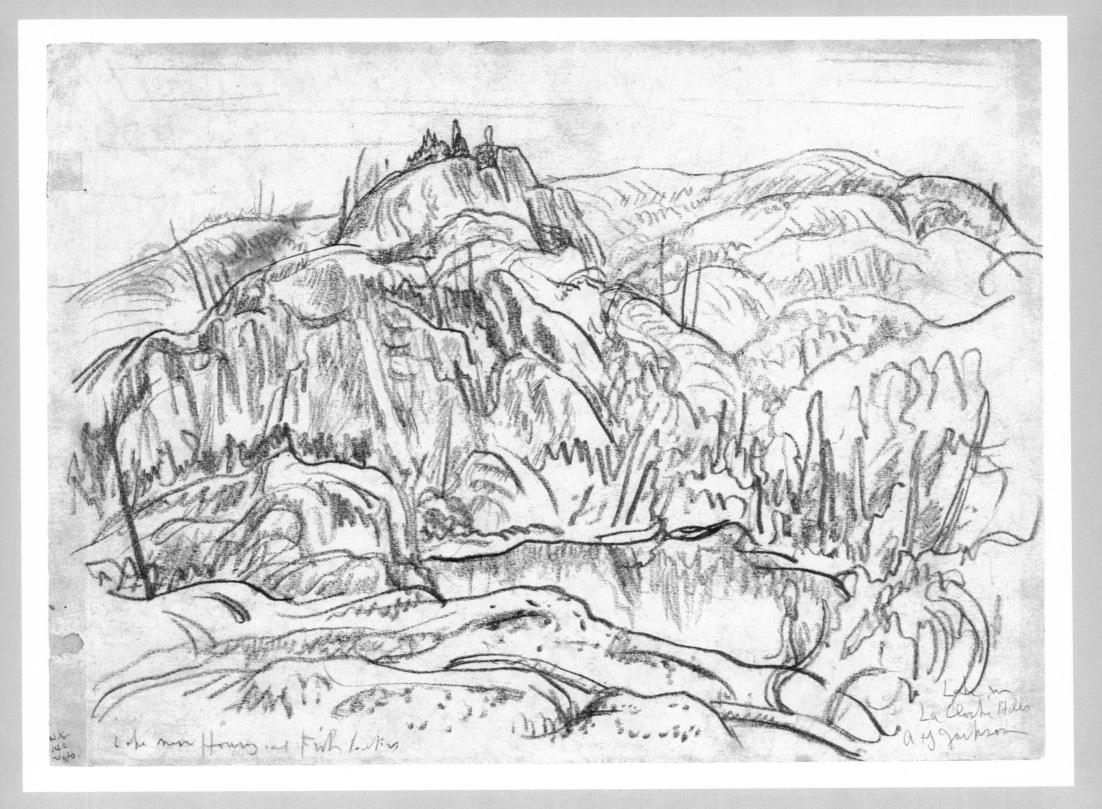

Lake near Haining and Frith Lakes

Lake in
La Cloche Hills
A Y Jackson

AY was in the region north of Lake Huron for two years in succession—autumns 1933 and 1934—following the habit he favoured of getting to know a particular stretch of country intimately in all weather conditions as the season advanced over a period of several weeks. He was back there again in 1938, 1939 and 1940.

This evocative drawing of a November day by a lake in Algoma was likely made in the same year in which AY wrote the letter from Grace Lake cited on the previous page and dated October 25, 1933. A firm basis for setting a date *ante quem* for the drawing is the handsome canvas, 26 by 32 inches, *Northern Lake, November*, given in the 1953 exhibition catalogue as "painted about 1934" and on loan from the Vincent Massey collection. The canvas was done direct from the drawing and recreates the same mood of this country once described by AY as "landscape untidy and ragged . . . swampy, rocky, wolf ridden, a land burnt or scuttled and flooded by lumber companies, with rivers and numerous lakes all over it. . . ."

Into the Ontario fabric of AY's life and of this present book, two Great Ones of the Seven—Lismer and MacDonald—have already been woven. Now we enter regions with which Lawren Harris had considerable contact. In AY's scrapbook there is a verbal description by Harris with which AY's drawing here shows affinity in subject and mood, possibly in actual location. This description is contained in a review by Harris of *Four Canadian Plays* by Merrill Denison. In the busy early 1920s, when the members of the new Group of Seven were bursting with vitality and interested in all things Canadian, Harris like Jackson often wrote articles and reviews for *The Canadian Bookman*, *The Canadian Forum* and other good local publications. This particular contribution was entitled "The Unheroic North" and describes the setting of one of Denison's plays as "existence in that tired sparse strip of land that lies between the healthy farming country and the vast northern woods, a country of silent drab sawmills, rotting lumber camps, stones, stumps, scrub growth and lonely rampikes. . . ."

Lawren Harris knew that fringe of the lumbering country personally, having worked around the town of Mattawa on the Upper Ottawa River, jumping-off point for generations of lumbermen. Harris' canvases of around 1920 tend to show deserted streets with bleak angular buildings, austere and perhaps harsher aspects than those expressed by AY. The latter somehow seems to sympathize more with the process of ageing, be it venerable barns, towns no longer active, or countryside that has been worked over, blasted to the bare bone by the passage of man, as has this lake with its denuded hillsides and half-submerged stumps. AY does not find it repulsive; he makes it beautiful.

While showing a slide of the canvas *Northern Lake, November* during a recent talk, AY mentioned this drawing made with such concentration and care: "It was done in Algoma East, in the district south of Sudbury, in the Collin Range of quartzite hills—a region all lumbered over and then flooded, which certainly produced interesting subjects for artists to tackle. It was early November when I was there, and the ice was beginning to form on the water around the tree stumps. In another week it would be all frozen up, but right then it made an exciting design. I did a very careful drawing and painted the canvas from it later."

No breath of wind stirs the surface's clear reflection, though mist lies wraithlike along the distant shoreline. The foregound is an almost surrealistic study of old tree forms, "stumps wet, warm blacks, colours flat, faint with blue." Overhead wing the wild geese, Indians' Wawa, last to leave the northland. Gone are Hahng the loon and Shuh-shuh-gah the great blue heron. One can think of many things that are gone:

> Gone the one-time lofty forest,
> Gone the "palisades of pine-trees"—
> (Lumbered over and then flooded)—
> Gone the birds and gone the fishes,
> Gone the pure and crystal waters;
> All along the lakes and shorelines
> White man's mess and rank pollution
> Threaten all the world of waters.
> "From the moorlands and the fenlands,
> From the melancholy marshes,
> Screams the heron, blue Shuh-shuh-gah,
> Screams Farewell, O Hiawatha!"
>
> (With vast apologies to H. W. Longfellow.)

PLATE 55

*Lake in Algoma East,
November [c. 1933]*

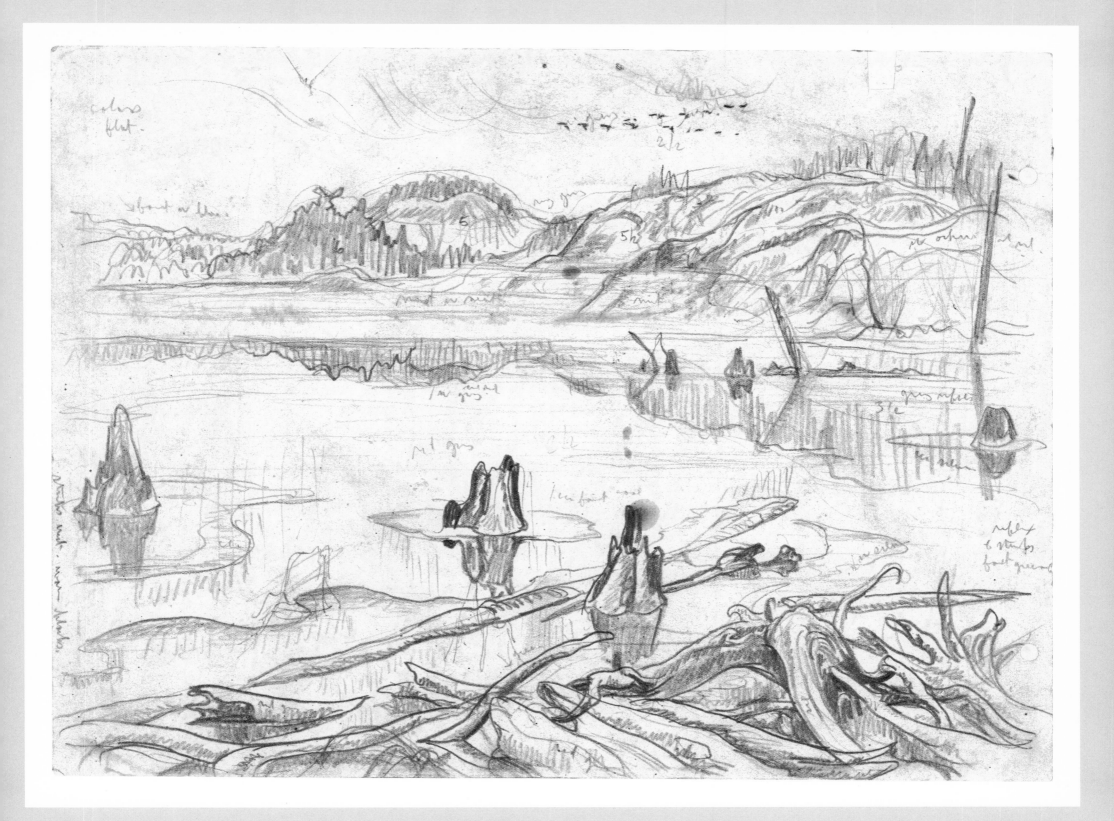

We have been watching AY find wonderful subjects in areas where the lumbermen had cleared out the forests and laid bare the rocky hills. In the same way he often finds interesting shapes in Ontario mining districts where our pre-Cambrian shield is being violently forced to yield up its hidden treasure.

The town of Cobalt lies some ninety miles north of North Bay. The 1956 edition of the *Columbia Encyclopedia* gives a surprising amount of irresistible detail on the subject of Cobalt, both the mineral and the town. How many Canadians know, for instance, that the word "cobalt" comes from the German word pronounced as in English but meaning "goblin" or "demon"? It seems that when the lustrous silvery white metallic element was discovered by Georg Brandt in 1735 it was taken for some form of iron or nickel, but refused to act like them under smelting. "This failure," the *Columbia Encyclopedia* informs us solemnly, "was attributed to the work of a demon or goblin. For a long time cobalt metal had no use. Today it is a component of certain steel alloys called high-speed steels, from which very hard cutting tools are made. . . . The element is found in meteoric metal, rarely by itself in nature." Among the many uses of cobalt is of course the one of most interest to artists, namely the preparation of pigments of high quality—cobalt blue, violet, green, etc.

The valuable cobalt ores, found in association with silver ores in which this part of Ontario is one of the world's richest areas, were discovered by chance in 1903 through railway blasting. The town of Cobalt sprang up as scores of mines were opened in the vicinity, reaching their zenith in 1911. Since then the town's population has steadily declined. Some mines were reopened in 1946, but many local businessmen now live in nearby Haileybury on Lake Timiskaming and commute by car. The *Columbia Encyclopedia* gives Cobalt's 1956 census as 2,376; the figure 2,200 was on the shield at the entrance to the somewhat spruced-up town in the summer of 1966.

AY's several visits to Cobalt were during the lull years of the 1930s. He tells how he enjoyed the subjects offered by its steep slopes, the jutting mineshafts and higgledy-piggledy houses built *before* the streets, which wended their way around them with such picturesque irregularity. "The palmy days were over by the time I got there, but the people had stayed on, subsisting somehow. It was a wonderful place to paint, especially under some snow. I can't find a thing to work on in towns laid out on a grid."

It is challenging to compare AY's treatment of Cobalt and old parts of Quebec City with the similar urban themes of Lawren Harris during the latter's socialist-expressionist stage in the 1920s. Harris presents grim warehouses and dreary city fringes, seen as stark, hard-edged blocks in cold metallic tones. There is a striking, little-known parallel to that stage of Harris' painting in a volume of his own poetry published in 1922 under the title *Contrasts, A Book of Verse*. (AY indicates that Harris inclined later to look upon this venture as a youthful extravaganza.) One of the poems in the section headed "People" contains lines of indictment against

Streets hard as steel; cold, repellent, cruel

. . . .

Dirty, musty, garbage-reeking lanes
Behind the soot-dripped backs of blunt houses,
Sour yards and slack-sagging fences.

It is enlightening to know that thoughts of protest against the ugliness of the modern city and the miserable fate of its inhabitants were in Harris' mind at the period when he did his city paintings. Perhaps the visual counterpart has been distilled into greater abstraction with a stark beauty of its own.

It is doubtful if AY at any stage even *saw* the city slums as Harris did, with the social reformer's eye. AY had worked his own way out of the industrialized metropolis by dint of his resilience, his ambition and energy, and his genius. He retained a liking for down-trodden corners. If we compare a Harris building with an AY building, there is something sharp-edged, crystal-hard, metallic, *mineral* about the Harris interpretation. In contrast, AY could be called *vegetable*. He lacks the biting edge of those "hard cutting tools" that Harris favours. AY's houses, shacks and sheds are never crystal-hard, seldom even geometrically cubist. They are living organisms with a sway, often a sag, to them; they tend to be time- and weather-worn, not rigidly impervious.

Even AY's blues lack the steely, indigo, almost sinister tinge we sometimes find in Harris. I don't think AY even used much Cobalt Blue! As for Cobalt Violet—after a big splurge he gave it all to Lismer to take to South Africa, a good place for it. AY's blues are more vegetable-dyed in character: larkspur, blue grape or purple hyacinth, at most turquoise or lapis lazuli.

Finally, as a last touch, small but possibly significant: in AY's copy of Lawren Harris' *Contrasts*, with its handsome orange and black end papers and pine tree cover (about the only *vegetable* nature in that book!) the pages of the beautiful heavy paper were uncut between 57 and 58—and what should that be but the poem about "sour yards and slack-sagging fences"! In this copy at least, AY, who *likes* his fences to sag a bit, did not get around to reading the end of the sad-street poem. A small touch, indeed, but perhaps significant?

PLATE 56
Cobalt, Ontario [1934]

This drawing of the town of Spragge fits into our present sequence of scenes along the north shore of Lake Huron and northward, that district so rich in natural resources and so poor in man's care and consideration for his surroundings. A poem by Lawren Harris called "Good Old Earth" speaks feelingly of "The gashes and long blunt wounds / And bleachings to lifelessness / Made by the pilgrimage / Of men. . . ."

Spragge can be further located as east of Blind River, west of Serpent River, from which the seventeen-mile spur runs north to Elliot Lake, another spot that has certainly had its ups and downs as "Uranium Capital of the World."

AY once spent a day working around Spragge, in which year it has not been exactly determined but probably in the early 1930s: "I was there for just one day. I remember arriving by train in a Pullman sleeper and being the only person to get off at Spragge. The train porter must have thought I was the manager of the big local sawmill, and he tumbled all over himself to look after me. Imagine if he'd known I was nothing but a bum artist!"

The one or two Spragge drawings on hand show the place in anything but a millionaire mood. They are careful studies, full of detail, which possibly indicates that the subject was not painted up at the time. The verbal comments support the serious mood effectively. "Grey purple" and "grey browns," the present drawing tells us, while another (njg 302) is more explicit, almost poetic in its own right: "All sombre . . . faded blue . . . lines decided but faintly blurred . . . boards have been taken off tops of old lumber piles."

The *verso* of the present drawing shows the stately Catholic church of Spragge, in nineteenth-century Gothic style with vertical clapboard walls and well proportioned lancet windows; in the churchyard under iron crosses "intense black" and "white stones bold" the dead are at rest from their labours. AY's drawings describe the visible surface of Spragge in a way which permits interpretation and penetration to deeper levels of meaning. Is there not a sort of dour dignity in the cluster of human habitations here? Those who have visited them know the warmth of hospitality and friendship within. As Lawren Harris writes at the start of his poem "The Earth Winds":

> The earth is such a pale thing in space,
> So drab a bleached grey—
> There are purer, richer, more translucent colours
> In the heart.

PLATE 57

Spragge, Ontario [*c. 1930s*]

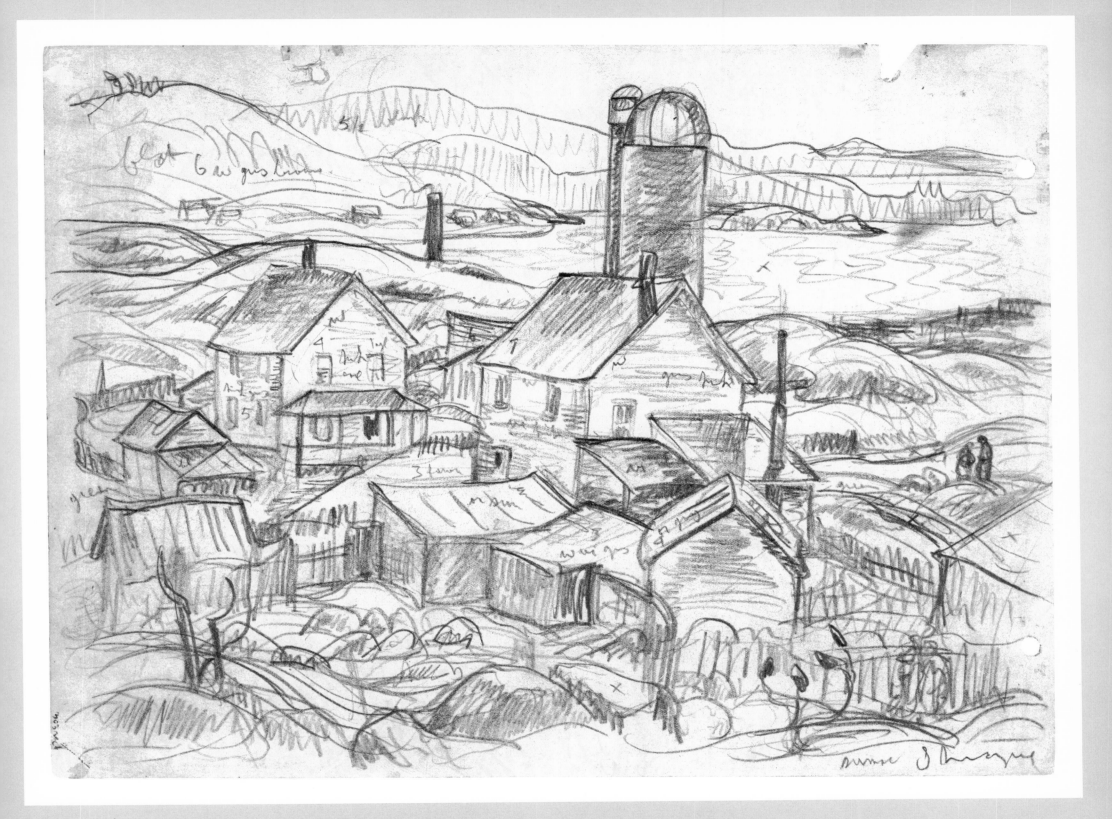

On that crisp fall day of October 2, 1925—one day before AY's forty-third birthday—it was not the wigwam of the Daughter of the Moon, Nokomis, that stood on the shore of the greatest of North America's lakes, but a couple of much less romantic tents belonging to a tough trio of artists named Harris, Carmichael and Jackson. These three had been camping near the tiny settlements of Jackfish and Coldwell on the north shore of Lake Superior and had made the trip out to the Slate Islands "in a gasoline launch with a fair rolling sea over a seven mile strip of Lake Superior," as F. B. Housser wrote the following year in his pioneer study of the Group of Seven, *A Canadian Art Movement*.

"It certainly was superior in all ways . . . that smooth glimmering infinity of waters . . . like a glimpse of God himself," wrote another member of the intrepid Seven, J. E. H. MacDonald, on his first glimpse of the "great rocky shores stooping grandly to the water. . . . I have not quite assimilated this experience yet. It is something to be quiet about and think over."

AY himself states in his autobiography, after long years of experience, "I know of no more impressive scenery in Canada for the landscape painter. There is a sublime order to it, the long curves of the beaches, the sweeping ranges of hills, the headlands that push out into the lake."

But of all the members of the Seven, it was Lawren Harris who really came into "his own country" when he reached that noble lake. Characteristically, it was he who discovered it for his fellow artists back in 1917 on a strenuous *convalescing* canoe trip with Dr. MacCallum that started at Manitoulin Island and reached the east end of Superior. The following year, Harris was the prime promoter of the famous box-car brigade up along the Algoma Central Railway, so vividly described in *A Painter's Country*. In the fall of 1919 AY was free of his war records work and joined the happy gang. Already by 1920 Harris felt the urge for something bold, dramatic and stark, less opulent than the hardwood-covered hills of Algoma, so later that fall he and AY pushed along the north shore as far as Rossport. Every autumn through the 1920s up to 1928 or so, Harris—and usually Jackson with him—could be found back in this grandiose terrain which has been interpreted in some of Harris' noblest canvases. As late as 1964 the artist was still extolling the "singing expansiveness and sublimity" of the lake he knew so well. More intensive study of Lawren Harris' creative development will doubtless do full justice to the present fleeting surmise that it was the experience of Superior's infinite space and light that formed the basis, or a basic component, of the mystic exaltation that henceforth filled that artist's work, expressed admirably in words in

his poem "Darkness and Light" in the final section, sub-titled "Spiritual," of his book of verse:

> And light has no weight,
> Yet one is lifted on its flood,
> Swept high,
> Running up white-golden light-shafts,
> As if one were as weightless as light itself—
> All gold and white and light.

We can picture Lawren Harris in those days: tall and slim, with his dark shining eyes and his aureole of silky hair, with his boundless energy and enthusiasm, up at dawn to concoct great pots full of Dr. Jackson's Roman Meal. And AY alongside him, equally resourceful, perhaps more resilient, not "running up white-golden light-shafts" in quite the same weightless way. The present vivid little AY drawing of the rugged island headlands and brilliant water beyond shows a concern for real rocks, real trees, real nature, that can only be Jackson and never Harris. If anything, the texture may be a trifle reminiscent of the MacDonald of Algoma days, but that texture is for AY part of the pencil study and will be swept along into the burlier rhythms of the canvas to come.

Yet AY appreciated the mystic quality in Lawren's work of the Lake Superior period and he felt that Harris matched that daring, dramatic country in spirit. He has saved among his papers a page, written in our late Cousin Isa Erichsen Brown's fine flourishing hand, on which is copied part of a letter written in February 1916 by D. H. Lawrence to J. D. Beresford, concerning the coast of Cornwall. Below it we read in AY's own characteristic small script: "Isa Brown suggests that this describes L. Harris' Superior canvases." It is interesting that D. H. Lawrence's prose here and Lawren Harris' mystic poems and paintings from Lake Superior all belong within the same decade in time as well as the same region of ideas—a region AY enjoyed contemplating from his own firm foothold. Here is part of the D. H. Lawrence passage: "The Shore is absolutely primeval: the heavy, black rocks, like solid darkness, and the heavy water like a sort of first twilight breaking against them and not changing them. . . . It is really like the first craggy breaking of dawn on the world, a sense of primeval darkness just behind, before, the Creation. . . . This cold light of the sea is really the eternal light washing against the eternal darkness, a terrific abstraction, far beyond all life, which is merely of the sun, warm. And it does one's soul good to escape from the ugly triviality of life into this clash of two infinities one upon the other, cold and eternal."

124

1925

Slate Islands
Oct 2 - 25

PLATE 58

Slate Islands, Lake Superior, October 2, 1925

"So the Canadian artist in Ontario was drawn north," wrote Lawren Harris in 1928 in his essay "Creative Art and Canada." Mention of this interesting essay fits well into the present time-and-place sequence of our book because it came towards the end of the period of closest companionship and inter-relationships within AY's circle of Ontario artist friends. And because the Harris essay concentrates upon Ontario, it will serve as the farewell we must now make before moving on across the country.

Words written in those very days have a bloom and freshness that later reminiscing sometimes lacks: "So the Canadian artist in Ontario was drawn north, and there at first devoted himself to nature's outward aspect until a thorough acquaintance with her forms, her growth and idio-

126

syncracies, and the almost endless diversity of individual presences in lakes, rivers, valleys, forests, rocklands and habitations, led him to feel the spirit that informs all these. Thus living in and wandering over the north, and at first more or less literally copying a great variety of her motives, he inevitably developed a sense of design, of selection, rhythm and relationship in individual conformity to her aspect, moods and spirit. Then followed a period of decorative treatment of her great wealth of material into design and colour patterns conveying the moods of seasons, weather and places. Then followed an intensification of mood that simplified form into deeper meaning and was more vigorously selective and sought to have no element in the work which did not contribute to a

unified intense expression. The next step was a utilization of elements in the North in depth, in three dimensions, giving a fuller meaning, a more real sense of the presence of the informing spirit."

Nearly four decades later, here is a late warm memory afterglow from Lawren Harris' essay of 1964: "We lived in a continuous blaze of enthusiasm. We were at times very serious and concerned, at other times hilarious and carefree. Above all, we loved this country, and loved exploring and painting it. Emerson once wrote: 'Every great and commanding movement in the annals of the world is the triumph of enthusiasm.' Please do not think that we had any idea of leading a great and commanding movement; but we did have enthusiasm."

PLATE 59a

Left: Jackfish, Lake Superior, 1924

PLATE 59b

Right: Coldwell, Lake Superior [early 1920s]

When AY heads across the great plains to the western prairies to work he is more on his own, as far as his Group of Seven connections go, than in any of the foregoing sections of this journey through Canada. The only member of the Group who represents the mid-west, Lemoine Fitzgerald of Winnipeg, joined the rather mythical and very elastic Seven in its last year of single existence, 1932. He was "the man who stayed home," in whose "solitary, reticent spirit" the Group recognized "a fellow pioneer in the enlargement of Canadian experience through art." But AY did not work much in Fitzgerald's province, in either sense of the word. To be sure, he occasionally visited Winnipeg to give a talk, as clippings from the *Free Press* show, just as he also touched on several corners of Saskatchewan over the course of the years—unfortunately not leaving much in the way of drawings on hand for our present purpose. But it is Alberta which has most often seen AY come to stay and work, chiefly in the region around Lethbridge and the south-west corner of the province. He has also worked farther north, using Calgary as headquarters after the summer session at the Banff School of Fine Arts, where he taught for six seasons in the 1940s.

Brief visits to Alberta, home territory of the western Jacksons (AY's elder brother, the late Ernest Jackson, and family), go back as far as 1914 to the year of AY's first trip west. In 1928 he and Dr. Banting, on their way to Great Slave Lake, liked the look of the region around Drumheller and stopped over for a day or so, as one or two vivid little dated drawings attest. But the fall of 1937 saw the first major visit for AY in that part of Canada. Being visible from a long way off on those wide stretches, symbolically as well, his presence made quite a dint in the awareness of the countryside and also made very good copy for the lively Lethbridge *Herald*. There is an endearing article by "F. G. C." (Frederick G. Cross) that conveys not only the Westerners' first impression of the visiting artist, but a graphic picture of all the things he looked at in that part of our Canadian world. Thanks to our Lethbridge kinsfolk, the exact date of the article is available, namely Saturday, November 13, 1937. It is headed "Distinguished Canadian Painter, Alexander Young Jackson, Gets South Alta. Scenes on Canvas" (a bit premature, as far as the *canvas* goes!). The article reads, in part: "During the past month a distinguished guest has been within our gates. With the countryside full of activity in an effort to garner the last fruits of the season before freeze-up, perhaps only a few noted his presence. Those who did, no doubt had their curiosity aroused at the sight of a sturdily built man of medium height with genial smile and a touch of white hair showing beneath an expressive fedora hat; a figure standing bolt upright by the side of a road, the edge of a coulee, the

outskirts of a little village, close up to a group of elevators, the corner of either a beet field or pasture of a typical Alberta farm; gazing at the pattern of strip farming or maybe at the more tragic pattern of soil drift; the more happier [*sic*] straw stack, horses, cattle, wagons, trucks, coal mines, oil derricks, or whatever we have. Lethbridge, Spring Coulee, New Dayton, Enchant, Cowley, Lundbreck, Porcupine Hills, etc.—always the same figure, bolt upright with a small sketchbook and pencil or perhaps canvas and brush; brains and fingers working in unison with startling rapidity and directness.

"Let Nature unleash her utmost vagaries of weather and drive the timid to cover—the upright figure remains to record the rhythm of movement of the heavenly forces. . . .

" . . . When A. Y. Jackson's paintings of our landscape are seen . . . in Eastern Canada, the rhythm, line and color will sing aloud of the West and a new chapter in the history of Canadian art will unfold."

Our first western drawing, lent by a friend out there and depicting a typical row of prairie grain elevators at Carstairs, north of Calgary, makes a good introduction to the West as seen through AY's eyes. Its rectilinear, delicate clarity is, oddly enough, not so radically different from the work of Lemoine Fitzgerald himself. During AY's many sojourns out west he developed a great liking for the clean angularity of the grain elevators, so different from his rolling Laurentian rocks and roofs. "The grain elevator is the only architecture that's of any importance at all on the prairies," he said after one visit. "Like France's cathedrals, the prairies have their grain elevators. White and silver and red—I think they're lovely things. I'd like to spend two or three months just kicking around Alberta towns painting them."

AY reached the West before the introduction of the long line of mechanical reapers that move systematically across the fields of harvest-ready grain. Never a horse or a solitary combine can be seen there nowadays. But AY saw and painted many a line of stooked grain and made careful pencil studies of individual threshing machines at work.

The analogy of the good, full harvest applies very happily to this artist's own productive life. Paul Duval, writing about the retrospective exhibition of a half-century of Jackson's work (opened at the Art Gallery in Toronto in the fall of 1953, then shown in Ottawa and Montreal), headed his column in *Saturday Night* "A Canadian Epic" and started off: "The waning harvest moon shone down on the most abundant crop ever gleaned by an artist from Canadian soil. A half-century of cultivation had gone to produce it, and what had once been mistaken for wild oats turned out to be a very hardy grade of No. 1 wheat."

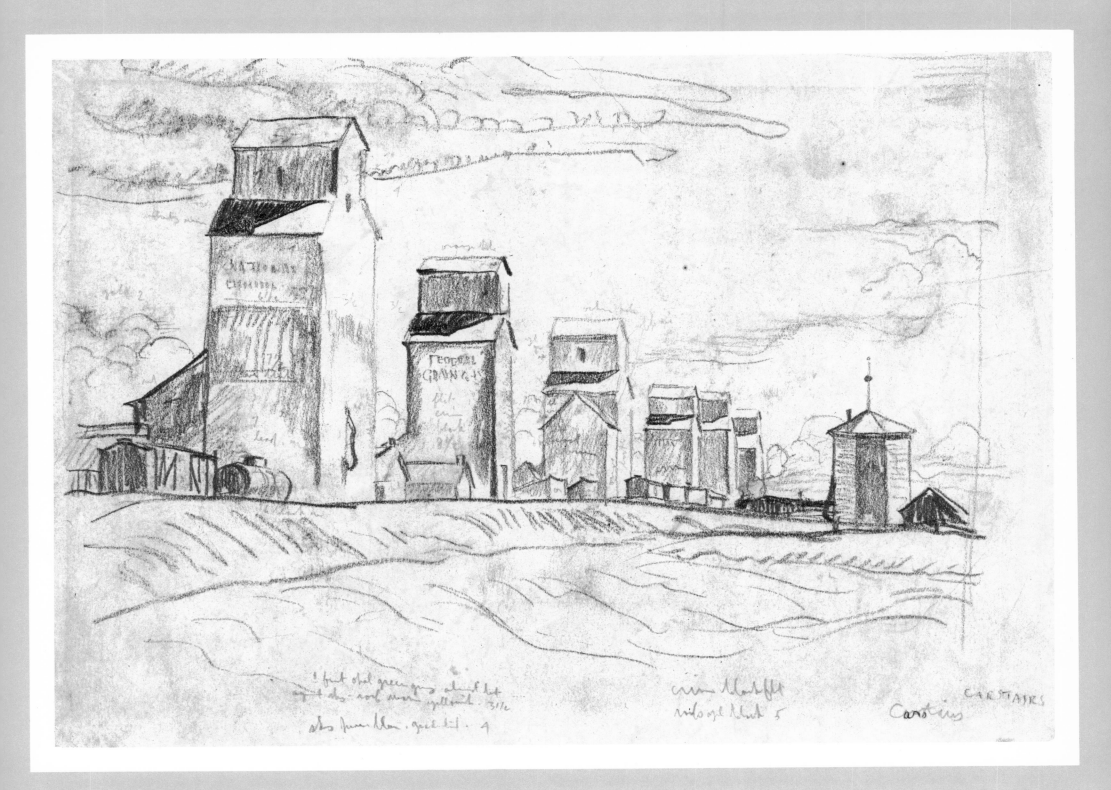

PLATE 60

Elevators at Carstairs, Alberta [c. 1940s]

The Calgary friend who owns the oil sketch of this subject, titled *Alberta Wheatfields* (njg 841r) and dated the same day as this drawing, recalls the occasion very clearly: "It was a Monday afternoon, and AY's birthday. We drove to De Winton, about twenty miles south of Calgary. Those elevators at the left are on the Blackfoot Highway. AY was on a wheatfield kick just then, and we stopped for him to make several drawings, which he painted up later.

"While he stood doing this scene from the edge of the wheatfield, the farmer and his collie dog came along to see what was going on. The farmer naturally thought that AY with his pencil and notebook would be figuring out the price to offer for the wheat, and he was all set to sell it to him. . . . Then when he saw the drawing he was none too pleased, either, because AY had left out one window in the elevator in the background!"

A canvas of the subject is in the collection of Ford Motors, Calgary.

PLATE 61

*South of Calgary, Alberta,
October 3, 1950*

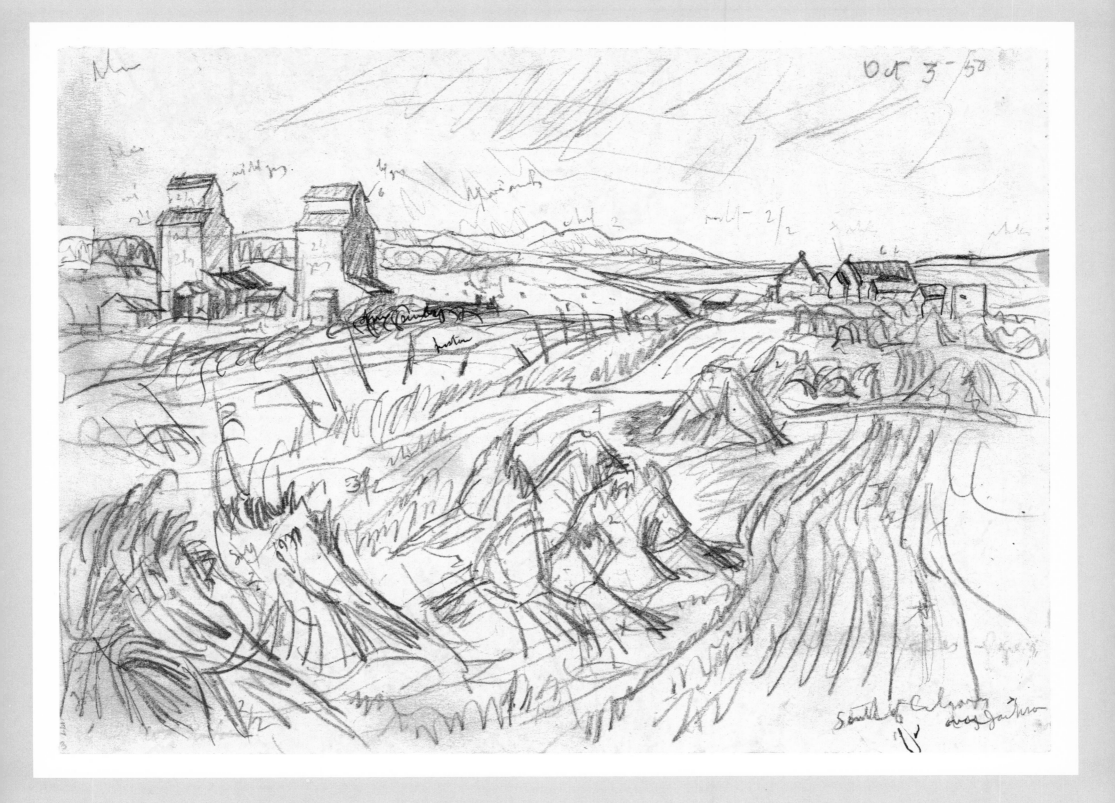

"What we really valued in a building was height," wrote Donald Buchanan, recalling boyhood days in Lethbridge in *To Have Seen The Sky*. This fine book of sensitive photographs and pithy, graphic prose was published in 1962, exactly forty years after Lawren Harris' *Contrasts*. It represents very worthily the work of the major wave of artists, writers, and styles which followed the generation of the Group of Seven. Donald Buchanan, twenty-six years younger than AY, recorded with nostalgia and a certain modern cynicism his memories of subjects that often have visual parallels in AY's work. Both, for instance, liked the line of elevators at Carmangay. Alongside his photograph of them Buchanan wrote: "What we really valued . . . was height, and so our five-storey post office [i.e. in Lethbridge], complete with clock tower, gave us a rightful pride. In the surrounding small towns and villages, the tall grain elevators standing sentinel-like in rows against the sky were the landmarks. From the constant talk of our parents about hopes of bumper harvests, our minds had become obsessed by the wheat economy of the prairies, and so we measured the importance of each hamlet by the number of red, brown, or white-painted elevators it possessed."

The mention of Donald Buchanan, whose accidental death in February 1966 deprived the Canadian art world of an original and important figure, is appropriate at this juncture. He was a native and a good interpreter of the western prairies, and he owned the fine 20 by 26 inch canvas *Elevators at Night, Pincher Creek, 1947*, with which the drawing presented here has considerable affinity, although the subject is not identical. The canvas shows three receding dark upright forms against a brilliantly light curved cloud, behind which the constellation of Ursa Major glistens greenly in the northern sky. This canvas was one of three western landscapes by AY which members of the Canadian Press presented to Donald's father, Senator William Buchanan, in 1954, on the fortieth anniversary of his founding of the Lethbridge *Herald*. Now, after the death of both father and eldest son, the canvas will be among those from the latter's valuable art collection bequeathed to the city of Lethbridge for its embryo Art Gallery. AY has himself always had the establishment of such a gallery at heart, and it seems most fitting that his dramatic night piece should come home to Lethbridge once more. (Note: This canvas was among the six by AY in the National Gallery's centennial exhibition *Three Hundred Years of Canadian Art* as Number 271, 19 by 25 inches, loaned by the Lethbridge Junior College.)

AY's work in general was well appraised in Donald Buchanan's *Growth of Canadian Painting*. Concerning AY's westward urge in the 1940s we read: " . . . the broad, unending horizons of the western plains have begun

to attract him more and more. Teaching now in the summer at the Banff School of Fine Arts, he frequently goes on sketching tours into the foot-hills of southern Alberta or farther north along the Alaska Highway.

"One need only look at a selection of his sketches to note how remarkable is the sensitivity with which he records such changes of climate and atmosphere. For instance, take his sketches of southern Alberta. A month previously he may have been in the Quebec countryside where, in the moist spring air, he would have been depicting, with what for him are rare touches of sensuous gaiety, those colourful scenes of melting snow and horses and red sleighs on drifted roads. But now in the west he starts in at once putting down, with sure strokes of colour and what is visible realism, even from the moment of his first arrival there, the dry brittle sense of distance in the prairie landscape or the deep cast of shadows marked by a harsh sun on a semi-arid range of hills . . . in his best canvases, he usually manages to preserve, without any noticeable loss of impact in the transition, the geographical validity of his original sketches."

As a final, diminutive, and humorous tribute to the Jackson-Buchanan-Lethbridge link, here is AY's drawing—a detail in natural size, about 1 by 1½ inches from a corner of njg 899—of that imposing five-storey Lethbridge Post Office, in which we are told each of the four clocks tells the time differently!

PLATE 62

Grain elevators and freight cars, western Canada [*mid-1940s*]

AY became greatly excited by the land formations in the south-west corner of Alberta. Some fifty miles west of Lethbridge is the Pincher Creek area ("a simply wonderful place") with the hills beginning about ten miles west of it again, and in about twenty miles or so, the mountains. Further southward towards Montana are the Sweetgrass Hills and the upthrusting buttes with their fantastic eroded forms—"that old battle-ground of buffaloes, cattle, cowboys and mounties," as AY described it to the Toronto critic Augustus Bridle, in May 1939: "It is a different glory from that of the sub-Arctic. . . . No wonder Canadians are cocky about their country. It's a prodigious cosmic thrill. That's what artists felt just before the war [i.e. 1914/1918] when they began to cut loose from pretty pastorals. That's what started the Group of Seven. Now they're all catching the glamour, and nobody bothers to think whether it's crazy or not!"

One can sense the cosmic thrill in the present masterly drawing, which probably belongs to the late 1940s and to the area around Pincher Creek. But like the monumental elevators of the previous page, it has a vast place-and-time-defying quality. AY must have sensed this himself, so instead of jotting down the exact location of the drawing, as he often does very matter-of-factly, he inscribed it grandly—and justly—"Alberta Rhythm." This is of course also the name of the large (38 by 50 inch) canvas of about 1949 for which AY utilized this delicate, precisely model-led drawing. The canvas was shown as No. 77 and "Collection of the Artist" in the 1953 retrospective and has subsequently been acquired by St. Hilda's residence in the University of Toronto. Here is "the dry, brittle sense of distance" and the "cast of shadows marked by a harsh sun on a semi-arid range of hills" of Donald Buchanan's words. But under-lying these surface aspects is the grandiose elemental cast of form that emanates the essence of the place.

Alongside such cosmic connotations it might be pleasant to place a few excerpts from AY's letters from the days when these drawings were done; they help to recreate the atmosphere of his life at that time. The first is headed "Lethbridge, Alta., October 17th" (1937) and was written to the niece just back from studies in Germany and starting graduate work at Harvard: " . . . Here we are two and half thousand miles apart again, old timer. . . . The Lethbridge Jacksons are a happy outfit . . . I expect the everlasting sunlight makes people cheerful out here. Not good sketching, weather hazy, and no kick to it. But it is a big spacious country. You can see the places you are going to twenty-five miles before you get there. If you stayed here for months, you could get some fine things, stuff that no one has done. . . ."

Seven years later, on November 1, 1944, AY wrote from Regina, Saskatchewan: "On my way home. Stopped off here to address the Women's Canadian Club yesterday, and tonight have to open an exhibi-tion of the Canadian Federation of Artists. Then on to Winnipeg, where I have to address the Federation tomorrow night. I'll be glad when I get home.

"It has been glorious sunshine for months, but November came in cold and rainy, and I had sent all my warm togs right through to Toronto, so I will just stick around the hotel. [Actually I believe he went out and did a drawing from the bridge, present whereabouts unfortunately not known; "Nearly froze, too!"]

"Have had a busy time sketching in Rosebud, Kamloops, Canmore, Cowley and Pincher Creek. . . . Getting to know the west."

Finally a letter from Toronto, dated November 21st, probably 1946, by which time the recipient was doing war relief work with the Quakers in Finnish Lapland and perhaps wishing to hear more often from her "Unk," to judge by the start of his letter: "Yes, I'm an old chump, but a busy one, and there are too many things to do. Covering the country both east and west is too much. Eighty-five sketches this year and a lot of canvases; being president of the Group [Canadian Group of Painters], on the council of the Federation, on various committees of the Art Gallery, on the Council of Canadian-Soviet Friendship, and general adviser to artists all over the country. . . .

"In today's papers it says there is three feet of snow in Cowley. I was sketching there not long ago. The station agent and I were batching, and having a grand time. There is some grand country in the west. The problem is that there is no place to stay where the best sketching is. You need a car and a trailer. That kind of art and adventure is to me what Canadians should be interested in, but hardly anyone is doing it. They are going abstract and pottering with new techniques. . . ."

PLATE 63
"Alberta Rhythm" [*1949*]

Alberta Rhythm   A. y. Jackson

AY has never owned a car and trailer for his sketching trips, nor a car of his own, and he never learned to drive. He has, however, always shown great talent for attracting good companions, most of them handy with the paintbrush themselves, to take him around the country. Such a one for southern Alberta in the 1930s, for instance, was Frederick Cross of Lethbridge, hydraulics engineer and irrigation expert, and in addition a keen watercolourist and occasional feature writer for the Lethbridge *Herald*, as we know from an earlier reference. Frederick Cross and AY ranged over hundreds of square miles in that spacious region, and one November day they stopped to sketch this scene on the Blood Indian Reserve south-west of Lethbridge, looking eastward towards the buttes.

There seems to be something arresting in the very name Blood Indian, which here combines with the season's sombre mood and the severe, uncompromising lay of the land to make this drawing heavily significant.

The Blood Indians are a subdivision of the once powerful and war-like Blackfoot nation, renowned as the Bedouin of the Plains. Their Algonquian dialect suggests an easterly origin in ages past. Making their way westward, they acquired the horse from tribes further south and became expert at hunting the buffalo and a terror as feuders and fighters. Their only cultivated crop was tobacco, grown for ceremonial purposes. By the early nineteenth century the Blackfoot tribes occupied immense territories from Lake Winnipeg to the Rockies. With the first coming of the white men they became wealthy through trade in pelts from their rich beaver streams, but the acquisition of firearms increased the deadliness of hunting as of feuding, and the Indians were an easy mark for southern traders of illicit whiskey. The fearful slaughter of the buffalo herds (32,000 in one kill in 1879) reduced their staple food; the treaty of 1878 with the British decimated their lands to a few reserves under government trusteeship. It was the white men who benefited from the surveying of the land, the fencing, the roads, the railway; the Indians of the plains, denied participation in the new economy of private ownership, deteriorated from opulence to rags. Recent figures for all Canadian Indians cite one-third on relief, three-quarters as earning less than $2,000 a year, twenty-four per cent illiterate. As for the six million acres held in trust for the Plains Indians (and the Bloods' Reserve is the largest in the country), an authority on the subject tells us: "Most of these lands lie fallow. A small part of them is cultivated by the Indians themselves. Much more is leased to the property-minded farmers whose productive acreage lies close by the reserve. In Alberta, a few tracts have been proved to be oil-bearing, and the bands fortunate enough to share in them are benefiting through the royalties which oil companies are paying to the Indian Affairs Branch as trustee for the Indian band members. But like most minor and lunatic beneficiaries of an estate, the Indian *cetuis-que-trustent* are uninterested. Life on the western reserve is largely a dreary and monotonous business, relieved only by the occasional wine orgy."

Perhaps this bitter knowledge about the once-proud Bedouin of the Plains pervades the empty angularity of AY's powerful drawing of the Blood Indian Reserve in 1937, with its vast horizontal stretches weighed down by the band of eroded hills. Does the work express something angry as well as angular? Something desperate as well as dreary? Its shape has a primitive quality. It is perhaps no accident that today when, as AY remarks, most Canadian artists have gone abstract and are "pottering with new techniques," there is one young mid-Western painter, forty-five years AY's junior, whose work shows this same primitive angularity and sharp emotional concern. In *Western Landscape*, 1962, William Kurelek uses strong horizontals, awkward diagonals, vast sky. His canvas, owned by Mr. and Mrs. L. V. Randall of Montreal, will have been seen by thousands in the centennial exhibition *Three Hundred Years of Canadian Art*. It is a pity that this show did not include AY's canvas of the Blood Indian Reserve, a sombre symphony of ochre, burnt sienna, black and grey, owned since 1946 by the Art Gallery of Ontario. AY considers it one of his most important works. Like this drawing, it has a great deal to say.

PLATE 64

Blood Indian Reserve, Alberta [*1937*]

"When A. Y. Jackson goes on a sketching trip in the Canadian hinterland," wrote Pearl McCarthy in her column "Art and Artists" in 1944, "he does nothing more pretentious than plod through mud, be a friendly stranger in far villages, and maybe drop into a movie. But the whole thing becomes a kind of public event, linking together sections of the country, because Dr. Jackson has that unaffected interest in his fellow men and the soil on which they live which is, probably, the finest patriotism."

The friendly stranger aspect of AY's visits was perhaps nowhere more vividly in evidence than out on the rolling prairies and in Alberta's foothill villages, where the arrival of a stranger by train was often a singular event. The story of AY's reception at Cowley, which is just down the line, east of the village of Lundbreck of our drawing, can serve as one instance of many. AY tells in his own inimitable fashion in the chapter "Painting in the West" of *A Painter's Country* how he got off the train in Cowley on a dark November night "with a howling wind blowing" and how helpful the stationmaster was, and furthermore how his wife all on her own connected the name Jackson with the Group of Seven. Now this stationmaster was the same one of whom AY wrote of "batching it" in that letter of November 1946. The late Mr. Clarence J. Bundy joined the Canadian Pacific Railway in 1910 and put in no less than thirty years in Cowley, followed by ten at Pincher Creek. The late Mrs. Freda Graham Bundy, who hailed from the Maritimes, had a real gift for writing. In Part 18 of her serial "Go West, Young Woman" she gives her version of how the friendly stranger AYJ turned up in their life: "Visitors —how we love them, invited ones and the most unexpected ones! . . . On one of those very dark nights, when neither moon nor stars were shining, the midnight train came in, C. J. met it, gave the OS to the dispatcher, blew out the office light and came into the house. A moment later there was a knock at the door and a passenger who had come off the train asked C. J. if he would tell him the location of the hotel.

" 'I'll do better than that,' said C. J. 'I'll get the flashlight and take you over.'

"A morning or so after, one of the merchants came into the station for express. 'My, the transients are traveling in style these days,' he said. 'There's one in town that carries his pack on his back and a camp stool in his hand.'

"It was not an hour later that I stood in the kitchen, baking, and through the window saw a man with a knapsack and a camp stool. There was something familiar about that set-up. 'Why, that's an artist,' I called to C. J. 'I wonder who he is?'

"Later in the day C. J. delivered a telegram at the hotel and returned, saying, 'That fellow's name is Jackson—he's the one who came off the train the other night. They don't know whether he is a real artist or not, his paintings are so queer.'

" 'Jackson—Jackson,' I muttered, then I cried excitedly, 'Why, it's A. Y. Jackson—I just know it is—he's one of the School of Seven.'

" 'Seven what?' inquired C. J.

" 'Seven artists that have set a new style of expression in painting,' I replied. 'I wonder if he has seen the south country—he'd like that.'

" 'No. They say he's been walking about town, painting some of the sheds and chicken houses.'

"I sent C. J. over to ask him if he would like to come over for supper . . . and what a wonderful evening we had. He told us of so many interesting things and places. . . . The next morning I packed a lunch for him, and before C. J. went to work in the office, he called for our new friend and drove him over to the South Fork Canyon where he spent the day sketching. We called for him after five o'clock and had a picnic down by the river. . . .

"That began a very precious friendship that has lasted down through the years, with a yearly visit. . . . Perhaps he'd be on his way back from the Cariboo, the Barren Lands around Coppermine, Great Slave Lake or Yellowknife. We scarcely could wait to have him open his bundle of sketches, and then we would have them displayed all over the room—on the piano, the mantel, the bookshelves—to enjoy during his visit. . . . We never have 'entertained' Alex, he just fits in as one of the family."

The western press in general appreciated AY's encouragement of painting activities among people in the smaller places. "In every village of 500 people in Canada there is probably someone who practises the art of painting," he told the Lethbridge *Herald* a quarter of a century ago. "It is time something was done for the isolated small town artist . . . working without honor or recognition . . . often the best person through whom to work in widening interest in the arts."

Lundbreck, in its day a coal-mining centre on the route into the Crowsnest Pass but now gone from the map, stands for many a small place in the "land of the last town and the distant point" where over the years AY visited, worked, and became friends with the local people. His drawings, full of characteristic features, are a record of things that have long since disappeared. Nowadays, oil, natural gas, sulphur and potash are the big things out west, and most of Alberta's four hundred coal mines and the villages that grew up around them have passed into limbo. And how long will there still be old-timers out west who recall the friendly stranger with the rucksack and camp stool?

Lundbreck Alberta 1936
a y jackson

PLATE 65
Lundbreck, Alberta [c. 1937]

It helps the balance of our book to include this dismal drawing of the disaster that befell the Canadian prairies in the 1930s—how well those can be named the Depression years. AY had firsthand experience of that grim situation when he stayed for a time in its midst, stopping over to visit the family of his cousin Jackson Hayward on his way back from sketching sojourns further west. Over the years this first cousin on AY's paternal side was bank manager in various small towns in all three prairie provinces (Coronation, Alberta; Wolseley, Saskatchewan; and Pilot Mound, Manitoba). Cousin Jackson gave AY an unforgettable description of how hard it was to be the so-called "manager" of a bank in those grim days. The local farmers, destitute and desperate, could not help blaming and hating the banker who was obliged to refuse so many requests for loans.

This drawing shows a drought-stricken farm in Alberta, but it could be anywhere out there in the mid 1930s. Its twin in photographic form in *Remember Yesterday*, showing a farm near Cadillac, Saskatchewan, "could be anywhere in southern Alberta, Saskatchewan, or Manitoba. The lush wheatfields, parched by lack of rain, have become a Sahara, given over to grasshopper and Russian thistle, plagued by hailstone and rust. More than half the families are on relief; most municipal councils are bankrupt and even the reeves and council members are on the dole. The topsoil, blowing with the wind, has become a black blizzard in the sky so that even those who can afford to are afraid to sink a plough into the land for fear it will all drift away."

The National Gallery of Canada has the oil sketch of this drawing; AY cannot recall doing a canvas. He remembers clearly driving a hundred miles or so through the terrible drought. "Everything was dead; the only thing growing was Russian thistle. There were drifts of dust a foot deep. The government kept people on the farms at a bare subsistence level. If they left, they could not get relief."

PLATE 66

Drought, Alberta [mid-1930s]

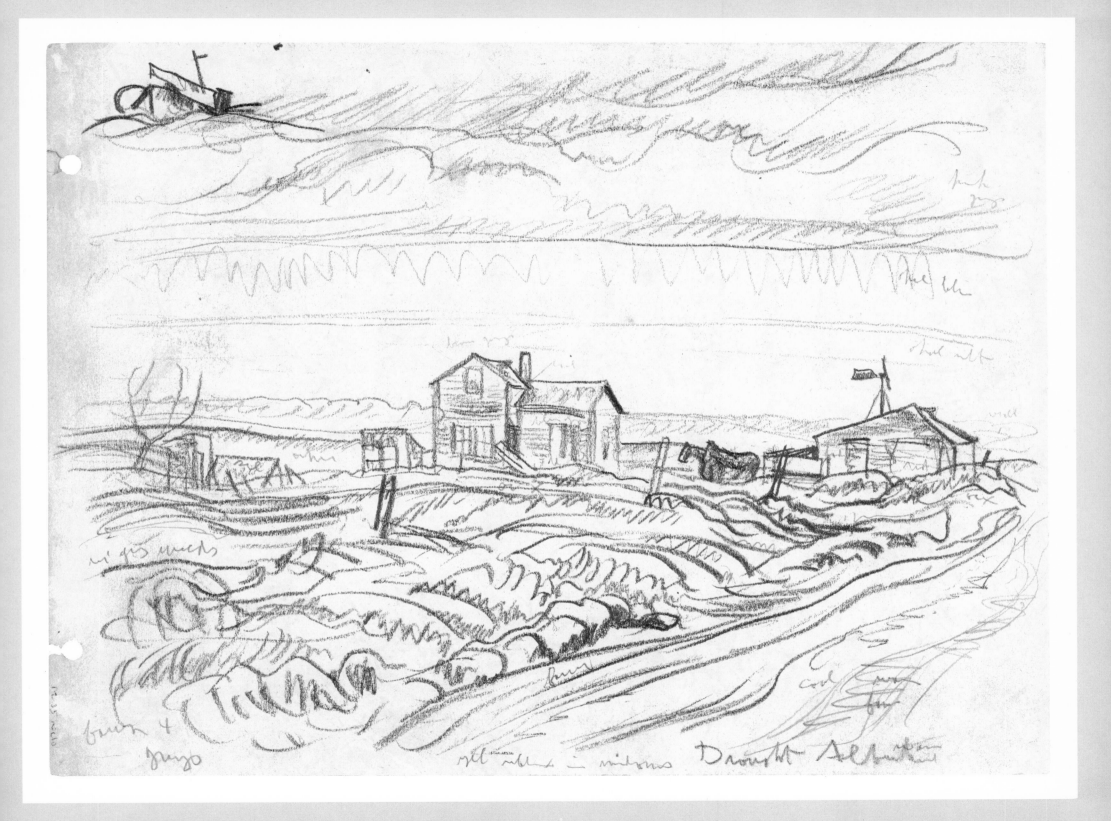

Drought Alberta

The enticing name of Rosebud, a spot north-east of Calgary on the railway towards Drumheller, appealed to AY and Dr. Banting away back in 1928, as they were heading north towards Great Slave Lake. But it was not until 1944, three years after the great doctor's tragic death, that AY actually visited that district to work. He tells most amusingly in his life story how he and the artist H. G. Glyde of Edmonton became fed up with the tangle of RCAF red tape surrounding their prospective work mission along the Alaska Highway, so AY said "To hell with them, let's go to Rosebud"—which they did!

This drawing presumably belongs to the fortnight the two artists spent around Rosebud, in September 1944. AY has one vivid memory of being driven along the unpaved highway which was deep with mud, called "gumbo" out there. "The car wheels had chains on but after a while we got stuck in the mud and realized that one chain must have come off. So Glyde stayed with the stuck car in case someone came along to help get it started, while I put on my rubber boots and followed the uneven track back almost two miles before I found that chain. I had to really pry it up out of that gumbo."

However, mention the name of Rosebud to any westerner and he won't be reminded of anything as gentle as flowers or even mud. He will immediately reply, "That's where Dick Cosgrave has his farm—didn't you know that?"

Dick Cosgrave is a grand western folk-hero connected with the Calgary Stampede since the early days of this century, world champion of the chuckwagon races and popular infield or arena director for many years. One western paper described him affectionately, and with characteristic western modesty in July 1960 as ". . . a big weather-worn man. . . . His voice is hoarse, his white hair sticks out in several directions. He holds a telephone between the thumb and two fingers of a hand big enough to swat down a Brahma bull. He rolls cigarettes as thick as cigars and tucks them in the corner of his mouth. . . . His decisions mould the success of the bronc-riding, steer-roping, wild cow milking, and chuckwagon racing that make the Calgary Stampede the greatest outdoor show on earth."

Richard Robert Cosgrave was born at the Blackfoot Indian Reserve south-east of Calgary in 1905 when his father, who hailed from Ireland, was farming instructor in charge of stock on the reserve. His maternal grandfather sat on the trial of Louis Riel. By 1923 Dick was a bronc rider, taking part in bareback and saddle events, steer wrestling and chuckwagon racing—that western specialty where teams of four horses with two outriders per team pull a covered wagon at breakneck speed over a tricky course, usually resulting in mammoth pile-ups with rearing steeds and

flying wagon wheels. . . . Dick Cosgrave's record feat was being winner of the chuckwagon race for a total of ten years. Here is the story of how chuckwagon racing started in Calgary, "by accident," in Dick's own words: "It was in 1919. There were two wagons lined up on the track and cowboys were dishing food from these. It was Pat Burns' birthday.

"After the cowboys finished dishing out the food, someone must have said something about racing to hitch up the teams. Anyway, they raced the hitching operations and then jumped in their wagons and started down the track. There were four roans owned by Cross and four greys owned by George Lane. The crowd got a great thrill out of it, and then one of the big roans piled up. That, I guess, was the birth of chuckwagon racing."

One of Dick's greatest wins was during the 1940s, when with only two weeks to go before the Stampede his barn at Rosebud burned and he lost all but one horse of his chuckwagon team. Some of his many friends who had already entered teams made up a chuckwagon team for Dick out of their spare horses. "I had Old Archie left out of the fire and that was all. I forget all the good fellows that gave me the horses, but I do remember some of the horses' names. There was Black Beauty, Blonde Burro. . . . They were good horses." So with four unmatched leftovers, whose names he remembers though he forgets who their owners were, the farmer from Rosebud was champion once more. This speaks well for the nourishing soil of that back-of-beyond countryside, which AY shows in the present dynamic drawing. Here are its typical long-rolling curves, its conglomerate of sheds, and the big haystack eaten away around the base by the livestock in winter, a scene appreciated by J. E. H. MacDonald in one of his *West by East* poems:

And cattle shove
To feed beneath the straw-stack's hollowed cove.

In the fall of 1944, when AY returned to Toronto with his rich visual harvest, including the season's drawings which were to be tucked away and forgotten for nearly two decades, Pearl McCarthy wrote these words which serve admirably to conclude our present theme: "Jackson picked himself about the most difficult material for artistic composition. He was in a country with a magnanimous sweep of undulating vista. To trap pieces of that on a unified canvas, without losing the dignity of its slow-moving rhythm, is a problem to be tackled only by a leading landscapist. The sketches have less drama, on the whole, than some former collections, but they have that high value which comes from Jackson's combination of human intellect and material reality, of mind and mud."

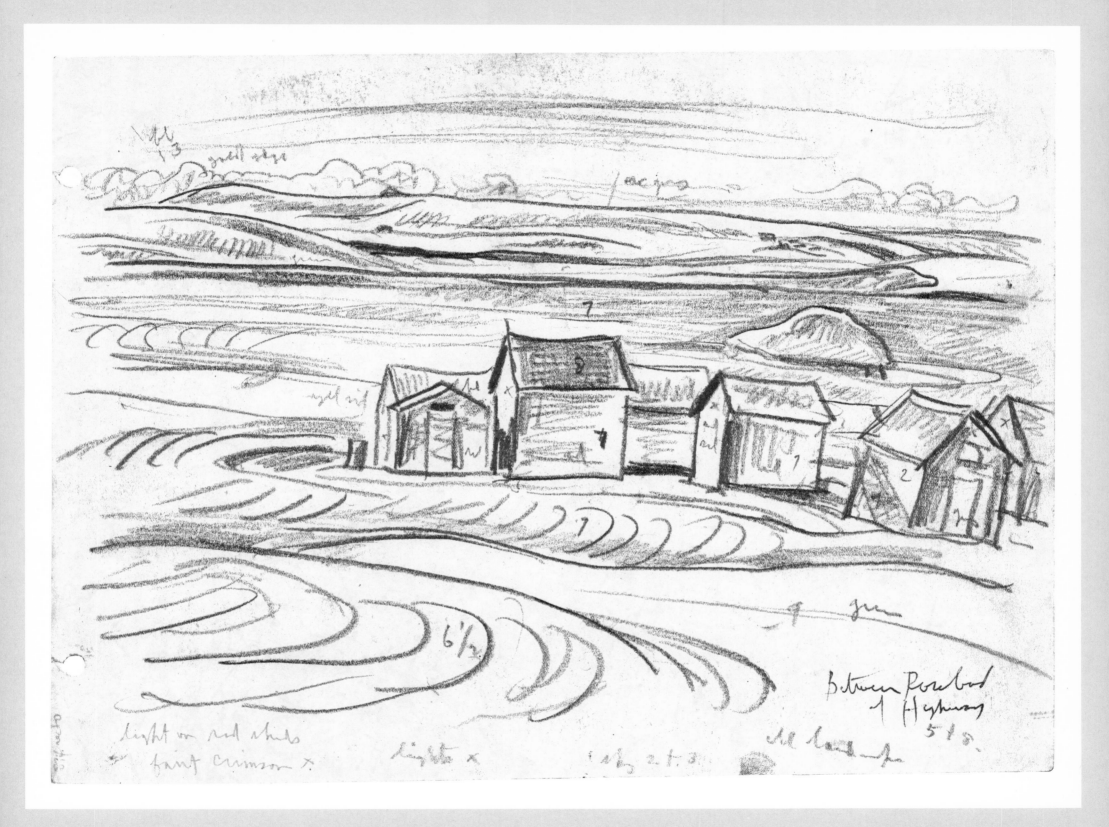

PLATE 67

Farm between Rosebud and (old) Highway 518 [c. September 22, 1944]

No wonder AY has enjoyed working around places with nice western names like Oldman River, Enchant, and Carmangay, or maybe even Pincher Creek! We have seen him pick Rosebud, and in due course he will visit Usk, inevitably calling one of his sketches *Usk at Dusk*.

The present drawing of the dynamic swinging curves of the Oldman River has another drawing on its reverse side dated September 1944, so presumably both sides belong to that rich period of AY's visits around the western countryside, after his summer school teaching at Banff.

The Oldman flows past Lethbridge in a great sweep, strengthened by the waters of many mountain streams from north, west and south of it— Willow Creek; Waterton and Castle Rivers; the Belly and the St. Mary that form the west and east boundaries of the Blood Indian Reserve south-west of Lethbridge—all favourite sketching grounds for AY. Most of these streams in the course of their journey down from the Rockies have cut their way through the rolling plains to such a depth that they can be called "hidden rivers," owing to the deep clefts or gulleys in which they lie concealed below the level of the surrounding plain. Donald Buchanan, who knew that country well, tells about the Oldman River: "The name of the river, like that of its tributary, the Belly, was a literal translation of the original Indian nomenclature. The Old Man could become almost a torrent in the spring, and so deep was the depression it had made in soil and soft rocks of the plains that it had left great cut-banks which often dropped sheer to the water. In other places the more sloping sides were indented with lateral ravines running far back into the open prairie. These were called *coulées*, the word being a relic of the earliest days when the buffalo hunters were French-speaking Métis." It was into such coulées, pronounced *coolies* out there, that part of a herd would be deflected and trapped. (Ralph Connor makes use of the device in *The Patrol of the Sun Dance Trail* for the horse-thieving activities of his hero's enemies.)

There is a fine panoramic photograph of the Oldman River among the numerous clippings that AY hoards in his studio as records of scenes and events of interest both for subject matter and for composition. (Some aeroplane crashes look like Abstract Expressionism, according to him.) The Oldman River picture was taken by the Lethbridge *Herald's* excellent photographer Orville Brunelle. AY's brother Ernest noted above the clipping: "Believe this is near the spot I showed you when here."

The present drawing actually bears considerable resemblance to the photograph, with of course the highly significant difference which exists between a photograph, no matter how good, and a drawing, provided it *is* good. Basically, the drawing eliminates the unnecessary and emphasizes the essential. In this instance, AY obviously finds the mighty curves of the Oldman most important, so he develops them in depth by rich powerful dark main lines supported by strong shadows blacked in with quick hatched strokes. The photograph by Brunelle, in contrast, shows airy light and shadow drifting across the vast, flattened-out landscape and delicately etching the ragged banks of the main gulley and its coulées. AY's concept is much more intense, by comparison, more concentrated, and—here come those inevitable words—more rhythmic and dynamic. AY sees his subject with a creative eye; so does Brunelle, but with a camera's eye.

On this subject of rhythmic design, which haunts all analyses of Group of Seven work, some of the most perspicacious remarks were made very early in the game by the late F. B. Housser in *A Canadian Art Movement*, published in 1926: " . . . allied to structure is the emphasis on rhythm. MacDonald can make a canvas rock with it, as in his *Wild River* and Lismer sports with it in *September Gale*. Jackson makes it the basis of his most intimate sketches. In Harris' work it is restrained but omnipresent. . . .

"Roger Fry the English art critic in an essay on the artist's vision [*Vision and Design*] refers in an illuminating way to rhythm: 'Almost any turn of the kaleidoscope of nature may set up in the artist this detached and unimpassioned vision. The (esthetically) chaotic and accidental conjunction of forms and colours begins to crystalize and as this harmony becomes clear to the artist his actual vision becomes distorted by the emphasis of the rhythm which has been set up within him. Certain relations of [or] directions of line become for him full of meaning. He apprehends them no longer casually, nor merely curiously, but passionately; and these lines begin to be so stressed and to stand out so clearly from the rest that he sees them far more distinctly than he did at first. In such a creative vision the objects as such tend to disappear, to lose their separate unities and to take their . . . places as so many bits of the whole mosaic of vision.' "

Sic Roger Fry *via* F. B. Housser, away back in 1926, but already with a rather abstract expressionist tone to his statement. This is definitely applicable to AY's habit of making a drawing to supplement the rapid colour sketch in which he has caught the first impression of the play of light. In the supplementary drawing the vision does indeed become more "passionate" in its rhythmic beat and stress. Sometimes one feels that the meaningfully accentuated drawing in its plain black and white garb may transmit the most dynamic rhythm and the purest passion of all the media at the artist's command.

PLATE 68

The Oldman River, Alberta [*c. September 1944*]

Harlands' ranch, Bar X, lies south of Pincher in the south-west corner of Alberta, down towards Montana. AY has stayed there many times. "The foothills of Alberta, with the mountains as a background, afford the artist endless material," he writes in his autobiography. Some years earlier he even said—at least he was *reported* as saying in the Lethbridge *Herald* (so there might be a slight bias!)—that "there is no better sketching ground in Canada than your Southern Alberta foothills!"

Now that was said on August 30, 1946, a fortnight or so before this drawing was done, when AY was happy to be "out of school" and able to spend a few weeks watching the western autumn come in. There is no use double-checking through past pages and reminding ourselves vexedly that he was also "never happier than sketching down on the South Shore of the St. Lawrence" or "up in the Barren Lands" because this is neither forgetfulness nor fickleness on AY's part, nor even a sweetheart in every port; it is simply the result of the artist's expansive love for the part of Canada that occupies the centre of his attention at the given moment.

A Painter's Country gives an affectionate description of the Harlands and their ranch with its bumper crops of hay and its wild flowers, its wonderful grazing land across which it is possible to ride anywhere by jeep. Behind the ranch rises the dramatic range of mountains of AY's drawing. And recently, as he tells us further in *A Painter's Country*, "on a ridge just east of Harland's, drillers put down a well twelve thousand feet and tapped a field of eighty million cubic feet of gas a day."

Nature can be very bountiful as well as very beautiful, but sometimes she hands out too much too suddenly. A couple of years ago an overload of snow and ice followed by a too rapid thaw caused a disastrous flood along Pincher Creek, ruining the Harlands' fine collection of books, pictures and other treasures. Such damage takes long to repair, although the elder Harlands take time to travel while the younger generation sees to the calving and other regular business of the ranch. But the welcome mat is always out for AY. "A Chinook in Winter, Calves in Spring, Always Welcome," is an old ranch saying out there. To which "AY Is Welcome Whenever He Turns Up" should be added.

Since this is our last midwestern or east-of-the-Rockies drawing, it seems a good point to recall what immense changes have taken place out there (and Alberta stands for the whole region) in the span of AY's working life. In September 1929, that fateful period that ushered in the Depression and, for the prairies, the Drought (also depicted by AY), there was a special supplement written for *The McGill News* by the editor of a western town weekly, Archibald Key. He called it "Culture in the 'Wild and Woolly' from an Albertan's Point of View." In part it reads:

"A spiritual vision peculiar to the west is undoubtedly materialising, but at present it is in nebulous form and practically indefinable. It is, however, manifesting itself in political life and in the arts as well as in educational circles where it is possible to interpret a certain cultural consciousness despite the apparently hopeless condition of the average educational mill in the cities, towns and rural districts.

" . . . the prosperity of the Province is dependent on the prosperity of the agriculturalist . . . in the public schools the study of weeds is considered of more importance than music, while to the laymen the major energies in the Provincial University appear to be directed toward grain and livestock. . . . The Calgary group of painters [unfortunately not named] . . . are interested in interpreting the mood of the west, but . . . their isolation has retarded their expression. . . . The official critics of the Stampede Committee, while accepting the R.C.A. show with its Group of Seven influence, succeeded in ousting the young men of the west who are refusing to conform to conventional expression."

That was in 1929. What changes have followed in the next third of a century, both for the "young men of the west" and for AY's progress in his chosen field! As our eye travels across the beautiful rippling foreground of AY's drawing (with all that natural gas away down below it!) towards the rising challenge of the mountains, we seem to follow the thin trail traced westward and upward. There is somehow a sense of mission here, of devotion, of single purpose, of solitude and of realization. On the back of one (njg 616) of AY's drawings of hills (not these, but from approximately the period when he discovered affinities in the western foothills) he has written down part of a poem by D. H. Lawrence:

> God, that I have no choice!
> That my own fulfilment is up against me,
> Timelessly!
> The Burden of self-accomplishment!
> The Charge of fulfilment!

And now we head for those hills. . . .

PLATE 69

Looking west from Harlands' ranch
[c. September 18, 1946]

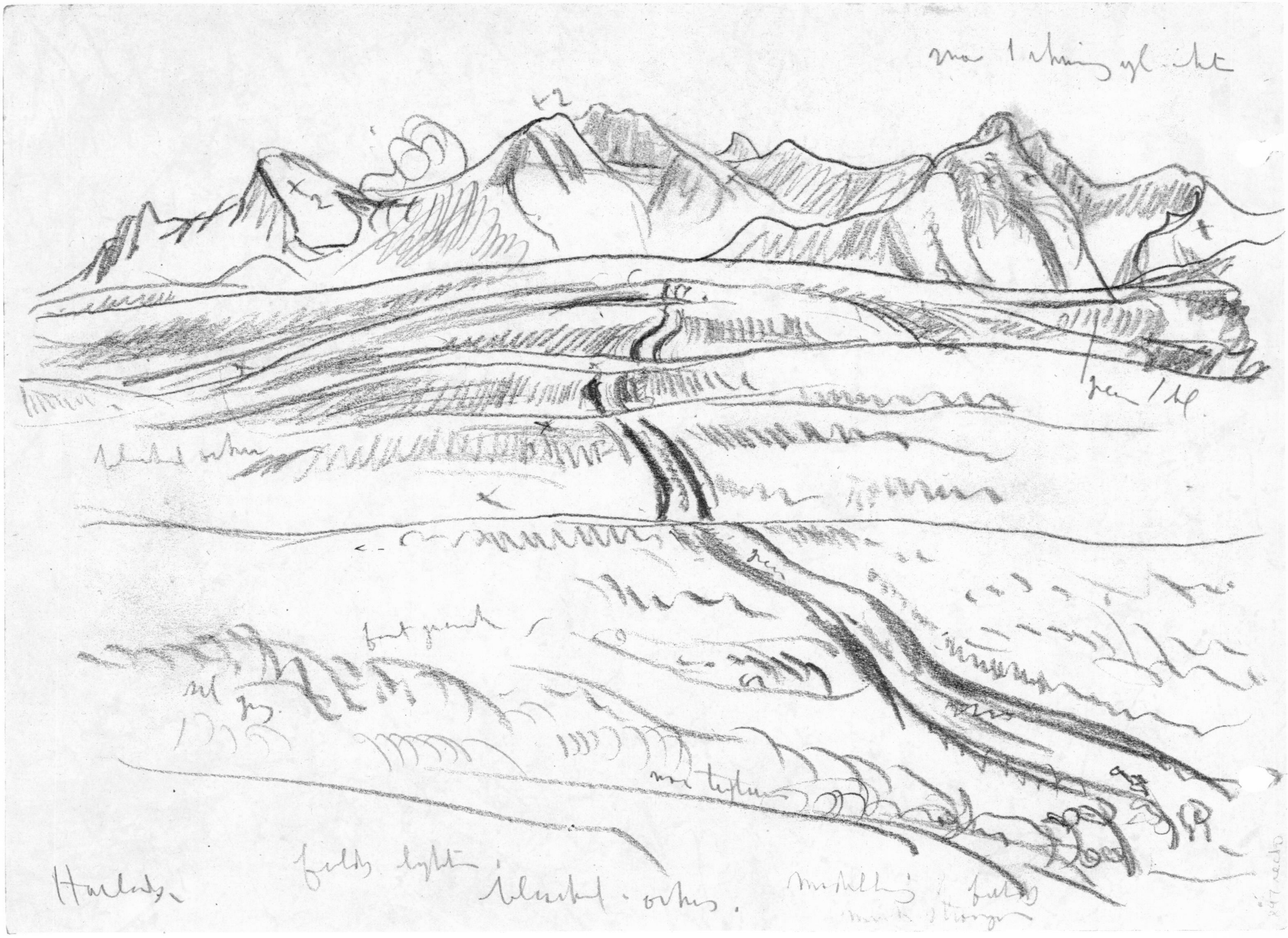

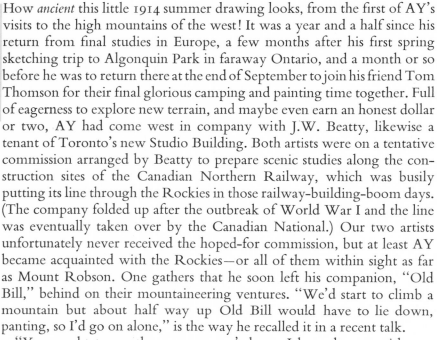

How *ancient* this little 1914 summer drawing looks, from the first of AY's visits to the high mountains of the west! It was a year and a half since his return from final studies in Europe, a few months after his first spring sketching trip to Algonquin Park in faraway Ontario, and a month or so before he was to return there at the end of September to join his friend Tom Thomson for their final glorious camping and painting time together. Full of eagerness to explore new terrain, and maybe even earn an honest dollar or two, AY had come west in company with J.W. Beatty, likewise a tenant of Toronto's new Studio Building. Both artists were on a tentative commission arranged by Beatty to prepare scenic studies along the construction sites of the Canadian Northern Railway, which was busily putting its line through the Rockies in those railway-building-boom days. (The company folded up after the outbreak of World War I and the line was eventually taken over by the Canadian National.) Our two artists unfortunately never received the hoped-for commission, but at least AY became acquainted with the Rockies—or all of them within sight as far as Mount Robson. One gathers that he soon left his companion, "Old Bill," behind on their mountaineering ventures. "We'd start to climb a mountain but about half way up Old Bill would have to lie down, panting, so I'd go on alone," is the way he recalled it in a recent talk.

"You ought to see those prospector's boots I brought out with me, worn all to bits. I've been climbing eight and nine thousand feet to sketch, and using them for a pillow at night," he wrote on a one-cent postcard headed "Lucerne, B.C., August 27th, 1914" and addressed to his helpful friend Dr. James MacCallum in Toronto, adding: "I am packing up now, expect to spend a few days on the prairies and then will go through to Port Arthur and take steamer to Port Colborne.... I have a whole raft of sketches, many of them up to the standard, but the country is less paintable than northern Ontario" (at that stage meaning Algonquin Park).

Judging by the full-brushed, richly gleaming mountain and cloud effects of the one or two oil sketches known to remain of that "whole raft," it is a pity that AY later "kept throwing the sketches into the furnace until there were none left." Only the ones already given away were saved. The only canvas that he can recall painting from that 1914 visit was titled *Mount Robson by Moonlight*, 40 by 50 inches. "It hung in the Arts and Letters Club in Toronto all the time I was away at the war," says AY, whose memory for the subject, size and fate of most of his works on canvas remains admirably keen. "Nobody seemed to like it much, so when I came back to Toronto in 1919 I had it returned to the studio, and later I painted something else on top—I think it was *October, Algoma*. That's in Hart House now, so I guess they've got two pictures in one. Mount

Robson, Canada's biggest mountain, all invisible! We ought to X-ray it some time."

As for drawings from the 1914 summer trip, AY has recently had to be restrained from subjecting the handful that remains to the fate of the all too flammable oil sketches—"Don't, AY, they're *historic!*"—One undated pen-and-ink drawing from that same year, *Vista from Yellowhead*, is in the National Gallery of Canada.

The present example in pencil is typical of AY's painstaking studies of the famous terrain around Yellowhead. He makes the beginner's typical mistake of paying so much attention to the illustrious "tops" that the middle and foreground suffer in comparison, as the Fraser River does here, scarcely visible as a weak strip across the bottom of the page. Adding to this the fact that the project of that moment involved future large canvases for railway hotel lobbies, where each mountain had to be recognizable to everybody, we can imagine how easily the end result might have been the type of "big bad mountain scenes" later decried by AY. His friend J. E. H. MacDonald was to grapple with the same problem of top-heavy composition during seven summer sojourns in the Rockies in the 1920s. He eventually conquered it by emphasizing the density of foreground and treating mountain crests as backdrops—a lesson hard to learn out there.

The reverse of this drawing bears AY's title *Seven Sisters*. That well-known range, however, is officially located east of the Skeena River and far from Yellowhead Pass. When this fact was brought to AY's attention recently, he merely murmured, "Oh well, this must be another family!" Then he seemed to delve deep into memories over half a century old, and came up with the cryptic remark: "I may have been thinking of the Seven Sutherland Sisters—they all had long hair." It seems that the famous demoiselles Sutherland used to sit on rocking chairs in shop windows (around 1900) and let their wavy locks billow over the floor, all to advertise an obviously efficacious hair tonic. (Maybe seven Yellowheads?!)

Back in 1914 the Group of Seven was not yet born, as a group, or at most was still very embryonic. There is a delightful parody written by the coming Group's poet, J. E. H. MacDonald, taken from Wordsworth's sentimental "We Are Seven."

> ... We are the leaven;
> We throw our pearls away; we stray
> In wilder regions every day.
> We want no dull or frigid gray
> Of old conventions in our way;
> We see the beckoning future ray:
> We are the Group of Seven.

148

PLATE 70

*Mountains, referred to by A.Y. as "Seven Sisters," and the Fraser River,
at the Yellowhead Pass, British Columbia, 1914*

The rarity of drawings from AY's next visit to the Rockies enhances the importance of extant examples. By 1924 his travelling companion was the energetic and creative Lawren Harris; indeed that single year saw no less that three Harris-Jackson trips together: to Algoma in the spring, to Jasper in the summer, and to Lake Superior in the fall. How the paint and the talk must have flown!

Details of the artist friends' summer expedition, recounted in letters from AY to their friend Fred Housser in Toronto, were published long ago in the latter's book, *A Canadian Art Movement.* The pair had a guide and four packhorses on their first trip of twenty-five miles, AY personally being better at walking than riding! Their two main objectives lay south of Jasper. The first was south-east to beautiful sombre Maligne Lake, down which they paddled some fifteen miles into a region of "great crumbling mountains like the ruins of a gigantic Nineveh." Later on that same jaunt they proceeded farther east of Maligne to the Colin Range—"a kind of cubists' paradise full of geometric formations, all waiting for the abstract painter."

We can see how well this terrain would suit the emerging trends in Lawren Harris' work and thought patterns. A drawing by AY of the Colin Range likewise shows considerable simplification and formal precision—a far cry from the Yellowhead days of a decade earlier! AY says that this drawing is the subject that he worked up into a canvas 36 by 46 inches, keeping the colours pale and the planes clearcut and geometric. "It developed into a good piece of painting, almost abstract, but nobody liked it in those days, so after it had sat around my studio for quite a while, taking up space, I destroyed it . . . Too bad—it would have been considered pretty good later on—an AY abstract!"

The second region visited by the Jackson-Harris team in 1924 lay west of the Athabasca River, in the valley of the Tonquin—"a journey of nearly twenty miles through the MacCarib Pass." Here the Continental Divide is established by the mighty Ramparts along the boundary of Alberta and British Columbia. On the careful drawing titled simply "Tonquin," AY has pencilled in lightly some of the picturesque names of individual peaks: Bastion, Redoubt, Dungeon, with Moat Lake at their base. This and another study of the rugged Ramparts under different light possibly formed part of the grandiose Harris-Jackson plan to collaborate on a set of large, strong, non-photographic, panoramic murals for the Canadian National Railway, a project which the latter favoured highly but finally never commissioned. A minor outcome of the studies was a travel brochure to which Jackson contributed six colour drawings, Harris

two, while J. E. H. MacDonald and Casson did pen-and-ink drawings—a good combination of talents.

One or two of AY's drawings indicate that he conceived of his composition as a poster design, writing in one place, for instance: "Poster scheme—pale blue, dark blue, warm buff." The flat-planed, abstract, posterlike quality is apparent in the style of several members of the Seven in the mid-1920s. Four of them were in the West that summer of 1924. Varley did little work at the time but eventually achieved wonderful misty and mystic mountain effects. MacDonald was in the Lake O'Hara district for the first time. "For Jim art was constantly full of experiments," said AY recently, "while for Lawren art was constantly a mission."

Harris was certainly in his element among those high places and altitudes of aspiration. The experience sustained him for several years and brought forth some really noble works, such as the canvases *Maligne Lake*, 1925, and *Mountain Forms*, 1927. Harris' oil sketches from the Rockies continue to impress us today with their handsome austerity. Like AY, Harris at that time did most of his drawings *after* he had made the sketch in oils, but unlike AY's, these drawings represented for Harris a *more abstract* stage of the subject and acquired symbolical content as a "vision of high things," in the words of his 1928 essay. Harris would then achieve the final stage of abstraction in his canvases, which were distilled out of elements in the drawings, hence tended to bear only a distant relationship to the oil sketch made on location. For AY—by and large—the drawings intensify the concrete presence of his subject; the canvases may simplify, but certainly retain, that natural presence.

AY obviously felt less at home in the sharp-peaked young Rockies with their upthrust, upstart ways ("and too many fuzzy trees around the base") than he did in the long-rolling rhythms of his beloved old Laurentians.

One senses a certain subjective disgruntlement in the two or three short essays which AY later wrote for *The Canadian Forum* and the Toronto *News* on the subject of mountains. One starts off: "Why is it that mountains which are so impressive in nature should be so unimpressive in a painting? . . . Few artists have enhanced their reputations by painting mountains and it would seem that the greater the mountain the more insignificant the artist who paints it becomes." Then, no doubt realizing that the work of his friends Harris and MacDonald did not in the least fit into this negative category, AY achieves a more objective conclusion: "Copying mountains literally has been done to death. As inspiring motives for the creative artist they are a source of unlimited wealth of design, rhythm, form and colour. The kodachrome boys can take care of the rest."

PLATE 71

Ramparts in the Tonquin [1924]

AY's third journey to the West was with an interesting team—Marius Barbeau and Edwin Holgate. The region was the Skeena River far up the north-west coast of British Columbia—the glorious, turbulent Skeena, celebrated for its Indian villages of the great old days. Along the Skeena's upper reaches lay the half-dozen tribal villages of the Gitksan, one of the three sub-nations of the Tsimsian Indians. Back in 1910 our notable anthropologist Marius Barbeau wrote his thesis at the Sorbonne on "Social organisation and 'totemism' among the Northwest Coast Indians of British Columbia." During the 1920s he had no fewer than seven sojourns among the West Coast Indians, the Gitskan being his special love—"his" tribe. In 1929 he published his first monograph on the totem poles, devoted to those of the Upper Skeena.

In the summer of 1926 AY and Edwin Holgate of Montreal, who eventually became the ninth member of the elastic Group of Seven, worked together for about a month and a half out west, during which time, Holgate recalls, they "cruised back and forth freely." AY stayed on for another month in the region. The main scene for the artists' activity was on the Upper Skeena among the Gitksan villages: from Kitwanga which lies about 150 miles inland, east to Gitsegyukla (Skeena Crossing), and north, up-river to Hazelton (formerly Kitenmaks) and Kispiox, as well as east of Hazelton a few miles to Hagwelget, a Carrier Indian village. AY did not reach Qaldo or Kiskagas to the north, both almost deserted by the 1920s, nor—most unfortunately—the fabulous but hostile Kitwinkul, which lies some fifteen to twenty miles north of Kitwanga on the old Grease Trail to the Nass River. The only white artist who ever managed to be accepted in Kitwinkul was Emily Carr, and her experiences there were harrowing enough, as we may read in the chapter "Kitwancool" of her book *Klee Wyck.*

Emily discovered the Upper Skeena between 1907 and 1909, soon after she had begun her ambitious project to depict all of the Indian totem poles in their native settings. Some of her Skeena studies were painted into canvases in 1912. It was thanks to an Indian from that district, William Beynon, assistant and interpreter for Dr. Barbeau, that the latter heard about Emily Carr's work and was instrumental in having it shown in eastern Canada in the fall of 1927. This led to Emily meeting the Seven and being encouraged to take up her painting again. By the summer of 1928 she returned to the Skeena to paint, this time achieving the great power of her maturity.

It was a marvelously rich territory likewise for Barbeau and his artist team in 1926. Holgate did elegantly disciplined portrait studies of Indians and a few fine solid landscapes with totem poles, which AY feels may well have influenced Emily's later style. AY's own work from the Skeena consisted of many delectable oil sketches on birch panels in the then-usual 8½ by 10½ inches; only *three* canvases later; one or two brilliant, very detailed watercolours for use as illustrations; and a rich crop of drawings. Several of the latter were reworked in pen and ink as illuminated initials for Barbeau's handsome book, *The Downfall of Temlaham,* now a collector's rarity, to which Edwin Holgate, Langdon Kihn, Anne Savage and Emily Carr also contributed illustrations.

All these recording visitors to the Skeena in the 1920s sensed its greatness and the threat of time's ravaging hand, and pleaded for its preservation in one form or another. AY contributed an article for *Maclean's Magazine,* illustrated by a pen drawing beautifully integrated into the text. Filled with insight gained from his sojourn there with Marius Barbeau, he wrote optimistically that there should be ". . . no great difficulty to overcome in making the Skeena country a centre for the study of the west coast Indian. . . . It is quite the most accessible country in America for such study. Here is a country rich in what most of Canada is lacking, a background. It has a history of invasion and conquest, adventures, myths and legends old enough for history and legend to become one. The whole setting is dramatic; its sharp peaks, its rushing rivers, its gorges. . . . Along with all this there is an imaginative side of life that delighted in dance and ritual, in painting, weaving and carving or other forms of art of which the totem pole was the last to develop."

The bright peaks of Mount Gitsegyukla rise south of the Skeena near the Crossing. Nowadays, by some sad transmutation, this 9,000-foot massif apparently bears the name of an Irish King, one Brian Boru. But it still gleams white in the dawn, or bulks up black as a panther against the setting sun, making a dramatic backdrop for the pageant of events along the Skeena.

In the drawing reproduced here, the grandiose theme of clear-cut peak behind wide-rolling middle ground with a hint of the village in the foreground left, the energetic sense of form, the cosmic mood—all recall once again the old "Flemish-eye Bruegel" panoramas referred to away back at the beginning of our book. Actually, though distant in space, we are close to them in time, for it will be the following summer, 1927, and again in 1930, that AY will bestride the heights of Baffin's Pangnirtung Fiord. This is the style and the mood of the mid-1920s for our artist. It is a time for the intense rendering of actualities. While Lawren Harris proceeded onward and upward towards his austere abstractions, AY reaffirmed his native realism, and nowhere more rewardingly than here along the Skeena River.

PLATE 72

Mount Gitsegyukla on the Upper Skeena River, B.C., October 1926

On the coastal region of British Columbia's Skeena River, where the annual rainfall is the highest in Canada, things are bound to be moist and green. The river seems to ooze straight from the low-lying clouds and the people say: "The mountains open to let the water out and to let the salmon in."

For how many ages have the salmon travelled up the Skeena to spawn? The icy grey-green water of the estuary stays salty for forty miles or so upstream. Here to this day the fishing from mid-July to the end of September is "absolutely dazzling," according to the fine notes in Peter Varley's *Canada*. In 1959, we are told, the biggest *tyee* or king-salmon on record (and the tyee is the largest and finest of the Pacific salmon) was taken on a rod—a ninety-two-pounder. Farther upstream lies the domain of the coho salmon. In spring and early summer the various tribes of these noble great creatures fight their way up the river, through two miles of canyon at Kitsalas where the turbulence is "one big boil," then onward for nearly two hundred miles, to reproduce and thereupon to die—one of nature's most incredible extravagances.

No wonder the Indians followed the salmon up the Skeena. The river, rich in food, was bordered by glorious tall red cedars that could be hollowed out into canoes so large that one tree-trunk could carry fifty people with gear, or could be split into building boards forty feet long and two feet wide for their entire length. No wonder the North-west Coast could once support an Indian population of up to fifty thousand well-established, wealthy, and wonderfully artistic people, the complex and cultured People of the Potlatch.

No wonder either, of course, that when other people arrived they also wanted to go up and down the Skeena: explorers, trappers, fishermen, missionaries, gold-mad miners, lumbermen, reckless captains and crews in wood-burning sternwheelers, railroad gangs, highway construction gangs, and finally gangs of tourists. By the early 1870s the Hudson's Bay Company had set up its trading post at Hazelton, and towards the end of the century the Skeena suddenly became one way to get to the gold in the Cassiar and the Yukon. By 1900 white infiltration and settlement in the Upper Skeena valley had upset the old balance of redman and nature.

On the south shore, near the mouth of the Skeena, the Tsimsian village of Spukchu (which sounded like Spokeshoot on a recent good CBC radio programme) became in due course a mission village, with a neat white wooden church, a Hudson's Bay Company post, and the English name of Port Essington. The main activity centred around the salmon cannery. During the fishing season the Skeena Indians used to be fetched downstream from as far away as Kispiox, some two hundred miles. Port Essington's heyday was around 1900, when it swarmed with people coming and going. Saloons flourished alongside the church; the high wooden sidewalks were slick-slippery after a week's continual rain—who knew in which direction you would fall! Nowadays, with both the railway and the motor road on the opposite shore, one searches in vain for even the name of Port Essington on the map.

AY came down the Skeena in 1926 by train, alas not by boat, but he did make a pencil study of an old dry-docked sternwheeler, as well as a number of exquisite little drawings of the river with its spectacular mountain shores and its islets plumed with cottonwood trees. He drew the high-legged piers and the swarms of fishing craft, the neat white church (since burned) and the small homes of the Indians surrounded by lacy foliage. Several studies of one peak-roofed house eventually became the canvas *Indian Home*, a mysterious, melancholy, green-toned work that AY still considers one of his best.

But lush green foliage is not the treat for AY that it was for Emily Carr, who would sit painting it until the rain ran down her neck and out her sleeves into her sketch-box, more or less. It is a great pity that Emily's most quoted remark concerning AY-and-the-West is the negative one from her autobiography written late in life, where she is madly monopolistic about "her" West Coast and "her" Indians, and very much the heroine solo versus all odds. (For instance, there are pages about how everybody made fun of her first exhibition out west, in 1913 or so, but not one word about Dr. Newcombe buying eight or more of her works at that time.) Of AY she wrote: "I always felt that A.Y.J. resented our West. . . . 'Too bad, that West of yours is so overgrown, lush—unpaintable,' he said, 'too bad!'"

It is therefore a good thing that we now have access to Emily Carr's immediate and spontaneous reaction to AY and his Skeena River works on the very day (November 14, 1927) on which she paid her first visit to the Studio Building in Toronto. The same evening she wrote in her journal: "I loved his things, particularly some snow things of Quebec and three canvases up Skeena River. I felt a little as if beaten at my own game. His Indian pictures have something mine lack—rhythm, poetry. . . . Next time I paint Indians I'm going off on a tangent tear. . . ." And the following day, after meeting Arthur Lismer, whom Emily found even "more poetical" than AY, she appraised the latter, her junior by eleven years, very interestingly: " . . . Mr. Jackson is steady and strong. His feet are planted firmly and he has the grit to push and struggle and square his shoulders and stand by others and by his convictions. He is still young in years but old. Probably the war did that."

PLATE 73

Indian home, Port Essington, B.C. [*1926*]

By the time of AY's visit in 1926, the site of the present drawing from the Upper Skeena was reached by "meek trains" that "slithered travellers through the forests to Hazelton," to borrow Emily Carr's vivid imagery in the absorbing essay "Eagles of Skeena River." Before that, long before, in the days before the white man had come, people travelling upstream "wrestled like salmon" against the swift-flowing Skeena, in dug-out canoes with high prow and stern, not unlike the one in our drawing. At the time of Emily Carr's earliest visits in the first decade of the present century, the journey was made in the daring little stern-wheelers that burned a cord of wood an hour and stopped about every twenty miles to replenish their fuel stock from woodpiles along the shore, each cord of wood costing $3. Emily tells how the sternwheeler had twenty Indian lads aboard, ready to leap into the icy water to push the vessel off the reefs as she worked her "fussing way" up the Skeena. It took twelve days or more to get up, and two or less to return, anchoring overnight, of course. "When she came to the end of steam navigation at Skeena Crossing, she was met by huge Indian dug-out canoes. Indians took the passengers the rest of the way. The finish of navigation was at Hazelton, which sat where the Skeena and Bulkley rivers meet, boiling into each other's faces like warring tom-cats."

The old canoe here in AY's drawing, a study of details made after the oil sketch (njg 393), is beached on the north shore of the Skeena, the river being merely indicated in the verbal directions "foam sharper gallop design." To the south of the river towers the famous form of Rocher Eboulé, which translates approximately to Rockslide Mountain—or perhaps more accurately Rockslidden Cliff. This French name may stem from some old voyageur's experience near the dangerous cliff, but it also recalls the local legend concerning that slope, in Indian Stekyawden, and its terrifying rockslides.

It seems that the Gitksan had their version of the almost universal myth of the Flood that once submerged the world. For them, the role of our Mount Ararat was taken by mighty Stekyawden, which rose above the receding waters. Against its lower reaches their rafts and canoes in due course came to rest, no doubt wave-battered like the craft in our drawing here. The survivors built their lodges on the shore at a fair site which became their Temlaham, good land of yore, an earthly paradise of peace and plenty. But eventually some of them disobeyed the advice of the sky-command and mistreated the offspring of their fellow creatures the mountain goats which they hunted along Stekyawden's slopes. One day four young strangers appeared, sheathed in robes of white goat fur, their faces painted white with red stripes around nostrils and eyes, and lured the people of Temlaham into the mountains for a great feast, only to hurl them screaming downwards in a fearful rockslide. There was a single "good" survivor to tell the tale, and in due course he adopted the crest of the single-horned Painted Goat for his family, which gradually recovered its prosperity.

Another Gitksan legend tells of the final dispersal of the people of Temlaham after they had again broken the taboos to be observed during the spring catch of salmon. The water spirits in anger caused the seasons to turn backwards so that snow covered the whole valley, and the people, all unprepared, froze and starved to death over their empty food trays. Only a few stragglers managed to dig tunnels down the river "towards sunset" and finally settled on the Segyukla tributary. "The former land of bliss and plenty had ceased to be. It has remained a barren prairie, forever desolate, forever accursed. . . .

"What is Temlaham to-day, what is it to us, who live on reserves conceded by the Ramkseewah, the White Man?

"A legend of the past, a barren stretch, two miles below Hazelton on the Skeena, a place which we still visit at times, when we are sad at heart.

" . . . We survive in a world greatly changed, greatly defaced, in a country that no longer remains its true self, that no longer abounds with game and fish, between mountain slopes repeatedly bleached by forest-fires, in a valley that has passed to other hands. . . . "

Can something of that desolate mood be read into the drawing before us? Or shall we simply look at it with detached objectivity and a sense of satisfaction at the way AY here exemplifies his own precept that a high mountain needs a good foreground with some "life interest" to it. Hence our rockslidden cliff and its battered old canoe.

PLATE 74

Mount Rocher Eboulé near Hazelton, B.C. [1926]

There is only one place in the world where the scene of this drawing—totem poles at home in their own surroundings—could be, and that is far up the West Coast of North America. Today, over forty years after AY's drawing was made, the only place on that same West Coast where such poles still stand in their original surroundings is along this same Upper Skeena River.

By the time AY arrived at this particular village, it contained only a handful of Indians and one white family, the Pratts, with whom our artist stayed for a few days. The place was given the name Skeena Crossing about 1910, when the railroad bridge was built over the river from south to north shore. Its Indian name is Gitsegyukla, variously spelled as Kitseukla, etc. The village as AY saw it dated from after 1871 when fire, reportedly caused by the carelessness of passing miners heading for the Cassiar goldfields, destroyed all the older wooden houses and the few totems that had already been erected. Gitsegyukla rose from its ashes, its lodges straggling along the steep gravelly bank of the river, in front of each lodge the family totem pole or poles. These faced towards the river to welcome kinsmen and to impress all passers-by—true "family trees" and status symbols that demanded not worship but reverence. Between the poles and the river appeared the occasional ornate little grave-house, while the glorious mountains provided a curving backdrop to the whole scene. Our aspect here is from the side-lines, so that houses and poles are in profile. A frontal, more formal view is presented in AY's watercolour made from across the river and reproduced in *The Downfall of Temlaham*.

AY's visit in 1926 fell about midway between the period of greatest prosperity on the Upper Skeena and the present, counting about forty years each way. The site, with its well-drained soil and its climate less destructively moist than in the coastal regions, would be relatively intact at the time of his visit. Marius Barbeau estimated that the cedar totem poles would last in good condition up to sixty years on the Upper Skeena, as against not much more than half that time on the rain-drenched coast.

According to Barbeau, the carving of the tall, free-standing totem poles may well have originated with the Tsimsian Indians of the Nass River just north of the Skeena, to be subsequently adopted by the seafaring Tlingit and Haida who came to the Nass for their *oolakan* fish oil. The first carvers on the Upper Skeena came overland along the Grease Trail from the Upper Nass, probably in the 1860s. Barbeau assigns to non-local, i.e. earliest, carvers some twenty of the just over one hundred poles he recorded during his visits in the district from 1920 onwards. Over thirty local carvers' names were remembered and reported to him.

The free-standing totem pole represents the final stage in the develop-

ment of West Coast Indian carving, which began with ritual masks and indoor house posts roughly hewn into cult figures, progressed to house-front posts with a hole for entrance and exit, and ended with the free-standing poles that could reach a height of fifty feet. As late as the 1920s an old Upper Skeena chief, Kweeyaihl (whose English name was John Brown!), recalled that when he was a boy in the 1850s stone-age tools were still used for carving. The rough work of cutting down the cedar tree was done with a stone axe, and the figures on the pole were outlined in the same way. For the finer part of the carving, sharp bone knives or chisels, made of the leg bones of bear or caribou, were used. The final finishing of the figures was done with the teeth of beaver—"four incisors lashed very tight together side by side onto a handle." With access to trade objects such as metal axes, knives and files, came the boom in the erection of the stately free-standing totems, the older type with a few mask-shapes evolving into the fully carved pole of beautiful fine-grained red cedar.

The erection of a totem pole was an important occasion, and the process was slow and costly, usually requiring no less than four gatherings of the clansmen of a particular phratry—namely on the Upper Skeena the Frog-Raven, the Fireweed, the Wolf, or the Eagle phratry. The pole would be erected to confirm the transfer of family patrimony in a village, usually after the death of a clan head-chief. The successor to his name and rank, a nephew on the maternal side, would often need two years to collect property in preparation for the first gathering, called the "hewing the pole" ceremony. It would cost him the equivalent of up to $800 to have a tall tree cut and hauled to the site. His maternal relatives—scores of them from far and wide—provided the labour and would of course be entertained and fed for days. For the actual carving of the pole before its erection, a relative on the father's side (nephew or brother of the deceased chief) would be professionally commissioned to carve the pole with the owner's crests—often a main family crest on top, to be recognized from a distance, followed by other emblems and symbolic devices inherited through the mother's line, down to the bottom of the pole, where usually some "important event" in the family could be seen and enjoyed at close quarters.

After another two years came the great feast or potlatch for erecting the finished pole. Clansmen from all the neighbouring villages were invited to help haul on the ropes, while the immediate family assisted by chanting with drum and dance—and by footing the bill for food and gifts to all guests: approximately the value of sixty dollars to headchiefs, fifty to lesser chiefs, and so on down the line. Gifts ranged from new canoes and

(continued)

PLATE 75

Skeena Crossing, or Gitsegyukla, B.C. [1926]

blankets, carved utensils and supplies of food, to as little as token strips of cloth. The cost of such a pole-raising could be well over the equivalent of $3,000. Careful count was kept of all gifts and they could be required back in kind by the giver—whence no doubt our usually misunderstood term "Indian giver." The principle of the potlatch was actually a sort of investment and banking system!

In due course, again two years or so later, a third meeting was called for "making dry the pole." For its protection against the elements the pole would be rubbed with grease and a modest amount of localized colour, soot-black and the earth colours, Indian red and ochre; a far cry from our garish commercial paints that took over in later years. AY's notes on the *verso* of our present drawing sound quite beautiful: "poles all warm grey, but some verging towards blue violet and others towards brown." Emily Carr admired the wonderful pinkish-grey colour of the bleached-out old poles she painted, some of them "bloomed over again with greeny-yellow mould."

With the fourth gathering, which Barbeau calls the *huks* or food-giving potlatch, the erection of the pole would be complete, and the social status of its owner well established. Each pole had its own proper name, its own personality and its own story to tell, vivid and unforgettable as the plot of a great novel. One can easily imagine becoming quite as addicted to totem poles as to other art forms with inner meaning. Consider one or two of the nineteen poles of the Fireweeds and Frog-Ravens in Gitsegyukla as Barbeau and AY saw them in the 1920s.

If we take our bearings in AY's drawing by the sun—whose rays are doodled in around a patched-up blob of turpentine—we see below the sun, in profile, a sharp-pointed pole facing the river. Read it from top to bottom—and there is our old friend, the Painted Goat of Stekyawden! There he sits on his haunches, his huge single horn atop his head. Even the red lines around his eyes and nostrils can be seen in close-up on another of AY's drawings. But this pole's proper name is not Goat; it is Pole of the Moon, and it belongs to Chief Gurhsan (meaning Gambler) of the Sky clan of the Fireweeds, an ancient family descended from the maiden Skawah of Temlaham. The Moon indicates Skawah's Sky connections, and this pole shows the Moon twice. (In the drawing here the Moon can be seen as foreshortened oval disks appended front and back.) Skawah is carved on each Moon, a square little woman holding an object that frankly looks like an overnight bag but symbolizes the Earthquake, another of Skawah's attributes. At the bottom of the pole is a delightful well-fed Owl; this is also a crest of the Fireweeds which will be encountered again later in our series of Skeena drawings.

The handsome pole just right of centre, with its long-billed Thunderbird (here named Weneel), belongs to Chief Weegyet, another of the Fireweeds, and an important personality in Barbeau's book on Temlaham. The first remote Weegyet was a wild character whose original name, Kip-ranaa, meant Small-frogs. (Strange that *ranaa* is also "frog" in Latin!) He broke a strict taboo by eloping with his own sister; they finally separated and he moved from the Eagles to the Fireweeds and changed his name as well. Later he married a woman in order to gain access to her uncle whom he killed in due course, along with the recently acquired wife. After all of which, Marius Barbeau remarks cryptically, "As acknowledgment of his exploits he became Fireweed head-chief of the Gitsegyukla tribe." This pole, one of three owned by the Weegyet connection, bears the strange name of Ladder in Steps and records, among other things, an adventure of Weegyet's maternal ancestors. A party hunting groundhogs at Place Uppermost (about fifty miles above Hazelton) conquered the Weneel monster, whose long nose protruded from a lake. In punishment they were imprisoned in a cave by a rockslide, but managed to escape by building a notched ladder which can be seen here at the bottom of the pole.

If we complete the "chapters" of Ladder in Steps from bottom to top, for an unorthodox change, we see between the notched steps and the Weneel a little man, one of a row of three carrying groundhogs under their arms. Above the Weneel is a crouching figure called Split Person; in front view he is cleft from top to toe, as was his unfortunate prototype in another grisly tale. At the top of the pole is a criss-cross pattern (drawn as a spiral here) representing a very ancient crest called Rafters or Wood of Hemlock, which goes back to the "supernatural discovery" of carved roofbeams when local hunters in ages past once visited Indian lodges on the lower Skeena River.

The totem pole closest to us in AY's drawing belongs to the Wild-rice clan of the Frog-Raven phratry, whose original home lay above Qaldo near the headwaters of the Skeena. Almost all their crests indicate that low-lying, damp area, as for example the frog hanging head down, below which are two rows of Three Beings Across, each manikin wearing a cedar-bark crown, the attribute of magicians. At the base is shown the Great Being Protruding from the Lake, sometimes called Reflections, stemming from the vision seen by a woman crossing a lake by raft. She saw children's faces in the water, and she and her companions heard a rumbling in the lake and beheld a huge human-like being emerging from the depths. Her clansmen had a pole cut to commemorate the vision, and the Wild-rice people adapted a special headdress named Of the Upper River, which shows two kingfishers sitting on the creature's head. The pole here has two kingfishers carved in the round atop it, but they do not show in this drawing.

Something else *almost* does not show here, or rather it shows in its final tragic ruins, lying broken across the middle ground. The short stakes perhaps once tried to give some last support. Here rests the once-great pole Snag of the Sandbar, erected four years after the fire of 1871 for the enterprising Weegyet of the Fireweeds, and carved by the Skeena's greatest artist, Haesem-hliyawn of Kitwinkul, who received the equivalent of four hundred dollars for his work. The pole fell in 1922, four years before AY got there and faithfully included its shattered remains in his careful drawing. But Marius Barbeau had studied it, and—perhaps even more important—Emily Carr had painted it, many years before.

Judging by the fine canvas *Kitseukla*, 1912, in the Art Gallery of Vancouver, Emily had placed herself over by the Pole of the Moon, perhaps sitting with her back against it so that the other silvery grey poles towered over her and filled the upper sections of her upright canvas, creating a majestic, almost mystic, effect that seems typical for Emily, just as the lengthways long view here is more typical for AY. The pole Snag of the Sandbar consisted of no less than four long-beaked Thunderbirds or Weneels, and we can imagine how they smashed apart when they fell. Between the huge figures of the birds were many small people and heads, referred to as Many Skulls. The story or supernatural experience here commemorated may well concern some fantastic pre-Gitksan cult in which human sacrifice was involved. It seems that three Indians fishing in the Skeena found an immense snag or partly submerged tree (and some of these can be eight feet in diameter). They tried in vain to pull it free from the sandbar. Along its shaft, between the projecting branches (possibly a source of the later beaks?) were fastened many skulls, some of them of children. At the bottom was a huge human face, Large Eyes, whose body could not be pulled out of the water. "The discoverers looked below the surface," Barbeau recounts, "there to behold a huge Grizzly-Bear-of-the-Water, on whose back stood the Snag. So they made it into a good crest."

The great Snag of the Sandbar crashed in ruins about a half century after its erection. But at least its memory lives: in Emily Carr's painting, in Marius Barbeau's tale, and here in the most modest form imaginable, yet none the less *imaginable* and full of secret spirit in AY's drawing.

A gallant attempt to preserve a score of fine old Gitskan poles in their own surroundings was made in Kitwanga, on the north bank of the Upper Skeena. AY recalls that he stayed there about a month with an Indian family, presumably that of Hlengwah, head-chief of the local Frog-Ravens, to whom several wonderful poles belonged. The restoration project was financed by the federal government. "The poles are sawn off at the base," AY wrote in his article for *Maclean's*, "and very carefully lowered to the ground; the centre is hollowed out and a new, well creosoted cedar pole driven in. The whole pole is soaked with linseed oil, painted as far as possible in its original colour and re-erected on a concrete foundation, the whole weight being taken by the new pole. In some cases the restoring is so perfectly done that there is no visible evidence of it, and yet the pole has been given another hundred years' lease of life."

AY's many pencil studies of the Kitwanga poles adhered faithfully to every detail. Often he drew the pole from three different aspects: full front, in profile, and, on one most interesting page, as shadowy silhouette in rear or three-quarters view. The line drawings in pencil are usually clearer and easier to identify than the corresponding photographs in Barbeau's monograph, as well as much more interesting aesthetically. As in each of the Gitskan villages in turn, every pole's tall tale has its own irresistible fascination. The three here in AY's drawing give us a tantalizing glimpse.

To the left is one of the most valuable relics of the Upper Skeena and by far the oldest pole in Kitwanga, dated by Barbeau back to about 1850. It is a rare example of the house-front pole, originally set against the centre of the front gable-end of a lodge, with a hole in it large enough for a man to crawl through but not to let the enemies in too fast! This pole fell in 1912, either along with or after its lodge. It was restored and re-erected in 1925. At the time AY drew it in 1926 it was only fifteen feet high, having lost the lower, most vulnerable part of its ceremonial doorway. It was formed of one side of a vertically split cedar log, with the soft core removed, which may have helped account for its longevity.

This ancient pole's proper name was The Bear's Den, and it belonged to the Eagle chief Sqayen, who at the time of AY's visit was a woman, her second name being Mrs. Maggie Wells. The pole featured two human figures, each with a round hole in his stomach "representing the entrance to the bear's den." The most famous of the many bear legends recounts how a beauteous Indian maiden walking along a trail one day slipped upon some bear dung and made rude remarks about bears in general. In almost no time she was overtaken by two bears in human form and led away to their den where she was compelled to marry the son of the chief bear. "She gradually changed into a bear herself," says the legend. Her two sons were half and half. One day she was able to attract the attention of her brothers by rolling a tiny snowball down the hillside. They followed the track to the entrance of the bear's den and trapped and slew their sister's bear-husband, who before his death taught his wife two ritual songs for hunters to use "to ensure good luck in hunting bears." (Animals are much nobler than people in these tales!) The two cub sons continued to behave like bears but helped their uncles to snare many more bears and the family grew very prosperous and naturally liked to use the crest of the "ensnared bear." Another much-favoured crest shows the Bear Woman with one or both of her cubs in front of her.

Below the bear-persons on the Kitwanga house-front pole is a Split Eagle with two heads and with wings spread to embrace the original ceremonial entrance hole, now embedded in the ground. A carved eagle, main emblem of the clan, and in one old tale representing a chief's eagle-wife waiting high on a tree while he hunted, originally topped this pole. But now the famous old relic stands disconsolate, *sans* lodge to be attached to, *sans* entrance hole at its base, *sans* eagle proudly atop it, *sans* everything save the view of the disreputable fish-smoking shed to our right of it in AY's drawing.

Farther along stand two more Eagle poles, these belonging to Chief Tewalasu. The one to the left, named Dog-Salmon and dating back to 1870, Barbeau considered one of the finest of the whole Skeena, and likely the work of a Nass River carver. The second, a much later work from around 1900/1905 is named On Top Sits the Squirrel. Anyone who takes this squirrel for a bear will be forgiven immediately because its legend tells of "apparitions of monster squirrels the size of bears."

So there in Kitwanga some of the poles still stand, stiffly erect, though AY preferred them leaning. (Emily Carr once remarked that the old poles that leaned backward looked stern, while the ones leaning forward looked sad.) And of course it was not possible to keep the Kitwanga poles in their original proud positions in front of their owners' lodges, facing the river highway of olden days. The railway line and station had to take priority of position in our twentieth century; the poles were placed in a straight row along the village's new main street, facing the road and the railway. Their ancient dignity was further impaired by commercial paint in the brightest of colours, chosen by the Indians themselves.

A gallant rescue project none the less....

PLATE 76

Totem poles and shacks, Kitwanga [1926]

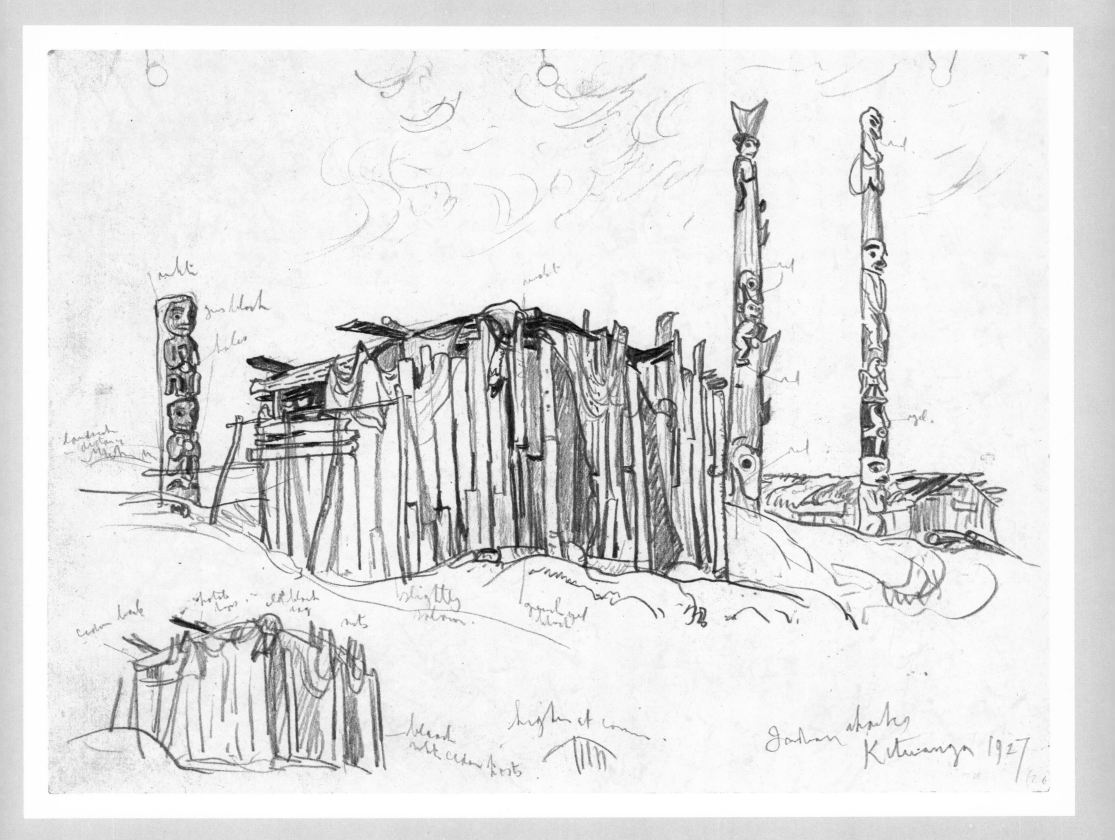

Our way takes us up the Skeena to the peaceful village of Kispiox—"a lovely little place," as AY today remembers it. "Holgate and I stayed there for about a week. I think we lived at the missionary's place; he was the only non-Indian there."

We are looking, in AY's careful drawing, along the rear of the "old" village's potlatch houses, with their storage sheds projecting towards us, while the tops of the totem poles in front of them loom up against the distant haze-dimmed mountain. The composition masses together well from this angle. AY drew the Kispiox poles in groups rather than as individuals, perhaps because so many of them were largely uncarved, with only a crest at the top and one or two figures at the base. Barbeau considered them less fully developed, more primitive, in some ways more intense, than those elsewhere on the Skeena. Their individual names help indicate their content, some weirdly evocative, such as Halfway Out, Person of the Smoke-hole, Sun-Dogs, or Tongue-licked. Thirteen poles in Kispiox were owned by the Fireweed phratry. The latter's principal crest here is the Owl. Many of their poles have a carved owl perched atop them. And what more natural than a dusky owl to look down upon ancient Kispiox? Let us lurk in this silent spot and allow the spirit of the Past to infuse the shape of the Present. . . .

We hear a buzzing and a humming. It is dawn of a day in late summer long ago, eighty years or more. The village buzzes with excitement, rings with laughter, hums with snatches of song. The people of Kispiox are famed for their fine singing. Today is a very special day, the day of the great annual Potlatch. The storehouses are crammed with rich products of the season—the most succulent salmon smoked and dried, flitches of mountain goat, baskets of berries dried in the sun, great tubs of *oolakan* oil brought from the Nass, bales of blankets from downstream trade, carved and inlaid utensils, garments new-sewn—far more than the families will need for themselves. All is carefully counted and ready to be bestowed upon the potlatch guests—even new canoes for visiting chiefs. There is a tangible, glorious sense of well-being and of being-well-off. And today come the late-summer visitors, all the people of the neighbouring clans: the Torchlight-fishers from Kitenmaks, the Rabbit People of Kitwanga, the Segyuklas from south of the Skeena, as well as the upstream neighbours from Qaldo and Kiskagas. What greetings, what dances and feasting with songs, what display of ceremonial regalia, and at last the great giving of gifts. They will come by the hundred and stay for a week—a Potlatch to remember!

Now mist and rainclouds roll down from the mountains. All is dark and wintry, grey and grim. It is the winter of 1888. Rain drips from the shingles, mist muffles the sounds. But the sounds are there: the sounds of the wailing of women, the drone of the death dirge, the piping and screeching to summon good spirits, to scare away the bad. The people are dying, dying by dozens, and no one can stop it. Some families have lost all their children—the young ones go the first; they get feverish, sicken and die. Some people blame *Ramkseewah*, the white men at Kitenmaks, the strangers whose skin is pale like a barkless log, for making black magic to kill all but themselves. The white men laugh: "It's only the measles! You don't die of measles!" But in Kispiox they die, in Kitenmaks and Kitwinkul. After this winter it will never be the same again.

And now forty years have gone. The time of year and day is hard to tell; it might be late afternoon, here in AY's drawing. The old potlatch houses stand empty, gape-windowed and silent. The people, what is left of them, have moved across the road, deserting their communal homes and their totem poles. In the "new" village are different, one-family homes, tall houses with upstairs windows, much like the houses of the white men whom the people work for now. Each spring the people migrate down-river, taking their children and dogs, down the Skeena to work at the canneries, canning the delicious salmon for others to enjoy. In the autumn they come back to Kispiox, bringing supplies from the store—mostly flour, sugar, and tea, not very hearty fare. They don't bother much about old things; they grin and are shy about legends: "That Owl? Well, my grandmother says our people had Owls as house-posts, back in the days when the Sky-clan of the Fireweeds still lived at Temlaham. The White Owl stole a child and fed it owl-fashion, and even after they got the child back it kept the habits of owls. There's lots of owls in Kispiox."

Artists seem to like owls, and artists have also liked Kispiox. Emily Carr got there first. She wrote a story on how the Indians carved their bird crests to surmount their tall poles, "carved with dignity and intensity. In primitive simplicity their calm seemed to pervade the village." Later came Langdon Kihn and Holgate, and George Pepper and Jock Macdonald and Art Price and others, not forgetting AY who drew every owl he could find. Some of his owls were used with pen-and-ink initials for *The Downfall of Temlaham*. One that he drew, a black owl, pleased his sculptor friend Florence Wyle, who was born one year before AY was. She worked from the AY drawing to model her own version of the wise little black owl, then cast it in sturdy iron, with a touch of red inside the beak and a touch of white in the watchful eyes. Happy the people now who possess their own Florence Wyle black owls, for surely they have special insight and luck!

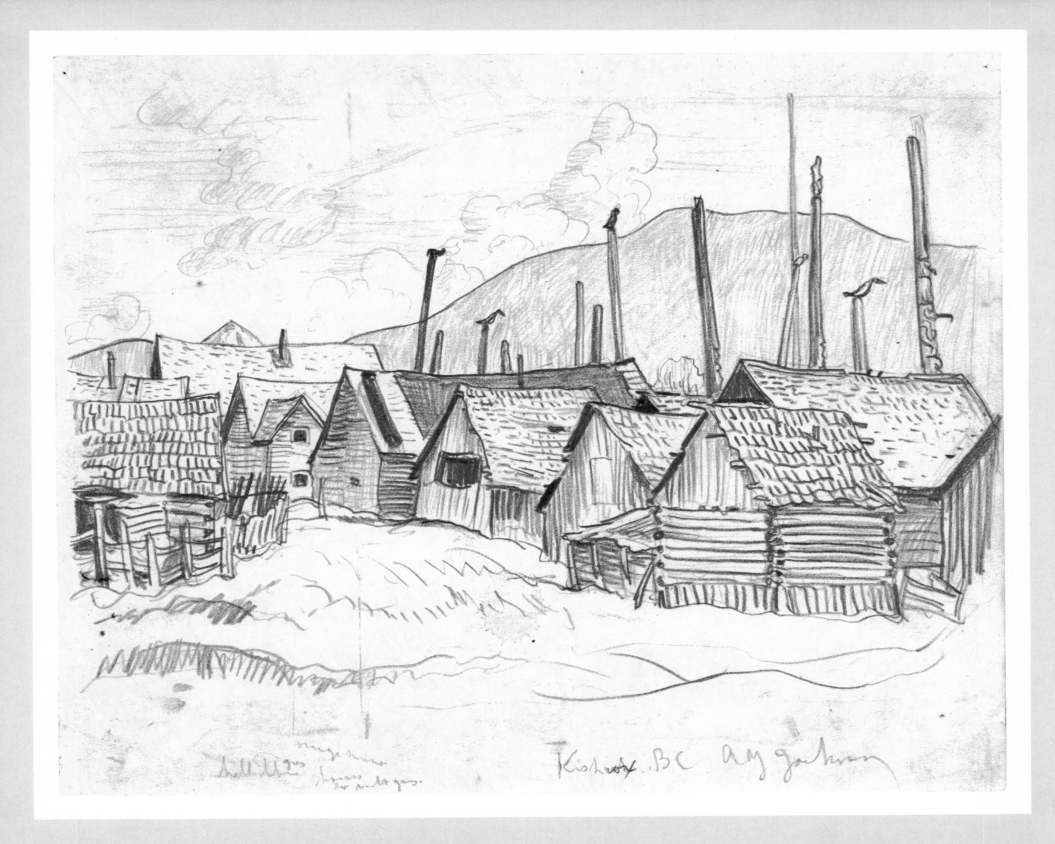

PLATE 77

Potlatch houses and totem poles in Kispiox on the Upper Skeena River, B.C. [1926]

Let the dead sleep,
They need not rise
To walk the earth again,
Except in other guise;
Nature needs no waste. . . .

How well the dead must sleep here in their own special houses within sight of the guardian mountains. It seems that on the Upper Skeena the dead were buried in shallow graves with a wooden superstructure placed over them as a post-mortem residence for the spirit. Many of these grave-houses display prized possessions of the deceased. The structures show an amazing variety of forms. Some look like little summer-houses or gazebos, some like small chapels, with a tiny glazed window and fretwork decorating their gable ends. (This fretwork could develop fantastic lacy intricacies.) Some grave-houses were built like step-pyramids, with an elaborate many-pointed ornament on top; others resemble richly canopied four-poster beds. In one or two cases AY's text on the drawing indicates that it is a reconstruction of some fallen monument, such as the Tomb of Beene at Hagwelget, with a carved beaver crest atop it and a steep shingled roof reminiscent of old Norwegian stave churches. One such reconstructed "house" looks like a shaggy-mane mushroom surrounded by a picket fence whose corner-posts are decorated with Elizabethan "melons" or vase-shapes. Colour notes on AY's drawings enhance the exotic effect, as for instance "salmon, crimson, ivory white." Occasionally AY jots down some detail concerning the contents displayed, such as "old clothes," and we may recall Emily Carr's touching story "The Blouse," in *Heart of a Peacock*, where she literally gave if not the shirt, at least the blouse off her back, to be placed on view as pièce de résistance among the effects of a dying Indian woman. Not to be worn—to be looked at.

Commenting upon these interesting structures in his 1927 article for *Maclean's Magazine* AY writes: "Beside the restoration of the totem poles it is hoped that efforts will be made to preserve some of the Indian cemeteries. The grave-houses are comparatively modern yet show an amazing number of architectural forms which no one has quite accounted for. Russian and Chinese influence seems to have pervaded the ones at Hazelton and Kispiox. They are all wood and rapidly rotting away. The Indian now having adopted the white man's tombstones, is not desirous that they should be preserved."

It would not seem that much, if any, of this restoration project of the hopeful pre-Depression 1920s was ever carried out. Recent travellers to the Skeena mention only the ruins of former grave-houses. It is sad to see the roofless wreckage of "Burial House, Kitwancool," plate 161 in Peter Varley's *Canada* and to recognize its crescent openings as those of the proudly intact grave-house painted by Langdon Kihn in 1924, and reproduced in colour facing page 3 in *The Downfall of Temlaham*. The whole of Kitwinkul, where Barbeau in the 1920s found "the finest cluster of totem poles still standing," today gives the impression of "fallen grandeur. The prostrate totem figures gaze upwards with their great eyes to the leaning totems ready to fall. Destruction and decay is evident on all sides."

Although many of the grave-houses drawn by AY in 1926 still look intact on the surface, the present drawing suggests the encroaching desolation. Recalling the time out there with AY, Edwin Holgate wrote recently, "I felt we were witnessing the rapid decline of a splendid race of creative and well-organized people. There persisted a brooding gloom which I found it impossible to dispel."

Somehow it seems right and fitting that rapid decay should follow upon that rapid and wonderful flowering. It is always a question as to how successful any major preservation can be if a work is to be pickled away as a "done," to paraphrase our picturesque Emily, and especially if a work intended to stand in the free outdoors is placed against a dreary wall in some museum in an alien land. Maybe it is better to allow the past to stand where it belongs and to lean and fall and lie in grandeur, "damp and lonely, in the undisturbed snow of the abandoned village," in the beautiful words about the visit of Diamond Jenness to Old Kuldo (our Qaldo) up above Kispiox in February 1924.

The evocative poetry of words such as these, the reaffirming power of good paintings and graphically descriptive drawings, the solid satisfaction of well-documented scientific records, all help to keep alive the indwelling spirit of Skeena Indian days. Emily Carr knew this as she huddled on her hard cot, miserably tormented by mosquitoes, outside the hostile lodge in Kitwinkul back in 1928, and whispered what have become the present writer's favourite lines in all those marvellous writings of hers, words of comfort in many a creative struggle: "My heart said into the thick dark, 'Why did I come?'

"And the dark answered, 'You know.'"

So let the dead sleep indeed. We yield to change and transformation as the past sinks away, intoning the old dirge of the Gitksan, the "song of withering change":

"My heart throbs at the memory of times that are past. When I look back I see the mountains, my birth-place, the high ridges wherefrom descends my path. My heart throbs at the memory of times that are past!

"The Chief of the Sky no longer fulfills his promises, no longer favours man with visions for him to tell, wherein all are alive that were dead. And the fallen no longer walk back to Temlaham through the fires of the setting sun. O, my heart throbs at the memory of times that are past!"

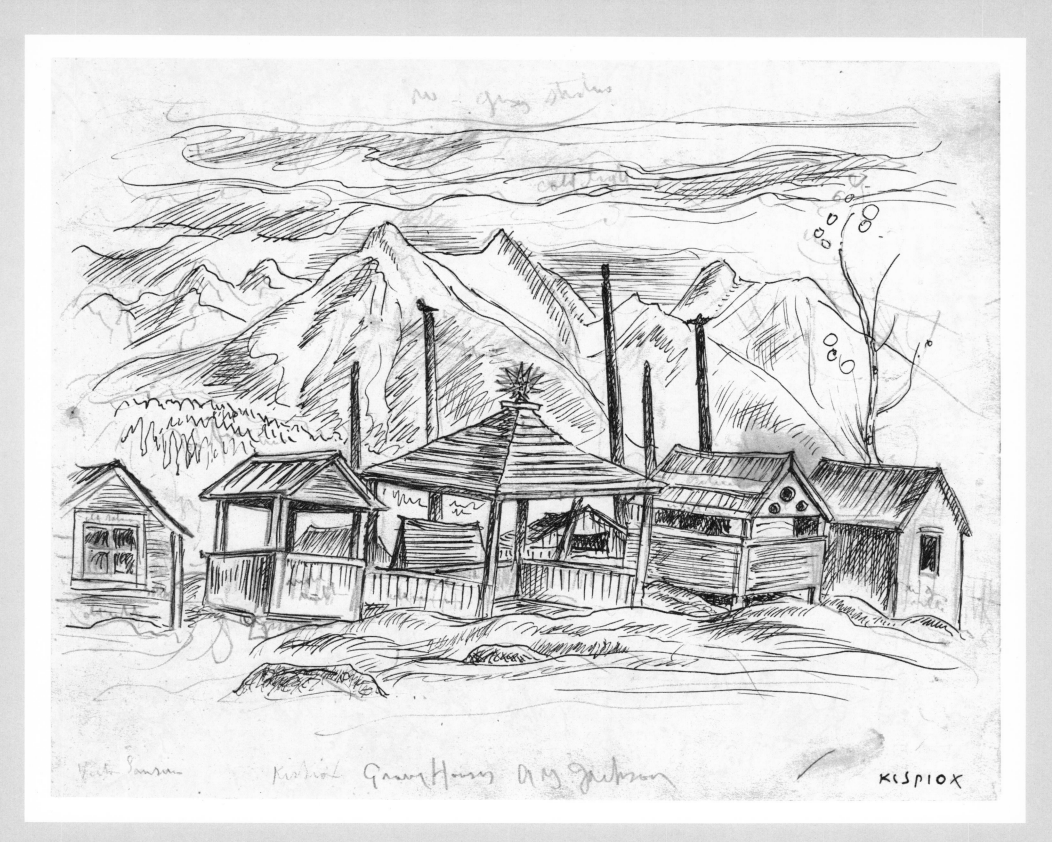

PLATE 78
Grave houses, Kispiox, B.C. [*1926*]

Indian House Port Simpson

house for Marius Barbeau's collection (njg 654) and drew several of the old fine houses at Port Simpson and Prince Rupert.

But why should we smile? We smile because we are not Indians and because we have discovered that nobody ever really *lived* in these houses. They were like totem poles, built for prestige, to be seen and admired and recognized, not to be used or lived in. At most, according to AY, the owners would live in one room on the ground floor—"sort of camping there in the place."

And how about a last smile from Kispiox away back up the Skeena? How can we tell it is Kispiox where the second little drawing was made? Believe it or not, we can tell by the small dark mark in the middle of the totem pole to the right: this hole represents symbolically an entrance hole to a potlatch house, with four people sitting around the hole. And this special crest, called Hole Through or Ceremonial Door, belonged to Klaem-Larhe, a Wolf of Kispiox. We would know his pole in a hundred, so pole-conscious have we become! Both the poles in this drawing are his,

Enough of old anguish; don't let's forget how to smile.

Can we for instance smile about Mrs. Musgrave's Victorian house? Mrs. Musgrave was born a Raven and she lived at Place-of-Wild-Roses, which in English is called Port Simpson. Mrs. Musgrave's house was one of the finest grand houses in the place, as fine as any in Victoria. It was built by one of the coastal Tsimsians with the money from furs and salmon, and from ample returns on potlatches, some time before 1900.

Mrs. Musgrave was the grandmother of William Beynon, who assisted Marius Barbeau in collecting many wonderful legends. When AY was with Barbeau in September 1926 they went up the coast by boat to Port Simpson, visited Mrs. Musgrave in her grand house and heard about many old traditions. AY sketched Mrs. Musgrave's Victorian

and oddly enough they both have the same official name, Running Backwards, which comes from the odd position of the legs of the lowest figure on each. A later photograph shows the right one tipped over almost touching the left one, obviously on the way down and out.

AY's name for these two poles, written on another of his drawings of them, was The Gossips. If we listen with the ear of our imagination we can hear what they are saying to each other—the left pole Running Backwards (with hands raised) to the right pole Running Backwards (with hands holding tummy):

"Do you remember away back in 1923 when young Gitludahl of the Fireweeds sold the very first totem pole ever to be cut down and taken away from our Upper Skeena? Remember those Americans who picked

out that pole? Its name was White Owl the First and it was carved by old Haesemhliwyawn a long while before he died. 'This is the best one,' they said, and they sawed it down and carted it away. . . .''

"Yes, but then do you remember what happened to young Gitludahl after that? How he was made to obey the old law and pay back all the people who had helped his ancestor put up that pole—pay them back the full amounts again? How many bales of Hudson's Bay blankets was it, with twenty blankets in each bale? And how many hundred skins? How many pounds of dried salmon? I'm sure it cost him all together much more than he got for the pole from those Ramkseewahs. That put a stop to the selling of poles, do you remember? Ha Ha!"

"Of course I remember. Potlatch handouts nowadays certainly aren't what they used to be; nowadays it's a brown paper bag you take to a party, and bring home a few biscuits, that's all. They don't have pole-raisings like when we were young, any more."

"Do you remember that nice pole with The White-man's Dog on top? That man's name was Mr. Ross but everybody pronounced it Maeselaws. That dog had such queer drooping ears that the first of our people who saw it considered it a supernatural experience, so they made it into a crest called Maeselaws' Dog."

"Yes, and remember that other funny dog, the one with the terrible temper, who used to scare all our big curs? It came with that white woman who did all the paintings, away back when was it? She had quite a temper too, but she liked to laugh a lot. Remember her hat? Made like the roof of a grave-house, a big mosquito veil all around, and with a glass window in front. And her trousers below her skirt, she called them 'duck pantalettes,' why duck I wonder? She'd be pretty old by now, she was a year or two older than I am—and I'm ten years younger than you are, don't

forget that, Running Backwards!"

"Maybe you are, Running Backwards, but at least I don't use paint to hide my age. And you're slipping faster than I am, that you cannot deny. I bet that you'll go before I do."

"Well, we'll all have to go some fine day, there's no doubt about that. I only hope that when I do go I'll bring down that new-fangled hideous house along with me. Huh."

"At least we won't be forgotten, with all the people that have taken our picture. Remember that nice little man that drew us, away back in '26? We may not be the beauties we once were but at least there's no one else like us, isn't that right, Running Backwards?"

"That's right, Running Backwards, that's right!"

Onward we move in time and in *AY's Canada*, and find ourselves in another phase of AY's western expeditioning. The date of our present drawing, 1943, marks the first occasion that AY went west in the summer to teach at the University of Alberta's Summer School of Fine Arts at Banff, establishing a summer pattern that lasted all through the 1940s. In 1943 he was helping out as replacement for his friend George Pepper, who was away on War Records duty. Here are AY's impressions a week after arrival at Banff, dashed off during a free moment on the first rainy day, August 3, 1943: ". . . It has been quite a busy week, taking out a lot of students, both morning and afternoon. They are a nice crowd, many of them quite inexperienced, but anxious to learn something. It is a good place to work in some ways—rather obvious stuff. It has the advantage that one does not have to go far, and owing to the gas shortage this is important. The boys I work with, Glyde and Phillips, are good heads and we work together very harmoniously. . . .

"School is over the end of August, then I hope to work on my own and kick around for a couple of months. We are having the Thomson film here and I have to give a talk on it. I guess it is a good thing to be useful.

"It is embarrassing to be so well known. I meet people who have come five hundred miles just to study with me.

"Well it is after midnight and I have to be up at seven, so cheerio old thing. . . ."

By 1946 AY was a well established fixture at Banff and the school had grown by leaps and bounds, with Pepper back and Jock Macdonald added to the staff. On August 10 AY wrote: "Two more weeks and we scatter. It has been sunshine ever since we arrived. Over two hundred art students. The East has invaded the West—there are as many students from Ontario as from Alberta. A lot of your friends are here from Montreal and Ottawa . . . and lots of Americans. It is easier to get gas, and the students are going farther afield this year. Plans are underway to build permanent quarters, dormitories for five hundred students, and a big central building. I am not sure I like to see it grow so large.

". . . Here in Banff we live very well, a little shy on butter and sugar. Prices are about the same as in Montreal. It is a happy little town, no snobbery, and very well managed. You meet people you know all the time, from all over Canada. . . ." (Think of all the people that would be, in six summers' time!)

AY's post-Summer School visits often took him to the hospitable home of some recent student at Banff—the Buckleys at Canmore, the Williams at Kamloops, or the Cowans at 150 Mile House in the Cariboo—and we can track round after him a bit to a few of those fascinating corners, start-

ing only fifteen miles east of Banff with the town of Canmore. This lies 4,295 feet above sea level in the valley of the beautiful Bow River, close by Mount Rundle and the Three Sisters (our mountain population is going downhill from the earlier *Seven* Sisters!). The name of Canmore is said to come from an ancient Scottish king, one Malcolm Canmore, and the place produces bituminous coal and mountain scenery, both in abundance. The Scottish aura may have appealed to one of Canmore's earlier famous devotees, known to the world in a double role—as Ralph Connor the novelist, and as the Reverend Charles W. Gordon the minister who came to the West as a missionary. One of AY's Canmore sketches (njg 834), privately owned in Calgary, is titled *Ralph Connor's Church*, so here the famous man's two roles have been blended. Some of Ralph Connor's dramatic tales of derring-do use this grand country as stage, especially those that deal with the RCMP and the powerful Indian tribes in the early days, eight or nine decades ago, when "east invaded west" in a different way. It was not very far from here that gallant Corporal Cameron got his man, that old snake Copperhead, the "illusive" Sioux chief, while towards the same glorious peaks of our drawing the charming Scottish Moira with her irrepressible brown curls rode out from "the busy, ambitious and would-be wicked little pioneer town" of Calgary in the days just prior to the Riel Rebellion. Ralph Connor's romantic adventure, *The Patrol of the Sun Dance Trail*, came out in 1914, the year AY also reached the Rockies. That seems very long ago, a lost world divided from ours by the great wall of World War I and the tough times since that have made us all tougher too. And yet today's Pop art produces heroines that look and talk just like Moira and nice plump pink Mandy, so maybe we are going in a big circle after all.

AY certainly circled around Canmore year after year in the 1940s; we can almost tell which inhabitants painted their garage doors a new colour from one season to the next. But topping all, the great romantic mountains retain their appeal through the decades. "Over all the blue arch of sky spanned the wide valley and seemed to rest upon the great ranges on either side, like the dome of a vast cathedral."

PLATE 80

Canmore, Alberta, 1943

Canmore. Alberta.
1943.

We now launch that hardy old Argonaut, AY, along another trail in search of treasure in British Columbia's manifold realm. This time he is headed through the Dry Belt towards the region of fable evocatively misspelled "Cariboo" back in the gold rush days of the 1860s. We can be sure that the type of pay dirt AY struck there in the mid-1940s contained as many good nuggets as any prospector ever uncovered—and AY's have probably afforded more lasting pleasure!

Westward from Banff about half the way to Vancouver the trail brought AY to Kamloops, where in 1943 he established a gold-hearted friendship with the Williams family—George R. the mayor, since deceased, and Dorothy his wife, an up-to-date art teacher who took refresher courses with AY at Banff. He stayed with them several times. "Making the odd sketch," says one letter headed Kamloops, August 30, "preparing a lecture and meeting lots of people. It's a strange country—a garden surrounded by a desert, with apples, pears, peaches and all kinds of trees here, but you go a couple of hundred feet up the hills and it is all gravel and sand, and only pine and spruce can grow."

Kamloops, major transportation and cattle ranchers' supply centre for the Thompson River district of inland British Columbia, and thirty years older than the provincial capital Victoria, lies at the confluence of the North Thompson (locally called North River) and the larger South Thompson which "runs in from the east between dusty, rolling hills. Nowhere is the desolate beauty of the Dry Belt presented on such a gigantic scale" writes Bruce Hutchison in his eloquent and richly informative book on the Fraser River and its tributaries. From that enjoyable work, supplemented by a well illustrated recent article "Kamloops: City in the Sage," by Donovan Clemson, we learn how the friendly local Shuswap Indians greeted the first white traders and fur trappers heading north up the Okanagan Valley in the winter of 1811/1812; how already by the end of 1812 Alexander Ross of J. J. Astor's Pacific Fur Company and Joseph Larocque of the North West Company had established their trading posts, the latter amalgamating in 1821 with the Hudson's Bay Company to become Fort Kamloops. This was half-way house along the Brigade Trail to the fur-rich wilds of the north-west, and here fresh packhorses were obtained and tired mounts were pastured. "As a brigade included several hundred horses, the post was a scene of great activity during the arrivals and departures. Livestock thrived in the vicinity and horses wintering on the open ranges were said to have been fat and sleek in the spring. . . . Old maps designate the region as 'undulating bunch grass country,' an indication that much of the range, covered mainly with sage brush today, has been degraded by overgrazing."

172

With the electrifying discovery of gold along the waterways west of Kamloops began the fantastic gold rush which by the fall of 1858 had brought over thirty thousand hopefuls to prospect up and down the Fraser. Many of them swarmed up the old fur traders' route through the Okanagan Valley and laid in their supplies at the Kamloops post. From another direction, down the North Thompson's 200 uncharted miles, came straggling, in October 1862, one band of the starving Overlanders, carrying on their raft the intrepid Mrs. Catherine Schubert and several of her children, the next child being extremely imminent. Bruce Hutchison describes very graphically the touch-and-go situation: the good lady was already in labour as the raft nudged ashore at Kamloops, and an Indian midwife, fortunately available, soon lifted the babe—first white child born in that whole region—and shouted "Kumloops! Kumloops!" Whereupon Mrs. Schubert christened her baby "Rose"!

AY says that this drawing of the old Indian village at Kamloops was made on the north side of the river opposite the present town, in the sharp angle where the two Thompsons meet. This was where the original trading posts also stood. Today the whole triangle has been engulfed by the rapidly expanding modern Kamloops, which in the decade 1954 to 1964 has grown from 16,000 to 35,000 people. There are still some Shuswap Indians along the river, but it is likely that this old village and its church have given way to the new area of motels and suburbia where a "genuine reproduction" of old Fort Kamloops is being constructed in a location convenient for tourists to reach from the Trans-Canada Highway by the fine new Overlanders Bridge. Does one somehow feel a sneaking sense of sympathy with the surly old Indian who came out with a gun while AY was sketching there, and threatened to shoot him? That old Indian's forebears are on record as having been "remarkably friendly" to the first white intruders. Today everyone is presumably friendly again. It is rather nice to have this small, rough nugget garnered by AY in the in-between stage.

PLATE 81

Indian village,
Kamloops, B.C. [c. 1943]

Indian Village Kamloops

How do we reach the Cariboo? We can trail AY down the Thompson River as far as Ashcroft, "this curious old town," as Hutchison calls it, asleep since the gold rush days, by-passed—unlike Kamloops fifty miles to the east—by our not always beneficial progress. On September 6, 1945, on his way into the Cariboo, AY drew Ashcroft's well-weathered wooden street façade, without a soul in sight. That drawing is now in the National Gallery.

The blue Thompson turns south at Ashcroft to join the muddy brown Fraser farther down at Lytton. We, however, leave both rivers for now and head north up the Cariboo Road, almost three hundred miles of which were hastily laid between 1861 and 1865 by Governor James Douglas' Royal Engineers to assist the tens of thousands of gold-mad miners struggling into the upper stretches of the Cariboo—and out again empty-handed, most of them. Nowadays ranchers and tourists and occasional modern miners use the road.

"It is a measure of how casual a land is the Cariboo that no man can say precisely where it is or what its boundaries are, except that it is up on the plateau country of B.C. It is, in truth, less a geographic location than a state of mind." Thus declared Philip Keatley, who produced that absolutely wonderful CBC television series *Cariboo Country*, which some of us feel should be re-shown at least once a year for the next hundred years or so.

Before we probe (properly casually, of course) into the Cariboo's state of mind, we might enjoy a quick moment's sharper focus upon its aforementioned geographic location, with Bruce Hutchison's able assistance:

"The Cariboo plateau, unique in the topography of Canada, is an oval about 125 miles across and 160 miles long. While its boundaries are vague, it may be said to lie between the Coast mountains on the west and the outer fringes of the Rocky system on the east. It stretches northward from the Thompson to latitude 56, even beyond the first sources of the arctic drainage system.

"On average the plateau is 4,000 feet above the ocean. . . . But the term 'plateau', though well understood by the natives, appears a misnomer to the stranger. Instead of a flat space . . . he finds a region of rolling range, low-lying meadows, a confusing skeleton of mountains sprawled in all directions, a maze of deep river gullies finally joining the central gully of the Fraser, and everywhere the unexpected bodies of upland lakes."

The Cariboo can be tangibly sensed in Hutchison's words. We can perceive how the Fraser has carved for itself "a yawning ditch through the yielding gumbo" and the vast open rangeland with its bunch grass and sage brush, its pungent glades of jackpine and balsam poplar, its clear

skies and clean upland air. We get a "feeling of unlimited open space," of "almost empty wilderness." Hutchison found the Cariboo "one of the loneliest stretches of settled country in America and, in our eyes, one of the most beautiful. . . . More than any other place in Canada it seems to offer sanctuary from the world. . . . From the days of the first gold miners, Cariboo has been a magic word."

So geography leads back to the state of mind. The ranchers and their beautiful straight-backed beefy Herefords have taken over after the miners and their diggings, but still the pioneer backwoods spirit lingers, "the quality that distinguishes all the people of the Cariboo—a complete detachment from the world, a steady feeling of security in good times and bad, and above all, a stubborn will to be let alone."

No wonder then that AY found the Cariboo to his taste, both the spirit of the place and the look of its broad open rhythms, uncluttered by too much fuzz, casual and non-glamorous after the Rockies' toothy peaks and the big panoramas of the Fraser farther south. "I found the intimate stuff more paintable, the creeks and the little lakes, the patches of small poplar or aspen growing in circular groups."

We were dubious, for a while, about including this drawing of Green Lake lying east of the Cariboo Road north of Clinton and 70 Mile House, thinking that it might be rather "slight." But it kept cropping up, it was so irresistibly typical of the magic Cariboo upland—a lovely little nothing-subject. Typical of AY magic too.

174

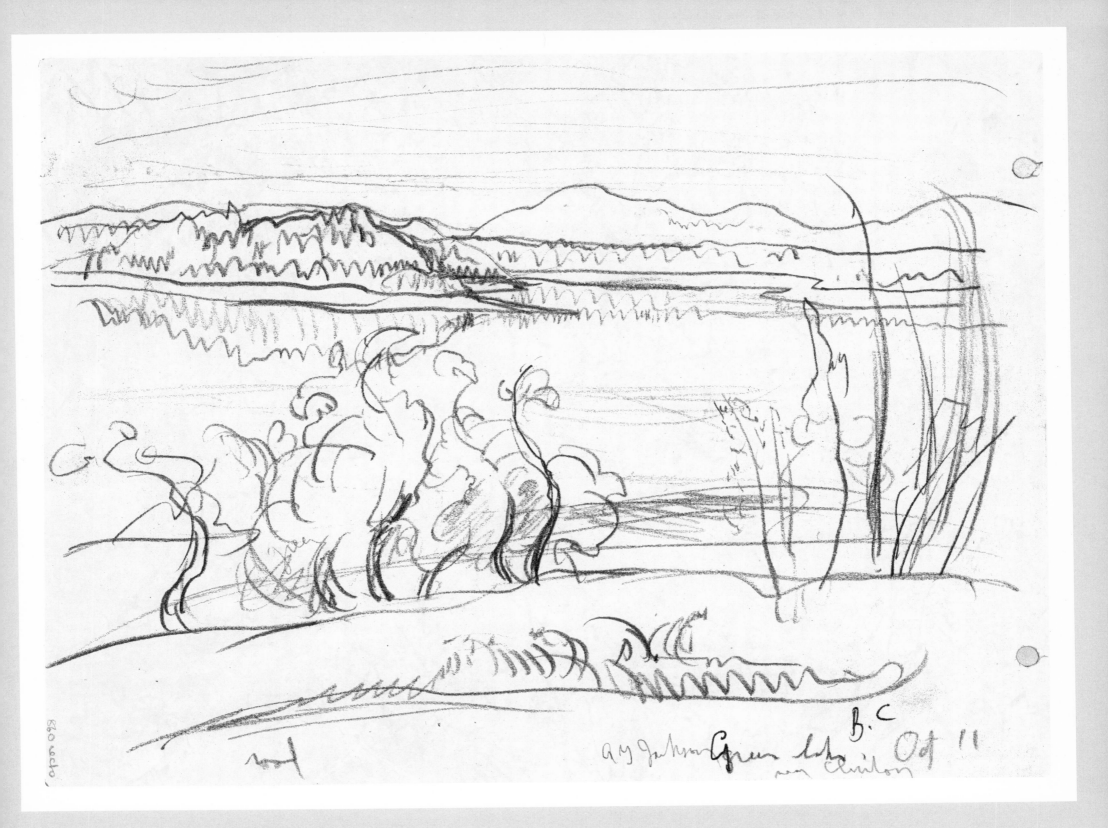

PLATE 82

Green Lake in the Cariboo, B.C. [mid-1940s]

When an official modern map of British Columbia gives us special-sounding place names such as Seventy Mile, The Hundred and Twenty-two, and 150 Mile House, we can tingle with secret pride at knowing that we have well and truly hit the famous trail of the Cariboo gold rush days of a hundred years ago. Alongside us still surge the restless ghosts of thousands upon thousands of hopefuls mad for gold who once swarmed on foot into the unbroken wilds of the hinterland. There hundreds found gold but thousands found only frostbite and semi-starvation. What did they care?

The responsibility of getting supplies in and getting both the destitute and the gold-bags out, of maintaining law and order, and—last but not least—of assuring some cut for the government in the treasure being garnered mostly by outsiders, all devolved upon Governor James Douglas, an astute and economical Scot. In order to by-pass the Fraser roaring grimly through its fifty-mile-long canyon, the Governor enlisted the free help of five hundred penniless prospectors to lay out a preliminary route, the Harrison Trail, which curved northward west of the Fraser, which it rejoined and crossed at Lillooet. From here a rough wagon road was laid north up into the Cariboo plateau, joining at Clinton with the old inland Fur Brigade pack-horse trail which, as we know, ran up the Okanagan from the Columbia River and via Kamloops along the Thompson River. The Harrison detour proved too much of a swampy tangle, so in the winter of 1861/1862 Governor Douglas set the sappers of the Royal Engineers to work with pick, shovel and dynamite to carve a northern road through the sheer rock of the Fraser Canyon from Yale below Hell's Gate, turning to follow the clay gorge of the Thompson up to Ashcroft and then the tributary Bonaparte up into the Cariboo "with its awful beds of miry clay." By 1865, 385 curvaceous miles of road "18 feet wide" had been laid from Yale up to Soda Creek, where river-boats took over as far upstream as Quesnel, while a final rugged sixty-five miles of road led in to the final goal of Barkerville on its gold-laden Williams Creek. That entire road, including innumerable bridges, some of them suspension, cost the canny Governor only $1,250,000, which needless to say he made up within a couple of years from tolls and taxes of one kind and another. Those were the days!

With the opening of the main Cariboo Road, the waterways of the Harrison Trail were almost abandoned, mule trains were replaced by horses and oxen, and the day of freight wagons and fast coaches began. Two trips a week were made without fail in the salad days of the 1860s and '70s between the coast and the interior—a distance in all of almost six hundred miles. By changing horses every thirteen miles and wasting

hardly a minute on the whole route, fourteen-passenger, four-horse stages could make the journey from Yale to Soda Creek in forty-eight hours—"an almost incredible feat," remarks Bruce Hutchison, "when you remember that this is a one day's drive today in an automobile.

". . . At every stopping place a hotel sprang up, the rude but well-fed mile houses of the Cariboo road, with new hay farms to support the horses.

". . . Until recent times it [the road] followed every twist and turn where the first builders could not stop to blast a rock or dig out a stump.

"In those days a mile meant something and every mile was marked. Starting first from Lillooet, as the jumping-off place of the Harrison route, and then from Ashcroft when Douglas' road was built, every stopping place along the way was called a 'mile house.' It had no name but its number. Even now you speak of stopping at the Seventy, or the Hundred, or the Hundred and Fifty. Since the old houses were measured from Lillooet and the later settlements from Ashcroft, a number is no guide to distance. The complete jumble of mileage never mattered in the least. Every house along the road was known, every bed and meal had its own special reputation with the freighters.

"In my young days, for example, we always tried to stop at the Hundred and Twenty-two, where I have seen such meals, such gargantuan breakfasts and steak dinners, such pies of wild raspberries, such lavish hosts and such red-faced cooks as a civilized man never encounters. Those days, alas, are gone."

There was another traveller in the stage-coach days whom we can almost recognize by her juicily descriptive words. "The C.P.R. train spat me out of its bouncy coach [at Ashcroft]"—Emily Carr again, to be sure. Emily paid a three-month visit to the Cariboo on her way back from five unhappy years in England, in about 1906. When Emily's stage-coach passed Cache Creek just north of Ashcroft on the way up, she just missed seeing the last of the twenty-one camels which an enterprising Mr. Laumeister had imported in the 1860s for use on the Harrison Trail, on the economical theory that one camel carrying 1,000 pounds for forty miles a day (at $1 per pound for the trip) can earn money faster than one

(continued)

PLATE 83

150 Mile House, British Columbia [1940s]

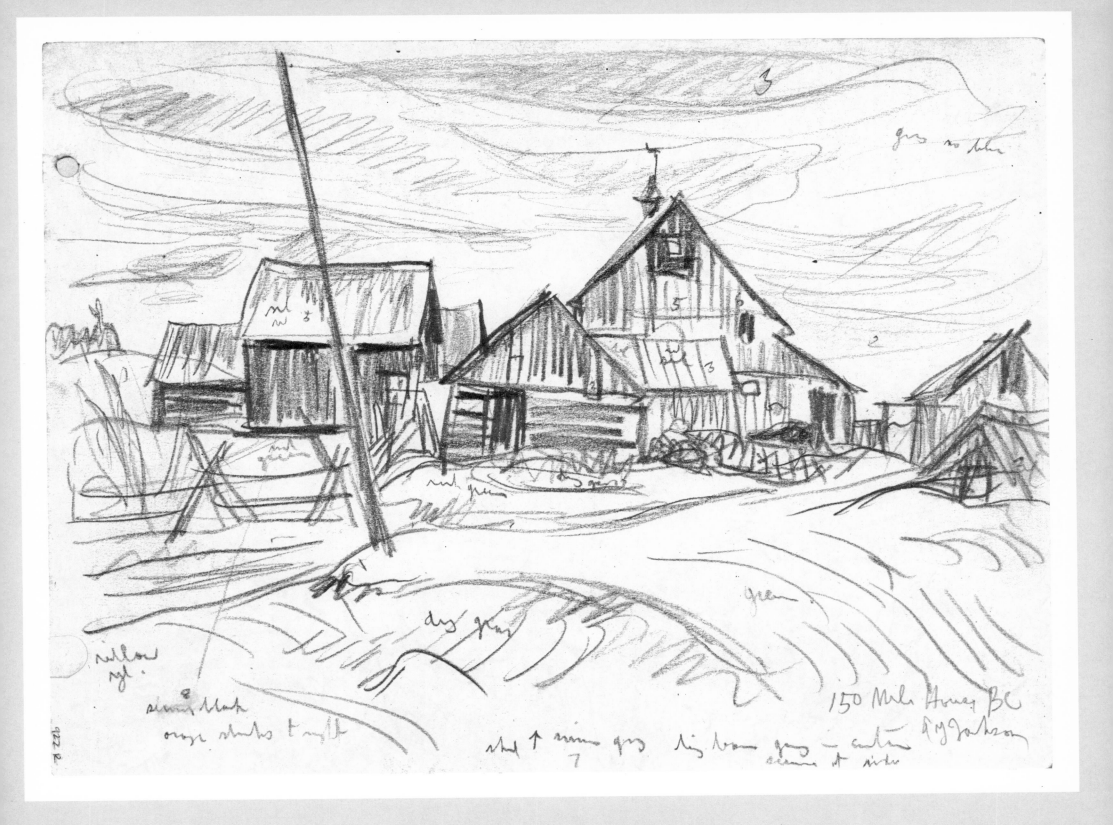

mule which only carries 250 pounds. The scheme did not work too well, but the last surviving camel completed its odoriferous existence in 1905.

Emily loved the Cariboo. "I did suffer two days of violence at the mercy of the six-horse stage-coach which bumped me over the Cariboo Road and finally deposited me at the door of the One Hundred and Fifty Mile House [See our drawing!] where my friend lived, her husband being manager of the Cariboo Trading Company there. It had been a strange, rough journey yet full of interest. No possible springs could endure such pitch and toss as the bumps and holes in the old Cariboo road-bed played. The coach was slung on tremendous leather straps and, for all that it was so ponderous, it swayed and bounced like a swing.

"A lady school-teacher, very unenthusiastic at being assigned a rural school in the Cariboo, shared the front top seat with the driver and me. She did not speak, only sighed. The three of us were buckled into our seats by a great leather apron. It caught driver round the middle and teacher and me under our chins. We might have been infant triplets strapped abreast into the seat of a mammoth pram. If we had not been strapped we would have flown off the top of the stage. At the extra-worst bumps the heads of the inside passengers hit the roof of the coach. We heard them."

One could happily go on quoting Emily Carr after that evocative three-word sentence, one of the high points in her style, as she recounts lustily how the horses pranced and showed-off as they neared the changing barns; how beautiful she found the open, rolling Cariboo (although she says she did no painting there); what lavish meals the road-houses provided: "We ate a huge meal and were then hustled off to bed only to be torn from sleep again at two a.m. and re-mealed—a terrible spread, neither breakfast, dinner, nor supper, but a 'three-in-one' meal starting with porridge, bacon and eggs, and coffee, continuing with beef-steak, roast potatoes, and boiled cabbage, culminating in pudding, pie and strong tea. The meal climaxed finally on its centre-piece, an immense, frosted jelly-cake mounted on a pedestal platter. Its gleaming frosting shimmered under a coal-oil lamp, suspended over the table's centre. At first I thought it was a wedding-cake but as every meal in every road-house in Cariboo had just such a cake I concluded it was just Cariboo . . . .

"At three a.m. we trembled out into the cold stillness of starry not-yet day. . . . Between teacher and driver I slept, cosy as jam in a 'roly-poly'."

Finally Emily reaches her—and our—destination.

"The Hundred and Fifty Mile trading post consisted of a store, a road-house where travellers could stop or could pause between stages to get a meal, and a huge cattle barn. These wooden structures stood on a little rise" and, we conclude happily, are almost without a doubt the very

178

buildings here in AY's drawing made a mere forty years after Emily's visit. He says they form "the very centre of 150 Mile House." At the time of his visit those old buildings belonged to his hostess, Mrs. Vivien Cowan, from whose hospitable Onward Ranch he wrote on October 4, 1945: "I am very happily situated, on a ranch eleven thousand acres. It is not very exciting country—it rolls gently, the ranches are all in the valleys, and surrounded by hills covered with spruce and fir. Mrs. Cowan was one of my students at Banff, and is a very charming person. . . . They have to do much of their own work these days. Her daughter has been busy plough-ing. She has eighty acres to do."

It is nice to know that although over twenty years have passed since AY wrote the above, things have not changed too much in that part of the Cariboo. Part of the Cowan ranch is now being run by the younger generation of the family, while Mrs. Cowan devotes her time to pro-moting several pottery-making groups among Indians in the vicinity. At Williams Lake, a few miles west towards the Fraser, the big cattle roundup is still held each fall, with the auctioneer's rattling singsong and the ranchers lounging about in their ripe old hats and high-heeled boots. Among AY's bits and pieces is a battered, three-folded sheet of paper containing a trio of quick pencil sketches of the cattle auction in progress during one of his visits to Williams Lake. On the front of the page are listed the Herefords to be auctioned, weights, owners, and so on. Even such a prosaic thing as this list breathes some of the atmosphere of the Cariboo: "20 2-year Steers owned by Mel Moon, net weight 22,000 average weight 1100 lbs. . . . 24 Heavy Cows, Mixed Ownership, average weight 1235 lbs. . . ." (Did someone say beef tenderloin is $1.99 a pound?)

Some of the Owners' names reveal distant lands of origin—names like Mikkelsen, Kinvig, Piltz, Faessler, Jefferson, even Lord Martin Cecil; others could be good farmer-names for the Ottawa Valley or for anywhere in Canada—Elmer Higgins, Orville Fletcher; still others make agreeable images—Sally House and Johnny Church, or even Maida Wright. It is impossible to resist making up our dozen here with the name of Pan Phillips who was so engagingly depicted in a weekend supplement of the *Ottawa Citizen*. This independent old Cariboo rancher disdains shipping his cattle out by truck and still drives them to the auction through 100 to 150 miles of wilderness on a two-week trek in the chill of October, sleeping outdoors on the way, as he has done for over thirty years. One of his tales is about the officious lady census-taker who insisted on knowing what his name "Pan" was the abbreviation of, so he told her it was Bed-Pan, and she said he was "a dirty old man."

Which may be a good place to move along, as we have come full circle to the "rude but well-fed" caption with which our piece began!

Well, here is the end of the Cariboo Road at famous old Barkerville, once one of the most important names on the map north of San Francisco, later Canada's first ghost town, then by the mid-1960s all gussied up into a museum piece and visited by over 150,000 sightseers in a single season.

AY's sojourn in Barkerville was back in the happy-medium limbo stage, his main visit taking place in October 1945, as he recalls: "I went on my own by the station wagon bus from Quesnel over on the Fraser, about sixty miles or so. I thought I'd get a room at the old Kelly Hotel, but they were all full up with people who were working a new mine at Wells, a few miles up the road. Luckily for me the proprietress saw my service button from the First World War and said, 'I will never turn away a returned man'—and next thing I knew she'd found a room for me. I poked around Barkerville for three or four days and did quite a few oil sketches and pencil drawings. I don't recall painting any canvases from my Barkerville subjects."

AY certainly had an easier time of it than did the first lot of prospectors to reach the area—William "Dutch Bill" Dietz and his two companions, in February 1861. With one pick among the three of them (Dietz had all his supplies stolen near Lillooet) they worked their way through eight feet of snow up Quesnel River and Keithley Creek, over the divide and into this valley where they struck "a dollar to the pan" in the gravel of the icy creek which today bears William's name.

On August 21, 1862, a colourful character, Billy Barker, a run-away Cornish sailor with daredevil blue eyes and big bow tie, made his first rich strike on a claim which netted $600,000 and gained for Billy a gay young widow to wife and a roaring time in the saloons—while the money lasted, which was not very long. In that same busy month of August 1862, a mile north along the creek from Billy's claim, John A. "Cariboo" Cameron staked his claim and on December 2 struck "more gold than he had ever dreamed of owning," as Bruce Ramsey relates with relish in his delightful, picture-filled book, *Barkerville: A Guide to the Fabulous Cariboo Gold Camp.* "Williams Creek has yielded more gold than any other creek in British Columbia . . . in early years, Steele's claim gave a maximum yield of 409 oz. or $6,544 a day. . . . [In] the deep ground below the canyon . . . it is credibly stated that . . . 200 lb. of gold worth $38,000 was obtained in one day."

No wonder that by the spring of 1862, a year after Dutch Bill Dietz got there, over 6,000 men were working the creek around Barkerville, while a few thousand additional feverish lunatics were milling about in the single nameless main street of the town that had mushroomed up, that "one-mile clutter of clapboard" hemmed in between the creek and the deforested hillside. The houses were built up on poles to help keep them dry when the creek overflowed and went roaring down the main street. Each house had its own bit of wooden sidewalk at a different height from its neighbours. No wonder that Bruce Hutchison can refer to it as "the maddest" of the goldrush towns in America. Until Governor Douglas got the Cariboo Road there in fall 1865, "You had to walk 600 miles from the coast to reach it. When you got there you paid $300 a barrel for flour, $2.50 a pound for dried apples, $50 for a pair of boots," with "champagne 2 ounces of gold per pint . . . and a stove $700."

By 1867, the year Canada was born, Barkerville's heyday was already over but it still contained many active business houses including 12 saloons and 10 stores. The Cariboo Amateur Dramatic Association performed regularly in the Theatre Royal, which stood on the site of the present community hall and fire department buildings. Perhaps the old theatre's aura can still be sensed behind the scene in this drawing, which shows the spacious community hall with its mansard roof and its imposing flight of steps leading to the round-topped door, flanked by the stately fire-tower whose bell has pealed forth many an alarm. In the olden days the fire-bell was atop the Theatre Royal itself, but was of little avail on that disastrous afternoon of September 16, 1868, when at 2:30 p.m. to be precise, an amorous miner (this part is legend) tried to steal a kiss (without paying beforehand) from a hurdy-gurdy girl at Adler and Barry's Saloon, in the process knocking over a stove-pipe and starting a fire which within eighty minutes had destroyed the entire town—one hundred and sixteen buildings along both sides of the long, narrow street—all except Scott's Saloon (not dry enough to burn?). This survived until the 1930s.

Fire moved fast in Barkerville, but so did rebuilding. Within six days, according to the *Cariboo Sentinel* for September 22, 1868, over thirty houses were rebuilt, "standing in symmetrical order on the old site," while the street was widened by a much-needed fifteen feet and the sidewalks were made uniform. This time great attention was paid to a new fire station, as Bruce Ramsey tells in the delightful section on "The Fire Department." A leather fire hose was procured by July 1869, but the fire reels imported from San Francisco did not arrive until October 1871!

We can visualize the intrepid Fire Brigade in their red shirts and shiny helmets tearing along the street of our drawing here, watched eagerly from the porch of the tiny house next door (centre in our drawing) by the little girls who in due course became "two old ladies who had been born in Barkerville and had never travelled farther from it than Quesnel. They had gone there to see a railway train. Having seen it, they were glad to come home again. Barkerville, they said, was good enough for them."

180

PLATE 84

Barkerville in the Cariboo, B.C., October 1945

Of course there were not only saloons and theatricals in bustling, brash Barkerville back in the olden days, but also at least five churches, including Roman Catholic, Anglican, Presbyterian, Wesleyan Methodist, and Welsh, as well as two Masonic Lodges, one of them Chinese. By great good fortune, one of the oldest church buildings has survived all the perils of time, of frequent hellish fires and of ditto, albeit well-meaning, improvements. This is the admirable little Church of St. Saviour's (Anglican), which held its first services in September 1870, and which today's photographs show in the same good condition it was in at the time of AY's drawing of October 8, 1945. Incidentally, an exact comparison between drawing and photograph, possible in this rare case, proves that such pencil studies by AY are extremely accurate as well as, at times, charmingly poetic. The diminutive scale of St. Saviour's here can be gauged by the fact that the width of the church (not including the attached vestry) is only twenty feet. Bruce Ramsey's book on Barkerville gives many details of its construction and illustrates the interior with its neat, unpainted, vertical board walls, its tall lancet windows in the curve of the choir, the lovingly embroidered altar cloth, the hand-hewn lectern and pulpit, and the pedal organ which looks as if it had accompanied the singing of faithful gold diggers and others through many long years.

The Anglican mission had already reached Barkerville in 1861, and by 1863 plans were advanced under the Reverend John Sheepshanks for a "small, substantial, well-proportioned building to be erected at a cost of $1,200." But the Cariboo was apparently too tough for the Reverend Sheepshanks; the mission fell vacant for two years, and it was September 1868 before the Reverend James Reynard from Yorkshire took over with fresh zeal, renting an old saloon for use as church cum school (which had 250 books). But within two weeks everything—including church vessels and vestments—was wiped out by the Great Fire. During the following terrible winter the Reverend Reynard, like many of his flock, survived on slim rations (potatoes on Sunday only, for instance). Despite all, he pressed onward with building plans, personally provided the design for the new church, and put a large share of his modest stipend into the building fund (which is more than his parishioners did, it seems!). Finally by discreet pressure on some of Barkerville's merchants, he succeeded within two years of the Fire in erecting what the *Cariboo Sentinel* called "an elegant structure. . . . The style is 'Early English' in which architectural effect is attained by due proportion of parts, bold and simple forms, rather than by elaborate ornament." And in the somehow movingly mid-Victorian words of its parson, it became "a church which shall prove that men working underground have still some hopes which go upward and heavenward."

Melancholy aftermath: the hardships the Reverend Reynard had suffered took heavy toll of his health, and within five years of the opening of his fine new church he had died, still a young man.

Early death through accident and illness befell many of those who now lie buried in Barkerville's old cemetery on the hillside north of the town. AY has commented on the fine original grave markers he saw there, handmade of wood, with black painted lettering which seemed to stand out in relief while the background weathered away—"some really beautiful," he says. Apparently many of these were made by a local character who sent them in place of a floral tribute. The oldest grave at present there is that of "Peter Gibson of Vankleek Hill, County of Prescott, Canada West, Who Died July 24th, 1863, aged 31 years." Another marker commemorates "Margaret Jane Blair, Beloved wife of John Pinkerton. Died May 30, 1880, aged 21 years 7 mos. Also their daughter, died April 19, 1879, aged 10 days:

> O cruel death; thou waster severe,
> To snatch so suddenly away
> This cherished loved-one in her prime
> To mix among the mouldering clay.

Another cherished wife and mother, perhaps the first to die in that area, lay for a time with her infant daughter in the cold earth beside Williams Creek. This was Sophia, wife of John A. "Cariboo" Cameron of Glengarry County. Their colourful wedding at Ottawa's famous old Russell House has recently been the subject of an article by Harry Walker in the *Ottawa Journal*. By one of the strangest ironies to come out of the wild past of the region, "Cariboo" Cameron's own grave is there in Barkerville, under a headstone donated by his friends after he died a pauper in 1888, having spent an immense part of his fortune keeping his promise to his dying wife to take her body back home to Cornwall in Upper Canada. Sophia died of "mountain fever" on October 22, 1862, six weeks before Cameron made the strike which within one year brought him $350,000. True to his promise to Sophia, he had her coffin dug up that same winter 1862/1863 (before the Cariboo Road was completed), and he and his partner packed it on horseback the hundreds of miles to the coast, through thirty-six days of sub-zero weather ("40 below" says Ramsey). A second provisional funeral was held on March 3, 1863 at Victoria, where Sophia lay until November 7, when her remains (Bruce Hutchison says preserved in alcohol) were shipped via Panama back to Cornwall for a third funeral. The rumour that the coffin was filled with gold, not with Sophia, caused her to be exhumed once more, then finally—for the fourth time—laid to rest in peace.

PLATE 85

The Church of St. Saviour's in Barkerville, B.C., October 8, 1945

Did someone like "Cariboo" Cameron once live in this rough but neat little hand-hewn shack which for about a century has perched against the hillside at Barkerville up in inland British Columbia? Did it once mean home for some colourful character like Billy Barker who "had gold in his poke but ended up broke"? Although it is estimated that in the twelve years up until 1871 about $25,000,000 in gold came out of the Cariboo, very little of the money seems to have remained with the original prospectors. Most of the memorable personalities seemed to end up in an Old Man's Home in Kamloops or in Victoria. Dutch Dietz was one who died in a Home a brief sixteen years after his original strike, "suffering great pain from a sickness developed in the Cariboo."

Some left a more cheerful story behind them, however, as for instance Twelve-Foot Davis, who lies buried over eastward by Peace River. Davis reached the gold fields too late to find land free for the regulation 100-by-100-foot claim, but, almost even better, he discovered that two other parties had staked claims that were a bit too wide, so Davis squeezed

in a twelve-foot-wide claim for himself in between the giants, and did very well thereby, completely protected by the law. On Twelve-Foot Davis' gravestone today is inscribed "He was Every Man's Friend and Never Locked His Cabin Door."

It is not hard to visualize Twelve-Foot's cabin as resembling this one here, which AY drew in 1945, when he recalls still seeing a few old-timers around. All over the West in the wake of the successive gold rushes, some individuals remained behind in their home-made shacks, not necessarily stranded or disgruntled failures who lacked the means or were ashamed to return to their original homes, but more probably strong-minded characters who preferred to stay on and eke out an independent livelihood by panning for a bit of gold or setting the occasional trap-line, rather than face the other kind of rat-race "out there." Perhaps they were "disillusioned but not defeated," as one roaming would-be prospector, whom we shall meet again later, described himself after two years of arduous and futile search for gold. "My fortune had not been made, but I was far richer in experience and in a knowledge of the rougher side of life." Some of those who chose to stay on in the wilds were men of culture—a graduate of Oxford who quoted Latin and Greek authors, a graduate of Toronto who was working on an essay about sources of modern slang in the works of Shakespeare. We can visualize the well-worn books on a shelf against the shanty wall alongside the pewter plate and cup and the battered teapot.

"Gold can be all to the good, and it is all right to grub for it in one form or another, but it's not all that important in the long run," was the timely and philosophical decision expressed by AY in a letter he wrote to me from the Cowans' ranch at 150 Mile House a couple of days before this drawing was made. I was at that time heading off to other northern wilds to spend four years as a relief worker with the Friends Service Committee in war-blackened northern Finland. (There the Quakers lived in barracks hardly more luxurious than this shack in the Cariboo.) AY wrote: "So you are making the big plunge. Your letter arrived yesterday on my birthday; I found it on my return from Horsefly Lake. Well, old timer, the only wealth worth acquiring is experience, and this promises to be a big chunk of it. . . ."

PLATE 86

Miner's shack, Barkerville,
October 7, 1945

Miner's Shack
A Y Jackson
Barkerville Oct 7/45

Now watch AY go over the top—northward across Latitude Sixty into that vast area—39.3% of Canada's broad domain—vaguely named Yukon and Northwest Territories (the latter north-*east* of the former). The subject of our drawing here is the swift and wicked little Smart River that snakes along the boundary between northern British Columbia and the Yukon Territory, forming part of the vast network of headwaters of the Liard River, which eventually joins the mighty Mackenzie to the east, for its last thousand miles to the Arctic Ocean.

The water route up the Liard and its tributaries and over the watershed to the upper reaches of the Yukon River was one way to head for the north-west in the olden days. It was a herculean struggle all the way for the men searching for an overland route to the Pacific, or for furs, or for gold. Close to the heart of this particular region, and of our story for some pages to come, is the epic told in *Son of the North* by the late Charles Camsell, geologist, explorer, faithful federal government functionary for forty-five years. Camsell, whom Malcolm MacDonald calls "child of this wilderness . . . and its most famous son," was six years older than AY. He was born in 1876 at Fort Liard, two thousand miles from a doctor, one of the eleven children of the Hudson Bay's Chief Factor for the Mackenzie District. These true sons of the north were the first of the white race to be born in the Northwest Territories.

The Upper Liard region was more or less Charles Camsell's own back yard, yet he and his party wrestled its icy streams for almost two years (1897 to 1899) along the route of the old voyageurs, forcing their way through Devil's Gorge, frozen in for months in winter, and nearly starving in their attempt to live off the land, without getting anywhere near their goal. That goal was the point where Dawson City now stands—at the junction of the Klondike and Yukon Rivers.

The great Klondike gold rush at the end of the century was one important factor in opening the interior of the Yukon wilderness. By another odd twist of fate, it took the Second World War to carry the process further. And it was the War which helped explain AY's presence in October 1943 on the ice-fringed marge of Smart River, not far from Watson Lake, on the Yukon's southern bounds.

Getting there involved no slow upstream struggle for AY, to be sure: no poling, tracking, portaging, no foundering of his equipment in icy depths. Being tough, AY could probably have made the trip that way if he'd had to, but it would have taken so long, there'd have been no time for art! In the fall of 1943, a mere forty-five years after that most strenuous of all gold rushes, AY *flew* from Edmonton, Alberta to Whitehorse in the Yukon in a matter of a few hours, covering 1,200 miles as the crow flies, only half the distance that previous travellers had to make by land and water. AY and his companion, the artist H. G. Glyde of Calgary, were undoubtedly the first Canadian artists to fly the route, several years before civilian air travel began in that region. Indeed, it was only eight years before, in 1935, that Charles Camsell, by then Deputy Minister of Mines and Resources, flew in stages from Prince Rupert to Fort Liard in a single engine Fairchild 71, to make the very first "risky pioneer flight across mountains that had never been crossed before by plane in that latitude."

The outbreak of war in 1939, with the ever-increasing threat of enemy

(*continued*)

186

PLATE 87

Smart River on the
Alaska Highway [*October 1943*]

torpedo attack along the west coast from Alaska southward, led to the speedy construction by the Royal Canadian Air Force of air bases along the inland route to the Yukon and Alaska; likewise to the building of the Canol oil line from Norman Wells on the Mackenzie through the mountains to Whitehorse. Equally essential was the construction, by engineers of the United States Army, of the great road that was first known as the Alaska Military Highway. This extends from the northern end of the existing road in the Peace River district at the Alberta-British Columbia boundary, across the northern reaches of the latter province and the southwest corner of the Yukon to Fairbanks, Alaska. A stretch of 1,527 miles, it was completed between March and October 1942—"a significant engineering feat because of difficulties of terrain and weather."

AY's sketching trip in the fall of 1943, while the new road was still in exclusively military use, can be correctly classified as part of his own personal "war effort." In younger days, during the First World War, he had proudly played an active part overseas in the newly established Canadian War Records. At that time Canada had been a pioneer in this field. Now, as we struggled through the first difficult years of World War II, AY felt that our art efforts were lagging rather sadly. He participated vigorously in an artists' symposium that was published in February 1942 under the title "Canada at War," in a special number of Walter Abell's lively brainchild, *Maritime Art*, shortly before this became *Canadian Art*. In September 1942, AY took part in a CBC radio discussion with

John Grierson of the National Film Board and H. O. McCurry of the National Gallery on ways and means in which Canadian artists could best help the war effort. Portions of that talk appeared on October 3rd, 1942, his sixtieth birthday, in the lively Toronto *News*, under the heading "Art and War." The article decried the scattered artistic efforts that "lacked spontaneity and guts," and deplored the entanglement in official red tape; it contained a strong plea for co-ordination of the visual arts to "sustain morale." "It is not too late yet," growled AY, "if it could be got into the heads of people in government that art is an active force in society and therefore has a definite job to do in a nation at war." Perhaps this helped jolt loose some funds to send the younger artists overseas late in 1943 and in 1944.

On the home front, meanwhile, it was AY who suggested the series of large silk screen prints to brighten the drab walls of military barracks and boost army spirit. There were thirty designs in all, donated by individual artists, and sponsored by private companies so that no less than 17,500 prints were made (without profit) by Sampson, Matthews of Toronto, and sent overseas. AY and Charles Comfort provided the first two subjects: Comfort, a rich brown and gold Ontario lake scene; AY, the village of St. Fidèle in winter, with the St. Lawrence in the background. AY's second design, for a series somewhat smaller in size, was made from the subject of the present drawing of Smart River, the silk screen being called *River on the Alaska Highway*. AY has always staunchly supported these rugged and handsome prints. The fine one of J. W. Morrice's *Quebec Ferry* (prepared by Sydney Hallam) still graces his kitchen wall in Ottawa, over twenty years later.

The second of AY's "war efforts" took him to the Yukon to make records of the Highway, the RCAF bases, and the Canol pipe line. He and Glyde went as free-lance artists sponsored by the National Gallery, and were given hospitality and transportation by the U.S. Army during their three weeks' stay. ("We were disgracefully comfortable!" he told the Lethbridge *Herald* soon after his return.) From Whitehorse they first drove west to Kluane Lake, than back along the full length of the Alaska Highway, "the great vistas changing with every rise or swing of the road," as AY recalled in a talk in November 1943 at the Art Gallery in Toronto. Their stops for sketching en route had to be limited to fifteen or twenty minutes, so AY did "innumerable pencil notes," most of which are still to be located and catalogued. From these were painted the oil sketches, about twenty by February 1944, and a number of canvases. AY's article "Sketching on the Alaska Highway" for *Canadian Art* in the spring of 1944 became the basis for the corresponding section in *A Painter's Country*. The 1944 article was well illustrated by three of H. G. Glyde's oil sketches, and two by AY; one was the *Smart River*, made from our present drawing, vivid and flashing, certainly a morale booster full of "spontaneity and guts" as specified; the other was a vista of the great highway between Watson Lake and Nelson, with the road telescoping off into the snow-covered mountains and a lone army truck bowling along. This subject has been used in a centennial issue of our Canadian postage stamps for the eight-cent stamp. "A good idea," says AY, "only I wish they had put the lettering of *Postes Postage* across the big empty road in the foreground, and left the white peaks visible."

Every time AY, with his wonderfully active visual memory, sees the drawing of the truly "smart" little Smart River, he recalls the exact second when he became aware of this exciting motif as they roared down the Highway. "That subject was such a beauty," says AY, "I simply had to yell STOP! to the driver—and he did!"

*   *   *

Letter from AYJ to NJ in Ottawa
Whitehorse, Yukon, Oct. 24th [1943]
. . . Came up here on short notice with Glyde of Calgary. Having a grand time but feel rather ineffective in portraying the Alaska highway in three weeks. It should be three months and then some. It's a grand country and no lack of stuff to paint. To really symbolize the whole thing is impossible—mountains, lakes, camps, old shacks, construction on a grand scale, airfields—it is endless and all we can do is see it and make a report, with drawings, notes and a few sketches.

We are guests of the U.S. Public Roads Administration, and they have been very kind to us. They are a swell lot of boys. We have had good weather ever since we arrived. It is cold at nights; the ground is frozen and the lakes, but no snow as yet. Tomorrow we start down the highway by motor for eight hundred miles, sketching as we go. We came in by plane, and it's quick but you don't see much. . . .

How well the name Whitehorse evokes the foaming crests of that perilous five-mile stretch of river that lies just inside the threshold of what was once "the front door to the Yukon"! Up the steep "front steps" in the gold rush days climbed the unending line of the thousands who had swarmed up the West Coast by boat, only to discover on landing that they had personally to pack their ton of required supplies either over the White Pass from Skagway ("the worst trail this side of Hell"), or over the Chilkoot Pass a few miles west, that "wall of glittering white, with a final slope so precipitous that no animal could cross it . . . only man could defy successfully its dizzy grade."

In the winter of 1897/1898 it took the average able-bodied man carrying a fifty-pound load on his back six hours to scale the final thousand feet— the Chilkoot's famous "Golden Stairs" at their angle of 35 degrees. Unless he paid $1.00 a pound to porters he would have to make forty trips back and forth to shuttle over his ton of goods, and this usually took him about three months because snow fell in the pass to a depth of seventy feet that winter and there were several avalanches as well. In spite of all this, as Pierre Berton recounts in *Klondike*, the Canadian North West Mounted Police at the international border at the top of the Chilkoot Pass checked through some *twenty-two thousand* individuals during that winter season— by that route alone. . . .

Once over the coastal barricade, the stampeders camped and built themselves boats of all sizes and shapes for their final half-thousand miles to the "city of gold." Not all of the 7,000 home-made craft made the journey intact. The fearful rapids of the White Horse alone claimed 150 boats and at least ten human lives. Yet it is fantastic what did get through— as for example the scow loaded with nothing but cats and kittens, along with their enterprising owner. Safely arrived in Dawson City, each fluffy feline fetched a whole ounce of gold dust (then worth $16.00) from miners lonesome for warm, soft—and relatively safe—companionship. Someone even got a cow alive over the White Pass in the spring of 1898 and sold fresh milk at $5.00 a mug. (An equal amount of whisky cost one-fifth that price at the time.) Getting things there was the trick.

Much busy boat traffic in 1897/1898 came the long way round (about two thousand extra miles) by sea and *up* the Yukon River. And by the 1940s the airplane in turn took over, so that Malcolm MacDonald, with Deputy Minister Camsell in their official private plane in 1942, "skimmed over [the rapids] and landed one mile away on the airfield at Whitehorse." Our artists AY and Glyde lumbered in almost as comfortably aboard their U.S. army transport plane a year later, in October 1943.

By then Whitehorse was a hive of activity for construction crews surfacing the Alaska Highway, air force people running the gigantic wartime air base, oil people running the refinery at the end of the Canol pipe line, plus the usual array of prospectors, miners, trappers, and Indians— "a most picturesque jumble, and we could have sketched there happily for a month," said AY, regretting the shortness of their three-week military travel permit.

In Whitehorse, the head of Yukon River navigation, the remains of many old river boats had found their last resting place and were drawn up along the river bank, disintegrating peacefully. Pierre Berton, born in Whitehorse in 1920, recalls playing among them as a small boy, and mentions two famous old ones—the *Yukoner* and the *Bonanza King*—at that time used for lumber storage. These may well be the very ones we see here in AY's drawing.

Back in the busy summer of '98 sixty steamboats, eight tugboats, and twenty enormous barges were in operation on the Yukon: "One Seattle shipyard knocked together ten or twelve sternwheelers for the Yukon trade and moved ten of them safely to their destination; they were 'built by the mile and cut apart in proper lengths' as one of their officers put it. There seemed, sometimes, to be a boat around every bend in the river. . . . Ship after ship puffed into town, many of them loaded with champagne and brightly plumaged dancing-girls, pennants, flags, and bunting fluttering gaily from their masts, clouds of white smoke bursting from their yellow stacks, a Niagara of spray churning back from their orange paddlewheels.

"Up the river at top speed that summer came the dashing John Irving aboard his trim steamboat, the *Yukoner*. . . . A great gold eagle was fastened in front of his pilothouse as a talisman, and a huge picture of a bulldog hung . . . in the dining-salon, while an enormous Negro bodyservant stayed constantly at his side during the journey. . . . An orchestra contributed to the general air of festivity and bonhomie."

The elegant *Bonanza King* was built by Nels Peterson who had grown rich from one of the early bench claims. He invested $90,000 in the two ships of his Yukon Flyer Line. The other ship, christened the *Philip B. Low*, sank so often that the wags referred to her as the *Fill up Below*, so she was changed to *Eldorado*. The extraordinary photograph at the back of Berton's *Klondike* shows the big sign advertising the *Eldorado* and the *Bonanza King* with the confident assertion, "ten days to Seattle and Vancouver" (not mentioning that a change of ship would be necessary!).

It is saddening to reflect that the old sternwheelers have now all disappeared from the Yukon River. Aeroplanes and automobiles have penetrated the wilderness; the steamers are obsolete.

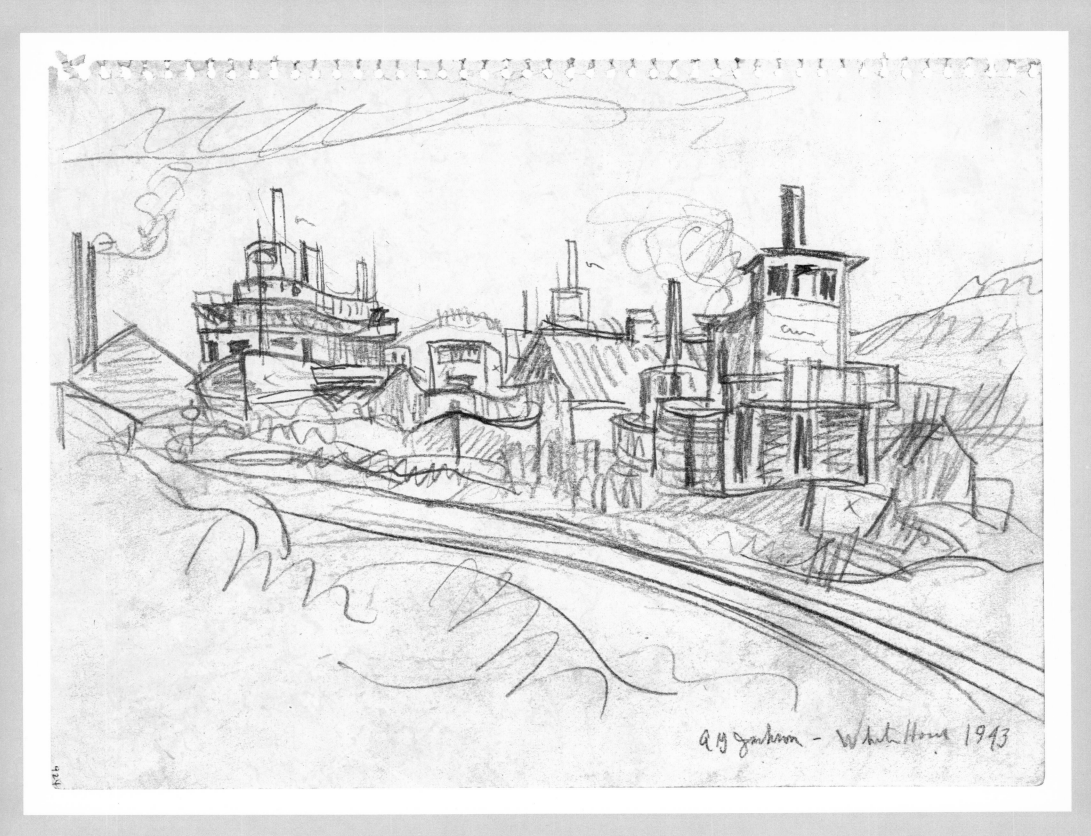

PLATE 88

Old river boats at Whitehorse, Yukon Territory, October 1943

Think of the Yukon before man got there—that distant, vast, and silent place of mountains and river valleys, without a boat, a road, or an airfield in its uncounted thousands of miles. Think of the rat-race for gold during the most spectacular stampede the world has known: rags to riches and back again within a score of months. Think of the racket—in every sense—around the spot where the little stream with the unpronounceable name Thron-diuck flowed into the mighty Yukon. In the year 1898, it is estimated, at least thirty thousand stampeders and their "friends" swarmed in and out of Dawson City at the mouth of the Klondike; seventy years later the city contained less than eight hundred inhabitants. In the interim about a quarter billion dollars' worth of "the yellow stuff" was taken out of the Klondike alone, and is now busily circulating somewhere else.

Think of the contrasting ways in which men lived and got about, then and now. AY's vigorous study of an old log shack near Whitehorse, drawn during his visit in 1943, shows one stage of an earlier "then." The name Alaska House sounds as if it might once have been a general stopping-place for stampeders heading for the Klondike or later for Nome, Alaska. It may even have been in use when AY himself was accepting the rugged but hearty hospitality of the U.S. Public Roads Administration which had authority along the entire Highway.

"Now" with all its changes can be shown with vivid directness by AY's return to the Yukon twenty-one years later, when he was approaching his eighty-second birthday. On September 9th, 1964, he left Ottawa, Ontario by regulation flight with Air Canada, in company with his artist friend Ralph Burton of Ottawa. At their destination they were joined by Dr. Maurice Haycock, government geologist cum enthusiastic landscapist. By September 11th, within two days of leaving Ottawa, Jackson and Burton had covered a distance that would have taken long months in the olden days.

"In Whitehorse," says AY's preliminary postcard greeting. "Had a grand day coming from Edmonton. Sunny all day, colour starting. In a Motel. We have rented a station wagon for five hundred dollars a month and expect to cover the country. Old friends have looked me up. All ready to start work today. . . ."

On the 15th of September, a growl from en route to Dawson: "This is the third rainy day in succession. Kind of fed up. Passed Mount Logan, couldn't see it. Went through some exciting country [i.e. Kluane Lake] but could not paint. We try hard: get up at six a.m. and to bed at ten. . . . We have been staying at motels, mostly doing our own cooking . . . bought two salmon from an Indian, ten pounds for a dollar. . . . A big change from when I was here last, twenty-one years ago. Whole towns have sprung up where there used to be nothing."

Letters from later in September reveal a cheerier mood: "Dawson City. Ten days since we left. 20 panels painted, apart from five or six scrape offs. The weather is nice again and we are very cosily settled in a bungalow (three beds, bathroom and stove for ten dollars a day). This town is not as dead as the reports you hear about it. . . . We went up Eldorado Creek; for ten miles it is just piles of gravel that has been washed for gold, several abandoned dredges, and a lot of miners shanties mostly empty and falling into ruins. . . . I've met lots of people. Talked to the kids in the High School and gave a half hour interview coming out on radio October 1st. Not much to draw in Dawson, mostly old houses—all empty. The whole town was laid out criss cross, and it makes poor compositions."

Later, on September 29th: "On the home stretch. . . . We went north for two days to the Ogilvie Mountains, got our first snow, and saw hundreds of caribou. Yesterday morning we headed for Keno Hill, about a hundred miles east and north of Dawson. We are guests of a big silver mine, United Keno. . . . The mines are all over the place, about eight of them. The highest one, the old Lucky Queen, is over six thousand feet. We climbed it in our motor car. On top it was like January—snow and cold winds, and mountains all around us. We almost froze. Some ravens were flying around, no other signs of life. They had taken out all the silver long ago."

Time, the magazine so nicely named to harmonize with our theme of Then and Now, caught up with AY just as his 82nd birthday was celebrated with a great party for old and new friends in the Yukon. On October 9th, 1964 *Time* printed Maurice Haycock's photograph of a rather frozen-looking AY hard at work as usual, over its "timely" text: "Painter Jackson at Mining Camp. Jackson, wearing a frumpy fedora [AY's best brown suede hat that also went to Baffin in 1965!]—sat on old boardwalks sketching. . . . Concentrating 'on the little things,' he sketched swayback stores, the sagging Third Avenue blacksmith shop and, on the bank of the Klondike River, the half caved-in log cabin once occupied by Prospector Robert Henderson, who was responsible for the Klondike's first discovery of gold at Bonanza Creek in 1896.

"At Dawson's Log Cabin Motel, Jackson held an impromptu showing for local teachers and amateur painters. Padding back and forth, he carried paintings from his bedroom into the kitchen, where he propped them against jam cans and ketchup bottles on an oilcloth-covered table. . . ."

Well—this picture of AY at eighty-two has a familiar look to us who have been following him through Canada for quite a while. Then and now—the teens, the thirties, the sixties—are not so different in AY's way of life. "Enough for a Group of Seventy," *Time* observed.

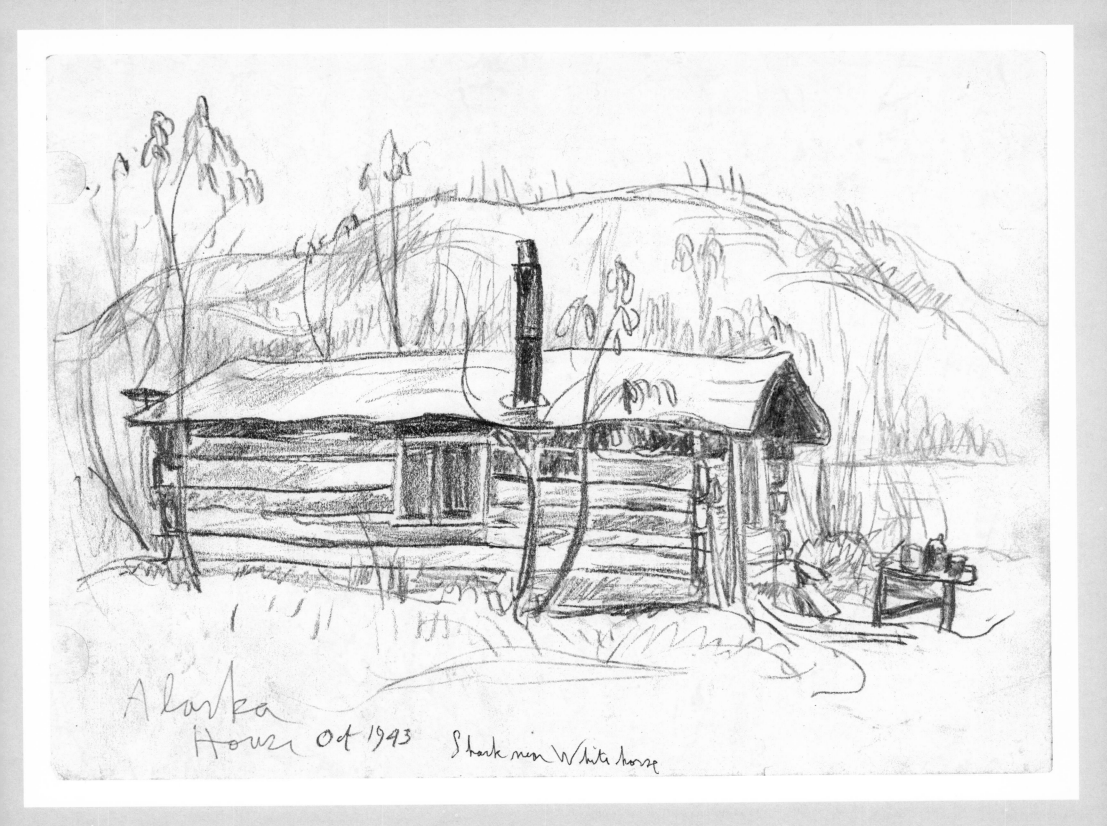

Alaska
House Oct 1943   Shack near Whitehorse

PLATE 89

Alaska House—shack near Whitehorse, October 1943

Now we trail the sturdy Jacksonian figure northward down the Athabasca and the Slave to the Northwest Territories and to places with sonorous, evocative names such as Great Slave and Great Bear, Fort Resolution, Yellowknife, Port Radium; then over the upper rim of Great Bear Lake into the Barren Lands; finally away east of the Coppermine to the September Mountains; then over and out into the ice again, where we came from in the beginning.

Flashback then, to scenes of old and to friends dear to the heart, as the *Manitoba Free Press* sets the frame of reference for the mid-1920s: "The West has now been opened up . . . . The new trend is to the north—to unlock the resources of regions that were formerly thought of little or no value or too inaccessible for development. . . . Mr. Jackson's bold venture might be regarded as suggestive of the new attitude of Canadians in general toward their vast domain in the north."

The bold venture here was AY's 1927 journey to the eastern Arctic with his new friend Dr. Frederick Banting. Now we watch the same two good companions set forth again, scarcely a year later, to explore the Great Slave Lake—"a part of the country few Canadians at that time knew anything about," writes AY in *A Painter's Country*.

How fortunate the pioneer artist and his keen amateur-painter friend were to be invited to accompany a Canadian who knew Great Slave probably as well as anyone alive at that time: Dr. James Mackintosh Bell, 1877/1934, distinguished geologist and consulting mining engineer, handsome, debonair, and "a great companion," according to AY. By 1899 Mackintosh Bell had paid his first visit to Great Slave Lake, wintering at Fort Resolution so as to make an early start the following spring. Then he and young Charles Camsell (our Son of the North), with three none-too-dependable local "assistants," made their memorable first exploration of an immense section north and east of Great Bear Lake, a stirring epic that both Bell and Camsell have described in their memoirs. In AY's well-worn copy of Bell's *Far Places* the chapter "Great Slave Lake Visited and Revisited" tells of six visits up to time of publication in 1931, and includes many details on the 1928 trip. At that time Bell would be in his 52nd, AY in his 46th, Banting in his 37th year.

AY found that "it was slow travelling getting to the Great Slave." First stage was by train from Edmonton to Waterways just east of Fort McMurray, Alberta. Ten years *later*, in July 1938, Count Gontrin de Poncins, heading for his *Kabloona* adventure, described the same journey on "a wonderful train with a stove in each car on which the passengers heated their tins of food; a train that carried trappers, Indians, and colonizers of every speech and nation into the North, cautiously covering the three hundred miles from Edmonton in twenty-two weary hours. . . ."

Even slower was travel for the Camsell family back in 1884. It took the Hudson's Bay Factor father, brave mother and five small children from June 10th to mid-September to proceed with their brigade of York boats from their home at Fort Simpson on the Mackenzie to Winnipeg—some two thousand miles in all. From age 8 to 18, ten full years, the schoolboy Camsell could not once get home to his family, for the simple reason that it took all summer to go one way.

AY missed by a mere nine years the adventurous Athabasca scow brigade which from about 1885 to 1919 carried in the entire provisions for the northern outposts and brought back the furs. Sixty to one hundred flat-bottomed scows, manned by Indians and Métis from Lac La Biche, made the annual dash down the swift Athabasca, which drops 360 feet in the hundred miles above Fort McMurray and contains sections meaningfully named Boiler, Crooked, Little Cascade, Big Cascade—a succession of thrills without equal in northern travel. How AY would have enjoyed that instead of the dreary train trip!

However, AY at least caught up with the picturesque wood-burning sternwheeler in which the travellers proceeded downstream from Fort McMurray, by way of romantic old Fort Chipewyan on Lake Athabasca, and on down the Slave River to the head of the rapids with their 100-foot drop above Fort Smith. Perhaps AY's sternwheeler stopped to "wood up" with some of the very logs cut and neatly piled by a memorable character at Fort Smith, one Edward Martin, who died June 13, 1928, and whose epitaph reads: "The Best Woodcutter of the North, he supplied fuel to steamboats. A silent and lone man who took pride in his work and built an honest pile."

The 16-mile portage at Fort Smith, across which little Charles Camsell had ridden proudly behind his father, where young Mackintosh Bell had struggled for "a day's journey with oxen along a trail, for more than half of which the animals sank to their bellies in a slough of mud and muskeg," had by 1928 become a fairly decent road with taxis for hire. After crossing it, AY and Banting at long last got their ride on a scow, pushed by the puffing little tug *Liard River* from Fort Smith down the winding muddy Slave.

And so they came safely to the Great Slave Lake and to the tiny settlement with the noble name Fort Resolution.

PLATE 90

Shoreline of the Slave River at Fort Smith, Northwest Territories, July 7, 1928

Ft Smith July 7 '28

How poetically Mackintosh Bell recalls his first arrival at the venerable trading post on Great Slave Lake in his youthful days, back in 1899: "On that first journey we reached Fort Resolution from Fort Smith, after four days' travel by canoe. My impressions of the settlement on that clear warm evening are still vivid. On a shelving shore in front of the Hudson's Bay post, the Catholic Church and the fur traders' establishment, stood a village of skin wigwams. From each rose a column of smoke—vertical and pink. Some canvas tents, scattered here and there, belonged to would-be prospectors, stranded on their journey to the Klondike. Indians of all ages squatted around, getting protection from the flies in the smoke of their camp-fires. There were dogs everywhere, all of the wolf-like variety, starved, and with last year's hair hanging in great chunks from their emaciated bodies. . . . Small canoes passed silently back and forth between the shore and the fish-nets in the open bay.

"In a few days all of the wigwams had vanished. Like a magic city they had disappeared overnight. The Indians had gone with the dogs to their hunting-grounds, not to return till Christmas."

Well, things have not changed very radically at Fort Resolution by July 10, 1928. A few tepees stretch along the beach in picturesque disarray, and still seem to be made of skin, although some Indians may have acquired the canvas tents that we see here. The stranded Klondikers have melted away, but a new wave of mining excitement has begun and prospectors are passing through again. The starving dogs still overrun the settlement.

The Indians that trade at Resolution bear the name Yellowknives, from their implements of copper once derived from deposits on the Coppermine River farther north. Always a small tribe, they numbered by 1928 not more than 150. Bell found that "they lack the gaiety of the Eskimos and the friendliness of the Algonquin tribes. Superstitious, not infrequently diseased, pursuing a highly precarious existence, and having no love for the white man whom not unnaturally they regard with suspicion as an intruder and the cause of the disappearance of game, their life is drab, sordid, and singularly gloomy. But . . . they are patient under misfortune, display remarkable endurance, and, though over-solicitous on their own behalf, are ready to treat hospitably those in distress, whether of their own race or another."

Camsell writes enthusiastically about the great banquet tendered him by Chief Little Dog of the Mountain Indians, to whom he travelled alone in winter. First, all present ceremoniously washed their hands in one small birchbark dish full of water; then they attacked vast quantities of cooked moose, caribou, beaver, and bear; eventually the old chief fell asleep in the

teepee with his bare feet sticking out from under his blanket and the snow blowing in on them all night. "The old fellow was tough," recalls Camsell happily. To which one can only add that Camsell was no tenderfoot either!

But for unequalled toughness and ability to adapt to native ways, as well as for an enthralling and blood-curdling tale of Northern Indian habits, of feasts of yore and of the tents in which they were held, we must turn to the man who from his twenty-fourth to his twenty-sixth year lived and travelled as sole white man with the Indians of the far north—none other of course than the redoubtable Samuel Hearne (1745/1792), the first person to *record* the existence of Great Slave Lake, and honoured as its discoverer. In the dead of black winter (1771/1772) Hearne and his party of Chipewyan nomads, at that stage in "twenty tents, containing in the whole about two hundred persons," pitched camp close to the spot where the tents drawn by AY stood in 1928, some 156 years later.

With vivid details of feast and famine and fortitude (intestinal as well!) *A Journey from Prince of Wales's Fort in Hudson's Bay to the Northern Ocean in the Years 1769, 1770, 1771, and 1772* tells how the area around Great Slave Lake abounded in game in those days. There were beaver, deer (both caribou and red deer), moose, and buffalo. (The last—a novelty on the white man's menu—Hearne considered "exceedingly good eating.") The lake contained great quantities of fine fish which could be caught through holes chipped in the eight-foot-thick ice. Hearne mentions the trout of 35 to 40 pounds, huge pike and whitefish or *tittimeg*.

The happiest Indians, Hearne observed, were those who lived free of the white man to whom they could only become enslaved as purveyors of furs. In 1771, the ravages of smallpox carried off nine-tenths of the Northern Indians, according to Hearne's estimate. At the time of AY's visit another plague of the white man, influenza, was sweeping the north. The natives fled from the danger of contagion at Fort Resolution; Mackintosh Bell, AY and Banting discovered lonely new graves on an island they visited. "Probably one-tenth of the native population died, and the mortality would have been even greater had it not been for the devotion of the missionaries at Resolution, Hay River and elsewhere."

Mindful of all that ancient desolation, we can take some comfort in the afterthought that now, by the latter 1960s, there is in Edmonton, Alberta a fine new hospital devoted particularly to Indians, Eskimos, and others flown in from the North. On July 1st of Canada's Centennial Year the whole world could watch by Telstar a fine healthy Indian baby boy in the process of being born—not in a caribou skin tent, but in the Charles Camsell Hospital, dedicated to the people of the North.

Fort Resolution July 10 '28

PLATE 91

Indian encampment, Fort Resolution, Great Slave Lake, July 10, 1928

Anyone asked to guess who uttered the above words could reasonably answer: "AY when he tackled this tough subject!" But the answer would be out by one hundred and fifty-six years and six months, almost to the day. The observation was made not in hot July 1928 but in cold January 1772, by Mr. Samuel Hearne, who had just reached Great Slave Lake in the hardest manner imaginable: on foot from Hudson Bay by way of the Arctic sea-coast at the mouth of the Coppermine River. Utterly dependent on the whims (occasionally murderous) of his Indian companions, Hearne must have walked in all some five thousand miles through the Barren Lands, whose name he so feelingly coined. His journal gives an admirable explanation for the presence of great masses of driftwood on the southern side of the lake near the outlet of the Slave River, which he called the Athapuscow, as he did the lake: "[On January 16, 1772] we arrived at the grand Athapuscow River, which at that part is about two miles wide, and empties itself into the great lake of the same name we had so lately crossed. . . .

"The woods about this river, particularly the pines and poplars, are the tallest and stoutest I have seen in any part of North America. The birch also grows to a considerable height, and some species of willow are likewise tall. . . .

"The bank of the river in most parts is very high, and in some places not less than a hundred feet above the ordinary surface of the water. As the soil is of a loamy quality, it is very subject to moulder or wash away by heavy rains, even during the short Summer allotted to this part of the globe. The breaking up of the ice in the Spring is annually attended with a great deluge, when, I am told, it is not uncommon to see whole points of land washed away by the inundations; and as the wood grows close to the edge of the banks, vast quantities of it are hurried down the stream by the irresistible force of the water and ice, and conveyed into the great lake already mentioned; on the shores and islands of which, there lies the greatest quantity of drift wood I ever saw. Some of this wood is large enough to make masts for the largest ships that are built."

Hearne made a drawing of the tall trees during the first week he was at Great Slave Lake, by far our earliest visual record of that part of the world. *A Winter View in the Athapuscow Lake* is reproduced in the 1911 edition of his journal, facing page 232. In the Introduction, the editor, J. B. Tyrrell, mentions that already as a child Hearne "was particularly fond of drawing, and though he never had the least instruction in the art, copied with great delicacy and correctness even from nature."

What sort of journal entry would have been made by Samuel Hearne, who searched with little success for copper, had he known that the wilderness scene here depicted by AY in its original state was to become the active centre of the greatest lead-zinc mining operation in the world—the tremendous Pine Point Mine?

At this location, some thirty miles west of Fort Resolution, the outcrops of metal had long been known to local Indian bands who fashioned lead pellets for fish-line weights and musket bullets. Gold rush prospectors heading for the Yukon in 1898 examined the site in high hopes but were disappointed to find "nothing but lead and zinc." Mackintosh Bell and Charles Camsell visited the spot at the turn of the century, and subsequent sporadic claims were made but later abandoned, mainly owing to difficulty of transportation aggravated by two World Wars and the great Depression. It took until the 1960s for the vast project to become reality, with federal government co-operation in the building of the Great Slave Lake Railway to Hay River and a spur line to Pine Point; in the laying of the Mackenzie Highway to Hay River and onward around the west end of the lake to Yellowknife; and finally in the provision of hydro power from a vast project east of the Slave River. Production at Pine Point was fully underway by the fall of 1965, with a capacity of 5,000 tons of lead-zinc ore per day, and "with indications of ore reserves of 17,500,000 tons averaging 4.8% lead and 7.4% zinc . . . [which] will increase Canada's production of both lead and zinc by 20%," according to a special Pine Point issue in the *Northern Miner*. A more recent official source states that Canada in the mid-1960s led the western world in the production of zinc, its output rising "to a record 832,000 tons in 1965, approximately 147,000 tons more than in 1964." A handsome "Special Pine Point Issue" was published in the Northern Administration Branch's magazine *North*, for May-June 1964. This included reproductions of a Great Slave Lake canvas by AY in colour for the cover and of two of his 1928 pencil drawings (among those in the present book), as well as two fine photographs of AY in action in the Barren Lands and in his studio—all embellishing a series of authoritative articles on the impressive development at Pine Point.

However, that great project of the future was "nothing but a little clearing and some holes in the ground" when AY and his companions got there in 1928, hiking the nine miles in from the shore, plagued by heat, mosquitoes, and biting flies. Those pests rendered outdoor sketching in oils impossible, so AY made pencil notes, including some for Mackintosh Bell which have not yet been located for examination.

A day or so later, on their way northward across the lake, the party became stormbound on an island which Bell in his memoirs calls Gros Galet, while AY on one or two drawings spells it Gros Goulet, the latter form being confirmed on later maps. AY, whose dynamo never runs

(continued)

South shore Great Slave Lake July 16: 1928

PLATE 92

Driftwood, south shore, Great Slave Lake, July 16 (or a day or two earlier), 1928

A.Y. Jackson Ft Smith 1928

PLATE 93

Tug pushing scows on the Slave River near Fort Smith, Northwest Territories, 1928

down, filled in the period of enforced waiting with pencil exercises that include exquisite studies of plants such as pyrola and bake-apple, and the surrealistic, abstract study of lichen that serves as end-papers for this book. In the high Arctic, lichen can grow two millimetres in fifty years, and its acids erode our ancient Canadian shield at about one-quarter that speed; so we will last for a while yet. "Rock rose-grey, almost covered with black," writes AY along the edge of the lichen design; "old lichen silver, new rich orange—pattern bigger and more form in silver lichen."

AY and Mackintosh Bell both tell in their memoirs the tale of the boat owned by a Syrian fur trader which likewise sought refuge on that same island in Great Slave Lake. *Far Places* gives fascinating details about the "incongruous human collection . . . Englishmen, Indians, half-breeds, and two Syrian traders and their Syrian wives. . . . The Syrian men strong, swarthy, and attired in semi-Indian clothing. . . . The women shy, delicate, retiring, and dressed in Eastern garments though unveiled . . . in fantastical contrast with that cold rocky environment."

AY's account in *A Painter's Country* is more brief, yet full of human warmth, this being one of the artist's favourite reminiscences. He recalls how the anxious Syrian with the beautiful wife so very ill with influenza was overjoyed to find a real live doctor on that windswept isle in the midst of nowhere; how he received immediate help for her and went away "much cheered up." In his pocket the grateful Syrian trader carried a little note which AY had scribbled in pencil on a page torn from his 5½ by 9 inch sketchbook, a note to his eldest brother who also loved the Arctic but had to do his travelling vicariously. The Syrian faithfully mailed the note, and in its small envelope bearing the postmark "Fort Smith, N.W.T., July 16, 1928" it has lain ever since among my father's papers. So here it is, mint fresh, to transport us into the midst of those distant days:

*   *   *

An island on Great Slave, July 14th. Stormbound.

My dear Harry,

It's a dirty day and we are waiting for it to clear so we can start on for Yellowknife River. A schooner bound for Fort Smith came in for shelter, so I will give them this letter. Our island is only a few acres of rock, treeless, but covered with shrubs—Labrador tea, which is in very full blossom; bakeapple, three weeks from being ripe; pyrola, sweet briar, etc.

The shore is piled with driftwood, and the muddy waters are pounding on the coast. We hit Fort Resolution a week ago and went west for thirty miles, hiked inland to see some lead and zinc claims. It has been boiling hot, up to 94° in the shade, and the mosquitoes and bull dog flies have lived up to the press reports. We keep a bonfire going against them.

The south shore is flat and monotonous, covered with mostly small jack pine, spruce and poplar; almost no life at all. The shore is piled high for miles with driftwood, and between it and the forest was a natural garden—orchids, paint-brush, honeysuckle and lots of other things. You would enjoy poking along it in spite of the heat and the bull flies.

The north shore is higher and rocky and we hope to get some sketching done. The water is clear, too. The Slave River fills this place with mud for miles out. Banting is touching up a sketch he made at eleven o'clock last night. It does not get dark here at all. Bell and Dawson are our geologists, then we have Gus and Jimmy, who look after the scow. It is a well managed party, with perhaps not enough work to do so far, but we hope to dig in more and explore on the north shore.

I expect Naomi is on the bouncing billows on her way to Europe. My kindest to Coralie and all the family.

As ever,

Alex

AY's hope, expressed in his letter of July 14, 1928, that the north shore of Great Slave Lake would prove good painting country, was fully justified. To be sure, back in January 1772 young Samuel Hearne had preferred the south side, remarking that "the scene was agreeably altered, from an entire jumble of rocks and hills, for such is all the land on the North side, to a fine level country, in which there was not a hill to be seen, or a stone to be found. . . ."

Needless to say, that jumble of rocks and hills, the edge of the Canadian Shield, was the very place for artists like Jackson and Banting, as well as for the geologists Bell and Dawson who hoped to find gold in a region that was complete wilderness at that time. The party went up the Yellowknife River and portaged over to Walsh Lake (now Wecho on our maps?). "This was good, clean country of open rock with patches of spruce, and fewer mosquitoes," writes AY in *A Painter's Country*, "so we were able to sketch. I made studies for a canvas of the shore line, which is now owned by the Rt. Hon. Vincent Massey."

The present drawing is one of those studies for *Walsh Lake, Evening, circa* 1928, sometimes called *The Lake* or *Northern Lake*, oil on canvas 32½ by 50 inches, and one of AY's favourite works. How well the balance of delicate verticals with peaceful horizontals, and the suggestion of limpid reflections, create the mood of twilit serenity, bringing to mind from some poetic depth the lines of Longfellow:

> Downward through the evening twilight
> In the days that are forgotten
> In the unremembered ages . . .

Perhaps an especially appropriate counterpart to the poetic mood of this subject, considering who has owned the canvas, can be found in some

lines which AY noted in late July 1930 at the Masseys' country place Batterwood, near Port Hope on Lake Ontario:

> Spend all thy days in dreaming,
> And all thy nights in sleep;
> Let not ambition's tyger
> Devour contentment's sheep.

To be sure, William Blake's beautiful lines apply better to the tranquil canvas and drawing than to the complete nature of the man who drew and painted them. AY has certainly never spent all *his* days in dreaming. The day after he sent his niece the good advice in the poem, he was off to the Arctic again, and not for the last time. Nor was AY's advice taken by Dr. Banting, although the latter *said* he planned to retire at fifty and devote himself to painting. After the thrilling Great Slave trip with AY there were to be only thirteen years more for the great doctor before death's "tyger" claimed him in the airplane crash over Newfoundland while on war duty—at the age of fifty-one.

But back in 1928 Banting and AY spent happy days sketching and fishing at Walsh Lake. AY's "Memories of a Fellow Artist, Frederick Grant Banting," made from a tape recording of an informal talk to a group of doctors at the home of Dr. R. A. Starrs in Ottawa, appeared in *The Canadian Medical Association Journal* in May, 1965. Here AY recalls some stories from the Great Slave trip, which will make a cheerful conclusion to the twilit mood of the days not yet all forgotten: "On the Yellowknife River where we remained several days Banting and I did considerable sketching in spite of the flies. The worst thing about black flies is you can make up your mind that you're not going to let them beat you—that you will let them chew you all they want. But what really stopped you was when they'd get in your paint. After a while you were painting with yellow black flies, blue black flies, and red black flies.

"Banting and I were fishing in Walsh Lake, hoping to get some nice big trout. We would throw out the line and pull it in—pike every time. Finally we had three really big fellows. Up north pike are pretty good, so we brought them back to camp. Next day we went off sketching with a tea pail and a lunch from the cook. When we unwrapped our lunches we each had a big slab of cooked pike—about a pound and a half—and that was all. This was cook's little joke for bringing in pike and a warning not to bring any more pike into his camp.

"Finally we turned back for Resolution and eventually reached civilization again."

PLATE 94

Yellowknife, Walsh Lake, Evening, 1928

At the end of the evocative chapter "An Arctic Holiday with Dr. Banting," AY's autobiography tells how the 1928 summer expedition returned south from the Yellowknife River: " . . . crossing Great Slave Lake, we travelled all night, though night is not the proper word, as it just got dark enough to see a pale aurora play across the northern sky."

The present little drawing is a modest but precious document of that nocturnal crossing. It shows the silhouettes of Mackintosh Bell and C. B. Dawson, the mining engineers; Dr. Banting taking one of his rare snoozes; Gus and Jimmy, the Indian guides; the two canoes trailing behind; the gleam of the sky reflected on the quiet lake—all observed and recorded by AY up in the prow.

Dr. Bell's book of memoirs, *Far Places*, adds the colour of further details. The vessel in which they crossed twice over what is considered one of the most treacherous water passages in the world—a lake as big as Belgium—was "a gasoline-driven scow—old, leaky and unseaworthy." The northbound passage was the "eventful" one: they were held up by high winds three times; they struck a submerged reef; and they re-discovered by happy accident the same island where Bell and Camsell had found iron about thirty years before. This they now duly staked and christened Housser Island, in honour of Fred and Bess. Bell called another island Jackson Island, but perhaps nothing remains of that name.

Of the southbound crossing Bell writes: "Our journey to Gros Cap was uneventful. About ten miles to the south of that landmark a freshening wind forced us to stop one evening at a small island. We went to bed early in order to get what rest we could, and to be ready to start on the long traverse to the south shore as soon as it grew calm. Shortly after midnight the energetic Dawson, the leader of our little party, awakened us; lake conditions were perfect, and by one o'clock we were off. It is never really dark in July at Great Slave Lake, and the night was further illuminated by the flickering diaphanous streamers of the northern aurora. These gradually faded as the north-eastern sky brightened, heralding the approaching dawn. The light slowly strengthened, the colours in the sky became warm and luminous, the smoothly billowing water scintillated like a vast opal. Yellowish pink, lilac, purple, greenish blue, pale blue, danced and shimmered, forming a magic foreground to the fantastic silhouettes of the dark rocky islands. . . ."

"No one spoke. All were enthralled by the splendour. Only the wheezy chug-chug of our awkward craft marred the majesty of the silence. At half-past three the sun rose, as we passed Gros Galet, crimsoning the few clouds which hung above the horizon. Slowly the colours paled, the clouds became grey, banners of misty white raced upward into the pale greenish-blue sky, the water turned cold yellow."

Between night and day of that distant August 1928, the old scow passed by with the good companions—the poetic, colour-sensitive mining engineer, the brilliant, energetic painter-doctor, the artist unusually aware of human and humorous aspects in the world around him. The memories of their journey echo in leisurely harmony.

Unless recorded in one form or other, events sink away beyond recall—"in the ages unremembered." What enrichment it is to our treasury of historic "images" to know that on a Christmas Eve almost two hundred years ago, the first white man ever to reach Great Slave Lake stopped to gaze across the frozen vastness, watched the aurora dance overhead, and *heard* it make "a rustling and crackling noise like the waving of a large flag in a fresh gale of wind."

How fortunate we are to be able to visualize the Camsells as they crossed the same lake later with their stately York boat brigade and to imagine Handel's "Water Music" played on the mouth organs of young Charles Camsell and his friends as their scows sped down the Athabasca.

Immense changes lay ahead in northern travel. Already by the mid-1920s the airplane appeared over the arctic horizon. In 1928 AY remarked upon two planes carrying prospectors to the Liard. Mackintosh Bell on his next trip (1929) came out by air. In so short a time change comes about.

So chug along, old-timers, into the past:

> above your head the cool and giant air
> and the future aching round you like an aura.

R Indian   Banting   crossing Great Slave Lake 1928.   McIntosh Bell
                                                                            Bartow
                                                                            Dawson.

PLATE 95

*Crossing Great Slave Lake
by night, 1928*

Things were different when AY paid his subsequent visits to the Yellow-knife area north of Great Slave Lake! Back in 1928 the richest sources of gold had not yet been discovered, though prospecting was underway. The big finds began in 1934; then came the boom, considerably aided by the rise in value of gold from $16.00 to $35.00 an ounce. In 1938 AY flew over the Great Slave en route to Great Bear Lake, whither we soon shall follow him. But it was not until 1949, by which time several major gold mines had been opened up, that AY was invited by Dr. Keenleyside, Deputy Minister of Resources and Development, to visit Yellowknife to paint.

"I was only too happy to get back there," says AY in the chapter "Tying up the ends," "Yellowknife was one of the friendliest towns I have ever been in—a real pioneer settlement." He flew back there the following year and again in 1951, the date of the present drawing. By that time the town had about 2,500 inhabitants, including several who liked to take him sketching, often by plane or helicopter. The canvas of this subject, one of several he painted for the federal government, is now at the Canadian Embassy in Stockholm, Sweden—"a very good canvas," says AY. The 10½ by 13½ inch oil sketch of the same theme was raffled in November 1953 in aid of the Vancouver Art Gallery. Perhaps its present owner will be alerted and "catalogued" some day in the ever-expanding AY files!

AY's pencil style had changed by the 1950s to this more open, casual manner.

Yellowknife's "style" has also changed. The place that was merely a huddle of Indian huts until the mid-1930s became, as of May 1, 1967, the capital of the entire Northwest Territories, with a population upwards of 5,000 and a five million dollar building programme underway. This has enabled the territorial commissioner and his advisory council (now five appointed and seven elected members, including at least one Eskimo) and their staff to be based permanently in the North.

The Yellow in Yellowknife's name can now stand for gold instead of copper. The area is ringed with gold mines, including Giant Yellowknife, Canada's largest, which has been disgorging from its depths of over 750 feet some 400,000 tons of gold-bearing ore per year. By 1965 four of the gold mines in the district together produced about thirteen million dollars' worth of gold each year.

Yellowknife is now an important way-point on the polar air route to other parts of the world, and is also reached by road from Edmonton along the great Mackenzie Highway. The town boasts, since 1963, Canada's most northerly museum of Eskimo and Indian artifacts and relics of explorers—including Peter Freuchen's wooden leg!

Off to the south across Great Slave Lake, Hay River has become the scene of constantly passing trucks, barges, and freight cars that ship out the annual million and a half tons of high-grade lead-zinc ore and concentrates from Pine Point Mine. "Much of the railway operation has been taken over by 37 Eskimos, who have an aptitude for mechanics." Hover-craft and Skidoos, "whirly birds" and "choppers" with clear plastic foreheads zoom across the wilds, summer and winter. "And it used to be so quiet around there!" remarks AY.

The Great Slave Lake itself continues to yield, on a sustained basis, the fishy riches once admired by Samuel Hearne. Four companies, using 42 gill-netters and 45 skiffs, employ some 300 men for two four-month seasons per year, summer and winter. Figures for 1964, for instance, show 7,000,000 pounds of whitefish and trout. Eighty percent of all lake trout now comes from Great Slave, since the Great Lakes further south suffer from pollution and lampreys. Ninety-eight percent of Great Slave's fresh-frozen delicacies are shipped direct by air to Chicago and New York, which seems rather a pity.

Venerable Fort Smith on the Slave River has an airport now and a side-road from the Mackenzie Highway. It has also a sense of the value of fine things, and many gifted, devoted teachers. Governor-General Vanier and Madame Vanier, visiting there in 1961, were treated to a concert by the Grade One band and were very impressed. Recently Sister Cécile of the Grey Nuns was in Ottawa learning to play the *saxophone* for the delectation of her Fort Smith classes. "The Indian children love music, all of them. It makes them open up like flowers."

"Canadians must become more aware of their North," roared the M.P. for the N.W.T. a short while ago, "and not just sit there down south in their living-rooms like puddings with the sauce of television being poured over them!" AY is one Canadian who doesn't sit like a pudding in front of his TV, except on Hockey Night in Canada. He likes the friendly people of Yellowknife and the North and they like him. The magazine *North* for May/June 1964 shows on its front cover a colour reproduction of the canvas of vast rolling country, *Between Yellowknife and Great Bear*. On the back cover is the well-known tough photo of AY in shirtsleeves, squinting through his cigarette smoke. The text alongside the photo says: "A. Y. Jackson has travelled the north from Labrador to Great Bear to Ellesmere. He is in the finest tradition of Canadian artists: a man whose genius has been inspired by adventure, wilderness and solitude.

"Honours to Dr. Jackson are routine, but this tribute carries a special meaning. It is one from the trappers, miners, pilots, and prospectors who have been his companions for a generation."

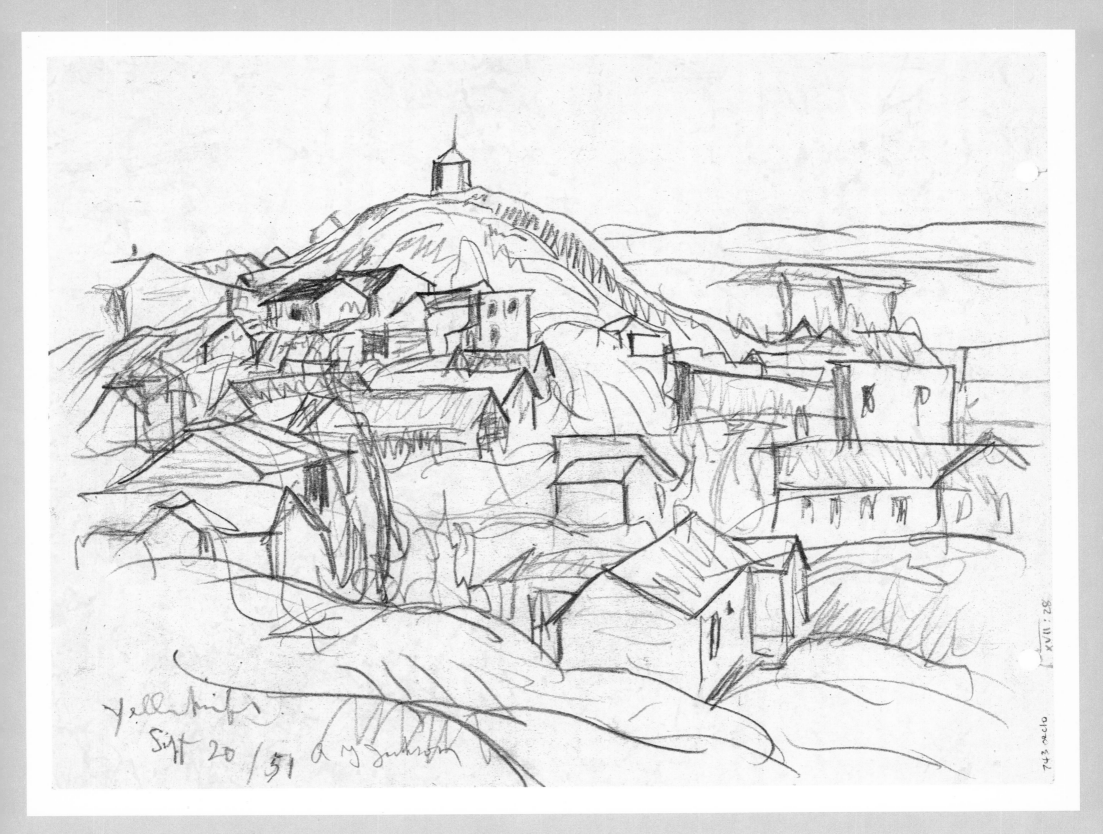

Yellowknife
Sept 20/51 A Y Jackson

PLATE 96

Yellowknife, Northwest Territories, September 20, 1951

In 1937, the year before AY reached Great Bear Lake, a region he had eyed with longing from afar, a perceptive French visitor to Canada, one André Siegfried, published his analytical findings on what is "peculiarly Canadian" about us, and observed: "The effect of the North on the Canadian individuality is noteworthy. Its importance lies less in its economic value than in what one may term its mystic appeal. Many countries—and they are to be envied—possess in one direction or another a window which opens out on to the infinite—on to the potential future. . . . In Canada . . . the North is always there like a presence; it is the background of the picture without which Canada would not be Canada."

Those words of the late 1930s already have a far-away, poetic look to our generation accustomed to jet travel, nuclear fission, radar, computers, and all-year-round Arctic sewer systems. "Economic value" has more weight, nowadays; and the "potential future" has become the present. And yet the mystique of the North somehow survives as a basic underlay, a sort of personality permafrost—and possibly for no Canadian more essential than for AY. "I guess I'm like a compass," he remarked recently in his own comfortable, unsiegfriedian way, "always heading north. I really do belong to the caribou country, not to the cow country."

How thrilling it was for AY back in 1938, when the "window on to the infinite" was flung open and he rode north on his first long-distance flight to claim the Great Bear and the Barren Lands for his own. It was then only *nine* years since a Canadian plane had crossed the Arctic Circle for the very first time, piloted by the intrepid Punch Dickins. On that occasion, looking down out of Punch's plane, the prospector Gilbert La Bine had observed, on the great rocks below, a mysterious "sign" he was able to recognize—cobalt bloom! In the course of the early 1930s a new Eldorado had sprung (or rather struggled) into being. And now, in August 1938, AY sat in the mining company's small plane along with a load of groceries, assorted steel pipes, and "several Finnish miners." They flew from Edmonton to Fort Smith, then on up across the Great Slave and the two hundred and fifty miles to the Great Bear.

The geologists tell us that the innumerable lakes which fill every hollow of that wild stretch were formed, like their huge brothers Slave and Bear, during the last retreat of the polar ice cap some ten thousand years ago, as the land was released from the pressure of the ice and gradually lifted and tilted. These northern lakes are considered unusually new and young, so Malcolm MacDonald was quite right, in his enthusiastic travel account *Down North*, to refer to the region as "a vast nursery devoted to the rearing of infant lakes."

The moment the Eldorado plane unloaded AY and the groceries at the site of La Bine's mine at the eastern end of Great Bear Lake, AY wrote a quick note that radiates the initial thrill of arrival: "Port Radium, Great Bear Lake, North West Territories, August 26th. . . . Just arrived and the plane is leaving right away. It was a grand trip. . . . Saw five hundred thousand lakes this morning. You just couldn't keep looking at them, hour after hour. Great Bear is surrounded by big rocky hills, open patches of spruce in places, but no farm lands. . . . Expect to be round about three weeks, but have to get out before freeze-up or stay another six weeks. A mail plane comes in once a week."

AY actually did stay for six whole weeks and had a marvellous time. On September 19 came another cheery note to "Dear Na yum e": "Our plane was supposed to be in today but had to go to the repair shops at Edmonton, so as it was a perfect sunny day, I did not give a hoot, and went off over the hills and away.

"Have only four panels left but I'll put a different little lake on each one. I can put on quite a show for the boys here now. It seems this is the most wonderful autumn they have ever had here, so I was in luck. I was supposed to come in with two millionaires but there was no room on the plane, so I spent four delightful days around Edmonton, and they returned on the plane I went north on, after they'd spent four cold rainy days here. Being rich does not get you everything.

"The country seemed monotonous at first, but gets better all the time. You don't get effects as you do down south. I suppose nature feels it isn't worth while putting them on for one artist. The skies are far away, and everything that takes place does it over a thousand square miles. . . ."

The present drawing was made from a relatively high point south-east of Port Radium, near the silver mine at Contact Lake. It looks out across some of those thousand square miles, and renders faithfully the wide vista in that "land of little sticks." At the same time, surely, it has some of the mystic quality of our infinite northland. It became the subject of a fine, rich-toned canvas titled *South of Great Bear Lake*, one of the first canvases ever painted of that part of the world.

AY was so enthralled with the Great Bear region that he returned there many times: in 1949 to Port Radium, which had changed considerably in the eleven intervening years; in 1950 when he and Maurice Haycock were air-lifted into the Barrens and camped near the Teshierpi Mountains; in 1951 with John Rennie farther north-east across the Coppermine to the September Mountains, then back westward to Hunter Bay; in 1959 around Lac Rouvier and Bathurst Inlet. Letters and an informal diary kept during one camping trip supplement the autobiography and the drawings, and radiate the living warmth of immediate experience.

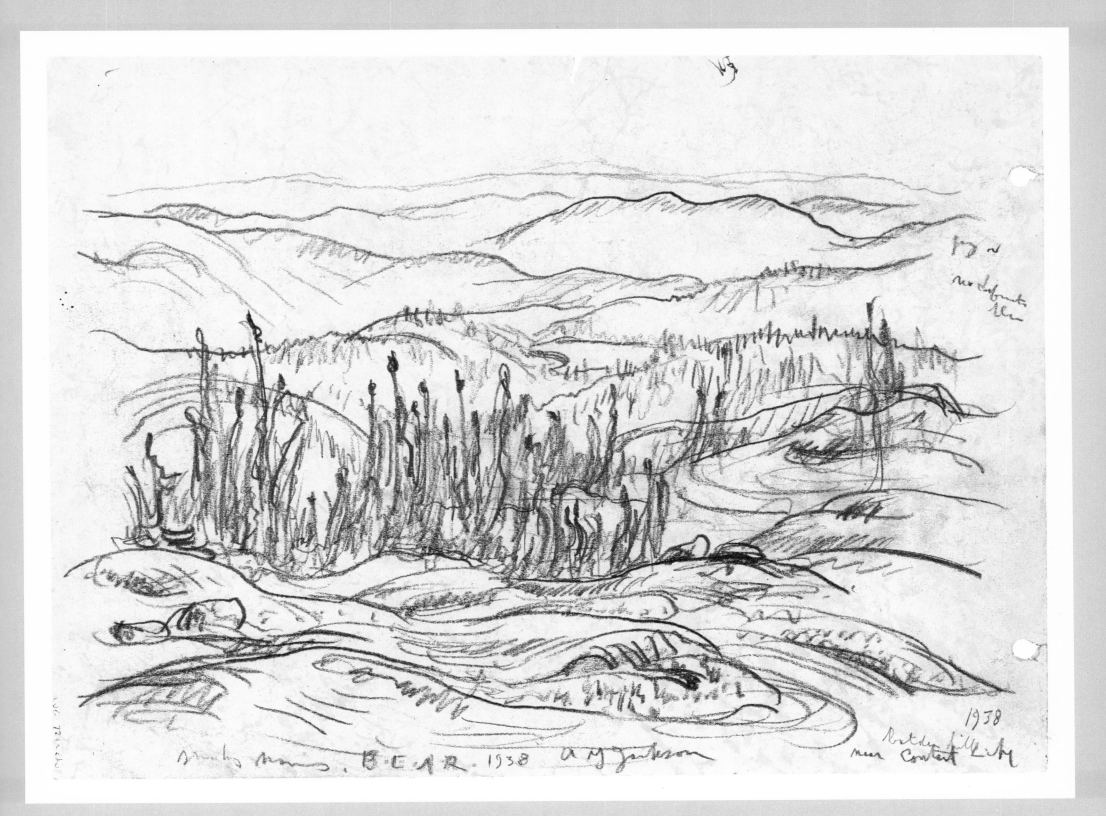

PLATE 97

Looking south from Great Bear Lake, 1938

Named for Richardson's Bear, the fearless Barren Lands Grizzly; located farthest north of earth's large freshwater bodies; Canada's greatest lake not shared with others; thrusting its arms with vigour in five different directions, glorious Great Bear stretches westward for some hundred and eighty miles from the mountain where AY stood one day and pencilled this cosmic vista.

It is easy to wax ecstatic over Great Bear's vital statistics. In area it is 12,029 square miles (of which 292 are islands). After brief storms "periods of flat calm may occur, when the whole lake surface is like a sheet of glass." (AY called it "the quietest lake I ever saw.") In content it has 528 cubic miles of H_2O, "probably the world's largest mass of cold fresh water." Cold water—so cold that the temperature in the main body of the lake barely exceeds 39° Fahrenheit even at the height of summer, when the air can rise to 85°F. Clear water—so limpid and crystal that a white rag can be seen on a line let ninety feet into the depths. And deep! Just six miles offshore from where AY stood, the lake bottom drops 1,482 feet to its deepest point, which is 974 feet below sea level. This is where the giant glaciers of the Late Ice Age plunged off the hard bed-rock of the Laurentian Shield on to the softer Cretaceous formation to the west, and gouged out this fourth deepest lake on the North American continent. The same grinding glaciers furrowed and fissured the edge of the Shield itself, forming the fiord-like bays which lace the eastern rim of McVicar Arm and leaving a fantastic array of islands along its shore.

Few rivers flow into Great Bear Lake and the precipitation is meagre, totalling only about 11 inches a year. (Ten inches of snow equal one of rain.) But evaporation is slow, due to permafrost and cold. In winter the temperature drops to 62° below zero Fahrenheit; which gives Great Bear a climatic range of 147 Fahrenheit degrees. The lake lies under ice from late November until the third week of July. All of the lake water flows westwards to the Mackenzie River by the sole outlet of the Bear River, "a very young river; very fast and full of rapids."

At the source of the Bear River, near where the Indian settlement Fort Franklin stands, are the earliest traces of occupation of the lake by man. Artifacts excavated recently were radio-carbon dated to about 5,000 years ago (before the Egyptians built their pyramids). "This would be approximately 3-4,000 years after the retreat of the ice from the neighbourhood. The culture of the people was very primitive and has affiliations with southern cultures in existence 4-5,000 years earlier. Associated with the artifacts discovered at this site were the remains of woolly mammoth, which apparently formed part of the diet of these peoples."

Those "peoples" of long ago would be the first heroes of Great Bear

Lake. Indeed, anyone who can survive up there is a hero, be he (or she) Indian, or explorer, or those who have come later. We muse, like ancient Chinese philosophers, on all such wonders of nature, and as we contemplate AY's rather oriental bay enclosed by its rocky arms, we can surely see how this particular stage seems set for the coming of a special hero of its own, some latter-day Arctic Ulysses. . . . Now! Watch that headland farthest to the right, for that's where he'll appear. He sweeps in from out of the north. He is age twenty-four; he paddles a strong canoe along with his three companions. A northern type indeed, this Ulysses—"tall and spare, with a sensitive face and keen yet dreamy grey eyes . . . that wise, witty, gentle and great Canadian, with a genius for story-telling," as one of his great admirers, the Right Honourable Malcolm MacDonald, has described him. His name is Charles Camsell, and he and his companion James Mackintosh Bell, along with their crew, are the first wanderers recorded in this region since the days of the search for Franklin.

The date of their entry on to the stage set by our drawing was August 24, A.D. 1900.

PLATE 98

The harbour at Port Radium,
Great Bear Lake [*1938*]

"On the 24th of August we took a latitude observation not far north of the point where the buildings of the Eldorado mine now stand, and that afternoon we were forced to seek shelter in a little bay behind this point. The bay was bordered by steep cliffs of rock which reflected the sound of our voices, and for that reason we called it Echo Bay. We camped in Echo Bay that night. It was a well sheltered camp and there was plenty of firewood available.

"The name Echo Bay has since been applied to the larger bay which runs back inland to the old station of Cameron Bay.

"Bell's notes on this locality refer to the colours on the rocks at the entrance to our Echo Bay, and in his official report published by the Geological Survey in 1901 there is this sentence: 'In the greenstones east of MacTavish Bay occur numerous interrupted stringers of calcspar, containing chalcopyrite, and the steep rocky shores which here present themselves to the lake are often stained with cobalt bloom and copper green.'"

So! Camsell and Bell are our heroes, and by artful northern alchemy are twenty-eight years *younger* than when AY and Bell travelled by scow on Great Slave Lake some time ago! And should anyone think that paddling along the Great Bear Lake in August need not be all that heroic, let him read in *Son of the North* the spine-chilling tale of treachery and near-murder that preceded the young adventurers' entry here. The little exploration party had already lost one man, and ahead lay hundreds of miles through unmapped wilds.

And now to that magic "cobalt bloom," the mysterious signal that lay buried in government files until the right man came along. Gilbert La Bine, having worked in Cobalt, Ontario, knew that "where there was cobalt, there should also be silver." La Bine's entrance upon the site of our drawing was heroic in its own way. In 1930, the year after he had seen the location from the air, La Bine came in on foot, or rather on snowshoe, since it was the month of May and of course still winter. *He* came in from the south, pulling his gear on a sled, his sole companion Charles St. Paul, snow-blind and helpless. A sturdy bush-plane had deposited the pair near Sawmill Bay in the south-east corner of McVicar Arm, a mere hundred miles or so down the rugged coast.

"They reached Echo Bay on May 14th. . . . On the 16th he located the occurrence that Bell had described . . . the cobalt bloom and also the native silver that he expected. Examining the exposure of rock more intensively, he broke off a piece of heavy black mineral which responded to all the field tests for pitchblende, which is the ore both of uranium and radium."

And so living history began to move in this remote spot where the pitchblende had lain waiting for one billion four hundred million years while heat formed rocks and ice gouged them off again up above it. Then it took a mere thirty years, from 1930 to 1960, "to alter the world forever," in the vivid idiom of the CBC television documentary, "The Secret Years." The great cycle began: from the silver came the profit to defray the enormous cost of mining the other precious finds; from the pitchblende came radium, a white powder glowing blue in the dark, present in the ratio of one part in three million. (Until La Bine's discovery, one gram of radium from the Belgian Congo cost seventy thousand dollars.) One by-product of the extraction process was uranium oxide, present in the highest concentration ever mined. From the radium and the uranium produced here came nuclear fission; the atomic bombs that fell on Hiroshima and Nagasaki; many later peaceful uses of atomic power—and what next?

AY's first visit to Port Radium, the little settlement that grew up around Eldorado Mine, took place only eight years after La Bine had trudged in with his snow-blind friend, and only five years after the mine had begun to produce. The present drawing emphasizes the rugged headland by then called Labine Point, and the famous diagonal bay, the subject of so many dramatic sketches and canvases. One handsome version, from a sketch in the National Gallery of Canada, fittingly graces the jacket of Malcolm MacDonald's book *Down North*. In the canvas entitled *Echo Bay, Great Bear Lake*, 25 by 32 inches, painted about 1945 for Dr. Charles Camsell, who by then was head of the Department of Mines and Resources and Commissioner for the Northwest Territories, the owner could recognize the very spot where he and Bell had camped nearly half a century before.

Though the manner of AY's arrival, along with the groceries and steel pipes, was unheroic, it nevertheless marked a "first" in the story of Canadian art. When AY was given an honorary degree at Carleton University in May, 1957, Dr. Claude Bissell, the President, referred to him as "the chief spokesman for Canadian art . . . an unsentimental and clear-eyed nationalist who knows and loves the face of his country . . . the true heroic voyageur of these times, ransacking nature, not for gain, but for beauty."

Thus AY plays his part in the living history of Great Bear and its mine. Here in the foreground of his 1938 drawing is the roof of the first structure, "a Rube Goldberg contraption evolved from scratch by the federal government," according to the CBC TV programme. La Bine's little mine had to close in 1940 on account of the war, with "the shafts all full of ice, since water freezes even as deep down as 250 feet, up there." Opened again in 1942 under the federal government, it was closed by 1960 when the uranium supply was exhausted. The premises are now used as a luxury camp for millionaires who pay $700 a week for the Great Bear trout.

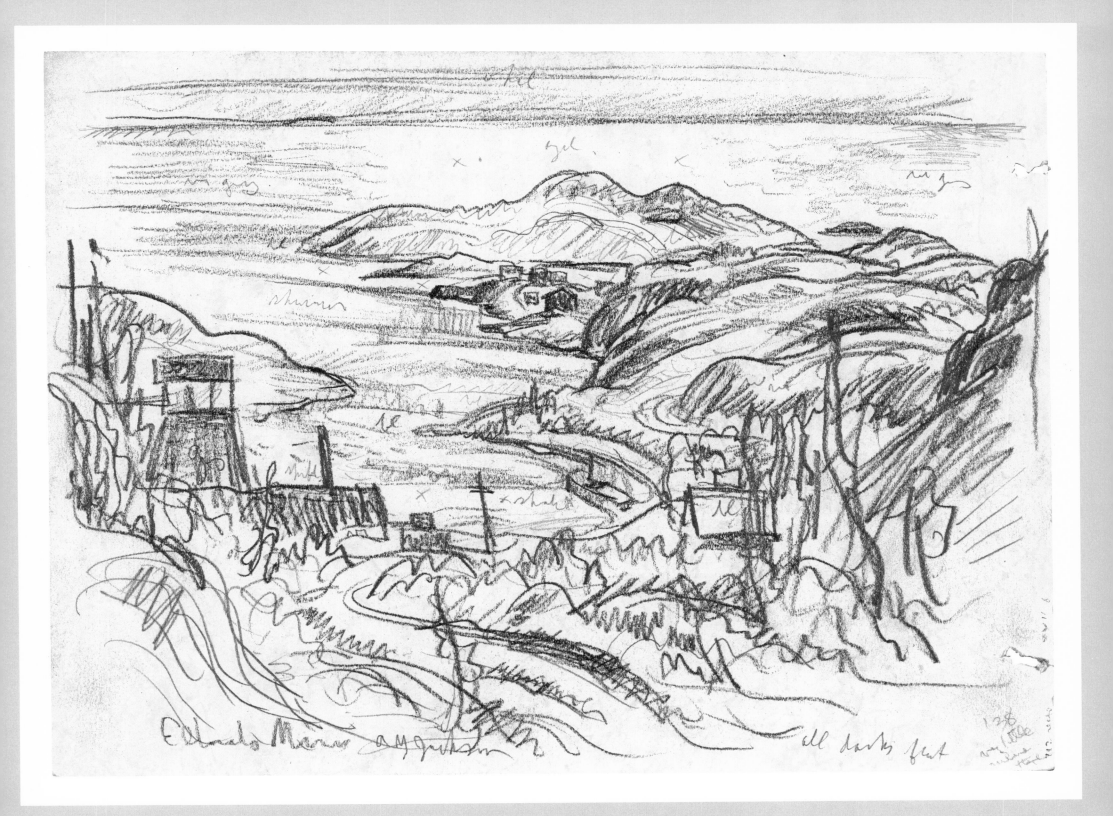

PLATE 99

Eldorado Mine on Echo Bay, Great Bear Lake [1938]

"Bonanza with Walli"—AY's own title for this energetic aspect of a mountainous shoreline—has an agreeably cryptic sound, which (more's the pity perhaps) can be reduced to common sense without much difficulty. Bonanza was the name of a silver mine thirty miles or so southward from Port Radium down the coast of McVicar Arm, the most easterly bay of Great Bear Lake. And Walli was Emil Walli, manager of the Eldorado Mine at the time of AY's first visit in 1938. "He was a fine big chap," says AY. "He'd been a geology student at Queen's and a quarterback on their football team. He wasn't afraid of any of the men in the mining outfit up at Great Bear, though some of them were pretty tough. He knew how to handle them."

During AY's six-week stay, he hiked all over the great rocky hills in search of subjects, often accompanied by Walli's dog Susie, the fearless Scottish terrier who was unmoved by the company of interested ravens, as AY tells in *A Painter's Country*. On at least two occasions AY enjoyed a jaunt with the mine manager, who took him by boat to visit the locations at Bonanza and Contact—the former on the coast, the latter inland over a portage of perhaps a quarter mile. The trip to Bonanza was taken at the request of J. B. Tyrrell, the noted geologist and explorer, at that time approaching eighty years of age, and keen to renew his acquaintance with the northland. Bonanza had already closed down by then, AY recalls. "Some crook had made quite a pile promoting it, but there never was very much there. At the time of our visit a bear had broken into the storage shed and spilled flour and other stuff all over the place—what a mess."

In the present drawing, made at Bonanza, the contours of the rugged shoreline, gouged out by glaciers back in the Ice Age, have their own tale to tell. "The constituent rocks, which are amongst the oldest sedimentary strata known [900-2,700 *million* years], are composed of sandstones and conglomerates with massive intrusions of granite. These intrusions have greatly modified much of the original material and have resulted in considerable mineralization taking place."

On the eve of La Bine's definite strike in 1930, and recalling the "cobalt bloom" he himself had been the first to discover, Mackintosh Bell notes in *Far Places* that the region's "hills of solid rock . . . are frequently table-topped and exhibit abrupt precipices of basalt toward their summits, and more gentle slopes of white quartzite or black shale below." This configuration is clearly visible in AY's drawing. Bell gave an eloquent description of the famous "cobalt bloom": "The variegated mineral staining—red, black, pink, white, and green—gave scintillating reflections in the deep, transparent water, and suggested a locality to lure the prospector."

Emil Walli enjoyed watching AY's sure hand extract the essence of the landscape before him with a few energetic pencil or brush strokes. When he saw this simple but meaningful drawing, he exclaimed: "You artists can draw rocks a hell of a lot better than we geologists can, and you can show what's in them far better than any blankety-blank photo can!" AY still chuckles with pleasure at that compliment.

Between them, the mining engineers and the artist made a good combination. They helped him to get to that glorious spot, where he garnered one of the best harvests of his life. He repaid their hospitality by showing them how a real artist handles his subject and makes a work of art out of what to them was "just rocks."

The relationship between this particular artist and the northern frontier was formulated by AY's old friend and admirer, the Montreal art critic Robert Ayre, writing on the occasion of the Montreal opening of the A. Y. Jackson retrospective exhibition in January 1954: "He is a Canadian because he is an outdoors man, an extrovert, fully conscious of the physical being of Canada and excited by it. He belongs to the tribe of explorers and pioneers . . . one with the adventurers who break into the North for oil, iron and uranium, the men who build railroads and airports, who divert rivers, drain lakes and make new ones . . . .

"In the past half century, with our growth and development as a nation, we have learned to take on the airs and graces of the sophisticated world. But this is only possible because of the wilderness and our energy in exploiting it. Jackson is not a documentary painter. He does not narrate the story of the exploitation. He shows us the country we have to deal with, what it looks like, what it feels like. . . . Cooped up in our cities, though we read about Kitimat, Leduc and Ungava, we are not always aware of that overwhelming hinterland that is Canada. Jackson keeps it in our consciousness."

PLATE 100

Coastline of Great Bear Lake, 1938

Bonanza
with Walli.

1938 a y Jackson

Southward along the shoreline from Port Radium, "about five miles," as AY recalls, lie the quiet waters of Cameron Bay, with what remains of the small settlement referred to by Dr. Charles Camsell in 1954 as "the old station." Cameron Bay enjoyed its brief heyday of frontier life back in the early 1930s when the great prospecting rush began as a result of Gilbert La Bine's rich strike of silver and pitchblende. In those days there was "a real mystique" to the very name of radium, and soon every available square foot of land (meaning rock) was staked in the vicinity of Eldorado Mine, quite without consideration of the practicability of the location, a thousand miles or so from "civilization."

Soon miners' home-made huts straggled along the shore at Cameron Bay; the mining claims recorder's office was established there, followed by the RCMP, the Hudson's Bay Company, and other enterprises of varying respectability. AY recalls that La Bine had very strict anti-drinking regulations at the mine, so on Saturday nights the miners used to sneak off to Cameron Bay to do a bit of boozing and gambling. Apparently one bottle of liquor per person per month could be imported in those days, so non-drinkers made quite a profit. AY usually refers to the location of this drawing as "the bootleggers' paradise in the olden days!" It is not certain if Cameron Bay was the hang-out of the character known as Calamity Jane, a cheerful, square-shaped "Indian" shown dancing a jig in an early film sequence taken at Great Bear Lake.

By the time this drawing was made during one of AY's later visits to Great Bear, the active frontier phase was over. Eldorado Mine was being developed by the government for uranium; Port Radium was "a happy little community" of some two hundred souls, including couples with their families, who had a school, hospital, and quarters with recreation facilities. Down along the shore at Cameron Bay, the old miners' cabins stood abandoned amid bright grasses and shrubs, providing many sketching themes for the artist. The place had been "given back to the Indians," to quote AY. "They lived in some of the old cabins and used the others as a handy source of firewood for their cooking. Saved walking half a mile to get fresh wood."

The drawing conveys the sense of idyllic aftermath. Its evocative notations indicate that it was to be painted up later: "Water warm silver; reflex green; willow bright orange; old fireweed; dwarf birch . . . ."

216

PLATE 101

Old buildings in Cameron Bay, Great Bear Lake, September 11, 1950.

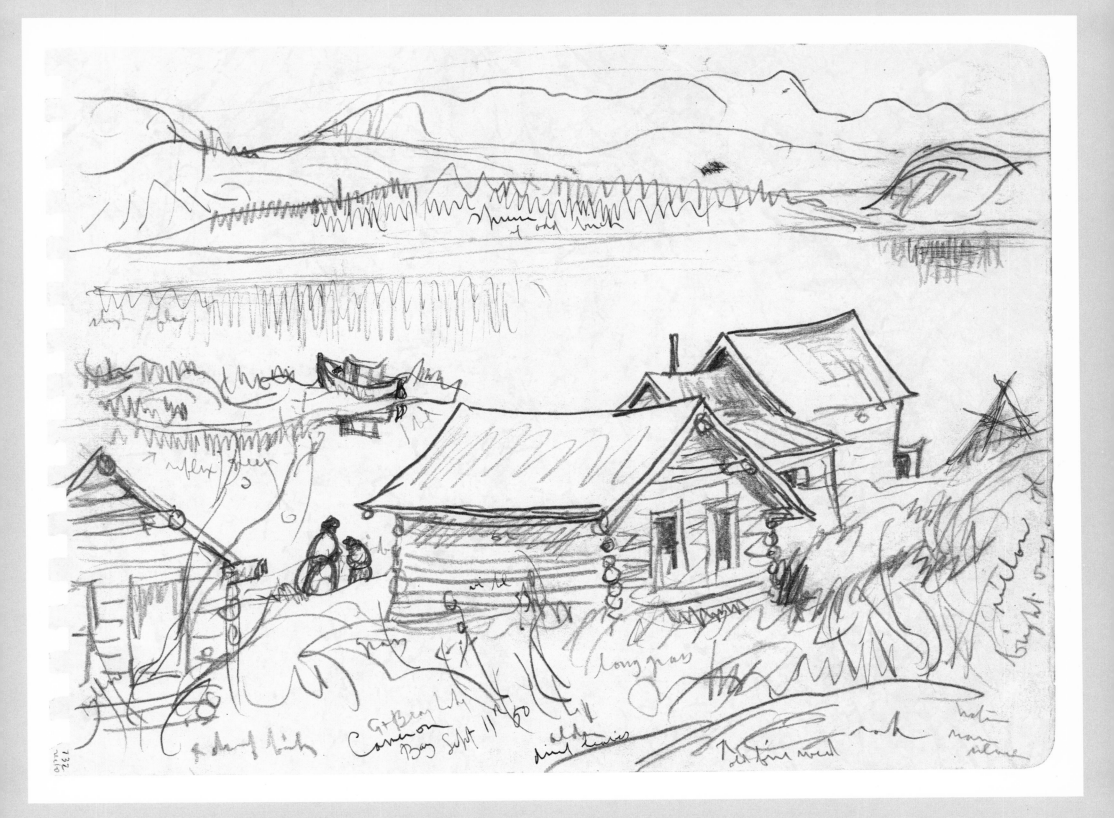

"The Canadian North today is like a great outdoor laboratory, training ground and treasure chest combined. Since the second world war, survey and research have advanced with considerable vigour to determine the value and richness of the Arctic . . . . Bit by bit the magic and mystery of the Arctic yield to man's energy, science and understanding."

Let the story of McDonough Lake, shown here in AY's drawing, bear witness to the brave words above and to those by Robert Ayre, already quoted in "Walli on the rocks," about man's ability to "divert rivers, drain lakes . . . ," and so on.

McDonough Lake used to lie in a hollow up among the hills about half a mile behind Port Radium. The name of the lake, inscribed here simply as "Lake near Eldorado Mine," was established from an old newspaper clipping with a photo of the artist alongside three of his oil sketches — one of them the counterpart of our present subject. The photo accompanied a long feature article by Betty Bletcher in the Lethbridge *Herald* for October 31, 1949, when AY visited the western Jacksons after spending six weeks at Great Bear and Yellowknife.

Piecing together the story of the lake: in the early days of La Bine's mine, when the quest was for silver and gold, the unwanted slag was dumped into nearby McDonough Lake. In due course, as radium and then uranium became the end-product desired, that slag was of interest again. So the engineers simply drained McDonough through a tunnel down into Great Bear. Out went the water; in came the mining equipment. And then the ore gave out, leaving the lake bottom flat and dry. This was referred to by the employees at the mine as "the most expensive baseball diamond in Canada."

"Thank goodness AY got there before the lake was drained!" is our unprofessional sentiment as we look at the peaceful scene of the noble ancient rocks and their clear reflection, set off by the "foreground interest" of the kind AY frequently favours. Occasionally when he sees works that he did during his early visits to Great Bear, such as the powerful canvas *Precambrian Hills* in the Art Gallery of Ontario, he murmurs: "There are tunnels under all those big rocks now." But the uranium ore gave out; the operation closed; all the tunnels are empty and the mountains are full of peace (and sadness) once more. The Eldorado Company has moved its centre of action to Beaverlodge, Saskatchewan and to Elliot Lake, Ontario.

Among the ironies of living history up there is the fact that silver seems to have been a much better paying proposition than the other more exotic-sounding minerals. During the early days the mining of radium never paid a single dividend, and it was the profits from silver which kept the venture going. AY enjoys success stories, but he also enjoys the irony of great efforts that produce puny results (the mountain-laboured-and-produced-a-mouse sort of thing) — or vice versa! He likes to recount how the mighty Smelters Corporation did a lot of work with diamond drills for samples up around there, without finding anything important. So they sold their rights to a group of young engineers who formed a private company and opened a new mine near the old Eldorado site. "*They* found all sorts of stuff — by now it's the richest silver mine in Canada!"

As the Lethbridge interviewer Betty Bletcher remarked in 1949, "A. Y. Jackson looks like a business man . . . there is none of that 'far away' look so often associated with artists . . . his feet are firmly planted on the good earth . . . ." AY keeps in touch with what the miners are doing under the earth as well. He does not feel "full of hills and sadness" as do some softer ones among us when we think of the fate of McDonough Lake. He records things as they are and keeps step with the spirit of change. No sentiment and gloom for AY: "Too bad to waste a good lake, eh?! But some day they can fill it all up with water again. All they need to do is plug up the hole!"

PLATE 102

McDonough Lake near Eldorado Mine [1949]

Lake near Eldorado Mines   A Y Jackson

During AY's later visit in 1951 he was flown along the coast of the big peninsula that separates McVicar from Dease Arm, as far as Hunter Bay and inland a bit to the good landing on a small lake amidst rather rough terrain described fifty-one years earlier by Mackintosh Bell: "Mural precipices descend to the lake front; a maze of peaks, with rough slopes and commonly uniform elevation, stretches inland. Between lie swampy valleys, with occasional lakes and patches of forest."

The angular vertical forms and wide intervening horizontals gave AY fine compositional themes, although some of the Hunter Bay subjects may deserve Farley Mowat's epithets for that land of "frost-shattered and malignant rock." No other part of Canada seems to have called forth such violent reactions—and language—as our Far North. Charles Camsell calls it ". . . a region that stirs strong emotions and takes a tremendous hold on those who know it. You either love it passionately or you hate it. . . . Your feelings about the north are never lukewarm."

"O outcast land! O leper land!" sang Robert Service, castigating the North for the "hate insensate of thy hand, Thy heart's abysmal loneliness," and indulging in "monster mountains" and wolves "gaunt against the gibbous moon." The northern valleys to him were "dreadly desolate," whereas Charles Camsell loved his "valleys unpeopled and still." Gontrin de Poncins in *Kabloona* describes the Arctic's "sapless and skeletal space," while Malcolm MacDonald wishes that he could live forever in "the wild and glorious north."

As for AY, we think we know what side *he* is on. "Jackson symbolise, à mes yeux, la sincérité pour ce qui a trait à la *forme* de ses tableaux, et l'amour du pays pour ce qui en concerne le *fond* . . . . Allons nous rafraîchir au contact d'un grand amour et d'une grande conviction." Paul Gladu's view was corroborated by Arthur Lismer when he described how AY could "grasp the breadth and depth . . . in his western paintings around the Great Bear, of vast stretches of lonely terrain, in a sweep of fervent affection for all that it means to him."

For AY it is affection, amour, love; we would concur. Yet not so long ago, in *The Listener* for August 29, 1946, a vividly differing view of AY's relationship to northern nature was included in a review by the writer-painter Wyndham Lewis. He considered AY "key man in this Canadian regionalist school," which according to him "adopted often the brutal methods of the bill-board artist to put their country across big and harsh and plain: with all its emptiness and savagery . . . this monstrous, empty habitat . . . ." He recounts with relish how AY went far afield "to Great Bear Lake and to the Polar Sea, and brought back grisly records of what he had seen . . . where there are few signs of man is where he really likes to be, where there is just Jackson and Nature . . . . In Jackson's case it is Nature-the-Enemy as known to the explorer.

"Yes, it is an affair of Jackson-against-Nature and vice-versa. Jackson being what is called a 'fighter' likes this situation. His painting expeditions are as it were *campaigning seasons*. . . . It is impossible to associate the notion of pleasure with these grim excursions, or at least nothing [i.e. anything] sensuous . . . .

"There is a gaiety somewhere in Jackson, but it is rationed. His vision is as austere as his subject-matter which is precisely the hard puritanic land in which he has lived; with no frills, with all its dismal solitary grandeur and bleak beauty, its bad side deliberately selected rather than its chilly relentings. This is a matter of temperament: Jackson is no man to go gathering nuts in May."

Poor Wyndham Lewis—so bitterly eloquent, and so subjective. Arthur Lismer once remarked alertly that "in standing before a work of art, it frequently judges us more than we it . . . . If we feel its bleakness and hate it, it is our own inner bleakness that hates, the finite part of us that dares not meet that infinite unfathomable thing—the wilderness."

And now how about asking AY himself if it is "impossible to associate the notion of pleasure with these grim excursions" of his. Hunter Bay is grim enough to fill the bill. Exactly five days after our present drawing was made, AY wrote as follows:

In a tent, Great Bear Lake. August 25th '51.
Sitting in my sleeping bag, and the Coleman stove down low, and the day's work done. A big hot meal inside me—life isn't too bad.

We are about finished our camping trip. No mishaps. My side kick John Rennie from Yellowknife is an experienced camper and good company. Our first camp . . . was all that could be desired. Last Sunday our plane swooped down and in a quarter of an hour we were away, not knowing where we would go next . . . . Well, we came down . . . just off the shore of Great Bear, swell campsite. Lots of wood to burn, which is lucky, as it has turned cold and windy. Rough country to travel over, all loose stones, with rocky escarpments rising up . . . . Lots of blueberries.

As a final, pertinent postscript, a few last words on the love-hate theme, written from Great Bear Lake just after the debacle at Munich in 1938: "Thanks for the photos. We have a lot of camera experts up here. They know all about lenses and exposures, but they don't see what a grand country it is. They are not artists . . . . The world needs more artists, music, poetry, love and such things. They don't need any boundaries, nor hate to feed on . . . . Cheerio, old thing. All the best from the Arctic, as ever . . . ."

PLATE 103

Hunter Bay, Great Bear Lake, August 20, 1951

Among AY's papers is a detail map hand-inked on tracing paper, crumpled by use, smudged here and there with traces of yellow ochre oil paint. It is plain to see that this map has travelled around in the Jackson sketch-box as an aid to general orientation while AY roamed the hills and valleys of the Barren Grounds—not a good place to go astray, indeed.

The little map shows the Teshierpi River which flows its swift course ("rap rap rap" on the map stands for rapids) from the watershed north-east of Great Bear Lake into the most southerly of the chain of Dismal Lakes. These in turn flow eastward by way of the Kendall River into the Coppermine and thence northward to the Arctic Ocean. Many small strokes on AY's map indicate the Teshierpi Range, south of which lies a small lake with a big red X beside it, and a note below: "camp Teshierpi."

This is the location described so graphically in *A Painter's Country* about the time AY, Maurice Haycock, and Bob Jenkins, an employee of Eldorado, spent in the Barrens in 1950. AY loved it. Three years before the autobiography was published he told Leslie Hannon: "Every chance I get I go by plane up into the tundra, into the Barren Lands. . . . I'm perfectly happy to be put down with my pack up among these rivers and lakes, perhaps two or three hundred miles from the nearest human being."

It was hoped, in seeking a good title for the present drawing, to call it *Looking from Teshierpi Mountain towards the Dismal Lakes*, which would have had a rich Canadian look. But alas the Dismals lay *north* of the camp (about ten miles, AY with his keen memory recalls) and the drawing specifically says "south," so the lake here must be that nice little "name-less" one that AY and his friends camped beside. (It can be *a* dismal lake if not *the!*) AY's casual diary from that trip gives wonderfully intimate, day-by-day glimpses of the artist at work:

"*Barren Lands, August 23/50 Wednesday.*

"Left Eldorado about 9.30 on Norseman, Don Ferris pilot. Bright sunlight, but after leaving Great Bear we soon ran into fog. Our destination was a lake a few miles south of Dismal Lakes. We had to find a lake big enough to land on safely, but not large enough to limit our sketching field by having to stay on one side of it.

"We intended to cruise around a while, but the fog made it difficult to see much. So as our lake looked promising we landed on west end of it, on a sand beach. Ferris spent an hour before leaving and put up the tent, while Bob Jenkins went after a caribou we had seen while landing. It does not feel much like summer. We had snow flurries all the afternoon.

"Haycock and I climbed a boulder-strewn hill and started work. It is a bold country of big bare hills, not much color, ochres and green-greys.

There is little wood, dwarf willow and dead birch twigs; it burns and helps out our gasoline supply. Not much life—a weasel, a skunk, a gull, a marmot or large gopher. There is a big hill on the north side of the lake, about a thousand feet, we should get a good view to the north if it clears. We have two small tents, one for dunnage, in the other we have our sleeping bags and should be comfortable.

"Dinner T bone steak and mashed potatoes and coffee. Jenkins went down towards Teshierpi River and found some spruce and brought back an armful of wood.

"*August 24th*. Heavy frost in the night, an inch of ice on the water pail. Sun shining so went out sketching with Haycock to south side of lake. It is like a vast pasture land with outcrops of rock rising to hills about eight hundred feet high. The east wind has been blowing every day, damp and penetrating, and there seems to be no shelter from it. There is very little autumn color so far, and we have been painting boulders. There are millions of them all shapes and sizes; it gives one a great deal of work. By noon it was all grey and cold winds make sketching difficult.

"We have two tents, a wedge and a pup tent, where we keep all our supplies. We have a gasoline stove, and we find enough scrub willow twigs to make a fire, which helps our cooking. The only place we can keep warm is in our sleeping bags. Made two sketches, scraped one off. Bob Jenkins shot a caribou, and after superhuman exertions brought the hind quarters back to camp.

"*Friday, August 25th*. We had caribou for breakfast, for lunch cold up on top of Teshierpi Mountain, and more for supper. Fresh wolf tracks on the sand forty feet from the tent this morning. Fog all over the hills this morning so we were late starting. We climbed the west end of Teshierpi Mountain, to get away from the cold wind. At noon the sun came out, and we could see for miles—long stretches of brownish hills, and lakes with low shores, not much variety in shape or color. Caribou trails every-where; they pick out the best routes. Not much life: a white butterfly, two grasshoppers, one mosquito, some small birds. From the big hill we could see a patch of spruce five miles away. Made two sketches.

"*Saturday, August 26th*. Cold morning, everything lost in fog, and a cold east wind blowing. Haycock moved the pup tent to the front of the wedge tent, so that they make one long tent; it stops the wind from blowing in. About noon it cleared and we went sketching. Got behind a ledge of rock and painted boulders. It greyed up and stopped us from making a second sketch. Saw a wolverine; it ran right in front of Haycock. I only saw it in the distance heading north. More color with an east wind, and it has been blowing steadily for four days.

"*Sunday, August 27th.* Strong east wind, grey but clearing towards noon. Dwarf birch coloring up. Made two sketches. Foregrounds are a problem —boulders covered with moss and lichen; the actual color of the rock is hardly discernible. Saw a couple of ravens. Expected J. W. Bennett [manager of Eldorado] to drop in on his way back from Coppermine, but he did not come. . . . T bone steak for supper. We turn in about 8.30—the only way we can keep warm.

"*Monday, August 28th.* It rained during the night and got milder. Grey morning, and the wind dropped for the first time. We went to the south side of the lake and were busy sketching when we heard a plane. We could see it come down to our camp, so we finished our sketches in a hurry and headed back to camp. Bob Jenkins arrived just before us. It was Don Ferris. Reports of bad weather all over made Mr. Bennett decide to take us out. So we packed in a hurry, and headed for Eldorado. Flew over some interesting country, much of it limestone. Ran into rain and fog over Great Bear Lake; raining hard when we landed, just in time for lunch. Unpacked our sketches, and a number of people have been in to see them."

* * *

So there we see AY, nearly seventy at that stage, sheltering behind his boulders, painting and drawing and faithfully keeping a diary even though there were three in one tent and they had to go to bed at 8.30 p.m. to keep warm, atop that permafrost. Being full of good food, however, including Bob Jenkins' caribou meat three times on the day he did this drawing, AY could probably keep going forever, quite in the tradition of others who had been there before him.

For it must not be thought that the Dismal Lake district is all that drearily empty and unknown, or an apt applicant for Stephen Leacock's famous phrase, "Nobody came and went. There was nowhere to come and go." That region happens to be part of a trail along which, since ages untold, people have come and gone: those from the south coming up from Great Bear and Great Slave to get copper; those from the north coming down to get caribou. The Dismals marked a sort of no-man's-land between Indian and Eskimo; long ago they were the southern limit of Dorset Eskimo culture. The place is full of ancient camp remains.

A few miles to the east of AY's camp, Samuel Hearne passed by in 1771 with his primitive Chipewyan horde thirsting for the blood of the Copper Eskimos. "On the 3rd [July], the weather was again very bad, but we made shift to walk ten or eleven miles until we were obliged to put up because of not being able to see, due to the drifting snow. By putting up, no more is to be understood than that we got to leeward of a great stone, or into the crevices of the rocks. . . . "

John Franklin, struggling back with his starving men from the seacoast towards the headwaters of the Coppermine on his "long, fatiguing, and disastrous" first expedition, entered in his journal for September 7, 1821: "In the afternoon we got into a more hilly country, where the ground was strewed with large stones. The surface of these was covered with lichens of the *genus gyrophora*, which the Canadians term *tripe de roche*. A considerable quantity was gathered, and with half a partridge each, (which were shot in the course of the day) furnished us with a slender supper, which we cooked with a few willows, dug up from beneath the snow. We passed a comfortless night in our damp clothes, but took the precaution of sleeping upon our socks and shoes to prevent them from freezing. . . . "

It was on August 5, 1900, half a century before AY's visit, and within five miles of the place where he made this drawing, that the two rash young explorers Camsell and Bell, half-frozen, their moccasins in tatters, hungry and with no ammunition to kill the caribou around them, "took shelter in the lee of a huge boulder . . . while the snow whirled about us." Through that snow they suddenly saw the looming forms of thirty or forty Eskimos, quite possibly hostile. With the courage of despair (and semi-starvation!) Camsell and Bell linked arms and marched forward, expecting a rain of deadly arrows every moment. But the Eskimos fled away into the snowstorm, abandoning their camp. There the two white men found plentiful supplies of caribou meat and fuel, to which they helped themselves, along with a moose-hide for moccasins. In payment they left one tin plate and three steel needles. This was probably the best trade ever made in the North, as it undoubtedly saved their lives, in every sense!

Within *one* mile of AY's camp, the man who gave the Teshierpi River its name camped with his party on two occasions in the years 1911/1912. This was George Mellis Douglas, author of *Lands Forlorn*, a beautiful book whose single edition in 1914 has long been out of print. Its 180 splendid 3 by 5 inch photographs give full visual documentation of the country at all seasons and of its inhabitants both Indian and Eskimo. Two men who were to become almost legendary in northern annals appear several times in pictures and in text: the Oblate missionary Father Rouvier who the following year, 1913, with his companion Father Le Roux, was stabbed to death by Coppermine Eskimos (later caught wearing the blood-stained surplices); the other, that vagabonding character Jack Hornby who eventually starved to death with two young companions, farther east in the Barrens.

The lake which Douglas named for Rouvier lies west of the Teshierpi, in the watershed between it and the Dease River, which flows into Great Bear. In 1959 AY made Lake Rouvier his headquarters for a time.

(continued)

look north
from Trstenik
MJ.
aug 25/50.

"We thought Teshierpi Camp the acme of comfort," writes the author of *Lands Forlorn*, deciding that although the upper Dismals were indeed "unspeakably dismal" the lowest lake near their camp was "most beautiful . . . a delightful sheet of water. . . . There is in fact something curiously attractive about all that country at the eastern end of the Dismal Lakes. . . ."

With the term "curiously attractive" we must concur, considering both the landscape and the thrilling epics of heroism and of perfidy that have come out of that one remote corner. Perhaps Wyndham Lewis had a point when he claimed that "this monstrous, empty habitat must continue to dominate this nation pyschologically, and so culturally." And if, as Robert Fulford has stated somewhere, the essence of Canadian art lies not in abstract-action of the American type, but in contemplation and symbolism, then we should continue to contemplate these symbols of our ancient, rugged, tenacious, mysterious, terrifying, rich-laden land, as seen through AY's eyes.

"If ever there is such a person as a Canadian artist," wrote Arthur Lismer in 1953, "Jackson fills the title role. . . . A topographical map of Canada would be dotted as with a rash marking the spots where he has painted—where he scraped his palette on the rocks—or cleaned his brushes on a pine log. . . . His trails cross and recross like the pattern of ski tracks on the fresh snow of a winter hillside. In all of these widely separated places where A.Y. has painted he has revealed their unique identity. In his hands and through his eyes they take on a new significance. They become integrated into our national consciousness."

*   *   *

An amusingly contradictory view to the theory that the "place" is important:

"He was to speak on Sketching Grounds in Canada. That was rather an illusion because geography has little to do with art: it's the season, the weather, and the artist's imagination. Artists don't have to be explorers but there is a lure to the unknown. Niagara Falls and the Grand Canyon are probably responsible for more bad painting than any other part of America. Rubens did a stable and Rembrandt a side of beef. Artists can express something out of almost nothing. A couple of haystacks, a barn, some plowed land—beauty is often in the eye of the beholder."

PLATE 104

Looking south from
Teshierpi Mountain in the Barren Lands,
August 25, 1950

Imaginative myths through the ages have explained how famous figures—especially those connected with the creative process—do not die an earthly death, but merely pass from mortal sight and continue their existence undisturbed. The North American Indians, who were the first to inhabit the half million square miles of our arctic tundra, named one such legendary figure Shagodyoweh—the world-rim dweller—a great medicine man and magician. When Shagodyoweh's work among men was done, he retired to dwell in the rocky hills to the west, near the rim of the world.

Samuel Hearne recounts the Chipewyan belief that long ago "a man of such a surprising height that his head reached up to the clouds, came to level the land, which at that time was a very rude mass; and after he had done this, by the help of his walking-stick, he marked out all the lakes, ponds, and rivers, and immediately caused them to be filled with water. . . ." After this creative—indeed artistic—act, the great visitor filled all spaces with fish, beasts, and birds, for the benefit of the first humans. Then "he returned to the place whence he came, and has not been heard of since."

AY's creative head does not reach to the clouds, to be sure, but he too has the northern nomadic urge, and goes off in search of his material, and never can stop too long. Away back at the ripe age of twenty-five, he wrote to his family from Florence: "The wanderer is still on the move, though if life was not so short he would like to stay here a while."

Life was to be anything but "short" for AY and he has been wandering indefatigably all through it: at 80 to the Yukon; at 81 to Labrador; at 83 to Baffin Island. "Storm Delays Show but not A.Y. Jackson" says the *Globe and Mail* in March 1960, as AY got through to the opening of his show at the Art Gallery of Hamilton, Ontario. And recently, going on 86, he left for Toronto on the noon bus from Ottawa to attend the memorial service for his old friends Loring and Wyle, and returned by the midnight bus that same night. "Too busy to feel old," is the way he likes to be.

The sturdy tent of this tough old nomad has been pitched in many places in the course of our present book: on a "delectable island" in Georgian Bay; beside Grace Lake and Superior; on the Slave River and up beyond Great Bear. Here now in our concluding tent scene he has put himself into the drawing—surely a magic act! He was camping with friend John Rennie in the September Mountains, which lie east of the Coppermine River, just where that glorious waterway turns sharply to the east, about sixty miles from its outlet. "It was a lovely country to walk over, with short grass and moss like a carpet, gently rolling hills with occasional rock outcrops and many little lakes." This camp was "all that could be desired," AY wrote in a letter after a happy week, so no wonder he pencilled in his own figure as a sort of reminder for later. No wonder, either, that Farley Mowat selected the oil sketch of this same subject to reproduce in the section "A Painter's North," with eight handsome pages of AY's work, in his book *Canada North*.

It seems quite natural to formulate a final "lasting" glimpse of AY sitting there by campfire and tent in that world-rim, lunar landscape—our Northland's *genius loci*, timeless and indestructible. Nor should he sit there alone, in our myth, for AY has never been a solitary recluse. The figure with him in this drawing can symbolize many a good companion in the Company of Arctic Cronies, creative persons, able to make and to muse. Someone like Samuel Hearne, who was "particularly fond of drawing"; or perhaps those dear chaps Mr. Back and Mr. Hood of Franklin's First Expedition, who "took beautiful sketches" of many a "majestic scene." On a hilltop in our myth sits Franklin's friend, the doughty Dr. Richardson, looking northward along the Coppermine, "contemplating the river that washed the precipice under his feet," and delighting in all those "primitive rocks" so carefully indicated in the beautiful maps of 1820/1821; while behind the great doctor are *nine white wolves* "ranged . . . in form of a crescent," quietly watching *him*. As a contrast, closer to AY's tent, can be Emil Walli's little black Scottie, watched by *her* circle of ravens—"merely curious," as AY said. Meanwhile, from off behind a boulder, there sounds a mournful *obbligato* played upon the French horn. That will be Maurice Haycock, another friend of the North.

Perhaps our final selection for AY's eternal companions should be some of those who have meant most to him during his lifetime. Any of the Seven, to be sure; or friends Thomson and Banting, or AY's own brother Harry, the one who started him sketching in the very early days. On the *verso* of this drawing is an antler and a large *boletus*; brother Harry would have been drawing that as well. "He can draw a mushroom better than anyone I know. . . . With Harry's prompting and companionship I came to love the country, and I still do."

PLATE 105

AY and John Rennie camping in the September Mountains, August 1951

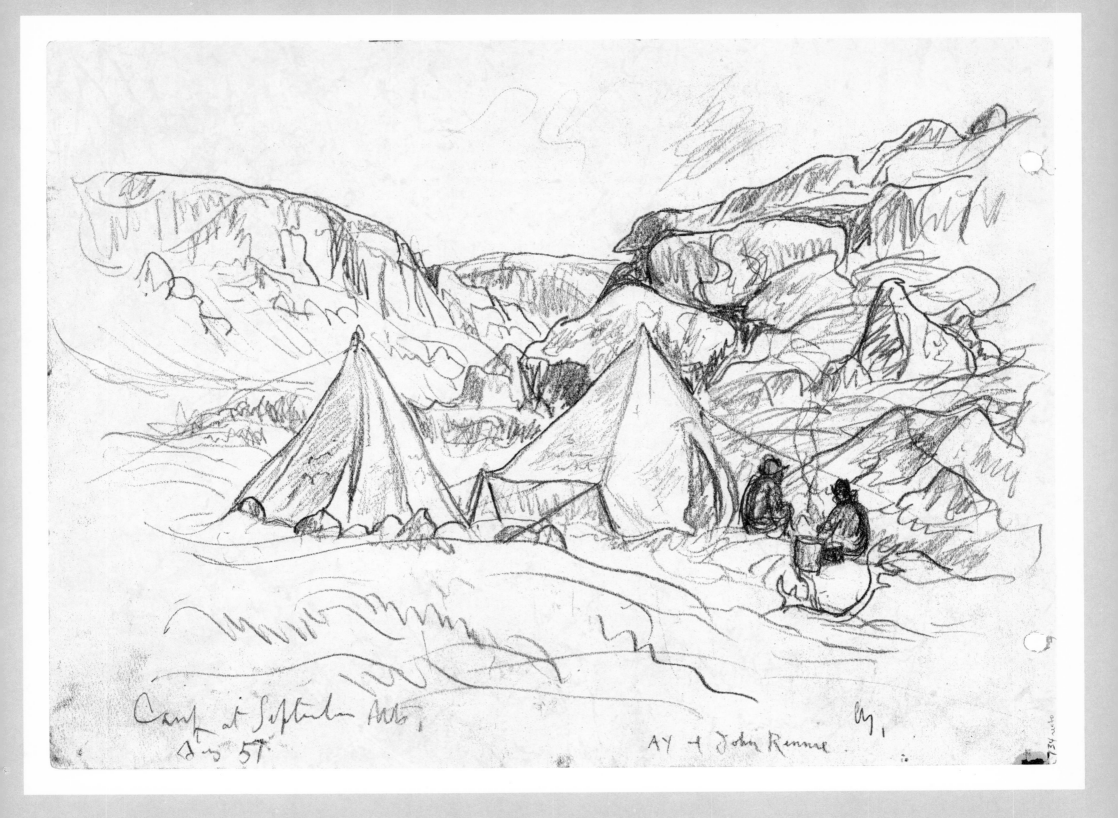

Camp at September Abry
Aug 57.

AY + John Rennie

What fateful symbolic finality can be conjured from this heap of bones and stones? What last message as we leave the "grisly" records of AY's "grim" excursions throughout our northern homeland?

Since we left the legend-artist at the door of his timeless tent on the rim of September Mountains, we have leapt in one leap fifteen hundred miles off to the north-north-east. We are back in the high Arctic islands where we came from in the beginning. Before us lie the ruins of an ancient Eskimo igloo located on the north-east tip of Somerset Island at the west end of Lancaster Sound. The ruins are part of what was a fair-sized settlement, long long ago. Radio-carbon dating reveals that they must have been there when Columbus sailed for America. They belong to the culture of the Thule Eskimos who were great sea-travellers and hunters of the whale. The immense bones here are whale jawbones and ribs used as framework for the roof of the semi-subterranean homes, completed with slabs of stone and turf, plus a blanket of snow in winter.

In due course conditions changed for the clever Thule Eskimos. Ice cap receded, land rose, channels became shallower; the climate probably grew colder. The whales left the district, then so did the hunters. . . . Later the white men tried to establish a post at Port Leopold but had to give it up—far too much ice for ships. The ruins have lain and looked like this for nearly five hundred years. Ross described them in 1832; a photograph taken in 1967 shows little or no change from the drawings AY did in 1927.

Will the whole world look like this some day? Or even our world here in Canada? Certainly this drawing shows the end of one kind of Canadian world, the world of the Stone Age people, the free hunters of the north. The past century has ended that world for them. And with our machine age phases becoming obsolescent every decade or so, who knows what lies ahead?

We can hope that some of the good genes of the people who coped with the North—capable, likable, cheerful Inuit—can stay alive to enrich our stock.

In some sense I think of them
as still here in the circle
the small brown men
they lived so strongly
with such a gift of laughter
. . . .
a thousand year old spell
relayed and handed down
a legacy
from the dead to the living

PLATE 106

Old igloo, Port Leopold,
Somerset Island, Northwest Territories,
August 9, 1927

A Y Jackson

old inglass. Port Leopold. Somerset aug 9th 1927

Blown down by the wind,
crushed by ice,
slowed in growth by adverse elements,
but thrusting up again when there's a chance;
roots tenacious and long-lived,
like the land and its peoples—tough to beat.

PLATE 107

Bent spruce, Great Bear Lake [*1938*]

Burnt spruce
Great Bear   A.Y. Jackson

Notes

All letters, unless otherwise stated, are to the author.

The njg notation refers to the sequence in which AY's works in all media are being catalogued by the author.

Measurements are given in inches, height before width.

END PAPERS   *Pattern of lichen on rock*, Great Slave Lake, 1928
njg 937   8⅜ x 10⅞

PLATE 1   njg 201   9 x 12
Reserved for the McMichael Conservation Collection of Art, Kleinburg, Ontario.
Ice mothers me   Scott, F.R., "North Stream," *Selected Poems* (Toronto, Oxford, 1966), page 18.
... Banting sat beside AY ...   Jackson, A.Y., *A Painter's Country* (Toronto, Clarke Irwin, 1964), paperback edition, page 18. Other editions of the same book include the 1958 hardcover edition (Toronto, Clarke Irwin) and the 1967 revised edition (Toronto, Clarke Irwin) which includes a new chapter and four additional colour plates to the eleven already present in the book. All references here to AY's autobiography are to the paperback edition.

PLATE 2   njg 754   7¾ x 10⅞
From the Collection of the Norman Mackenzie Art Gallery, Regina, Saskatchewan.
... AY's little book ...   Jackson, *Banting as an Artist* (Toronto, Ryerson, 1943), page 15.
"A land very high ..."   Davis, John, c. 1585. *The Voyages and Works of John Davis, the Navigator*, A.H. Markham, ed. (London, Hakluyt Soc. 1880). With thanks to the Reference Librarian, National Library, Ottawa.
"a place of anchorage ..."   Sverdrup, Otto, *New Land* (London, Longmans, Green, and Co., 1904), Vol. 1, page 210; "as ever, had aspiring tendencies ..." *Ibid.*, page 213.
... heading towards the North Pole ...   Jackson, *A Painter's Country*, page 114.
"Sketching was done ..."   Banting, F.G., Introduction, *The Far North* (Toronto, Rous and Mann, 1928), first page of Introduction.

PLATE 3   njg 191   7½ x 11
Reserved for the McMichael Conservation Collection of Art, Kleinburg, Ontario.
The loveliest island ...   Jackson, *A Painter's Country*, page 117; "an exciting place to paint" *Ibid.*, page 132.
"No one lives ..."   Jackson, *The Far North*, unnumbered page (6).

PLATE 4   njg 187   9 x 12
Private Collection.
A land of vast spaces   Jackson, *A Painter's Country*, page xv.
"the eye penetrated ..."   Blake, W.H., *Brown Waters* (Toronto, Macmillan, 1915), page 132 of the 1948 reprint.

PLATE 5   njg 196   7½ x 11
Reserved for the National Gallery of Canada.
Vignette   *Three seated figures*, detail from njg 202 [1927]. Private Collection.
"Three police ..."   Jackson, *The Far North*, unnumbered page (4).

PLATE 6   njg 758   10⅞ x 7⅝
From the Collection of the Norman Mackenzie Art Gallery, Regina, Saskatchewan.
Vignette   *Eskimo in kayak*, detail of njg 1324 [1927 or 1930].
"They fell down ..."   Capt. McClintock, *A Narrative of the Discovery of the Fate of Sir John Franklin and his Companions* (London, John Murray, 1859), page 275; "in excellent order ..." *Ibid.*, page 172; "And so HE bringeth ..." *Ibid.*, page 174.
"It is a bleached out ..."   Jackson, *The Far North*, page (4); "The Mary ... waiting ..." *Ibid.*, page (5).
"a trader named James ..."   Jackson, *A Painter's Country*, page 118.

PLATE 7   njg 209   9 x 12
Reserved for the McMichael Conservation Collection of Art, Kleinburg, Ontario.
Vignette   *Eskimo sled with whale-bone handle*, detail from njg 1277 [1927].
"the metropolis ..."   Jackson, *op. cit.*, page 120.
"several hundred millions"   Davidson, A.T., "Some factors regarding northern oil and gas," *The Arctic Circular*, Vol. 12, No. 4, page 58 (Published by the Arctic Circle, Ottawa, April, 1960). Thanks to Colonel P.D. Baird, also to Geneva Jackson Petrie for first-hand observations on Pangnirtung's telephone poles as "status symbols."

PLATE 8   njg 751   5 x 8
Private Collection.
"Cleopatra seemed the obvious name ..."   Manning, Mrs. Tom, *Igloo for the Night* (First printed in England by Hodder & Stoughton, 1943; first Canadian edition Toronto, University of Toronto Press, 1946), page 193 f. of the Canadian edition.
... the dogs that Varley drew ...   *Eskimo* (Toronto, University of Toronto Press, 1959).

PLATE 9a   njg 206r   5 x 8

PLATE 9b   njg 205   5 x 8
Private Collection.
"strange gothic-looking formations"   Jackson, *The Far North*, page (5). Sincere acknowledgement is given to Lawren and Bess Harris for helpful comments on sketching trips in the past.

PLATE 10   njg 75   9 x 12
Reserved for the McMichael Conservation Collection of Art, Kleinburg, Ontario.
On 30th August ...   Jackson, *A Painter's Country*, page 132.
... one John White ...   and   "The observed detail ..."   Hulton, Paul, "John White, Artist," North Carolina Museum of Art *Bulletin*, Vol. 5, Nos. 3 and 4 (Spring/Summer, 1965), pages 2-43, with special reference to Plate 7, pages 10-11. John White's two watercolour studies of the Eskimos were exhibited in *Pageant of Canada* at the National Gallery in 1967, catalogue Nos. 4 and 5.

PLATE 11   njg 338r   9 x 12
Reserved for the McMichael Conservation Collection of Art, Kleinburg, Ontario.
Vignette   *The Beothic*, detail of njg 202 [1927].
"shippes of fishers"   Captain Robert Hay in Story, G.M., "Newfoundland Dialect: An Historical View," *Canadian Geographical Journal*, Vol. 70, No. 4 (April 1965), pages 128-9.

PLATE 12   njg 339r   9 x 12
Reserved for the McMichael Conservation Collection of Art, Kleinburg, Ontario.
Fishermen's boxy wood houses ...   By J.W. Bacque from *Canada* by Varley, Peter and Dobbs, Kildare, published by The Macmillan Co. of Canada Ltd., and Thames & Hudson Ltd., London, 1964, page 36.
"We Newfoundlanders of the older generation ..."   Premier Smallwood on a CBC

radio programme entitled "The Canadian Mood," April 11, 1965.

PLATE 13 njg 341 6⅝ x 8½
Reserved for the McMichael Conservation Collection of Art, Kleinburg, Ontario.
"a big black ball . . ." and "a dull reverberating roar . . ." Halifax *Mail-Star*, December 6, 1965. Grateful acknowledgement is made to Mrs. William ("Mac") Barnes for obtaining this information about the Explosion.

PLATE 14 njg 343 6⅝ x 8½
Private Collection.
Vignette Home-made anchors or *killicks*, detail from njg 348r [1936].
Together Lismer and AY . . . Jackson, *A Painter's Country*, pages 50-1.
"scarcely one was sold" McLeish, John A.B., *September Gale; A Study of Arthur Lismer and the Group of Seven* (Toronto, Dent, 1955), page 63.

PLATE 15 njg 340r 9 x 12 including margins; drawing itself is 7½ x 9
Reserved for the McMichael Conservation Collection of Art, Kleinburg, Ontario.
"When the little spent winds . . ." Roberts, Charles G.D., "In the Night Watches," *Willison's Monthly*, January 1927, pages 288-9. The poem was written in Toronto in December 1926.

PLATE 16 njg 347r 9 x 12
Reserved for the McMichael Conservation Collection of Art, Kleinburg, Ontario.
Vignette Detail of a sailboat, from njg 1331r, undated.
Le premier touriste AY in a letter dated April 6, 1936.
"being overthwart the said River . . ." Richard Hakluyt in Clarke, J.M., *The Heart of Gaspé* (New York, Macmillan, 1913), page 111.

PLATE 17 njg 344r 9 x 12
Reserved for the National Gallery of Canada.
Capes and rivers . . . Clarke, J.M., *The Heart of Gaspé*, page 65.
"lies a buried rock platform . . ." Clarke, *op. cit.*, page 47; . . . place names . . . *Ibid.*, pages 259, 267-8, 269, 60.

PLATE 18 njg 344v 9 x 12
Reserved for the National Gallery of Canada.
"Here is great fishing . . ." Clarke, *op. cit.*, pages 172-3, 176, 191-2.

PLATE 19 njg 669r 9 x 12
Reserved for the National Gallery of Canada.
"the new road . . ." Clarke, *op. cit.*, pages 59, 40, 274, 58.

PLATE 20 njg 594 7⅝ x 10
Private Collection.
The first time . . . Jackson, *A Painter's Country*, page 71; "It was old . . ." *Ibid.*, page 69.
"old rural life-ways . . ." Miner, Horace, *St. Denis, A French-Canadian Parish* (Chicago, University of Chicago Press, 1939; reprinted 1963), page vi of Foreword written 1963.

PLATE 21 njg 598 7⅝ x 10
Private Collection.
Vignette *Driver, sleigh (and horse?)*, detail from njg 597v. Private Collection.
A very picturesque place . . . Jackson, *op. cit.*, page 70; "Towards spring . . ." *Ibid.*, page 69.

234

"a whole parish . . ." Rivard, Adjutor, trans. Blake, W.H., *Chez Nous* (Toronto, McClelland and Stewart, second printing, 1924), pages 117-18.
"The dark earth lifting through the sinking snow" MacDonald, J.E.H., from "March Wind," in *West by East & Other Poems* (Toronto, Ryerson, 1933), page 6. Grateful acknowledgement to Thoreau MacDonald for providing the exact source.

PLATE 22 njg 602r 8⅜ x 10⅞
Reserved for the National Gallery of Canada.
Trying to make . . . Jackson, letter from the South Shore. A few South Shore drawings bear the date 1926, probably added some time later. AY was only on the North Shore in 1926; only on the South Shore in 1927. The same size drawing paper seems to have been used both years.
"Here we are . . ." Jackson, *A Painter's Country*, pages 73-4; "a dead little sawmill town" *Ibid.*, page 76.
"I suppose I get bored . . ." Jackson, letter of April 9, 1940.

PLATE 23 njg 353 8⅜ x 10⅞
Private Collection.
Canvas *Early Spring, Quebec*, 1927, Art Gallery of Ontario.
Vignette *Pig*, detail of njg 614v.
Jackson gives the drabness . . . McInnes, Graham, *New World Illustrated* (Toronto), April 1940, page 26.

PLATE 24 njg 679r 8⅜ x 10⅞
Private Collection.
Vignettes *Bic Steeple* and *Horse and wagon*, details of njg 498 [1927].
All day long the sullen sky . . . Rivard, trans. Blake, *Chez Nous*, page 149.
Les Prices Broders . . . Begun in the early nineteenth century by William Price, the lumber industry of the Price Brothers flourished on into the twentieth.
"probably the oldest of the Indian legends . . ." Information most generously provided by Miss Hagar of Bic, to whom many thanks.
"This morning . . ." Traill, Catherine Parr, *The Backwoods of Canada*, 2nd edition (London, Knight, 1836), pages 15-16.

PLATE 25 njg 355 8⅜ x 10⅞
Private Collection.
"And I thought . . ." Jackson, *A Painter's Country*, page 75.
. . . there is a wonderful book . . . Ouellet, Gerard, *Ma Paroisse, Saint-Jean Port Joly* (Quebec City, Les Editions des Piliers, 1946), *passim*.

PLATE 26 njg 603 8⅜ x 10⅞
Reserved for the McCord Museum of McGill University.
Vignette *Ancient bread-trough*, detail from njg 481.
"with the vast panorama . . ." Jackson, in a letter of June 9, 1948.

PLATE 27 njg 357 9 x 11½
Private Collection.
Vignette *Study of an old mill, probably St. Jean Port Joli*, from njg 486b [1927].
Private Collection.
A first class spring . . . Jackson in a letter from Ste. Louise.

PLATE 28 njg 643r 9 x 11⅞

Private Collection.

The oil sketch of this subject is in the Royal Collection, England.

The Right Honourable Malcolm MacDonald has kindly consented to the inclusion of parts of his letter to A.Y. Jackson.

PLATE 29   njg 356r   9 x 12
Private Collection.

Blodwen Davies' book . . .   Davies, Blodwen, *Quebec: Portrait of a Province* (London, Wm. Heinemann Ltd., 1951; New York, Greenberg, 1951). The sugar lore is drawn from pages 188-95.

". . . knows as much about art now as Morgan Powell . . ."   The late Morgan Powell was a literary critic in Montreal with whom the Group of Seven tangled on several occasions.

. . . had *sunk* to 165,000 gallons . . .   Of the 70,000,000 sugar maples in Ontario, only 1,000,000 are being tapped at present.

PLATE 30   njg 359r   9 x 12
Reserved for the McMichael Conservation Collection of Art, Kleinburg, Ontario.

PLATE 31   njg 360r   7⅝ x 11
Private Collection.
Vignette   *Old house, Ste. Famille, Isle of Orleans*, from njg 474r [1925]. Private Collection.

"This is possibly . . ."   Jackson, "In the Realm of Art," *The Canadian Bookman* (November 1925), page 186.

"Perhaps other houses . . ."   Rivard, trans. Blake, *Chez Nous*, page 20.

"Winter blasts and summer storms . . ."   Barbeau, Marius, *Quebec, Where Ancient France Lingers* (Toronto, Macmillan, 1936; Quebec, Librairie Garneau, 1936), page 12.

PLATE 32   njg 370r   9 x 12
Private Collection.
One of the places . . .   Jackson, *A Painter's Country*, page 78.

PLATE 33   njg 411   8⅜ x 10¾
Reserved for the McMichael Conservation Collection of Art, Kleinburg, Ontario.
Vignette   *Horse and carriage*, detail of njg 511. Private Collection.

The name Côte-de-la-Misère . . .   Barbeau, M., "Le pays des gourganes," *Mémoires de la Société Royale du Canada*, Section 1, 1917, page 220.

"With heavy robes . . ."   and   ". . . It was a stormy passage . . ."   and   "Eight o'clock . . ."   Blake, W.H., "A Christmas Jaunt," *Brown Waters*, pages 122, 123-4, 129.

PLATE 34   njg 600r   8⅛ x 10¾
Reserved for the McMichael Conservation Collection of Art, Kleinburg, Ontario.
"The true range of . . ."   Blake, *Brown Waters*, pages 57-9.

There are several versions . . .   The earliest dated AY drawing of this subject to turn up so far is marked April 4th, 1929, 7⅝ x 9⅞, njg 412. One canvas of the scene, *Grey Day, Laurentians* (1929), 25 x 32, is in the Montreal Museum of Fine Arts. It was the first shown in the Salon d'Automne 1929 and is reproduced in the Centennial Edition of *A Painter's Country*. A sunny version, dated 1933, and titled *Winter Morning, Charlevoix County*, 25 x 32, belongs to the Art Gallery of Ontario; it is reproduced as Plate 51 of *Canadian Painters* (Oxford, London, Phaidon Press, 1945), Vol. 1.

PLATE 35   njg 413   7¼ x 9¼
"Spring must be here . . ."   Pearl McCarthy's words are taken from an undated clipping on page 14 of AY's Scrapbook.

And last of all . . .   Scott, Duncan Campbell, *The Village of Viger* (Boston, Copeland and Day, 1896). This collection of thumbnail sketches was republished by The Ryerson Press in 1945, with fine black and white illustrations by Thoreau MacDonald.

PLATE 36   njg 1094   8⅞ x 11⅞
Reserved for the National Gallery of Canada.
Vignette   *Rocking chair*, detail of njg 612. Private Collection.
"St. Hilarion is like . . ."   and   "Grandpère Tremblay's own rocking chair . . ."   Jackson, *A Painter's Country*, page 74; "There was something about . . ."   *Ibid.*, page 72.

PLATE 37   njg 371r   9 x 12
Private Collection.
. . . a whole monograph . . .   Séguin, R.-L., *Les granges du Québec, du XVIIe au XIXe siècle* (Ottawa, Queen's Printer, 1963).
". . . au centre . . ."   Venne, Emile, *La Renaissance*, Montreal, November 23, 1935.

PLATE 38   njg 410   9 x 12
Reserved for the McMichael Conservation Collection of Art, Kleinburg, Ontario.
"the head of Seal Skin . . ."   Mrs. Simcoe, *Diary*, Ed. by Mary Quayle Innis (Macmillan St. Martins, 1965), page 147.
"The rush down steep . . ."   Blake, *Brown Waters*, page 132.
"The changes in this village . . ."   Jackson, "A Changing Paradise," Toronto *News*. AY's essay has the date '46 added in his own hand beside the clipping on page 110 of his monumental Scrapbook.

PLATE 39   njg 585   7⅜ x 9⅞
Reserved for the McMichael Conservation Collection of Art, Kleinburg, Ontario.
Vignette   *Profile of Quebec*, detail of njg 586 [1922].
Quebec . . . sits bristling . . .   Jameson, Anna, *Winter Studies and Summer Rambles in Canada*, Selections (Toronto, McClelland and Stewart, 1965), page 104.
". . . Robinson and I went . . ."   Jackson, *A Painter's Country*, pages 71, 72.
. . . for the two-page spread . . .   Beston, Henry, *The St. Lawrence*, page 53.

PLATE 40   njg 363r   9 x 12
Private Collection.
Vignettes   *Three children under an umbrella*, detail from njg 460. Private Collection.
          Snow plough, detail of njg 504.
          Horses and sleighs, detail of njg 437.
"At 7 I looked out . . ."   Mrs. Simcoe, *Diary*, pages 38-9; "a covered Carriole . . ."   *Ibid.*, page 140.
"At ten last night . . ."   Mrs. Traill, *The Backwoods of Canada*, 2nd edition, 1836, page 22ff.
"giddy heights"   and   "this Gibraltar . . ."   Dickens, Charles, quoted in Percival, W.P., *The Lure of Quebec* (Toronto, The Ryerson Press, 1941), pages 15-16; "Probably no city on earth . . ."   *Ibid.*, Introduction, page xvii.
". . . a quaint oasis . . ."   Barbeau, *Quebec, Where Ancient France Lingers*, pages 1, 3.
". . . The *ancien régime* . . ."   Beston, *The St. Lawrence*, pages 19, 20.

... the agreeable widow ...   Jackson, *op. cit.*, pages 71, 72.

Anyway, Blodwen Davies ...   Davies, B., *The Storied Streets of Quebec* (Montreal, L. Carrier & Co., 1929), page 66.

In the research for ...   Sincere and grateful acknowledgement is given to Dr. and Madame B.T. Denis of Quebec City for all their research on behalf of AYJ and NJG and historic Quebec.

PLATE 41   njg 364r   9 x 12
Private Collection.
"la belle de Québec"   Percival, *The Lure of Quebec*, pages 42-3;   ... and once the home of ...   *Ibid.*, page 160.

On leafing through ...   Ed. by Berton, Pierre, *Remember Yesterday, A Century of Photographs* (Toronto, McClelland and Stewart, 1965), The Canadian Centennial Library, page 57.

PLATE 42   njg 365r   9 x 12
Private Collection.
Vignette   *Pointe Lévis*, detail of njg 362r [1941].
... as in Claude Picher's unforgettable ...   C. Picher's photograph, "Entrance to East Wing," is on page 245 of *Canadian Art*, Vol. 18, July/August 1961. Many thanks to the Reference Librarian at the National Gallery for locating this exactly.
... an English lady artist of great talent ...   No less than twenty-three of Mrs. M.M. Chaplin's exquisite little works were reproduced for the first time in Marius Barbeau's *J'ai vu Québec* (Québec, Librairie Garneau, 1957);   *I Have Seen Quebec* (Toronto, Macmillan, 1957).
... as Dr. Percival's book shows ...   Percival, *The Lure of Quebec*, page 13.
... there is a pen-and-ink version ...   Beston, *The St. Lawrence*, page 264.
"I always like Quebec ..."   Jackson, The *Toronto Daily Star*, May 1939. This clipping is found on page 99 of AY's Scrapbook.

PLATE 43   njg 627   8⅞ x 11⅞
Reserved for the McMichael Conservation Collection of Art, Kleinburg, Ontario.

PLATE 44   njg 628r   9 x 12
Reserved for the McCord Museum of McGill University.
One of the most beautiful ...   Lebensold, Fred, as quoted by Johnstone, Ken, in "Montreal's Vieux Quartier," *Maclean's Magazine*, March 6, 1965, page 21.
... is naturally none other than ...   McLean, Eric, *Montreal* (Montreal, McGill University Press, 1964). The quotation is on the unnumbered pages between plates 44 and 45. Mr. Eric McLean's assistance is gratefully acknowledged.

PLATE 45   njg 143   9 x 12
Private Collection.
Vignette   *Oak leaves in the wind*, detail of njg 14v, undated, courtesy of the Art Collection Society of Kingston, Ontario.
The clear crisp air ...   Jackson, *A Painter's Country*, page 16.
"You say you fear ..."   Traill, *op. cit.*, pages 203-4, 205; "zig-zag fences ..." *Ibid.*, page 56.
"straggling over the untidy ground ..."   Jackson, *Mayfair*, September 1954, page 61.

PLATE 46   njg 321   8¼ x 10¾
Reserved for the McMichael Conservation Collection of Art, Kleinburg, Ontario.
Vignette   *Mullein*, detail of njg 892. Private Collection.
"In Pennsylvania ..."   Séguin, *Les granges du Québec*, page 77, Plate 40.

PLATE 47   njg 327   9 x 12
Reserved for the McMichael Conservation Collection of Art, Kleinburg, Ontario.
Most of the above ...   Card, Darius King, *McClure Heritage* (Printed for its author by the Picton Gazette Publishing Co., Picton, Ontario, 1966).
Sincere thanks are due to all who helped obtain information on the Maynooth area, in particular the Reverend N.E. Schamerhorn of the United Church, Maynooth, who did a great deal of research; Dr. R.A. Starrs, Miss Mae Mulvenna, the Reverend Fr. L.P. Casartelli, P.P. of St. Ignatius Martyr Parish, Maynooth, who kindly brought the excellent publication by Mr. Darius King Card to my attention; finally the Pembroke Chamber of Commerce, where I learned that Maynooth was in Hastings County not Renfrew!

PLATE 48   njg 326r   9 x 12
Reserved for the McMichael Conservation Collection of Art, Kleinburg, Ontario.
When the landscape ...   Jackson in November 1918, referring to Southern Ontario, in his Introduction to the catalogue for the Tom Thomson show held in Montreal in 1919.
... as he tells in his autobiography ...   Jackson, *A Painter's Country*, pages 143-4.
"Far off the beaten ways ..."   Walker, Harry, "Tales of the Valley," *The Ottawa Journal*, November 5, 1963.
... her neighbours were ...   *1000 Islander* (Gananoque, Ontario), August 13, 1966. With thanks to Cousin Fran Hayward Cloke and to Mr. Don Strikefoot.

PLATE 49   njg 323   9 x 12
Private Collection.
Vignettes   *Poplar and sumac*, detail of njg 1338
          Canoes, detail of njg 1340
          Old houses, Toronto, detail of njg 1336.
The Shack is ...   Jackson, *op. cit.*, page 55; "One day ..." *Ibid.*, page 31; "a prospector ..." and "Hell Rosa" *Ibid.*, page 53.
These words were published ...   Housser, F.B., *A Canadian Art Movement* (Toronto, Macmillan, 1926); ... J.W. Beatty and J.E.H. MacDonald did ... *Ibid.*, page 95. The style of the scene on the dust jacket is AY's, but the hand is that of Thoreau MacDonald.
... according to the late Miss Blodwen Davies ...   Davies, Blodwen, *A Study of Tom Thomson* (Toronto, Set by hand by the author, an edition of 450 copies, printed at the Discus Press, 1935), page 36; "making notes ..." *Ibid.*; The following year ... *Ibid.*, page 48. Republished 1967 by the Mitchell Press, Vancouver, with a Foreword by AY, and added colour plates.
All that film ...   Hubbard, R.H., *Tom Thomson* (Toronto, McClelland and Stewart, 1962); "Jackson & myself ..." *Ibid.*, page 8.
"You liked Thomson ..." and "Tom was packing up ..."   From two mimeographed sheets in AYJ's files.
... brought from Italy ...   They were brought the year before.
"When I remember ..."   *Mayfair* (Montreal, Maclean Hunter), September 1954.
"MacDonald, Jackson and I ..."   Harris, Lawren, *Story of the Group of Seven* (Toronto, Rous & Mann Ltd., 1964), page 16.

"they worked and cheerfully . . ." Davies, *op. cit.*, page 81; . . . Miss Davies' chapter on the Shack . . . *Ibid.*, pages 95-104; "that winter the shack . . ." *Ibid.*, page 96.

"not a banquet . . ." *Maclean's Magazine*, September 1, 1956.

The spelling of McIver was AY's own. The correct spelling however is MacIver.

The author is grateful for access to original letters and other Thomsoniana in the McMichael Conservation Collection at Kleinburg.

PLATE 50 njg 278r 9 x 12
Private Collection.

Happy hunting grounds Jackson, *op. cit.*, page 60; "many memories . . ." *Ibid.*, page 87.

"We sketched on . . ." From two mimeographed sheets in AYJ's files.

McIver See note under Plate 49.

PLATE 51 njg 285 7¼ x 11
Reserved for the McMichael Conservation Collection of Art, Kleinburg, Ontario.

Some large blasted pine . . . Mrs. Simcoe, *Diary*, page 34, October 29, 1791.

A Northern Lake is reproduced in Hubbard, R.H., *Tom Thomson* (Toronto, McClelland and Stewart, 1962), Plate 5. The book is dedicated to AY.

. . . reproduced on the cover . . . Hunter, E.R., *J.E.H. MacDonald, A Biography and Catalogue of His Works* (Toronto, Ryerson, 1940).

"three of the finest paintings . . ." Jackson and Casson, A.J., a CBC broadcast of July 31, 1966.

"who made us see . . ." Jackson to Robert Ayre, "Artist's Island," *Weekend Magazine*, Vol. 3, No. 41, 1953.

"after blowing . . ." Jackson, *op. cit.*, page 90; "in outward appearance . . ." *Ibid.*, page 31.

PLATE 52 njg 284v 9 x 12
Reserved for the National Gallery of Canada.

"Paddling around the islands . . ." Jackson, *op. cit.*, page 31.

"His attitude toward . . ." Lismer, Arthur, *A.Y. Jackson: Paintings 1902-1953* (Retrospective Exhibition), 1953, Introduction, page 4.

PLATE 53 njg 308 9 x 12
Private Collection.

I always think . . . Jackson, *op. cit.*, page 56.

"a grander, more sombre . . ." Jackson, "J.E.H. MacDonald," *The Canadian Forum*, January 1933.

"in the joyous young days . . ." Ayre, Robert, "The Magic Is Still There," *The Montreal Star*, February 12, 1966.

"A picture is a perfect enclosure . . ." Nancy Robertson quoting MacDonald, "J.E.H. MacDonald, R.C.A. 1873-1932," J.E.H. MacDonald Exhibition Catalogue (1965), page 7; "the remoteness" *Ibid.*, page 11.

Miss Nancy Robertson, Director of the Norman Mackenzie Art Gallery, has been most helpful in matters pertaining to J.E.H. MacDonald.

McIver See note under Plate 49.

PLATE 54 njg 140r 8½ x 11 (sight)
Private Collection.

Inland there are . . . Jackson, *A Painter's Country*, page 57.

"we perceived in the east . . ." Jameson, Anna, *Winter Studies and Summer Rambles in Canada*, Selections (Toronto, McClelland and Stewart, 1965), page 139.

McIver See note under Plate 49.

PLATE 55 njg 306 9 x 12
Reserved for the McMichael Conservation Collection of Art, Kleinburg, Ontario.

"landscape untidy and ragged . . ." Jackson, quoted by Delzell, Sylvia, "Art Brushes," Hamilton *Spectator*, Fall 1953.

"existence in that tired . . ." Harris, "The Unheroic North," *The Canadian Bookman*, February 1923, page 37.

Both Dr. Grant Darker and Mrs. G.E. Wilson kindly loaned copies of *Hiawatha*.

PLATE 56 njg 301r 9 x 12
Reserved for the McMichael Conservation Collection of Art, Kleinburg, Ontario.

. . . of his own poetry . . . Harris, Lawren, *Contrasts, A Book of Verse* (Toronto, McClelland and Stewart, 1922); "Streets hard as steel . . ." *Ibid.* Reprinted by permission of The Canadian Publishers, McClelland and Stewart Limited. With most grateful acknowledgement to Lawren Harris for permission to quote from these poems, and regrets that space limitation prevented inclusion of more.

PLATE 57 njg 303r 9 x 12
So drab a bleached grey Harris, "The earth winds," *op. cit.*, page 122; "Good Old Earth" Harris, *op. cit.* Both quotations are reprinted by permission of The Canadian Publishers, McClelland and Stewart Limited.

PLATE 58 njg 295 8⅜ x 10⅞
Reserved for the McMichael Conservation Collection of Art, Kleinburg, Ontario.

By the shining big-sea water Longfellow, Henry Wadsworth, "Hiawatha."

"in a gasoline launch . . ." Housser, *A Canadian Art Movement*, page 198.

"It certainly was . . ." MacDonald, quoted by Hunter, E.R., *J.E.H. MacDonald, A Biography and Catalogue of His Works* (Toronto, Ryerson, 1940), pages 56-7.

"I know of no more . . ." Jackson, *A Painter's Country*, page 57; . . . the famous box-car brigade . . . *Ibid.*, pages 56-7.

"singing expansiveness and sublimity" Harris, *Story of the Group of Seven*, page 20.

"Darkness and Light" Harris, *Contrasts*, page 91. Reprinted by permission of The Canadian Publishers, McClelland and Stewart Limited.

"The Shore is . . ." Lawrence, D.H., Letter to J.D. Beresford, February 1916, *Collected Letters*, Ed. by Harry T. Moore, Vol. 1. Exact source kindness of Miss Peggy Blackstock of Shirley Leishman Books, Ottawa.

PLATE 59a njg 297 5⅝ x 8⅞

PLATE 59b njg 315 5⅝ x 8⅞
"So the Canadian artist . . ." Harris, Lawren, "Creative Art and Canada," *The McGill News*, December 1928.

"We lived in a . . ." Harris, *Story of the Group of Seven*, page 16.

PLATE 60 njg 842 9 x 12
Private Collection.

A very hardy grade . . . Duval, Paul, "A Canadian Epic," *Saturday Night*, November 14, 1953, page 20.

"the man who stayed home" Ayre, Robert, "Painter of the Prairies," *Weekend Magazine*, Vol. 8, No. 12, March 22, 1958.

"The grain elevator . . ." Jackson, "Search for Beauty Still Concerns A.Y. Jackson," Hamilton *Spectator*, November 26, 1959.

The author acknowledges the kind assistance of the Reference Librarian of the National Gallery for obtaining bibliographical information.

PLATE 61 njg 997r 8¾ x 11¾
J. Gordon and Wilhelmina Morris McIntosh Collection of the University of Western Ontario.
Vignette *Threshing*, detail of njg 858. Reserved for the McCord Museum of McGill University.

PLATE 62 njg 893r 9 x 12
Reserved for the McMichael Conservation Collection of Art, Kleinburg, Ontario.
Vignette *Lethbridge Post Office*, detail of njg 899. Private Collection.
"What we really valued . . ." Buchanan, Donald, *To Have Seen the Sky* (Toronto, McClelland and Stewart, 1962), pages 4, 6.
"the broad, unending horizons . . ." Buchanan, *The Growth of Canadian Painting* (Toronto, Collins, 1950), page 29.

PLATE 63 njg 144 9 x 12
Private Collection.
"It is a different glory . . ." Jackson to Augustus Bridle, *Toronto Star*, May 1939.
The Canadian Group of Painters was the outgrowth of the Group of Seven. It began in 1933 with about forty members, and has at present approximately sixty members.

PLATE 64 njg 1236r 9 x 11⅞
Reserved for the McMichael Conservation Collection of Art, Kleinburg, Ontario.
The Blood Indians . . . Barbeau, Marius, *Indian Days on the Western Prairies* (Ottawa, Queen's Printer, 1965), pages 37-8; also *Columbia Encyclopedia* (2nd edition, 1956), pages 206, 207.
"Most of these lands . . ." Schumiatcher, Morris C., "Canadians with Nothing to Celebrate. 1, The Plains Indians," *Saturday Night*, June 1967, Vol. 82, page 27.

PLATE 65 njg 895v 9 x 12
Reserved for the McCord Museum of McGill University.
"When A.Y. Jackson . . ." McCarthy, Pearl, "Art and Artists," Clipping from *The Globe and Mail*, 1944.
. . . AY's reception at Cowley . . . Jackson, *A Painter's Country*, pages 147-8.
"Visitors—how we love them . . ." Bundy, Freda Graham, "Go West, Young Woman," from an undated newspaper clipping (probably the Lethbridge *Herald*, c. 1955), supplied by Miss Claire Jackson of Lethbridge.
"In every village . . ." Jackson to C.F.S. (C.F. Steele), "Lights and Shadows," Lethbridge *Herald*, October 1943.
"land of the last town and the distant point" Anderson, Patrick, "Cold Colloquy," *The Blasted Pine* (Toronto, Macmillan, 1962), page 5.

PLATE 66 njg 1235r 9 x 11⅞
"could be anywhere . . ." Ed. by Pierre Berton, *Remember Yesterday, A Century of Photographs* (Toronto, McClelland and Stewart, 1965), The Canadian Centennial Library, pages 94-5. Reprinted by permission of The Canadian Publishers, McClelland and Stewart Limited.

PLATE 67 njg 894r 9 x 12
Reserved for the McMichael Conservation Collection of Art, Kleinburg, Ontario.
He tells most amusingly . . . Jackson, *A Painter's Country*, page 175.
"a big weather-worn man . . ." *The Calgary Herald*, July 12, 1960; "It was in 1919 . . ." *Ibid.*, July 3, 1954; "I had old Archie . . ." *Ibid.* With many thanks to Cousin Kenneth Henry Jackson of Calgary for the Cosgrave bits.
"And cattle shove . . ." MacDonald, J.E.H., From the title poem in *West by East & Other Poems*, page 1, published posthumously by Thoreau MacDonald (Toronto, Ryerson, 1933). With grateful acknowledgement to Thoreau MacDonald.
"Jackson picked himself . . ." McCarthy, Pearl, Clipping from *The Globe and Mail*, Fall 1944.

PLATE 68 njg 896r 9 x 12
Reserved for the National Gallery of Canada.
The Oldman River jus' . . . Lethbridge *Herald*, caption to photograph by Orville Brunelle.
"The name of the river . . ." Buchanan, *To Have Seen the Sky*, page 12.
Ralph Connor makes use . . . Connor, Ralph, *The Patrol of the Sun Dance Trail* (Toronto, The Westminster Company Limited, 1914).
"allied to structure . . ." Housser, *op. cit.*, pages 152, 153.

PLATE 69 njg 897r 8⅞ x 11⅞
Reserved for the McMichael Conservation Collection of Art, Kleinburg, Ontario.
"The foothills of Alberta . . ." Jackson, *op. cit.*, page 146; "on a ridge" *Ibid.*, page 148.
"Culture in the 'Wild and Woolly' . . ." Key, Archibald, *The McGill News*, September 1929.
"God, that I have no choice! . . ." Lawrence, D.H., Last stanza of the poem "Humiliation," *Complete Poems*, Ed. by De Sola Pinto and F.W. Roberts (London, W. Heinemann Ltd., 1964). Source and correct form kindly traced by Miss Peggy Blackstock of Shirley Leishman Books in Ottawa.

PLATE 70 njg 906 8¾ x 11
Private Collection.
We Are (not yet) Seven The title with apologies to William Wordsworth.
"kept throwing the sketches . . ." Jackson, *A Painter's Country*, page 37.
One undated pen-and-ink . . . *Vista from Yellowhead*, accession No. 3171, page size 10⅜ x 13½, actual drawing size 7⁹⁄₁₆ x 10¼.
"We are the leaven . . ." MacDonald, J.E.H., quoted by Jackson in a paper read for him by William Dale at a meeting of the Royal Society of Arts, in London on December 14, 1948; "The Development of Canadian Art," *Journal* of the Royal Society of Arts, January 14, 1949, Vol. 97, No. 4786, pages 129-43.
With thanks to Dr. D.B.O. Savile for obtaining data from the Toponymy Division on all possible *Seven Sisters* out west!

PLATE 71 njg 1197 8⅜ x 10⅞
Reserved for the McMichael Conservation Collection of Art, Kleinburg, Ontario.
A single simple vision of high things Harris, Lawren, "Creative Art and Canada," *McGill News*, December 1928.
. . . the two artist friends set out . . . Housser, Fred, *A Canadian Art Movement*, page 193ff.
"great crumbling mountains . . ." Jackson, quoted by Housser, Fred, *op. cit.*, page 194.

"a kind of cubist's paradise . . ." Jackson, *A Painter's Country*, page 107.

"a journey of nearly . . ." Housser, Fred, *op. cit.*, page 193.

"Why is it that . . ." and "Copying mountains literally . . ." Jackson, from undated clippings in his Scrapbook.

PLATE 72 njg 907 8 x 10
Reserved for the McMichael Conservation Collection of Art, Kleinburg, Ontario.

The mountain tops brighten . . . Barbeau, M., *The Downfall of Temlaham* (Toronto, Macmillan, 1928), pages 29, 38.

". . . no great difficulty . . ." Jackson, "Rescuing Our Tottering Totems," *Maclean's Magazine*, December 19, 1927.

Mt. Gitsegyukla's distinctive peaks show in Holgate's canvas *Totem Poles, Gitsegiuklas* (1927, 32 x 32, National Gallery of Canada) facing page 167 of *The Downfall of Temlaham;* also wreathed in cloud in Jackson's watercolour facing page 54. Exact information on the Holgate canvas was kindly provided by the Registrar of the National Gallery of Canada.

PLATE 73 njg 1186 5⅝ x 8⅞
Private Collection.

"absolutely dazzling" Varley, Peter, *Canada*, page 54.

Several studies of . . . *Indian Home* (c. 1927, 21 x 26, owned by Miss Isabel McLaughlin).

"I have always felt that AYJ . . ." Carr, Emily, *Growing Pains* (Toronto, Oxford University Press, 1946), page 321; Clarke Irwin (owners of copyright), 1946.

"I loved his things . . ." and ". . . Mr. Jackson is steady . . ." Carr, Emily, *Hundreds and Thousands, The Journals of Emily Carr* (Toronto, Clarke Irwin, 1966), pages 5, 6.

PLATE 74 njg 911 8⅛ x 10⅞
Reserved for the McMichael Conservation Collection of Art, Kleinburg, Ontario.
Vignette *Hahao animal*, njg 1190. Reserved for the McMichael Conservation Collection of Art, Kleinburg, Ontario.

"When she came to . . ." Carr, Emily, *The Heart of a Peacock* (Toronto, Oxford University Press, 1953), page 60; Clarke Irwin (owners of copyright).

"huge Indian dug-out canoes . . ." There is a fine detailed description of how the red cedar dug-out was made by the West Coast Indians in *People of the Potlatch* (Vancouver Art Gallery, 1956), pages 31-2.

It seems that the Gitksan . . . and Another Gitksan legend . . . and "The former land of bliss . . ." Barbeau, M., *The Downfall of Temlaham*, pages 242-3, 244.

PLATE 75 njg 913 8 x 9⅞
Private Collection.
Vignette Detail of *pole with Painted Goat*, njg 1171r. Private Collection.

Forms to fit the thoughts Carr, Emily, *Klee Wyck* (Toronto, Oxford University Press, 1941), page 72; in paperback (Toronto, Clarke Irwin, 1965), page 51. All references to this book from now on will be to the paperback edition.

"four incisors lashed . . ." Barbeau, M., *Totem Poles of the Gitksan* (Ottawa, Queen's Printer, 1929), page 91.

"bloomed over again . . ." Carr, Emily, *Klee Wyck*, page 13.

"As acknowledgement of his exploits . . ." Barbeau, M., *Totem Poles of the Gitksan*, page 104.

There is an excellent colour reproduction of Emily Carr's 1912 canvas *Kitseukla*.

"The discoverers looked below . . ." Barbeau, *op. cit.*, page 106.

PLATE 76 njg 916 8⅜ x 10⅞
Private Collection.

Rescuing our tottering totems Jackson, "Rescuing Our Tottering Totems," *Maclean's Magazine*, December 15, 1927, pages 23, 37; ". . . The poles are sawn off . . ." *Ibid.*

It was restored and re-erected . . . A brief footnote on page 141 of Barbeau's monograph *Totem Poles of the Gitksan* says the rare house-front pole was re-erected "through the initiative of the Totem Pole Committee of Ottawa." It is described on pages 140-2.

"apparitions of monster squirrels . . ." Barbeau, *Totem Poles of the Gitksan*, page 139.

PLATE 77 njg 912 8 x 9⅞
Reserved for the McMichael Conservation Collection of Art, Kleinburg, Ontario.
Vignette *Raven*, side and rear views, njg 1372. Private Collection.

The colour version of this drawing faces page 70 of *The Downfall of Temlaham*.

"carved with dignity . . ." Carr, Emily, "Indian Bird Carving," *Heart of a Peacock*, page 84.

PLATE 78 njg 917 8 x 10
Private Collection.

Let the dead sleep . . . Wyle, Florence, *Poems* (Toronto, Ryerson, 1959), Ryerson Poetry Chap Books, page 16.

. . . we may recall . . . Carr, Emily, "The Blouse," *Heart of a Peacock*, page 42.

"Beside the restoration . . ." Jackson, "Rescuing Our Tottering Totems," *Maclean's Magazine*, December 15, 1927.

"the finest cluster of totem poles . . ." Barbeau, *Totem Poles of the Gitksan*, page 2.

"fallen grandeur . . ." Clemson, Donovan, "Scenes along the Skeena," *Canadian Geographical Journal*, May 1966, Vol. 72, No. 5, pages 154-9.

"I felt we were . . ." Holgate, letter of November 29, 1966.

"done" Carr, Emily, *Klee Wyck*, Foreword.

"damp and lonely . . ." Swayze, Nansi, *The Man Hunters* (Toronto, Clarke Irwin, 1960), page 88.

"My heart said . . ." Carr, Emily, *Klee Wyck*, page 101.

"My heart throbs . . ." Barbeau, *The Downfall of Temlaham*, page 38.

PLATE 79a njg 1174 5½ x 8⅞ Private Collection.

PLATE 79b njg 915 5⅝ x 8⅞ Private Collection.

The author gives grateful acknowledgement to Mrs. Duncan de Kergommeaux for information on present-day potlatches.

. . . with that white woman . . . Carr, Emily, "Greenville," *Klee Wyck*, page 50.

PLATE 80 njg 918 8⅞ x 11⅞
Reserved for the McMichael Conservation Collection of Art, Kleinburg, Ontario.

The East has invaded the West Jackson, letter of August 10, 1946. from Banff.

A canvas very similar to this drawing was reproduced in *The Christian Science Monitor*, October 29, 1948, courtesy of the Dominion Gallery, Montreal.

. . . the "illusive" Sioux chief . . . and "the busy, ambitious and would-be wicked . . ." and "Over all the blue arch . . ." Connor, Ralph, *The Patrol of the Sun Dance Trail* (Toronto, The Westminister Company Limited, 1914), pages 70, 86, 129.

Useful information was provided by M.P. Hess and by the Glenbow Foundation of Calgary, for which many thanks.

PLATE 81   njg 859   8⅞ x 12
Reserved for the McMichael Conservation Collection of Art, Kleinburg, Ontario.
"runs in from the east . . ."   Hutchison, Bruce, *The Fraser*, page 275. Copyright 1950 by Bruce Hutchison. Reprinted by permission of Mr. Hutchison and of Holt, Rinehart and Winston, Inc., New York (New York, Holt, Rinehart and Winston, Inc., 1950; Toronto, Clarke Irwin, 1950). First published in paperback format by Clarke Irwin, 1965.
. . . a well illustrated recent article . . .   Clemson, Donovan, "Kamloops: City in the Sage," *Canadian Geographical Journal*, January 1967, Vol. 74, No. 1, pages 18-27; "As a brigade . . ."   *Ibid.*, page 19.
Acknowledgement is given to D.B.O. Savile for information on Kamloops today.

PLATE 82   njg 860r   9 x 12
Private Collection.
Vignette   *Kettle Valley*, detail from njg 929.
The Cariboo . . .   Keatley, Philip, *CBC Times*, January 29-February 4, 1966, page 5.
"this curious old town"   Hutchison, Bruce, *The Fraser*, page 268.
"It is a measure . . ."   Keatley, Philip, *CBC Times*, January 29-February 4, 1966, page 5.
"The Cariboo plateau . . ."   Hutchison, Bruce, *op. cit.*, page 244; "a yawning ditch . . ." *Ibid.*, page 8; "feeling of unlimited space . . ."   *Ibid.*, page 245; "the quality . . ." *Ibid.*, page 223.
"I found . . ."   Jackson, *A Painter's Country*, page 151.

PLATE 83   njg 922r   9 x 11⅞
Reserved for the McMichael Conservation Collection of Art, Kleinburg, Ontario.
Vignette   *Quick studies of cattle auction, Williams Lake*, detail of njg 930. Private Collection.
The rude . . .   Hutchison, *op. cit.*, page 85.
"with its awful beds of miry clay"   Hutchison, *op. cit.*, page 81 quoting Mr. Justice Denis Murphy speaking in 1925 at Yale; "18 feet wide"   *Ibid.*, page 83; "an almost incredible feat . . ."   *Ibid.*, page 85; "Until recent times . . ."   *Ibid.*, page 250.
"the C.P.R. train . . ."   Carr, Emily, *Growing Pains*, page 263; "I did suffer two days . . ."   *Ibid.*, page 264; "We ate a huge meal . . ."   *Ibid.*, page 266; "The Hundred and Fifty Mile . . ."   *Ibid.*, page 267.
. . . who was so engagingly depicted . . .   Hanlon, Michael, "The West's Last Cattle Driver," *Ottawa Citizen*, January 28, 1967.

PLATE 84   njg 920r   9 x 11⅞
Reserved for the McCord Museum of McGill University.
Of all the gold towns . . .   Hutchison, *op. cit.*, page 73.
"more gold . . ."   Ramsey, Bruce, *Barkerville: A Guide to the Fabulous Cariboo Gold Camp* (Vancouver, Mitchell Press), page 10; "Williams Creek has yielded . . ."   *Ibid.*, page 14. Bruce Ramsey quotes here from a report by Dr. George M. Dawson, Director of the Geological Survey of Canada.
"one-mile clutter . . ."   Ed. by Berton, Pierre, *Remember Yesterday, A Century of Photographs* (Toronto, McClelland and Stewart Limited, 1965), The Canadian Centennial Library, page 43.
"You had to walk . . ."   Hutchison, *op. cit.*, page 73; "champagne 2 ounces . . ." *Ibid.*, page 170.

. . . active business houses . . .   Ramsey, *op. cit.*, page 28;   *re* "The Fire Department" *Ibid.*, pages 55-7 *passim*.
"two old ladies . . ."   Hutchison, *op. cit.*, page 169.

PLATE 85   njg 921r   9 x 11⅞
Private Collection.
Some hopes which go . . .   Rev. James Reynard, as recorded by Ramsey, *op. cit.*, page 62.
"small, substantial . . ."   Ramsey, *op. cit.*, page 62; "an elegant structure . . ."   *Ibid.*, page 62; "Peter Gibson . . ."   *Ibid.*, page 72; "Margaret Jane Blair . . ."   *Ibid.*, page 68; "40 below . . ."   *Ibid.*, page 10.
"Cariboo" Cameron . . .   Hutchison, *op. cit.*, page 163 refers to the alcohol preserving Sophia.

PLATE 86   njg 919r   9 x 11⅞
Reserved for the McMichael Conservation Collection of Art, Kleinburg, Ontario.
Vignette   *Western Tavern*, detail from njg 931. Private Collection.
Well, old timer . . .   Jackson, in a letter to the author, dated October 4, 1945.
"suffering great pain . . ."   Ramsey, *op. cit.*, page 4.
. . . Twelve-Foot Davis . . .   Gamester, Stephen Jones, "Journey to the Last Frontier," *Maclean's Magazine*, February 19, 1966, pages 20-34 *passim*.
"My fortune . . ."   Camsell, Charles, *Son of the North*, page 8. The graduate working on Shakespeare is referred to on page 185.

PLATE 87   njg 923r   9 x 11¾
Private Collection.
Vignettes   Details of *U.S. Army trucks on the Alaska Highway* from njg 1220r and 1221.
. . . the epic told in . . .   Camsell, Charles, *Son of the North* (Toronto, Ryerson, 1954).
"child of this wilderness . . ."   MacDonald, Malcolm, *Down North* (Toronto, Oxford, 1943), page 74.
"risky pioneer flight . . ."   Camsell, *Son of the North*, page 72. The latitude referred to is Lat. 60.
"a significant engineering feat . . ."   As it is put mildly in the *Columbia Encyclopedia*, 2nd edition, 1956.
He participated vigorously . . .   Jackson, "Canada at War," *Maritime Art, A Canadian Art Magazine*, Halifax, N.S., February/March 1942, Vol. 2, No. 3, pages 83-91.
On the home front . . .   Surrey, Philip, "Silk Screen Prints Enlist," *Canadian Art*, December 1943/January 1944, Vol. 1, No. 2, pages 58-61.
"the great vistas changing . . ."   AY quoted by Pearl McCarthy in *The Globe and Mail*, November 22, 1943.
A.Y.'s article . . .   Jackson, "Sketching on the Alaska Highway," *Canadian Art*, February/March 1944, Vol. 1, No. 3, pages 88-92.

PLATE 88   njg 924   9 x 11¾
Reserved for the McMichael Conservation Collection of Art, Kleinburg, Ontario.
In Whitehorse the glamour of early days . . .   Jackson, *A Painter's Country*, page 173.
"the worst trail . . ."   MacDonald, Malcolm, *Down North*, page 87.
"wall of glittering white . . ."   Berton, Pierre, *Klondike* (Toronto, McClelland and Stewart Limited, 1958), pages 244, 245. Reprinted by permission of The Canadian Publishers, McClelland and Stewart Limited. "city of gold"   *Ibid.*, page 268; scow loaded with nothing . . .   *Ibid.*, page 291.

"skimmed over [the rapids] . . ." MacDonald, *Down North*, page 83.

"a most picturesque jumble . . ." Jackson, *op. cit.*, page 173.

"One Seattle shipyard . . ." Berton, *Klondike*, page 307; "Up the river . . ." *Ibid.*, page 308. Both quotations are reprinted by permission of The Canadian Publishers, McClelland and Stewart Limited.

Mrs. Len Tyrrell kindly provided data on the old riverboats.

PLATE 89 njg 925 9 x 12

Reserved for the National Gallery of Canada.

Thron-duck flowed . . . This spelling occurs in Berton, *Klondike*, page 38.

"Whole towns have sprung up . . ." This is along the Road; on the River the opposite is the situation.

PLATE 90 njg 233 8⅜ x 10⅞

Private Collection.

"The West has now . . ." *Free Press*, July 5, 1927 and July 8, 1927. Clippings supplied by Miss Claire Jackson of Lethbridge.

"a part of the country . . ." Jackson, *op. cit.*, page 122.

Among Mackintosh Bell's . . . Bell, James Mackintosh, *Far Places* (Toronto, Macmillan, 1931); The chapter . . . *Ibid.*, pages 3-33.

"it was slow travelling . . ." Jackson, *op. cit.*, pages 122-5.

"a wonderful train . . ." de Poncins, Gontrin, *Kabloona* (New York, Reynal & Hitchcock, 1941), page 6.

. . . adventurous Athabasca scow brigade . . . Alcock, F. J., "Scow Brigade on the Athabasca," *Canadian Geographical Journal*, February 1932. This was reprinted in the same journal for March 1967, Vol. 74, No. 3, pages 92-9.

"The Best Woodcutter . . ." Inglis, John, "An Honest Pile," *The Beaver*, Winter 1966, page 34.

"a day's journey . . ." Bell, *Far Places*, page 10.

PLATE 91 njg 682 8⅜ x 10⅞

Private Collection.

In the summer the Indians . . . Jackson, *A Painter's Country*, page 123.

"On that first journey . . ." Bell, *Far Places*, pages 11-12.

The Indians that trade at Resolution . . . Bell, *Far Places*, page 6. They used to be called Copper Indians or Red Knives.

Always a small tribe . . . The population figure of 150 is found in Jenness, Diamond, *The Indians of Canada* (Ottawa, Dept. of Mines, National Museum of Canada, 1932), Bulletin 65, page 389.

"they lack the gaiety . . ." Bell, *Far Places*, page 8.

"The old fellow . . ." Camsell, *Son of the North*, page 57.

"twenty tents . . ." Hearne, Samuel, *A Journey from Prince of Wales's Fort in Hudson's Bay to the Northern Ocean In the Years 1769, 1770, 1771, and 1772* (First published posthumously in 1795; in Toronto by the Champlain Society in 1911 in an edition of 500, edited by J. B. Tyrrell; and in Toronto by McClelland and Stewart Limited in 1958, under the title *Coppermine Journey* in a vivid and shortened arrangement by Farley Mowat. Unless otherwise stated, pages refer to the 1911 edition.), page 277; "exceedingly . . ." *Ibid.*, page 257.

"Probably one-tenth . . ." Bell, *Far Places*, page 31.

PLATE 92 njg 238 c. 8 x 11

Reserved for the National Gallery of Canada.

". . . we arrived at the grand . . ." Hearne, *A Journey from . . .*, pages 267-8; "was particularly fond . . ." *Ibid.*, page 2.

"with indications of ore . . ." *Northern Miner*, August 19, 1965, 51st year, No. 22.

"to a record . . ." *Canada One Hundred 1867-1967* (Queen's Printer, 1967), page 159.

"Special Pine Point issue" *North* is a bi-monthly publication of the Northern Administration Branch, Dept. of Northern Affairs and National Resources, Ottawa, May/June 1964, Vol. 11, No. 3.

"nothing but a little clearing . . ." Jackson, *op. cit.*, page 124.

"incongruous human collection . . ." Bell, *Far Places*, pages 27-8.

"much cheered up" Jackson, *op. cit.*, page 124.

PLATE 93 njg 234 8⅜ x 10⅞

Reserved for the McMichael Conservation Collection of Art, Kleinburg, Ontario.
Private Collection.

PLATE 94 njg 243 8⅜ x 10⅞

Reserved for the McMichael Conservation Collection of Art, Kleinburg, Ontario.
Vignette *Bakeapple on Goulet Island, Great Slave Lake*, detail of njg 934.
Private Collection

"the scene was agreeably altered . . ." Hearne, *A Journey from . . .*, page 255.

"This was good, clean country . . ." Jackson, *op. cit.*, page 125.

"Downward through . . ." Longfellow, H. W., "The Song of Hiawatha," *Longfellow's Poetical Works* (London, Geo. Routledge & Sons, 1889), page 120.

But back in 1928 . . . Jackson, "Memories of a Fellow Artist, Frederick Grant Banting," *The Canadian Medical Association Journal*, Ed. by Dr. J.B.R. MacKendry, 15 May, 1965, No. 92, pages 1077-84. Courtesy of Mrs. R.A. Starrs.

PLATE 95 njg 240 5½ x 9

Private Collection.
Vignettes *Studies of heads, Mackintosh Bell and Indian*, from njg 1223. Reserved for the McMichael Conservation Collection of Art, Kleinburg, Ontario.

"crossing Great Slave Lake . . ." Jackson, *A Painter's Country*, page 125.

"a gasoline-driven scow . . ." Bell, *Far Places*, page 27.

"Our journey to Gros Cap . . ." Bell, *Far Places*, pages 29-30.

"a rustling and crackling . . ." Hearne, *A Journey from . . .*, page 235.

"Above your head . . ." Anderson, Patrick, "Cold Colloquy," *The Blasted Pine* (Toronto, The Macmillan Co. of Canada Ltd., 1962), page 5.

PLATE 96 njg 743r 9 x 12

Reserved for the McMichael Conservation Collection of Art, Kleinburg, Ontario.

"I was only too happy . . ." Jackson, *op. cit.*, pages 182, 183.

By 1965 four of the gold mines . . . *The Ottawa Journal*, September 16, 1965.

. . . Canada's most northerly museum . . . Inglis, G. E., "Museum of the North," *Canadian Geographical Journal*, November 1967, Vol. 75, No. 5, pages 174-7.

"Much of the railway . . ." McCook, James, "The North's Visible Assets," *The Ottawa Journal*, February 16, 1967.

The Great Slave Lake . . . The statistics noted here are from *Canada One Hundred 1867-1967* (Queen's Printer, 1967) and from Green, Earl, "Fishing, Gold Mining Keep the N.W.T. In Operation," *The Ottawa Journal*, September 16, 1965.

"The Indian children . . ." CBC radio, August 7, 1967.

PLATE 97 njg 721r 8⅞ x 11¹³/₁₆

Reserved for the McMichael Conservation Collection of Art, Kleinburg, Ontario.

"The effect of the North . . ." Siegfried, André, *Canada* (London, Jonathan Cape, 1937).

"several Finnish miners" Jackson, *A Painter's Country*, page 149.

The geologists tell us . . . See "Great Bear Lake" by Lionel Johnson in the *Canadian Geographical Journal*, August 1966, Vol. 73, No. 2, pages 58-67 for an excellent article on the region's ecology.

"a vast nursery . . ." MacDonald, Malcolm, *Down North*, page 219.

The canvas *South of Great Bear Lake* measures 32 by 40 inches, was painted around 1939, and is now in the collection of the late J. S. McLean of Toronto. It was reproduced in the catalogue of the 1953 retrospective as Plate 15, and in *Mayfair* of September 1954 on page 29.

PLATE 98 njg 714v 9 x 12

Private Collection.

"periods of flat calm . . ." Johnson, Lionel, "Great Bear Lake," *Canadian Geographical Journal*, page 63.

"the quietest lake . . ." Jackson, in a 1939 interview with Augustus Bridle, Scrapbook page 99.

"probably the world's largest mass . . ." Johnson, "Great Bear Lake," page 64; "a very young river . . ." *Ibid.*, page 62.

"This would be approximately . . ." Johnson, "Great Bear Lake," page 59.

"tall and spare . . ." MacDonald, Malcolm, *Down North*, pages 74, 79.

PLATE 99 njg 712r 9 x 12

Reserved for the McMichael Conservation Collection of Art, Kleinburg, Ontario.

"On the 24th . . ." Camsell, *Son of the North*, page 131.

"where there was cobalt . . ." Camsell, *Ibid.*, page 132.

"They reached Echo Bay . . ." Camsell, *loc. cit.*

"to alter the world . . ." *CBC Times*, January 6-12, 1968. The programme itself was on January 11, 1968.

The present drawing . . . A similar drawing, dated September 6, 1938, is in the National Gallery. It was a gift of Dr. J. O. Firestone, of Ottawa. The subject of the *Echo Bay* canvas for Dr. Camsell closely resembles the drawing in Plate 98.

"the chief spokesman . . ." *The Ottawa Journal*, May 18, 1957.

PLATE 100 njg 717r 9 x 12

Reserved for the McMichael Conservation Collection of Art, Kleinburg, Ontario.

Walli's dog Susie . . . Jackson, *A Painter's Country*, page 150.

"The constituent rocks . . ." Johnson, Lionel, "Great Bear Lake," *Canadian Geographical Journal*, page 61.

"hills of solid rock . . ." Bell, *Far Places*, page 65.

"The variegated mineral . . ." Bell, *Far Places*, page 66.

"He is a Canadian . . ." Ayre, Robert, *The Montreal Star*, January 30, 1954.

PLATE 101 njg 723r 9 x 12

Vignette *Study of mushrooms* (*boletus*), detail of 734v. Private Collection.

"the old station" Camsell, *Son of the North*, page 131.

AY recalls . . . Jackson, *op. cit.*, page 150.

. . . character known as Calamity Jane . . . The CBC TV programme "The Secret Years," January 11, 1968.

"a happy little community" Jackson, *op. cit.*, page 182.

The Glenbow Foundation, Calgary has one of the oil sketches of an old miner's shack at Great Bear Lake, dated September 1950, and numbered JA 55.30.1.

PLATE 102 njg 718r 9 x 12

Private Collection.

But I am full of hills . . . Anderson, Patrick, "Cold Colloquy," *The Blasted Pine*, page 5.

"The Canadian North . . ." and "Bit by bit . . ." Van Steenburgh, W. E., Fortier, Y.O., Thorsteinsson, R., "Scientific Research in the Arctic," *The Unbelievable Land* (Ottawa, Queen's Printer, 1964), pages 108, 109. This extract is reproduced with the permission of the Queen's Printer, Ottawa.

. . . a long feature article . . . Bletcher, Betty, "Noted Artist Urges Creative Work for Young Canadians," Lethbridge *Herald*, October 31, 1949. By the courtesy of Miss Claire Jackson of Lethbridge.

Piecing together the story . . . This much appreciated information came from Mr. Nuttall who worked at Eldorado Mine as an accountant from 1955 to 1959.

PLATE 103 njg 738r 9 x 12

Reserved for the McMichael Conservation Collection of Art, Kleinburg, Ontario.

"Mural precipices . . ." Bell, *Far Places*, pages 65-66.

"frost-shattered . . ." Mowat, Introduction, *Coppermine Journey*.

". . . a region that stirs . . ." Camsell, *Son of the North*, page 62.

"hate insensate . . ." Service, R. W., *Songs of a Sourdough* (Toronto, Wm. Briggs, 1908), page v; "monster mountains" *Ibid.*; "gaunt against . . ." *Ibid.*

"valleys unpeopled . . ." Camsell, *Son of the North*, page 62.

"sapless and skeletal . . ." de Poncins, Gontran, *Kabloona*, page 17.

"the wild and glorious . . ." MacDonald, *Down North*, page 4.

"Jackson symbolise . . ." Gladu, Paul, "La nature: Pour ou contre?", *Notre Temps*, page 4. Also in AY's Scrapbook, page 135.

"grasp the breadth . . ." Lismer, Arthur, *A. Y. Jackson Paintings 1902-1953*, pages 6, 7.

"key man in . . ." Lewis, Wyndham, "Canadian Nature and Its Painters," *The Listener*, August 29, 1946. A review of the Phaidon Press *Canadian Painters;* "to Great Bear Lake . . ." *Ibid.*

"in standing before . . ." Lismer, Arthur, from Housser, F. B., *A Canadian Art Movement* (Toronto, Macmillan, 1926), page 190.

PLATE 104 njg 730r 9 x 12

Reserved for the National Gallery of Canada.

"Every chance I get . . ." *Mayfair*, September 1954, page 67.

"nobody came and went . . ." Leacock, Stephen, "My Remarkable Uncle," *My Remarkable Uncle and Other Sketches* (Toronto, McClelland and Stewart, 1942). With thanks to Miss Peggy Blackstock of Shirley Leishman Books, Ottawa.

"On the 3rd . . ." Mowat, *Coppermine Journey*, page 64.

"In the afternoon . . ." Franklin, John, *Narrative of a Journey to the Shores of the Polar Sea, in the Years 1819-20-21-22* (2nd edition, London, John Murray, 1824), Vol. 2, page 256.

"took shelter in the lee . . ." Camsell, *Son of the North*, page 124.

. . . a beautiful book . . . Douglas, George, M., *Lands Forlorn / A Story of an Expedition to*

Hearne's Coppermine River (New York, G.P. Putnam's, 1914). A portrait of G.M. Douglas, 1911, hangs in the National Gallery, Ottawa.

"this monstrous, empty . . ."   Lewis, "Canadian Nature and Its Painters," *The Listener*.

"If ever there is . . ."   Lismer, Arthur, Introduction, *A.Y. Jackson Paintings 1902-1953*, pages 4, 7.

"He was to speak . . ."   Gibbons, Lillian, "Personality Parade," Winnipeg *Free Press*, Fall 1943.

PLATE 105   njg 734r   8⅞ x 11⅞
Private Collection.

"a man of such . . ."   Hearne, *A Journey from . . .* , pages 324-5.

"The wanderer is still . . ."   Jackson, letter to his mother, April 24, 1908.

"It was a lovely . . ."   Jackson, *A Painter's Country*, page 184.

No wonder either . . .   Mowat, Farley, *Canada North*, The Canadian Illustrated Library Series (Toronto, McClelland and Stewart, 1967).

"particularly fond of drawing"   Hearne, Introduction, *A Journey from . . . .*

"took beautiful sketches"   *Franklin's First Journey*, Vol. 2, page 247; "contemplating the river . . ."   and   "ranged . . . in form of a . . ."   *Ibid.*, Vol. 2, page 166.

"merely curious"   Jackson, *op. cit.*, page 150.

"He can draw mushrooms . . ."   *Mayfair*, page 58. See vignette with Plate 101, showing the *boletus* drawn by AY on the *verso* of the present drawing.

PLATE 106   njg 388   7 x 10⅜
Private Collection.

. . . a photograph taken in 1967 . . .   *The Unbelievable Land* (Ottawa, Queen's Printer, 1967), Plate 21.

"In some sense I think of them . . ."   Purdy, Alfred, From "Tent Rings," *North of Summer; Poems from Baffin Island*, with oil sketches of the Arctic by A.Y. Jackson (Toronto, McClelland and Stewart, 1967), pages 68-9. Copyright 1967 by Alfred Purdy, reprinted by permission of The Canadian Publishers, McClelland and Stewart Limited, Toronto.

PLATE 107   njg 724r   9 x 12
Reserved for the McMichael Conservation Collection of Art, Kleinburg, Ontario.

Index

244

245

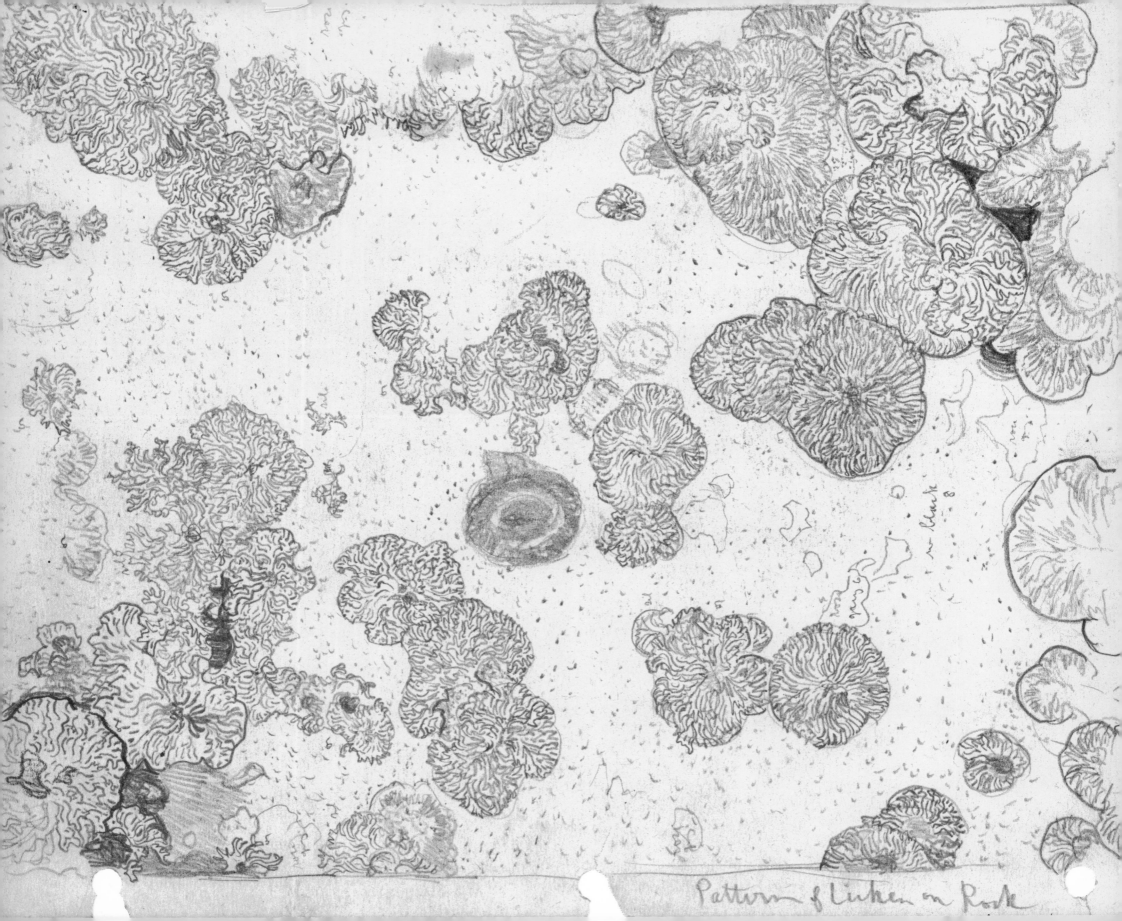

Pattern of Lichen on Rock